Christopher Simon Sykes grew up at Sledmere, and went on to become a journalist, photographer and writer. His work has appeared in *Vogue, House & Garden*, the *Sunday Telegraph* magazine and *Architectural Digest* amongst others, and he wrote and presented *Upper Crust*, a six-part series on country house cookery for BBC Two. He has written six and photographed fourteen books, including *The National Trust Country House Album*, *The Rolling Stones on Tour* and *The Garden at Buckingham Palace*. Christopher Simon Sykes is married with two children and lives in North London.

For automatic updates on Christopher Simon Sykes visit harperperennial.co.uk and register for AuthorTracker.

From the reviews of *The Big House*:

'Brilliantly written and researched . . . a revealing social history of England . . . It's a riveting read from start to finish, and should be a must for a full-scale BBC drama'   *Observer* Books of the Year

'Written with sympathy and insight, this is an irresistible portrait of the Sykeses of Sledmere'   *The Spectator* Books of the Year

'*The Big House* . . . left me moved, gripped and unwilling to leave its author's warm and generous presence'   *Independent on Sunday*

'Sykes's history is a meticulously researched labour of love . . . an enjoyable record'   *Daily Mail*

'Entertaining, instructive and engaging . . . a treat'
    Sunday Telegraph

'Witty, absorbing and touching . . . Good rollicking stuff; a splendid book'   *Sunday Times*

'Romantic, accessible and absorbing history . . . I cared passionately for everyone of these people and wanted the book to continue indefinitely . . . dive between its pages and . . . and sloping lawns for myself'   IE MYERSON, *Daily Telegraph*

THE
BIG
HOUSE

The Story of a Country House
and its Family

Christopher Simon Sykes

HARPER PERENNIAL
London, New York, Toronto and Sydney

To the memory of my grandfather, Mark Sykes, and
for the new generation, my children, Lily and Joby.

Harper Perennial
An imprint of HarperCollins*Publishers*
77–85 Fulham Palace Road
Hammersmith
London W6 8JB

www.harperperennial.co.uk

This edition published by Harper Perennial 2005
2

First published by HarperCollins*Publishers* 2004

A catalogue record for this book is available from the British Library

ISBN 0–00–710710–2

Set in Bembo by
Rowland Phototypesetting Ltd, Bury St Edmunds, Suffolk

Printed and bound in Great Britain by Clays Ltd, St Ives plc

CONTENTS

ACKNOWLEDGEMENTS   vii
SYKES OF SLEDMERE FAMILY TREE   ix
PROLOGUE   1

   I   The Merchant   5
  II   The Parson   36
 III   The Architect   56
 IV   The Collector   86
  V   The Squire   114
 VI   The Eccentric   136
 VII   Jessie   150
VIII   Sykey   167
 IX   Lady Satin Tights   189
  X   Mark   211
 XI   The Traveller   235
 XII   A Restless Spirit   261
XIII   A New House   282
XIV   Richard   313
 XV   Sledmere Reborn   342

EPILOGUE: My Unexpected Uncle   377
NOTES   387
BIBLIOGRAPHY   405
INDEX   409

'When I come back here, all the time I have been away seems like a dream. Everything is exactly the same here; the same conversation, the same jokes, the books in the same place on the same tables. My rooms just as I left them. One cannot believe that five months of incident and excitement have passed away. Home seems very calm and comfortable; a refuge quite inaccessible to any of the vexations and troubles of the world.'

Christopher Sykes, March, 1854.

ACKNOWLEDGEMENTS

First and foremost I am indebted to my brother Tatton for allowing me to undertake this project with no strings attached, and for giving me complete access to all the Sykes papers. No author could have asked for more. The book would have been far longer in the writing had it not been for the great kindness of John Popham in allowing me to read and quote from his unpublished manuscript, *The Economics of Elysium*, which provided me with invaluable information about the life of Sir Christopher Sykes. I thank him unreservedly. I am also eternally grateful for their assistance to Brian Dyson and his staff at the Brynmor Jones Library in Hull University, where the majority of the Sykes family papers are lodged; to Ian Masson and Clare Boddington at the East Riding Archives in Beverley, home of the Strickland-Constable family papers, to which Sir Freddy Strickland-Constable gave me generous access; to the staff of the Yorkshire Archeological Society, and to Nick Scheetz and his staff at the Georgetown University, Washington, Archives for photocopying the correspondence between my Uncle Christopher and his siblings.

Many other people have helped me in a variety of ways during the writing of this book, from sharing their memories of past events and lending me letters and documents, to providing me with generous hospitality while I was undertaking research. My heartfelt thanks therefore go to Professor Roger Adelson, Jack and Lilian Clark, Debo, Duchess of Devonshire, Mark and Val Elwes, Denise Lady Ebury, Desmond and Penny Guinness, Anne Hines, the late Mrs Odile Hourani, Theresa 'Baby' Jungman, Zita Jungman, Sir John Leslie, Jeremy Lewis, Julian and Victoria Lloyd, the late Lady Dorothy Lygon, Hector MacDonnell, Hugh Massingberd, Maggie Phillips, John Richardson, Ben and Veronica Roberts, Adrian Robson, Lady Sibell Rowley, Molly, Marchioness of Salisbury, Tessa Scott, Adrian Scrope, and Tony Wilson. In addition I would like to acknowledge the encouragement and enthusiasm given to me by my agent Ed Victor and my editor, Mike Fishwick, and express my deep gratitude to the staff of that peerless institution, the London Library, where most of the book was written. No author could hope for a better place to work. And thank you, my new friends at HarperCollins, for your great enthusiasm about the book.

Finally, darling Isabella, I thank you unreservedly for your patience while I was at work on this project and for never complaining about having to listen day after day to stories about the Sykeses. I only hope that it hasn't put you off them (and me) forever.

SYKES OF SLEDMERE

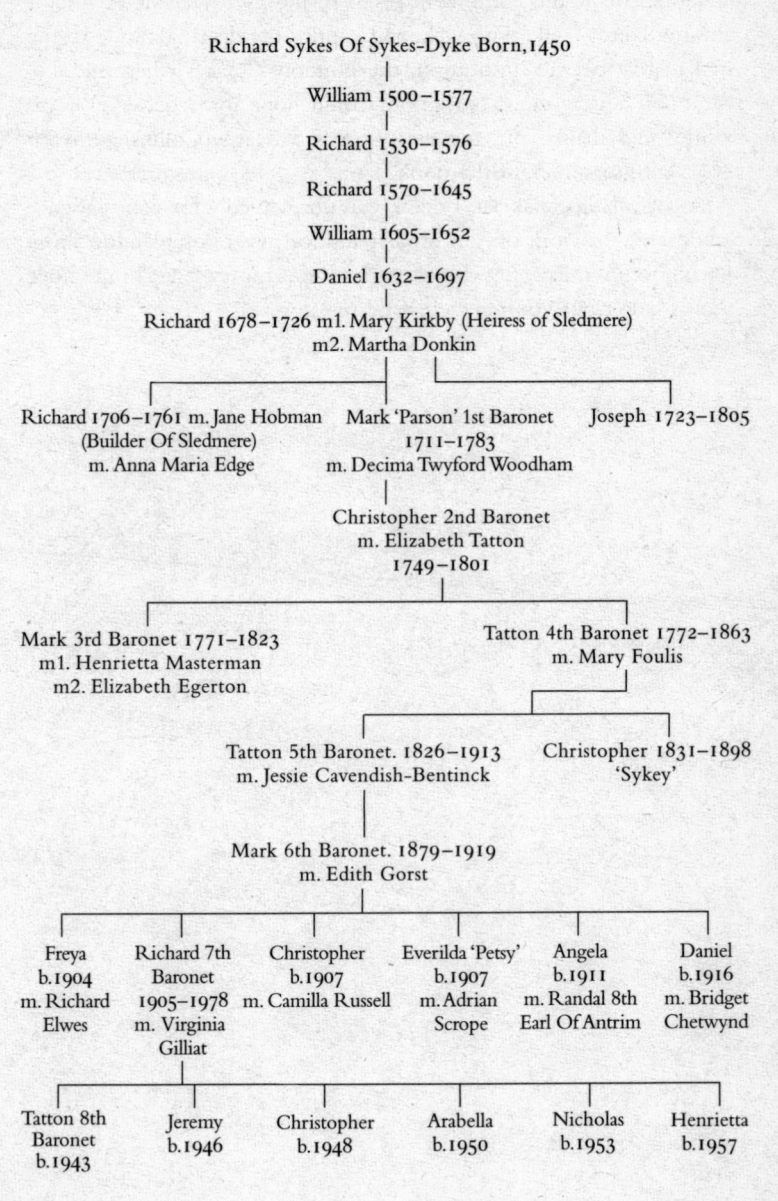

Richard Sykes Of Sykes-Dyke Born,1450
|
William 1500–1577
|
Richard 1530–1576
|
Richard 1570–1645
|
William 1605–1652
|
Daniel 1632–1697
|
Richard 1678–1726 m1. Mary Kirkby (Heiress of Sledmere)
m2. Martha Donkin

Richard 1706–1761 m. Jane Hobman   Mark 'Parson' 1st Baronet   Joseph 1723–1805
(Builder Of Sledmere)   1711–1783
m. Anna Maria Edge   m. Decima Twyford Woodham

Christopher 2nd Baronet
m. Elizabeth Tatton
1749–1801

Mark 3rd Baronet 1771–1823   Tatton 4th Baronet 1772–1863
m1. Henrietta Masterman   m. Mary Foulis
m2. Elizabeth Egerton

Tatton 5th Baronet. 1826–1913   Christopher 1831–1898
m. Jessie Cavendish-Bentinck   'Sykey'

Mark 6th Baronet. 1879–1919
m. Edith Gorst

| Freya b.1904 m. Richard Elwes | Richard 7th Baronet 1905–1978 m. Virginia Gilliat | Christopher b.1907 m. Camilla Russell | Everilda 'Petsy' b.1907 m. Adrian Scrope | Angela b.1911 m. Randal 8th Earl Of Antrim | Daniel b.1916 m. Bridget Chetwynd |

| Tatton 8th Baronet b.1943 | Jeremy b.1946 | Christopher b.1948 | Arabella b.1950 | Nicholas b.1953 | Henrietta b.1957 |

PROLOGUE

In the afternoon of Tuesday, 23 May, 1911, in the village of Sledmere, high up on the East Yorkshire Wolds, a passer-by would have been confronted with a shocking and terrifying sight. The large grey stone Georgian house, dominating the village and clearly visible from the main road, was ablaze, thick black smoke and flames pouring from its roof. Had they been there around three o'clock, they would have met with the heavy horses and wooden wagons of the Malton Fire Brigade, at the end of an arduous journey of twelve miles, which had included the navigation of two long steep hills, come to join their fellow-firemen from the other local town of Driffield, and the entire population of the village as they fought to save whatever they could of the contents of a house that had been at the centre of their lives for over 150 years.

The fire had started because a roof-beam protruded into the chimney above the kitchen in the north-east wing. It had probably smouldered for days before igniting, and even then the progress of the flames was slow, inching their way forward until they made contact with other beams supporting the roof. So it was that by the time the first suspicious wisps of smoke were seen oozing out of the brickwork of a chimney, the fire had really begun to take hold. The alarm was raised at about noon, just as the elderly owner of the house, Sir Tatton Sykes, was sitting down to his lunch. The great bell of the hall was rung, and all the men employed on the estate, farmhands, grooms, coachmen, foresters, bricklayers and carpenters, were summoned to help. Even the children were called out from the village school. The agent, Mr Henry Cholmondeley, burst into the Dining-Room to tell Sir Tatton that the house was on fire and that he must leave at once. His warnings went unheeded, for at that moment the old man was interested in nothing but his food. 'I must finish my pudding,' he said, 'finish my pudding.'

There were two fire brigades in the district, the nearest at Driffield, eight miles away, and the other four miles further still, at Malton. Both were summoned. In the meantime, Henry Cholmondeley, who had no illusions about how long they would take to arrive, organised all present into a human chain and began a bucket service from the reservoir which supplied the house. Just as this was beginning to prove useless, since it was impossible to get access to the seat of the fire, a neighbour from Malton, Mr Freddy Strickland, arrived by motor car, bringing with him Captain Jackson of the Fire Brigade and a quantity of hose. This was attached to fire hydrants near the house and ultimately unsuccessful attempts were made to play water on to the flames now issuing from the roof at the north-east corner.

Henry Cholmondeley then took a vital decision. Seeing that the fire was still burning fairly slowly, he ordered his human chain to concentrate all efforts on salvaging as much of the contents of the house as possible, many of which were great treasures. Starting on the upper bedroom floors, with the men at the head, then the women and finally, spilling out on to the lawn, the children at the far end, they began by rescuing anything that was easily movable, such as china, glass, pictures, carpets and smaller pieces of furniture. In the vast Library another group was engaged in throwing the thousands of books out of the windows into sheets and blankets held by those below. Others were unscrewing fine mahogany doors, prising out marble chimneypieces and carefully taking down the collection of family portraits.

'The servants behaved with wonderful pluck and coolness,' observed a reporter from the local paper, 'in removing furniture from the burning rooms, the maidservants acting as coolly and bravely as the men. The fire, however, was now gaining rapid hold and was fanned by a slight breeze, which caused all the upper rooms of the east wing to blaze fiercely.'[1] At half-past two, the Driffield brigade finally arrived, but, in spite of the fact that there was no shortage of water, their manual pumps proved quite inadequate to the task, the pressure from the reservoir, used solely for household purposes, being far too low. Shortly after three, the Malton Brigade were on the scene, but even their powerful steam-driven pump, which was able to send streams of water on to the roof and into the blazing upper storeys, did no good, the fire being now quite out of control. The best they could do was to keep the walls of the rooms sufficiently cool while the salvage work continued.

The roof of the east wing was the first to go, falling in with a 'great crash', but this seemed merely to strengthen the determination of the workers. 'Notwithstanding the menacing nature of their task,' commented the local paper, 'the rescue parties worked most splendidly, and the way in which the rooms were emptied of their principal contents without confusion or disorder was really wonderful.' A new hazard was caused by the large quantities of molten lead from the roof, which poured down the walls and threatened to splash anyone who came too close to it. The men worked on undeterred. As one huge painting was carried precariously down a burning staircase, supervised by the under-gamekeeper, he was heard to mutter, 'Now lads, don't damage t'frame.'[2] There were many narrow escapes. 'A long ladder was placed against an upper window, from which a large wardrobe was being lowered, two men standing on the ladder to steady it. An ominous swaying of the ladder was followed by a crack, and a moment later the ladder snapped, carrying the two men with it. Fortunately they were unhurt beyond a shaking, though the wardrobe was smashed.'[3] In the Library, the roof above crashed in and pierced the ceiling, sending burning debris raining down on the group working there, a heavy beam narrowly missing one of their number as it fell thirty feet to the floor. They made their escape down ladders from the open windows, and helped to load the huge quantity of books on to wagons which carted them away to be stored in the church.

The scene on the lawn was extraordinary, if piteous, with furniture and fittings, china, bed linen and mattresses, statues, gold and silver plate, paintings and books strewn around as far as the eye could see. In the midst of it all the melancholy figure of Sir Tatton paced up and down, his hands held firmly behind his back. He had one last request. In the Hall there stood a very fine piece of sculpture, a copy in marble of the famous Apollo Belvedere which had originally been part of the Duke of Devonshire's collection at Londesborough. It had been left till last since it was thought it might escape the flames. However, since the centre of the house was by now blazing and roaring as through a gigantic chimney with temperatures that must have been close to 1,000°C, it was obvious that the statue had no chance of survival. Sir Tatton asked if it might be saved, a difficult task as it was reckoned to weigh close to a ton, and though the ceiling of the Hall was still intact, the back and east sides were fiercely blazing. 'Scores of hands volunteered to remove the statue,' recorded the correspondent of the *Yorkshire Post*. 'Jets of water were poured on the ceiling, and the hall flooded. Water was also poured on the walls behind the statue, which was itself drenched, to render it cool enough to handle. The front door was removed, and the jambs wrenched down to admit the passage of the large life-size figure. With admirable skill it was lowered from its pedestal into the arms of the stalwart farm labourers and helpers, and finally carried out, with barely a break or scratch to the lawn.' It was the last act of salvage possible.

Throughout the night the fire brigades worked to keep down the flames, but it was not until noon of the following day that the fire was finally extinguished. Little was left at the end beyond the four outer walls. Looking into the roofless building, one of the more curious sights was a fire-place on the first floor which had miraculously escaped the flames and which remained ready for lighting, complete with paper, sticks and coals. 'Although I did not see the fire,' wrote one of Sir Tatton's grandchildren in later years, 'the shock and horror among the household, and the blackened ruin with the pungent smell, filled me with fear for a long time.'[4] Sir Tatton himself showed stoicism in the face of such disaster. 'All he said when a word of sympathy was offered,' commented the *Yorkshire Post*, 'was, "These things will happen, these things will happen", repeating the words with resigned fortitude and recognising the utter hopelessness of it all.'[5] But the correspondent of the *Yorkshire Post* had not reckoned with the absolute determination of the family who had built and loved this house that it would live again.

CHAPTER I

The Merchant

A house is more than bricks and mortar. To those who inhabit it, it lives and breathes. It has moods. It has a smell, an indefinable scent that is as peculiar to it as a genetic code is to a human being. It is made from the peculiar mixture of paint, polish, carpets, dogs, leather, wood-smoke, dust, fabrics, plaster, wood, cooking, flowers and numerous other aromas that exist in a home. Pluck me from my bed, blindfold me, drop me anywhere in the world and I could pick out the smell of Sledmere from a thousand others. This is the house in which my family have lived for 250 years. It is where I was brought up and spent my adolescence. Though I left it when I was eighteen, I still feel attached to it as if by some invisible umbilical cord. I do not live there yet my roots are there. For good or for bad, it inhabits my soul.

From the outside, Sledmere is a plain building, built of grey stone, with a lack of embellishment that makes it seem a little austere. This suits its setting, high up on the Yorkshire Wolds. It is a large country house, always known in the village as 'the big house', but it is not a palace like its neighbour, Castle Howard. I know every nook and cranny of it and, sometimes, if I am lying in bed at night trying to sleep, I play a game in which I return home and take a journey round the rooms.

I walk through the back door, the way in which everyone enters the house, and on the left is the Lift Room, depository for all coats, hats and boots. A large cupboard which faces me is filled with bric-à-brac – discarded shoes, old kites, tennis rackets, dog leads etc. – its drawers overflowing with objects that remain there year after year. In one corner there is a rack full of walking sticks, which immediately remind me of my late father. When my brother's bull terrier, Lambchop, occupied the room for years, it became known as the Dog's Lobby. To the right is the lift, to which the room owes its name. Built by Pickerings of Hull, it has steel folding doors with a small viewing window. As a child I was terrified of getting stuck in it between floors: something that did occasionally happen and, even today, my brother, Tatton, who now inhabits the house, won't travel in it alone at night.

Beyond the lift, a stone passage runs the width of the house, leading on the left to the Staff Cloak Room, the Brush Room and the Servants' Hall, and on the right to the Kitchen, the Small Dining Room and the Pantry. It is a hive of activity, particularly in the mornings, with Sue, the housekeeper, and her ladies arriving at eight to clean and dust, Maureen, the cook, soon afterwards, to prepare breakfast, and from then on a succession of callers – the postman, the gardeners, the works department – coming to conduct their business. This is where I spent much of my childhood, in and out of the Kitchen, the Servants' Hall and what was then my father's secretary, Mouzelle's room, now the Small Dining Room.

I pass through a heavy swing door, halfway up the passage, which leads into the main part of the house, the first space being the stairwell of the back staircase, known as the Blue Stairs. It is dominated by a vast marble Roman statue of Caesar Augustus, which throws eerie shadows on the wall at night. Opposite the stairs, a door leads into the Turkish Room, decorated from floor to ceiling with twentieth-century copies of ancient Iznik tiles. This was my grandfather, Mark Sykes's folly, a monument to his love of the Middle East, and if his ghost walks anywhere in the house, then it is in here. In the nineteen-sixties, I used to set up my music in the Turkish Room, fill it with candles, and come and smoke and chill out in it. Below it, down a flight of stone steps, are the Gentleman's Cloakroom and the Gun Room.

Walking past the Turkish Room and turning left, I reach the Entrance Hall, which is the main entrance into the house. It is dominated by a huge statue of Laocoon and his sons being devoured by serpents, another object which generated fear when I was little. There are muskets on the walls that were used by a regiment raised by my Great, Great, Great Grandfather, Christopher Sykes, during the Napoleonic Wars. Walking out of the left-hand door, I find myself in the Stone Hall, which occupies the central space on the ground floor, and whose tall windows look south across the park. Looking down towards the windows, the first room on the left is the Horse Room, formerly my father's study, the walls covered with paintings of horses. Next comes the Music Room, painted in shades of grey and pink, which is the comfortable family sitting room containing the drinks tray and the newspapers. The room opposite is the formal Drawing Room, with its highly decorative ceiling. It is dominated by a great equestrian portrait of my Great, Great Grandfather, Tatton Sykes, mounted on his favourite hack and carrying a walking stick, which sits on the side table below it. If I turn left out of here, I find myself first in the Boudoir which, though now changed beyond recognition, fills me with memories of my mother, since it was once her sitting room, and then in the Dining Room, with its beautiful portrait by Romney of Christopher Sykes and his wife.

At the north end of the Hall, I ascend the grand stone staircase leading up to the most unexpected room in the house, the Library. Nobody entering this room for the first time, through its plain mahogany door, could help but catch their breath at the sheer audacity of its monumental scale. Two storeys high, with a vaulted ceiling inspired by the Baths of Caracalla and Diocletian in Rome, and running the entire width of the house, with nine windows overlooking the landscape, the 120-foot long polished oak and mahogany floor was a paradise to slide about on as a child. The other three sides of the staircase have a balcony running round them, overlooking the Hall, behind which runs a bedroom passage. There are six bedrooms and a pantry on the first floor, including the last bedroom I slept in before leaving home, the Orange Room, which includes a charming portrait of my Great Grandmother, Jessica Sykes, as a child. There are a further nine bedrooms, another pantry and the linen cupboard on the top floor, which once upon a time was the nursery floor where we spent the first few years of our lives.

Turning left at the top of the Blue Stairs and immediately right through tall, double, glass-fronted doors, I push open a grey door on the left and climb a narrow metal staircase which winds up into the attics, a rabbit warren of passages, long-abandoned servants' bedrooms, spacious galleries lit by glass domes and dark, ghostly areas of roof space. I then take the lift down five floors to the cellars, and walk down dark passages to the very back, beyond the wine cellar, where there are remnants of ancient walls dug from the local Garton Shale, which makes up the ground beneath the house. In the seventeenth century the builders would have carved their cellars straight out of this material, which forms the foundations of the house. The vaulted arches are extremely well built, as good as anything you will see. I walk past the wine cellar, through the first arch, turn left and through the next arch, and look at the wall on the left leading up to the door. Garton Shale and an immensely thick opening make me believe that this is probably where the house was born.

Sledmere is one of those houses in which very little has ever been thrown away. Every drawer in every desk or cabinet seems to be stuffed with an eclectic mix of papers, photographs, letters and objects, which spill out when you open them. I was always fascinated by these as a child and spent many happy hours rifling through seemingly endless repositories of treasures. In the attics there were wooden chests filled with minerals, cupboards full of old glass bottles, huge leather trunks overflowing with old clothes, and ancient suitcases containing loose negatives and faded photographs. I particularly loved the large partners' desk in the middle of the Library, whose multitude of drawers revealed, when opened, all kinds of curiosities: old coins, medals, bills, pieces of chandelier, seals, bits of broken china, etchings, ancient letters and the charred foot of an early Sykes martyr.

These early explorations awoke in me a passion for the history of the house, which was further fuelled by the discovery of a remarkable collection of photographs, some loose and scattered about in various chests, others in photograph albums. Most of these were kept in a cupboard in the Music Room, and chronicled the comings and goings of the family since the early 1850s. I became fascinated by these images of my ancestors, the earliest of which is a splendid portrait of my

Great, Great Grandfather, Sir Tatton Sykes, who was born in 1772. It was taken in 1853 and he is sitting in a high-backed chair, his left arm resting on a table. His thick white hair is swept back from his forehead, and his strong features bear the ghost of a smile. His clothes are curious, for he is not dressed in the fashion of the time, but wears a long-skirted high-collared frock coat with a white neck-cloth and frilled shirt, together with breeches and mahogany-topped boots, the manner of dress of an eighteenth-century squire. He is undoubtedly a 'character' and I find it impossible not to like him.

But what of the first builder of Sledmere, my Great, Great, Great, Great, Great Uncle Richard Sykes, a man who died ninety years earlier, in an age when there were no photographers to record his image? The house is crammed with family portraits. They line the reception rooms, the passages, the back stairs and the bedrooms; full-lengths, half-lengths, heads and shoulders in oils, pastels and watercolour, of relatives both close and obscure. They are objects of such familiarity that until now I had never really looked at them properly. Richard Sykes hangs in the best bedroom in the house, the Red Room, at the top of the stone staircase on the right. He is just to the left of the door, and his portrait shows him to have been a well-fed looking gentleman. He is wearing a long black velvet jacket with a frilly lace shirt and cuffs and breeches with diamond buckles, and is seated at a desk surrounded by books. He has a prominent down-pointed nose, a pinkish complexion and he looks . . . well, thoroughly pleased with himself.

He had every reason to be. The eldest of six children, he was rich from the success of his family's various mercantile ventures in Hull. He had status, having been appointed High Sheriff of Yorkshire in 1752. Best of all, however, was the fact that he had succeeded, on the death of his uncle in 1748, to substantial estates on the East Yorkshire Wolds, an area of undulating chalky hills, not unlike the Sussex Downs, that run from east of York nearly all the way to the North Sea. His uncle, Mark Kirkby, had been the richest and most important merchant in Hull. He had used part of the great fortune he had amassed to buy Sledmere and the surrounding estates, and went to live in the Tudor manor house which then stood there and was used mostly as a hunting lodge. He loved it, and the memory of him still survived in my Grandfather's time.

Sometime in the middle of October, 1748, a year in which the first excavations were made at Pompeii, Samuel Richardson published *Clarissa*, and the Peace of Aix-la-Chapelle ended the War of the Austrian Succession, Richard set out on a journey to look at his uncle's land. Leaving his house in Hull, he rode north, first to the nearby market town of Beverley, made prosperous during the days of the medieval cloth trade and dominated by its cathedral-size Minster, then followed the course of the River Hull through flat wetlands to Great Driffield. Here he began a slow laborious climb uphill, passing the tower of St Michael's Church at Garton, pushing his horse on until he reached the summit of Driffield Wold. This is where the Kirkby land began, thirty miles north-east of Hull.

The Yorkshire Wolds were then a Godforsaken place, being little more than a tract of barren wasteland, much of it one vast open field destitute of hedges and ditches, with stones here and there to mark where one property ended and another began. There were no roads as such, only grass tracks, most goods being carried to market on the backs of horses rather than by cart. Though the hills had once been covered with woodland, these had been cleared by the end of the eleventh century, leaving scarcely any trees, and thin and stony soil. There were the occasional scrappy fields of oats or barley and whatever grassland was not in use for grazing sheep was fenced off into rabbit warrens. Less than a century before, wolves had roamed the area freely. Daniel Defoe, writing in 1720, described it as being 'very thin of towns, and consequently of people',[1] most of the villages having been depopulated in the sixteenth century to make way for sheep. It cannot have appeared to Richard as the most congenial of environments.

After a few miles' ride across the top, from where, if the day was a clear one, he would have caught a glimpse of the North Sea glinting to the east, where the source of his wealth, a fleet of ships, plied their trade out of Hull with the Baltic, he came to a dip in the land. Pausing to give his horse a rest, he looked down upon what he had come to see. The village of Sledmere, which lay at the heart of the Kirkby estate, stood in the bottom of the valley straddling a Roman road, which ran from York in the west to Bridlington on the east coast. It had a church and a large mere, a pond used for the common watering of livestock and from which the village got its name, translating literally as 'pool in the valley'. Little had changed there since 1572 when it was described as consisting of 'thirty messuages, ten cottages, ten tofts, five dovecots, forty gardens, forty orchards, 1,000 acres of land, 100 acres of meadow, 1,000 acres of pasture, forty acres of wood, 100 acres of heath and furze and . . . Free Warren.'[2] According to Nicholas Manners, a Methodist missionary who had been born there in 1732, its inhabitants were 'extremely ignorant of religion, wild and wicked'.[3] As Richard surveyed the scene below him, his eyes were drawn to a building which stood to the north-west of the village, on rising ground overlooking the mere. This was 'the manor house of Sledmer upon the Woulds',[4] the home of his recently deceased uncle.

As Richard rode his horse slowly down the hill, memories of his Uncle Mark came flooding back. Daniel Defoe had written of 'that glorious Head of Commerce, called *the Merchant*', and in Hull, they had called Mark Kirkby 'the Merchant Prince', for at a time when trade with the Baltic was booming and merchant families were amassing great fortunes, he was the richest of them all. He had bought the land at Sledmere in order to pursue his favourite sport of hunting, and during the season would move into the manor house where he liked to surround himself with his sporting cronies. He was known to be fond of the bottle, a trait which he shared in common with all the squires of the day, and Richard smiled as he recalled the agreement that his uncle had once made with his Coachman, that they should never get drunk the same evening. Instead each should have the privilege on alternate nights. It had not been a success, for on the very first occasion that it had fallen to the Coachman's turn to be sober and Uncle Mark was indulging himself without restraint at some friend's house, early in the evening his enjoyment had been disturbed by the entry of his Coachman into the room crying 'Tak care o'yesell Master, I'se going fast.'[5]

Richard also remembered an occasion when he had attended a supper given by his uncle for all his tenants and other dependants, at which, owing to the bottle having circulated the table one too many times, the general tenor of the evening had deteriorated and the mirth had become too uproarious. At this point, 'Old Mark Kirkby', as he was known in the neighbourhood, had risen somewhat unsteadily to his feet, his florid face beneath its flowing periwig contrasting vividly with his favourite blue velvet coat, and loudly rapped the table crying 'Mark Kirkby is at home!' It was evident that to all those gathered round the table this was a well-known signal at which all merriment was to be hushed and the proper decorum restored. However much of a good fellow the Merchant Prince may have been, he did not like his guests to forget their place.

Like Kirkby, the Sykeses were successful merchants. Originally yeoman farmers, they had come from a place called Sykes Dyke, near Carlisle. One of their descendants, William Sykes, had left Cumberland in about 1550 and settled in Leeds where he had set up as a clothier. He could not have timed his arrival better. The town, which is conveniently situated on the borders of the industrial West Riding and the predominantly agricultural North-East, was on the move. The textile industry was expanding rapidly, spreading wealth through the valleys and uplands west and south of the town. Cloth woven in the outlying villages was brought into Leeds to undergo all the various finishing processes and was then marketed by local merchants whose fortunes snowballed. As industry developed the population doubled and by the middle of the seventeenth century Leeds was the epicentre of woollen manufacture. Clothiers and merchants thronged the huge cloth market held on and around Leeds bridge. The town's inhabitants, wrote Macaulay, 'boasted loudly of their increasing wealth, and of the immense sales of cloth which took place in the open air on the Bridge. Hundreds, nay thousands of pounds had been paid down in the course of one busy market day.'[6] Within two generations the family had accumulated so much money that William's grandson, Richard, who had risen to being Alderman of Leeds and was the first 'private gentleman' in the city to own a carriage,[7] was able to leave each of his three daughters the sum of £10,000, a staggering sum for those days, as well as vast estates to his five sons.[8]

While this branch of the family continued to prosper in Leeds, one of Richard's grandchildren, Daniel, set up in business as a merchant in Hull, seeing the great opportunities that were opening up in the city from its burgeoning trade with the Baltic. Hull, whose port arose around the confluence of the Rivers Hull and Humber, had risen to greatness in medieval times when her proximity to the vast sheep runs of Yorkshire and Lincolnshire had stood her in good stead in the important wool trade. When cloth eventually replaced wool as the major English export, her fortunes had temporarily waned, the London merchants having a virtual monopoly in everything except raw wool, but they had risen rapidly again in the latter half of the seventeenth century with the opening up of direct trade to the Baltic. 'There is more business done in Hull', Daniel Defoe had observed in 1724, 'than in any town of its bigness in Europe . . . They drive a great trade here to Norway, and to the Baltick, and an important trade to Dantz-ick, Riga, Narva and Petersburgh; from whence they make large returns in iron, copper, flax, canvas, pot-ashes, Muscovy Linnen and yarn, and other things; all which they get vent for in the country to an exceeding quantity.'[9] By the time of his death in 1697, Daniel Sykes's firm was part of an oligarchy of two or three dozen great merchant houses, which handled most of the goods passing through the port. He had been twice elected Mayor of Hull and had built up a fortune to leave to his son Richard, an equally successful merchant, who in 1704 further consolidated the family's position by marrying Mary Kirkby, the sister of the Merchant Prince and co-heiress to Sledmere. It was a classic case of trade marrying into land, a formula which was to be behind the building of many of the most important houses in Britain.

Though Richard must have visited Sledmere there is no record of him ever having lived there. It was his eldest son and namesake, born in 1706, who was destined to be the first Sykes to move out of Hull to the country, though not until, like his father and grandfather before him, he had made his name in his native city. The family had recently built a new house in Hull High Street on a site which they had acquired in 1725 and which extended to the river. It is described as having been 'a fine strong structure, built a little way back, with iron palings in the front. You ascended to the street door by a flight of marble steps.' It also had a 'coach house and stables belonging to it with substantial cut stone doorways . . . reached by a short passage on the opposite side of the street'.[10]

From here young Richard had immersed himself in the family business. With a fleet of seven ships, two of which were named *The Richard* and *The Sykes*, he carried on and expanded the family's considerable trade with the ports of Scandinavia and the Baltic, exporting mostly large quantities of woollen cloth and importing iron. Swedish iron, which was high-grade, malleable iron, produced under stringent controls from the finest ores, was then regarded as the best in the world. It was considered the only iron fit for steelmaking. A number of firms built up a very great business on the basis of trading in this commodity, of which Sykes & Son became the largest. Richard was made Sheriff of Hull in 1740, and in 1745, when the Young Pretender was leading his rebel army on a gradual procession south, he was appointed Captain of a regiment of volunteers, composed of the chief Merchants of Hull, the purpose of which was 'to take up arms on His Majesty's behalf for the common defence of the Town of Kingston upon Hull'. These orders were signed the month after the Battle of Prestonpans, the same month that the Pretender was marching upon Derby and when such a panic prevailed throughout the northern counties that even the Archbishop of York, Dr Herring, thought it his duty to muster and levy troops, to attend Reviews and to urge all country gentlemen to take up arms in defence of the Protestant Religion. In the event of the triumph of the Pretender, Richard Sykes's signature on such a document would certainly have pointed him out as being worthy of ruinous fines and penalties, and possibly have cost him his head.

These civil troubles were long passed when Richard rode out to his uncle's house on that October day. He had made his fortune and his reputation, and he was ready for a change. It is quite clear that improvement of his new property was on Richard Sykes's mind from the very beginning. He was married to Jane Hobman, the daughter of Hesketh Hobman, another important Hull merchant whose family had extensive interests in Danzig, and if he were to bring a wife to live in such a desolate spot, especially one who was used to living in some luxury in their Hull mansion, then he would have to make it worthy of her. No picture exists of the house, which was described variously as a 'manor house' and a 'hall house', and was probably a gabled Tudor building, which she would certainly have considered old-fashioned. The surrounding landscape was largely treeless, with the exception of the odd orchard and the occasional hedgerow in the vicinity of the village, and so Richard decided to concentrate on planting first.

Landscape gardening was all the rage at the time, largely due to the influence of a local man, William Kent, whose family came from Bridlington. The son of a coachman, he had as a young man spent a number of years painting and studying art in Italy, where he had fallen under the spell of the works of Claude Lorrain and Salvator Rosa, whose depictions of the Italian landscape showed a nature that had been improved or 'methodised'. On his return to England in 1716, under the patronage of the Earl of Burlington, he worked as a painter and architect, and passed on to fashionable society his enthusiasm for all things Italian. He became *the* oracle on matters of taste and his influence was soon widely felt when he took up designing gardens in 1730. 'He leaped the fence,' wrote Horace Walpole, 'and saw that all nature was a garden. He felt the delicious contrast of hill and valley changing imperceptibly into each other, tasted the beauty of the gentle swell, or concave scoop, and remarked how loose groves crowned an easy eminence with happy ornament.'[11]

Richard's designs were, to begin with, on a relatively modest scale, being confined to the planting of an Avenue radiating out from the house on either side of the Mere. To assist him in carrying out this scheme he employed a firm of nurserymen from Pontefract called Perfects, which had its origins in the local industry of liquorice growing. John Perfect, an ex-mayor of Pontefract and 'a Person well known in the North for his Skill in Nurseries and Planting of all Kinds',[12] had worked on designs for the gardens at another Yorkshire house, Nostell Priory, as well as supplying plants to Harewood and other mansions in the neighbourhood. There was another factor that might have played its part in swinging him the job and that was, as Richard commented to a neighbour in December, 1749, 'Mr Perfect likes this Air very well.'[13]

Mr Perfect soon found his employer to be an impatient man, wanting his Avenue to be planted and then appear as if by magic. Richard was annoyed when the first consignment of trees turned out to be too small, Perfect having miscalculated the depth of the soil where they were to be planted, and he immediately ordered much larger ones. 'I have planted some Beeches sixteen feet high,' he wrote on 2 February 1750, 'which I Expect will answer at the end of my Avenue, and the firrs will be larger than we first talked of as we find the soil much better than expected.'[14] He delighted in the planting of his trees and in the period 1749–1750 is known to have planted 20,000 Beech, Sycamore, Wych Elm and Chestnut.[15] The completed Avenue, a great and almost triangular belt of trees, enclosed a hundred acres of parkland. At its southern end the focal point was a gap in the peripheral belt in which a gate was set. At the northern end there was the Mere and the House, which Richard intended to rebuild.

Though his wife was the catalyst for all this work, scarcely had the project begun when tragedy struck. In the autumn of 1750, Jane fell ill. In spite of being sent by Richard to one of the best physicians in London, Dr James Munro, a man of 'great Experience and knowledge',[16] she did not improve. In June of the following year, Jane's brother, Randolph Hobman, wrote to Richard from Danzig, thanking him for a melancholy gift, 'the Wearing Apparel which you was pleased to be ordered to be distributed between my Wife and Sister here'. He added 'My Wife . . . assures me as long as it may please God to spare her life, she will wear those things in a most grateful acknowledgement of your Brotherly Love . . . as also in a continual remembrance of my most dear beloved Sister deceased.'[17] Jane was forty-seven years old and she died childless.

After her death, Richard immersed himself in the building of his new house and on 17 June 1751 recorded the starting date with one short line written in his pocket book: 'Laid the first Stone of the new house at Sledmere.'[18] As to the actual position of the house, a contemporary witness, one Richard Kirkby, stated that 'Richard Sykes . . . built the present Mansion house at Sledmire near the Plot of Ground where the Old House stood.'[19] Richard himself made virtually no mention of the building of the house in his letters, apart from the occasional order for materials. 'Please to send first a sample of two sizes of your Mortice Brass Joints for Doors,' he wrote to Richard Pardoe & Son, on 9 June, 1752, 'as also of iron, and your lowest prices of each sort with Screws proper for Screwing them fast, and the price of them. As the Doors are eight feet high, I have some thoughts of having three Joints to a door.'[20] Others have him asking for 'thousand four foot pail boards and please to let them be very good ones', and 'two Baggs of Nails such as you sent me last for pailing 15,000 of 6d, 40,000 of 3d and 10,000 of 2d Sprigs as all these sorts are greatly wanted'.[21]

As work on the new house progressed, Richard turned his attention once again to the landscape, and with the help of Mr Perfect set to work planning a garden. According to Richard Kirkby, whose family were tenants of the estate, 'in order to make out Buildings, Gardens, Lawns and other necessary Conveniences to the New House, he took the old Pond or Marr into the ground called the Lawn, which then might contain an acre and upwards and before that Time laid open to the York, Malton and Scarborough roads . . . he also removed a Hill called Green Hill, along the North and South side of which the Roads went to York and Malton and to the Church, and inclosed the Hill and both the Roads within this Lawn by a Brick Wall.'[22] This brick wall, which remains today, was in fact an elaborate form of ha-ha, with triangular, rectangular and semicircular buttresses, which marked the end of the garden. At either end were quite grand pavilions, long since gone, which faced up towards the house, each consisting of three buildings and a yard. To complete the scheme there was a general clearance of all enclosures or buildings that might spoil the view up the Avenue from the House.

On 2 January, 1752, Richard received a welcome letter from George Crowle, one of the MPs for Hull and a commissioner for the Navy Office. 'I am at this moment come from Court,' he wrote, 'and I should not have forgiven myself if I slip't the first opportunity of acquainting you what was hinted me by a person in power, that it is almost determined upon in Council to appoint you High Sheriff of Yorkshire this Year. I heard you mentioned with great honor.'[23] The appointment came through in the spring and he was soon busying himself with all the details of taking up his new post, such as organising his livery – 'the High Sheriff's Livery is blew faced with red, the jacket red, white and green, gold coloured lace on the hatts . . . the expence of furnishing one man and hors with the livery for two assizes is this year Sixteen Shillings, som years are more and som less',[24] appointing a Chaplain – one applicant whom he turned down was the Revd Lawrence Sterne, soon to become the acclaimed author of *Tristram Shandy* – and dealing with approaches from various tradesmen. Amongst the latter was a curious letter endorsed 'my Lady Elizabeth Burdet, 16 Jan., 1752' in which she stated that she was the widow of Sir Francis Burdet of Braithwaite in the West Riding, who had invested and lost his entire fortune in the South Sea Scheme, the notorious 'Bubble'. After Sir Francis's death Lady Elizabeth had been obliged to take up the Coal Trade. She begged his permission to allow her to supply the Judges' lodgings with coal: 'our applications has been for ye Quality & Gentry not hoping for any regard from ye low sort of persons'.[25]

Richard's appointment as High Sheriff was indicative of the high esteem in which he was held, a fact which was further borne out in August of the following year when the Prime Minister himself, the Right Hon. Henry Pelham, wrote to him to try and persuade him to stand as MP for Hull. They had met in Scarborough, then a fashionable spa in which it was said 'earls, marquesses and dukes' could be found 'as thick as berries on hedges',[26] and where Pelham was indulging in the popular pastimes of drinking the waters and outdoor bathing. 'There is no man I should wish to see more in Parliament than yourself,' he told him, 'and indeed the unreserved civilities I have received from your countrymen must always make me partial to Yorkshire . . .'[27] Richard declined, and the position was taken up by Lord Robert Manners, Pelham's brother-in-law, who put Sykes's refusal to stand down to his preoccupation with Sledmere. 'Till Sledmere is quite completed,' he wrote to him, 'the delight you take in that pretty place I dare say will not let you stop your hand, but afford you daily employment & the most delightful amusement. I hope all your improvements there answer your most sanguine expectations.'[28]

The real reason, however, that Richard was never able to take up a serious career in politics was that he suffered from very poor health. This already interfered with his position as High Sheriff. 'Your Lordship I am afraid will think me remiss,' he wrote to Sir Thomas Parker, one of the Assize Judges, on 6 June, 1752, 'in not acknowledging the receipt of your kind favour till now but . . . I have been chiefly confined to my Bed by a Sharpe fitt of the Gout, the pain of which I thank God is greatly abated and if no relapse think I may flatter myself with the pleasure of attending your Bro: Judges at the Ensuing assizes in person.'[29]

Gout, which was the common enemy of the country gentleman, was caused mostly, and certainly in Richard's case, by an excessive fondness for Port.

> Yes, one Failing he has, I recollect that
> He prefers his Old Port to a Velvet 'Old Hat'

wrote his younger brother, the Revd Mark 'Parson' Sykes, in a poem he entitled 'Verses in praise of my Brother'.[30] The size of Richard's appetite for Port is made clear in one of many similar letters to Robert Norris, one of his shipping agents. 'When you have any extraordinary Pipe of Old Red Port Wine, let me know and will take sixty or seventy Gallons of it, but will have it drawn into bottles with you and well corked any time betwixt now and the latter end of April.'[31] Among the daily dining, supping and drinking companions listed by Richard in his pocket books are numerous parsons who shared his enjoyment, such as Parson Ferrit, Parson Morice and Parson Lazenby, but none more so than his own chaplain, a drunken old clergyman by the name of Parson Paul. 'Parson Paul and the tenants of Sledmire dined with me,' he recorded on Christmas Day, 1752; then on Boxing Day, 'Parson Paul supp'd with me', and on the following day, 'Ditto breakfast with me and returned home', no doubt much the worse for wear.[32]

Though one might be tempted to smile at these exploits, the subsequent Gout is an extremely painful condition, in which excess uric acid crystals are deposited in the joints of the big toe, the ankle and the knee, causing protuberant swelling and acute attacks of pain. 'The victim goes to bed and sleeps in good health,' wrote Dr Thomas Sydenham, who himself suffered from the disease. 'About two o'clock in the morning he is awakened by a severe pain in the great toe ... so exquisite is the feeling of the part affected that it cannot bear the weight of the bedclothes nor the jar of a person walking in the room. The night is passed in torture.'[33] The condition was caused not so much by the ingestion of alcohol, but by the fact that the port was contaminated with lead, regular doses of which can induce the disease. The contamination came either from the port having been stored in lead lined casks or from contact with leaded pewter drinking vessels.

Gout plagued Richard's life. 'The Top of my Great Toe,' he wrote to his doctor on 11 October, 1759, 'began again to be inflamed and uneasy at night ... I bathed it with Brandy ... and continued to do so twice a day. Monday night it was very much inflamed and painful and kept me awake all night. . . . Wednesday morning pressing of the flesh of the toe close to the nail, there issued out white matter. I bathed my toe with Brandy . . .'[34] There were times when the pain was quite devastating. 'I am now confined to my chamber in the Gout,' he wrote to Dorothy Luck, the wife of one of his tenants, on 30 December, 1753, 'and have been very much afflicted therewith for these twelve months past (which prevented me coming to see you as I intended) in such a degree that life has become a burden and not worth desiring even amongst the abundance of the Riches of this World which God Almighty has been pleased to entrust to my care.'[35]

To cure him of his afflictions, he had entrusted himself into the care of a certain Dr Chambers, whose practice was in the nearby town of Beverley. Though Gout was the worst of these, and self-inflicted, he was plagued by other illnesses, the minutest details of which were communicated to the doctor in a series of almost daily letters. They included the 'Scorbutick disorder'[36], endless colds ('coughed much and my lungs wheezing like a Broken Winded Horse . . .'),[37] toothache ('I have had a very great pain in my Teeth Gums and Roof of my mouth much Swelled as well as on the right side of my face',[38]) piles ('my piles are yet very troublesome but not so much Heat or Inflamation about the Fundament'),[39] and very unpleasant rashes ('my Wife tells me my back and shoulders are full of red and blue spots with an itching and my armpits full of scurf').[40] In return the good doctor kept him well supplied with a battery of different remedies. There were Physick, the Electuary, Asthmatic Elixir, Virgin Wax Sallet Oil, Camomile Tea, Saline Julep, the Spring Potage, Sassafras, Mr Bolton's Ointment, Rhubarb Tea, Apozem and Basilicon to name a few. Richard lapped them up. 'I have pursued Dr Chambers directions hitherto in every respect,' he wrote to his brother Joseph in September, 1759, 'and am now waiting for what more he may please to send me.'[41]

All indications are that the new house at Sledmere was completed by the end of 1753 and Richard was certainly living there the following summer, for in August he advertised for a butler. 'I yesterday received your favour of the 23rd,' he wrote to a friend, Thomas Sidall, 'informing me you have heard of a Butler that you think will do for me. I want one and such a one as is not fickle as I do not love to see new faces. I beg you will not only be particular in your inquiry if good natured, for I can't brook with an ill temper or impertinent answers . . . As I can't shave myself he must shave as he will chiefly attend me wherever I go.'[42] The annual salary was £15. 2s. and William Shawe, who was hired to fill the post, was to find himself working in a household of twelve. His fellow servants were listed along with their wages by Richard in his pocket book for 1756 as 'Sam Hirst, my Coachman. Wages £12. 12s.; Edward Guthrie, my Gardiner. Wages £16. 16s.; Mary Brocklesby, my Housekeeper. Wages £8. 8s.; Thomas

Porter, my Groom. Wages £5. 5s. 8d.; James Wellbank, my Postilion. Wages £3. 3s.; Mary Mitchell, my Chamber Maid. Wages £3. 3s.; Mary Banks, my Chamber Maid. Wages £3. 0s.; Susanna Anderson, my Cook Maid. Wages £4. 0s.; Mary Thornton, my Dairy Maid, Wages £3. 5s.; and Robert Collings, Odd Man. Wages £3. 3s.'[43]

A drawing dated 1751 of the design for the principal elevation shows the new house to have been a solid comfortable building, three storeys high and of seven bays. It was built in brick with rather heavy stone facings and rusticated windows, and was more typical of the kind of gentleman's house that would have been erected in the Queen Anne period. A detailed inventory made in January 1755, listing each of the rooms and their contents, shows it to have had eight bedrooms, two dressing rooms, a dining room, drawing room and study ('my Own Room'), a hall, with a service area which consisted of two kitchens, servants' hall, butler's pantry, servants' bedrooms, a laundry, dairy and brewhouse, and extensive cellars.

> This Pile is polite! Free from Frogs & from *Dykes*
> And was raised at th'Expense of Worthy Dick *Sykes*
> The Pond, Full in view is clear of all *Stench*
> Stock'd with Mackrel, with Carp and gold bellyed *Tench*,
> The Master is generous! Free from envy and pride
> Loves a *Pipe* in his Mouth, A *Friend* by his side.

wrote Richard's brother 'Parson' in another of his poems entitled 'Upon the New Structure at Sledmere & the Master'.[44]

Richard's inventory gives a clear idea of how the house was furnished. Since carpets are listed in a number of the rooms one must presume that where they are not mentioned, the floor was simply wooden boards. Such was the case in Richard's sitting room, which is referred to as 'My Own Room'. It had 'A Large Stove Grate, A fine open Fender, A Shovel, Tongs & poker, A Sconce Looking Glass, and A Marble Chimney Piece & Hearth'. There were 'Six Wallnutt Tree Chairs Leather Bottoms, One Liber Stool Cover'd with Leather,

One Wallnutt Tree Arm Chair Ditto'. There was 'A Mahogany Square Table & Tea Chest, One fine Large in Laid Scruetoire & Bookcase, One Mahogany Shaving Stand, with a Glass, A Large Chest mounted with Brass two drawers, and set upon pedestals, A Mahogany Round table a yard Diameter, A Perspective Looking Glass and an Iron Holland Chest'.[45] There appear to have been no pictures. Those were reserved for his bedroom, described as the 'Lodging Room Over Kitchen', which was delightfully comfortable.

The bed was a four-poster 'with Mahogeny Poles, Blue Merrine Furniture, two Window Curtains of the same to draw up, a Feather Bed, a Check Cover, a Bolster, two Pillows, a Check Mattress, Three Blanketts and a Blue & White Linnen Quilt'. In this room there were 'Two Old Bedside Carpets'. The other furniture consisted of 'an Arm Chair Leather Bottom, Six Mahogeny Chairs Covered with Blue Merrine with Check Covers, A Lib. Stool with a Leather Bottom, A Wallnutt Tree Sconce Looking Glass, A Close Stool with a Pott, A Leather Seat, A Bureau, An Oval Table of Mahogeny, A Wainscott Reading Machine, A Large Mahogeny Book Case with Sash Doors and presses below, A Little Camp Bed with Furniture compleat and A Dressing Table with drawers & a Swing Looking glass'. Then there were 'Three very fine Blue & White Delph Jarrs with Tops, two Chocolate Cups and saucers, 2 Milk potts, 4 Shoker Basons'. Finally he mentions 'three Small pictures and My Uncle Mark Kirkby's Picture'.[46]

The latter, a half-length portrait, which today hangs in the Red Bedroom at Sledmere and shows him looking rather pompous dressed in his blue coat, has an amusing anecdote attached to it. While my Grandfather, Mark Sykes, was engaged in researching an unpublished Sykes family history, his house carpenter, an old boy called John Truslove, once told him that when he was a very young man and had been employed to move some pictures in the house, he had slipped while taking down the Kirkby portrait and was obliged, with some trepidation, to tell the housekeeper, 'I've cut Mark Kirkby's throat!'[47] To confirm the truth of this story I climbed up a ladder and gently touched the lace bands round his neck. Sure enough I felt the place where a gash had been repaired.

The only other pictures mentioned by Richard in this inventory were 'Two pictures' in the Servants' Hall, 'Three Black & White prints' in the Store Room, 'my Bro. Joseph Sykes picture' in the Crimson Dressing Room, and 'My Niece Polly's Picture', which hung over the chimneypiece of the dressing room adjoining 'my Best Lodging Room'. This is where he would have kept his clothes, also minutely catalogued under the heading 'My Wearing Linnen' and including such finery as 'fine Point Ruffles, Dresden Ruffles, fine Mechlin Ruffles, Fine New Holland Shirts, Ruffled Shirts, A Velvet Suit, Coat, Waistcoat & Breeches, a Light Gray Coat Lined with Crimson Silk Trimed with Gold Lace, a Flowered Silk pair of Breeches, etc, etc.'[48]

So proud did Richard soon become of his new house that he would take great umbrage if it came to his notice that strangers to the neighbourhood had been to visit the much grander house at Castle Howard but had not been to Sledmere. He was thus delighted when, in April, 1755, he was approached by Edwin Lascelles, one of the richest men in Yorkshire, who was about to start work on building a new house at Harewood, near Leeds. He too had inherited an old manor house, Gawthorpe Hall, and was looking to Richard for advice on how to go about starting anew. 'I am going into Mortar Pell-Mell,' he wrote, 'and shall stand much in need of the experience and assistance of such Adepts as you. The first step, I am told, is to provide the main materials; & wood & Iron being of the number, I flatter myself I shall learn from you, the Lowest price of the latter.'[49] Drawing on the wealth of experience he had gained in the previous four years, Richard's advice to Lascelles was to start by appointing a first-class foreman to oversee the work and to fix upon a plan from which he should not vary. He should then make sure that all the materials he needed were not only on hand, but prepared. Finally he should fortify himself 'with a multitude of patience'.[50]

Though the house at Sledmere may have been finished, the work of landscaping continued. An undated design, probably from the mid-1750s, shows Richard to have contemplated the creation of an oval carriage drive in front of the house, between it and the Fish Pond, with planting to the west of the house to include a formal ride up to a garden temple.[51] This work was never carried out, but in January, 1756, he wrote to Lord Robert Manners sending his 'best respects to my Lord James and thank him for his kind wishes of the Improvement and Increase of my Nursery. I have been planting and transplanting for these six weeks past the Season, for that business has turned out very favourable and my trees come forward and grow almost beyond all imaginary expectations and great pleasure when I view them.'[52]

He also had a thriving kitchen garden of which he was especially proud. Back in December, 1752, he had written to Richard Lawson, a broker friend in London, asking for advice on buying a glass house: 'Not having acquaintance with any in or about London, I hope you will excuse the trouble in desiring you to recommend one that will serve me with a Good Comodity. I have only got at present a few sash frames finished which gives me an opportunity of taking an Exact Measure of the Squares . . . & as they may be larger than Common I could like to have it of Crown Glass to be run or cast somewhat stronger and better if allowed a half penny a foot more than the usual price . . .'[53] By August, 1760, he was able to write to his brother Joseph, 'I perhaps may cut upwards of a hundred Pine Apples this year'[54] and when he went on his annual trip to Harrogate to drink the waters, cargoes of nectarines, peaches, plums and melons followed him there.[55]

With the house and gardens completed, Richard needed a new wife to share his good fortune, and on 1 November, 1757, he married for the second time. He had not had to look far, for his bride was his first cousin, Anna Maria Edge, the widow of a Hull merchant, Thomas Edge. She was described in a local newspaper as being 'a Lady of the most distinguished merit, & blessed with every amiable qualification that can adorn her sex'.[56] She also had three children, Dicky, Bella and Kitty, to whom Richard appears to have been a most affectionate stepfather. 'If at any time you should think my advice may be of Service,' he told Kitty, 'upon application I will give it to you honestly and sincerely to the best of my judgement, just the same as if you was my own Child.'[57]

Comfortably settled in his new home, Richard immersed himself in the life of a country squire. 'Gentlemen from Hull hunted with me,' ran his diary entry for 23 February, 1756, and on the subsequent days through until the 29th he wrote, 'Ditto. Breakfasted, dined and suppd with me.'[58] He hunted hares with a pack of harriers and frequently alluded to his runs in his letters. 'My brother Parson and his wife came to see us the 11th of this month,' he wrote to Bella Edge on 23 October, 1759, 'and returned to Hull on the 21st. The day before they were a-Hunting in the Lawn with very great diversion. Killed and Eat four Brace of Hares and two Couple of Rabbits.'[59] In December he told his niece Polly, 'I have been able to mount my Hunter and ride a Chaise. Your Aunt and Kitty goes in the Coach a Hunting when the weather will permit. Once, twice or three times a week I accompany them therein to the field and back.'[60]

The daily entries in his pocket books show that scarcely a day went by without him entertaining somebody, either to lunch or dinner. If it wasn't Parson Paul, then it was family or his tenants and neighbours. No doubt they relished their visits to Sledmere, for Richard was nothing if not a bon-vivant. They would have expected to find copious amounts of game on the table, such as hare, partridge and venison, but there were often surprises in store. In October, 1759, for example, he thanked his Danzig brother-in-law, Randolph Hobman, 'for the kind present of the bagg of Sturgeon',[61] while in December he received 'a forequarter of very fine Lamb and some Oysters'[62] from 'Brother Parson Sykes'. The same year he wrote to Joseph Denison in London to thank him for the olives that had been sent and proved 'very good and acceptable', and to order 12lbs of chocolate. He sent bottled mushrooms and potted hare to his friends in London, but a gift of potted char sent to him by his brother Parson got left behind in Hull, his servant Bob 'not knowing what it was'.[63]

> Your Melon was good
> The Flesh red as blood
> The flavour & juices how fine!
> Here's a health to 'Squire Sykes'
> Whom no man dislikes
> I'll drink it as oft as I dine.

wrote Parson Walmisley from Malton on 11 August, 1759.[64] He would have found no shortage of drink with which to charge his glass. The new Cellar contained 'twenty-four New Hogsheads Iron Bound, seven half Ditto, ten Twenty Gallon casks, Eight Gantrys'[65] and it was well stocked, for Port was not the only drink for which Richard had a fondness. In November, 1759, he wrote of having received fifty-nine dozen bottles of wine from Robert Norris, and in the following January told him 'I have been inspecting into my Stock of Madeira and to oblige you I have sent you seven Doz. by my Market cart . . . and can spare you 5 Doz. more.'[66] This was in addition to eight dozen bottles of 'Old Hock' which he had pledged to spare him from his cellar only a few days earlier, while February found him writing once more to Robert Norris, inquiring anxiously, 'When do you draw off the Red Wine? I must have some fit to drink about next October.'[67] For the chosen few there was a rare treat, the 'water of life': 'I got one Mr Richard Lawson, a Broker in London,' he wrote to Joseph Denison in November, 1759, 'to Buy me two or three bottles of Usquaba. The best of my remembrance he bought it of one Burdon, famous at that time, and having none Left desire you will buy me two Quart bottles of it, the best and send it by the first ship to Hull.'[68] The good life that Richard was enjoying is reflected in his portrait, which he commissioned from Henry Pickering, an artist who liked to paint people 'in character'. Richard was rich and successful, he had a delightful new house, and he now had an instant family. Childless himself, Richard had a warm and affectionate nature which reveals itself best in his relationship with two close members of his family, his half-brother Joseph and his favourite niece, Polly, portraits of whom hung in his dressing room.

Joseph Sykes was Richard's junior by seventeen years and was the product of their father's second marriage to Martha Donkin. Since he never really knew his father, who died in 1726 when he was only three, Joseph had always looked to his older brother for support. He worked in the family business and Richard thought so highly of him that in 1753, when Joseph had just turned thirty, he made him a partner. 'I have turned over the Charge of the Counting House,' he wrote to his brother-in-law, Randolph Hobman in August, 1753, 'to my Brother . . . for I am mostly in the Country when in Health.'[69] That summer Richard went to a lot of trouble to help smooth the path for his brother to get married to a Miss Dorothy 'Dolly' Twigge, against the express wishes of his mother. 'I observe that Mr Jos. Sykes', wrote the prospective bride's father, Nicholas Twigge, in June, 1753, 'has communicated to you what passed at his last visits betwixt him, myself and Dolly, the Substance of which was that he made an offer of himself of which I disapproved but my Daughter accepted . . . I always thought the consent of Parents and nearest relations necessary for the happiness of the young ones.'[70] He did, however, go on to say that he believed 'as do you, that their affections are mutually engaged and so engaged that if I was now to attempt to break the affair, I should be under the greatest fear for the consequences'. He finished by asking 'In the meantime if Mrs Sykes has any particular reason why she would not have her son's marriage to take place, I should be glad to know it . . .'

It turned out that Joseph's mother did indeed have very strong objections, which Richard laid out in his reply. 'She says the frequent Headaches your daughter had at Hull must frequently disable her from looking over her family, that her son's Industry must be spent at the discretion of Servants, and that she has instances in her family of great Miscarriages from the Mistress being Sickly . . . indeed there seems so great an aversion that it will be impossible to get over it. I need not tell you how bad a prospect there is where the Mother is so averse to the Lady.'[71] Richard did not give up, however, for he could not bear to see Joseph so unhappy, and in the end he persuaded both sets of parents to allow the marriage, which took place in June, 1754 and turned out to be a very happy one. In spite of Joseph's mother's fears that Dolly's health would lead to her having endless miscarriages, she gave birth to seven children, all of whom survived into adulthood, and she lived to the ripe old age of sixty-nine.

Richard's niece was the only daughter of his younger brother, Parson Sykes, the Revd Mark Sykes, Rector of Roos, and although she was christened Maria, her Uncle always affectionately referred to her as

Polly. His correspondence with her shows him to have taken an almost paternal interest in her upbringing. For example, in a letter to her dated 2 July, 1753, when she was fourteen, he gently chastised her for her last letter, which contained little more than 'compliments love & duty', expressing hope that 'your next will be more entertaining . . . by giving me a description of your Journey as well as the Country Situation and prospect from your friend's House and Garden'; he offered her advice on healthy eating – 'The latter abounds with fruit. I make no doubt but you have been tempted to taste thereof. A little at proper times may be both good and wholesome as too much hurtful. I hope you are so prudent as to require no reminding you of that or anything else which may contribute either to your health or benefit', and made a few suggestions of a more personal nature – 'You will be very observing to give your friend as little trouble as possible, and do you mind to lay by your things in a careful manner and not to litter up your room with them. The one is commendable, the latter a sluttish and an indolent disposition and an unpardonable fault in a young lady.'[72]

A pastel portrait of Polly, done when she was in her early teens, shows her seated on a red stool wearing a white dress with a blue sash. She has thick curly brown hair to her shoulders and a sweet intelligent face wearing a mischievous smile, in which one can detect a touch of the 'gidiness' to which her uncle referred in his next letter. The time had come, he said, to cast this off 'and become more Circumspect and thoughtful'. He showed his pious nature when he urged her not to forget her daily prayers, nor to 'repeat them as a Girl at School does her Lessen but in a most humble posture with a devout Mind in such a manner as will be most acceptable to that Good and Gracious God your Creator'. He ended the letter 'God preserve you Bless you and make you a good Woman.'[73]

When Polly was twenty, she was courted by and became engaged to John de Ponthieu, the eldest son of Josias de Ponthieu, the head of a successful Linen trading company, based in London but with strong links in Hull. It was a good match, the young man having a reputation for being 'lively and active' and 'indefatigable in business'.[74]

He was also well-off, having an inheritance of £6,000, which being added to Polly's expectations of £4,000 enabled them to begin life on the not insubstantial sum of £10,000. They would have a house in London in Friday Street, and the free use of his family's two villas, one on the outskirts of London, the other in Sir Thomas Egerton's park near Manchester.

It was quite clearly the intention of Polly's future father-in-law to keep a close eye on the young couple, and he set down his advice to them in no uncertain terms. He exhorted them 'not to set out in an expensive way, to have every day a regular table of two dishes with vegetables & fruit pyes, & for desert the common fruit in season – to have no more servants than what are useful, a coachman, a footman, a cook, a chambermaid & the housekeeper; to dine and sup out very seldom, except with select friends with whom we make no ceremony; & who afford great satisfaction & pleasure & little expense; for I put it down as a known maxim that no person can receive much company & treat in an elegant manner but they must have great anxiety & trouble which overbalances the pleasure such company can afford them; besides the expense which is always considerable, everybody vying who shall exceed in luxury, or as they call it Genteel Taste.'[75]

'Tho' my Vanity will not permit me to think myself *dirt* yet I must acknowledge in point of fortune Polly might have done better,' John wrote to her father, Parson, who appears to have at first opposed the match, 'yet in Birth, Virtue and Honesty, I will give up to none.'[76] Uncle Richard, on the other hand, was delighted and soon after her wedding on 5 June, 1759, wrote her a charming letter in which he reminded her of the particular care and regard which he had always entertained for her and her happiness. He hoped that her husband would find that the marriage state was 'a Heaven upon Earth'. 'Now my Dears,' he continued, '. . . May the Day of your Marriage continue to the day of your Deaths, that you may Enjoy not only all the Happyness this world can afford but also all those in that which is to come. Our sincere Love waits upon your Father . . . and all the Families of your New Relations unknown to us and it will give us great pleasure if at any time their Affairs will permitt them to come here to partake of my One Dish which is a Friendly and Hearty welcome, and if any of the gentlemen like Hunting, perhaps I can in the Season here entertain them both as to the Country and Diversion. I wrote to your Pappa at Hull how we celebrated the day here at night. I exhibited some fireworks. We received the cakes and gloves for which we return you thanks for your kind remembrance of us both.'[77]

What hope there was for these two young people! A pair of portraits painted on the occasion of their marriage show her clutching a posy of roses, looking elegant and pretty, and him dressed in a coat edged with gold braid, positively oozing bonhomie and self-confidence. They moved to London from where John wrote rapturously to his father-in-law soon after the wedding, 'from my Wife, my Servants, my Coach and my horses, one may truly say *I'm a Lucky Dog*'.[78] He seemed particularly pleased with his mode of transport. 'Our Equipage is as genteel a one as any I've seen, not Gaudy but gay; it's painted Crimson mosaick; a pair of good horses, bays; they cost seventy guineas.'[79] He also dwelt with great emphasis upon 'their Assembly'. Assemblies were all the rage in London at the time. 'There is not a street in London free from them,' wrote Lady Mary Wortley Montagu, 'and some spirited ladies go to seven in a night.'[80] These gatherings, which mixed conversation and cards with dancing, took place in the evening, and while they had begun their life in the early part of the century as quite small affairs, they had since developed into something much bigger, with the numbers of those attending running into the hundreds. 'We have at length concluded the Assembly to the satisfaction of everybody; the number we have limited to 150 which is filled by the most considerable Merchants we have. We have about fifty petitioners desirous of being admitted in case of vacancies. The subscription price is two Guineas. I have sent you enclosed a Copy of our regulations, with a list of the Subscribers, which no doubt you will be glad to see; as I daresay nobody in Hull has it, and it has become a general topick of converstaion here in London – I shall by this means keep up the Connections that will be useful to us in business without having the trouble and expense of seeing them at home.'[81]

To cap it all, Polly was three months pregnant. 'God Grant that you may arrive to your full time and then to a Speedy Delivery, as well as recovery,' wrote Uncle Richard in September. 'I am very much pleased to learn of your rising at six of the Clock, for when the days are so long as to permit it, tis certainly the most pleasantest part of the day.'[82] When he wrote to her on 3 December, however, he noted that she had been 'put under some restraint', and counselled her that 'if you were not so careful of yourself as you ought to have been, it may now be necessary for your future health.'[83] A letter written by Richard to his brother, Mark, a week later revealed that a shadow had fallen across the young couple's happiness. 'I am not a little uneasy for Polly's second Miscarriage and wish the advice they have consulted may have the desired effect for the future.'[84] By March, Richard was extremly worried. 'I am under great concern for our niece de Ponthieu,' he wrote to his brother Joseph. 'Brother Parson gave me but a very disagreeable account of the state of her health.'[85] He wrote to Mark suggesting that a trip to Sledmere might do Polly the world of good. 'I think it was well Judged to come down to try her Native Air since the Doctors that have been consulted could not do her any service. As soon as she is so much better and dare venture to under go the fatigue of a Journey here . . . I will meet her God permitting at Beverley with our Coach to conduct her here, and I am not without hopes that this air may partly contribute towards re-establishing her in her former state of Health.'[86]

But it was not to be. Worn down and depressed after her miscarriages, Polly was wasting away, suffering from what appears to have been Anorexia. 'Her appetite is so bad,' wrote Richard to Joseph on 20 March, 'that she does not take nourishment sufficient to support nature, so must in consequence rather lose than gain strength.'[87] Richard hoped she might be tempted by the Sledmere dishes she had loved in the past, and in April wrote to John de Ponthieu suggesting that she 'perhaps could eat a Sledmere Pidgeon or a young Rabbitt . . . and if she can think of anything Else that Either this place or the Neighbourhood can produce that will be acceptable, let me know and will do my best endeavours to obtain it for Her with all the pleasure imaginable'.[88] By 1 June, however, he noted that 'every letter gives less encouragement of hopes of our Dear Polly's recovery', and went on to admit 'I must own to you I have been preparing myself for the change these two months past, but while there is Life would hope for the best and pray God support you all and all of us against the Severe Tryal with Christian Patience.'[89] On 18 June poor old Uncle Richard made the following entry in his pocket book, 'Niece Polly de Ponthieu died at 7 o'clock of the evening at York.'[90]

The tragic loss of his beloved Polly receives remarkably little mention in Richard's correspondence at this time. He took a stoical view, dealing with her death in the same way that, a few months later, he advised his friend Joseph Denison to cope after the death in the same week of both his father and his son. 'Though these trials to our frail nature ... appear very severe requiring great Fortitude of Mind to reconcile ourselves to the all Wise God dispensing providence,' he wrote, 'yet we must believe what ever he orders and directs is for the best ... Let us sit down and seriously Consider asking ourselves at the same time will my Anxious Soul be benefitted by my unreasonable fretting? Will it not rather Endanger my future Health and constitution, or will it bring him to life again?' When he had finished dispensing advice, he turned at once to other important matters. 'Please to buy for us 2lb of best Hyson Tea, 2lb of Fine Green, 4lb of Gongs and 12lb of Common Breakfast Bohea Tea for the servants and send it by shipping to Hull directing it for me to be left at my brother Joseph's.'[91] Life must go on.

The death of Polly may well have been tempered by his growing fondness for his three stepchildren, of whom Bella seems to have been a favourite, and many amusing letters passed between them. He praised her artistic endeavours. 'Shell work properly adapted and a Geneous to Imitate Nature,' he told her, 'is not only an agreeable amusement, but very delightful and Entertains both oneself & friends. I apprehend by this time, as it was your Taste before you left Sledmire, that you are a perfect Artist thereof and that you will be able to decorate every Room here where it wants your finishing Handy Work.'[92] When she took up singing, he gave her a new nickname. 'I think I must now drop all those familiar Names by which I out of my affection used to

Apeller you & as you are become an Italian Singer I must now name you "the Belle Italienne" till another opportunity offers to change again for the better.'[93] But perhaps what really drew them together was their shared love of pigs.

'One of your Grunting Queens was brought to bed of eleven last week but one dead,'[94] he wrote to her in October, 1759. The sow in question, nicknamed 'The Chinese Queen', had been a gift to Bella during the summer, so the news must have delighted her. The second litter, however, were all born dead. 'I informed you what had happened to Her Majesty the Chinese Queen,' Richard wrote the following January to Robert Norris, who had procured him the sow, 'and desired to know what could be done for Her to prevent the like for the future, but you are silent.'[95] Better news and a mystery followed in April. 'I have had an uncommon increase of my family within this month past,' he told Bella; 'a Sow brought me Ten Piggs, six of which were Still Born, the remaining four by their Colour being mostly Black. By their form and shape we have strong suspicion to believe that His Chinese Majesty has not been so Chaste and Continent to Her Empress, who has not long to go before she will lay in, as becomes a faithful Husband. I can't tell how John Yatton may not be to Blame in this affair, for you know he is their Guardian, and am afraid he has connived to their Love Meetings . . . If I conjecture right, the Emperor has by some token or other given him to understand that as he is an unmarried person he would make him a Present of One of the Princesses when fitt, and I have heard it reported of him that he is a great Lover of such Princesses, that he is for having two at a time, one not contenting him.'[96]

Richard's new marriage brought great happiness to him and life into Sledmere with all the hustle and bustle and comings and goings that a family with children brings. These were amongst the best years of his life. His love of his house, his pride in his achievements – in his richly laden ships, his acres of land, his plantations and his gardens, his harriers and his pineapples – and his affection for his family are all self-evident. Sadly he had precious little time to enjoy them. 'I fully intended coming over the next rent day,' wrote Richard to John

Rhodes, one of his tenants, on 9 January, 1761, 'had it pleased God to have kept me well and free from Gout, but I have been confined to my Chamber since the 27th of last month with a very Severe fitt.'[97] Yet in spite of the fact that he was suffering so much, and having constantly to surrender to Dr Chambers's never-ending battery of remedies, he could not put aside his fondness for the bottle. Only four days later he wrote to his brother Joseph, 'I thank you for your tender for some Butts of mountain wine at £23. 10s. I expect I have so much old Mountain left as will last my time or longer.'[98] Prophetic words. On 19 January, he told 'Brother Parson' 'I would flatter myself that this fit of the Gout is almost gone, but has left a great weakness.'[99] A few days later he was dead.

The following epitaph, intended for a monument to him to be erected in the church, but never used, was written by his brother:

> He was of strict Integrity
> Universal benevolence
> And a fast Friend
> All the general Virtues shone conspicuously in him
> Save Ever easy & cheerful in himself
> Like Light he reflected
> Joy, Pleasure & Happiness on all around him
> He was a Grace to his Fortune
> An Honor to his Country
> True to his King and his God
> Beloved while living–Lamented now Dead.[100]

CHAPTER II

The Parson

Richard's heir, Parson, was five years younger than him and conspicuously lacked his charm and *joie de vivre*. His portrait by Sir George Chalmers, which hangs to the left of the bed in the Red Room, shows him seated in a heavy wooden chair, dressed in powdered wig, black gown and bands. In his hands he holds a Sermon, the text of which is 'Without Charity all is unavailing towards Salvation. Charity is the Chief Benefit of the Suffering and Death of Jesus Christ.' He is thin and slightly bent, and though there is something of an expression of kindness and benevolence in his eyes, his demeanour is a solemn one. This may have something to do with the fact that of his six children, only one survived beyond the age of twenty-one.

Relatively little is known about the life of Parson Sykes. He was educated at Cambridge, where he became a fellow of Peterhouse College, and it was while he resided there that he met and fell in love with Decima Woodham, the daughter of a Cambridgeshire surgeon, Twyford Woodham of Ely. She was said to have been 'remarkable both for beauty and cleverness'.[1] Her portrait, painted when she was in middle age, hangs on the other side of the bed in the Red Room, and inspired my Grandfather to describe her as 'gorgeous in white satin, lace and diamond buttons – very handsome and commanding looking'.[2] They were married in 1735, on which occasion Parson's uncle, Mark Kirkby, presented him with the Living of Roos, near Hull, thus setting him up for life in the style to which second sons of the Gentry were accustomed. They moved into the Rectory, an imposing red brick house, where their first child Polly was born in 1739, followed two years later by a son, Mark. A second boy, Richard was born in 1742, but died in infancy, while a third, also Richard, born in 1743, survived. After the death of their fourth son, Joseph, who was born in 1744, there was a gap of five years before the birth of their sixth and final child, Christopher, on 23 May, 1749.

Mark, the eldest son and heir, seems to have shown some promise at an early age, if one can believe the rather gushing words of the Rector of the nearby Parish of Patrington, Mr Nicols, who wrote to Parson in 1748, 'I can hardly say which gave me most pleasure, whether to see the first Essays & Blossoms of a fine Genius in Master Mark's letter, or the Rich Fruit & perfection of one in your Composition.'[3] A year later Mark was writing to his father in a manner which suggests a precociously polite little boy. 'Honored Sir, My Mama & I received an unspeakable pleasure at hearing that you was very well,'[4] he wrote, the large scrawling handwriting of a boy of eight contrasting curiously with the quaint formality of expression. It is reassuring to learn that he was not all good. The year 1754 found Uncle Richard writing to Mark's sister, Polly, 'Your Brother doubtless has transgressed in a very high degree having forgott his duty to his Creator, Father, Mother and his other relations.' Whatever the temptation was that he had succumbed to at the age of twelve remains a mystery, though it was serious enough for his uncle to state, somewhat dramatically, 'the End I am afraid must be endless ruin and destruction of both Body and Soul'.[5]

There is a painting of Mark which hangs in the Red Room, next to that of his mother. He is wearing a beautiful red velvet suit with a richly embroidered matching waistcoat and lace jabot. His hand is resting on a globe. He has youthful good looks and a faint smirk playing across his face. 'Look how fortune has smiled upon me', he seems to be saying. Perhaps he was planning his Grand Tour, or which of the great universities he was going to attend. The label on the painting tells the sad truth; Mark Sykes 1741–1760. He died aged nineteen, the same year as his sister, two years before his younger brother, Richard.

Only two children survived to witness the move to Sledmere, which Parson inherited on the death of his brother, and which then consisted of an estate of just over five thousand acres. They moved in at the end of the summer. 'I am curious to know how you pass your time in

Sledmire,' wrote his son-in-law, John de Ponthieu, on 10 September. 'Pray do you delight in Gardning – how are your Trees, do they get the better of your Cold Climate, have you pine Apples in perfection? I should think in so private a place as Sledmire Gardning would be a very great amusement, especially as you cannot hunt – I intend you a parcel of Shrubs this Autumn. I desire you would order a spot to be dug up in your garden for them, as much sheltered as possible otherwise they might die.'[6]

Reading through the considerable volume of Parson's correspondence written after he moved from Roos, gardening appears to have been the last thing on his mind. Scarcely was he settled than his son Richard fell ill. 'I am very sorry for the account you give me of poor Cozen Dicky,' wrote his banker and cousin by marriage, Joseph Denison, in November 1762. 'I am very sensible of the affliction you must be under as a Parent, having felt it myself, when I lost both my boys in the same year. I have never heard of his being so ill before.'[7] The following April he was sending his condolences 'on your late severe loss, which has given both me and my Wife much sorrow'.[8] There were frequent attacks of the gout, rendering him often bed-ridden, as well as keeping Dr Chambers as busy as he had been with Sledmere's previous incumbent. Much of Parson's time was taken up with clerical business and his high standing was reflected in the fact that on three occasions he was chosen to represent the Clergy of the East Riding in Convocation. That he had a high opinion of himself in this field is shown by the fact that when one local clergyman, the Rector of Hunmanby, wrote him a letter saying that he was considering standing himself, Parson scrawled across the letter 'the man must have been drunk when he wrote it'.[9]

His primary interest however was making money, in particular by investment in mortgages and speculation in government bonds. He was described by one contemporary, John Courtney, a wealthy young financier, as 'an artful cunning fellow, ready to take all advantages where he can'.[10] Numerous letters he wrote to his London banker, Joseph Denison, testify to his love of speculating. Denison, who had also looked after his brother's affairs, was an extraordinary figure, a former Leeds bank clerk who moved to London and prospered to such a degree that he came to own his own bank. He married Sarah Sykes as his first wife, who was a distant cousin of Parson's. Celebrated for his spectacular meanness as he clawed his way to riches, he left great fortunes to his children, principally to his son, William Joseph Denison, who became one of Yorkshire's biggest landowners and left a fortune of £2,300,000 in 1849, but also to his daughters, one of whom, Elizabeth, married the Marquis Conyngham, and became notorious as the mistress of George IV. 'I wish most heartily I had now your £10,000 by me,' began a typical letter from Denison to Parson, written in November, 1762. 'I would lay it out this very day, & I am very confident I could clear you 10 p.ct in a few months . . . but it must be done immediately . . . you may Judge what an immense profit will be and is made.' The letter concluded with a hint of his tightfistedness, conveniently blamed on his client. 'I was once going to send this by Express, but I did not know if it might be agreeable to you, or whether you would think the expense too much.'[11] Parson celebrated the profits from one deal early in their partnership by paying £1,000 for a single diamond, equivalent to approximately £50,000 in today's terms, which he made into a ring which graced his finger for ever after.[12]

Denison, with a canny eye for the future, was also careful to cultivate ties with Parson's son and heir. 'Your Son was heartily welcome,' wrote Denison in March, 1770, 'to any small Civilitys it was in our power to show him during his short stay with us . . . He is a very worthy young Gentleman, & you are very happy in having so pleasing a prospect of his future amiable conduct and usefulness.'[13] Parson's only surviving son, Christopher, was twenty at the time and down from Brasenose College, Oxford, for a brief spell in London as the guest of Mr and Mrs Denison at their house in St Mary Axe. He had gone up to Oxford in the autumn of 1767, where, after the obligatory period of idleness and tomfoolery, requiring many parental admonitions, he appears to have grown into a model student. 'I have not at any period studied harder than at present,' he wrote to his father early in 1770.

Christopher's decision to devote himself to study appears to have been inspired by the love of a woman. 'I solemnly declare,' he told Parson, 'it was my attachment to Miss B. which alone brought to light what little abilities I may now possess; it was the desire I had of rendering myself worthy of her which first roused me to pursue my studies with application. They cost me for some months many hours of pain, but by a resolute pursuance they afterwards became a pleasure & now I may safely say the pursuit of knowledge is my only pleasure in the absence of her.'[14] He studied law, history, botany, French and drawing under men who were the experts in their field in the world, such as 'the famous Scotchman Williamson'[15] who taught him mathematics and Thomas Hornsby, his astronomy tutor, one of the leading scientists of the day, whose observations of light ascension and declination were not surpassed in accuracy until 1925, and who went on to build the Radcliffe Observatory. There seems to have been no stopping Christopher in his pursuit of learning, all of which contributed to his development as a perfect example of the Renaissance Man. 'I have begun a new study,' he wrote on 6 May, 1770, 'to add to all my other business. Music as far as it depends upon Mathematical principles, & strum a fiddle an hour or two every day.'[16]

The woman he loved, 'Miss B.' or 'my dearest Bessy', as he commonly referred to her, was Elizabeth Tatton, the daughter of William Tatton Esq. of Wythenshawe in Cheshire. She was a friend of long standing who was referred to in one letter as being 'a woman I have from childhood adored'.[17] It was a match that both his parents had apparently vigorously promoted. 'When my heart was free and unconquered by Miss B.' Christopher reminded Parson, 'I well remember how many arguments you both used to persuade me to call upon her in a morning to walk out, & how you forwarded every opportunity of bringing us acquainted.'[18]

Writing to his father from the Denisons', Christopher made quite clear his intentions so far as Bessy was concerned, strengthened all the more by his admiration for his hostess. 'I am very fond of Mrs Denison,' he told him; 'she seems to be a very amiable & agreeable woman & of the sweetest temper; surely with such a woman the marriage State must be the happiest Mortals here enjoy (& such my Bessy is) for without good sense & a sweet temper every little accident will embitter its pleasures & any very unfortunate one even destroy its happiness . . . If unjust pray correct me for as I shall shortly (with the blessing of God & my Parents approbation) marry my Bessy, I could wish to know whether I have formed a right opinion of that state.'[19]

Soon after Parson received this letter, he gave his consent to the marriage. 'I already perceive it will require the greatest economy to make my allowance serve till I am married,' Christopher told him, echoing the familiar cries of incautious students down the ages. 'Notwithstanding the many bills I have already paid, there still remains to pay as far as I can guess £170 – I have now by me £50.' He was keen to show his father that in his opinion not one penny of the money spent had been wasted. 'I shall send into the country goods to a very considerable amount: a very valuable collection of books in most branches of science; a much admired collection of prints of the best Masters which will be of infinite use in drawing & in forming a pure & just taste; a collection of coins not to be despised; Mathematical instruments & many miscellaneous things of less moment, with a set of beautiful specimens of the various kinds of Fossils collected by a man the most famous in the Fossil world; all these may most fairly be valued at £500. & I hope I may without vanity say that I either am now or shall shortly with the blessing of God be able to make a considerable use of the articles here contained.'[20]

The marriage between Christopher and his 'beloved Bessy' took place on 23 October, 1770, at St Wilfred's, Northenden, the Tatton family's parish church. As well as personal happiness, it brought him great riches, for not only did he officially become the inheritor of Sledmere and all its estates, but Bessy brought with her a considerable dowry from her father, in the form of two banker's drafts, one for £10,000, the other for £2,542. These were the first payments as part of the terms of the marriage settlement which had been signed on 1 September, under which Christopher was to receive a total of £16,000 out of the fortune left to his wife by her maternal aunt, Elizabeth Egerton of Tatton.

Though he took his bride to Sledmere on 29 October and stayed for five weeks, it was never Christopher's intention to move into the house, as might have been expected, preferring instead to allow his parents to live on there, while he removed his bride to Wheldrake Hall, a modest house owned by the family to the south-east of York. After Christmas the young couple travelled together to London for an extended shopping spree, taking lodgings at Jewels Hotel, Surrey Street, which ran from the Strand down to the Embankment.

This was an important time in London's history, with the City growing in power as a financial centre and rapidly expanding its banking, shipping and trading activities, and as they stood on the terrace of Somerset House, a few minutes' walk from their hotel, looking out over the Thames, Christopher and Bessy surveyed a scene which had changed little since Canaletto had painted it twenty years previously. As they looked west up to the Banqueting Hall, Westminster Abbey and Westminster Hall, and east down to St Paul's, a view which took in numerous facades of fine waterfront mansions and the myriad spires of city churches, dozens of small boats sailed the water: lighters, barges, brigs, hoys, dinghies, bum-boats, ferry-boats, packets and wherries all scuttling about and connected in some way to their larger cousins, colliers from the North, whalers from Greenland, merchant ships from the Continent, East Indiamen and West Indiamen, and square riggers from America who plied their trade in ever increasing numbers in and out of the port of London. To the east stood a monument to the man who had restored the greatness of Britain. The newly completed Blackfriars Bridge, opened in 1770, was named Pitt Bridge, after William Pitt, whose successful, almost single-handed, prosecution of the Seven Years War had brought France to her knees and Canada under the British flag. What a sense of excitement and pride the young couple must have felt.

In accordance with their new status, there was much shopping to be done, details of which Christopher meticulously recorded in neat, tiny handwriting in his account book. A large quarto volume protected by a pale calfskin dust jacket, and stamped on the front with the initials, C.S., and the date 1770, it was discovered a few years ago hidden away in the Estate Office, and has now been restored to the Library, where it is one of the most important books to have survived. It tells us in the first few pages exactly the kind of things a fashionable young couple down from the country would be buying to take home. For Christopher there were new clothes – pairs of breeches, a waistcoat, gentlemen's ruffles, a sword and belt – and a visit to his tailor, while Bessy visited the milliner, and the barber 'for curls', and bought two gowns, one of India silk, lace trimming, a fan and cloak, and shoes. On 28 February her new husband took her to Mr Young, the antique dealer, and spent the not inconsiderable sum of £106. 14s. 6d. on jewels. They also went food shopping and ordered a whole Parmesan cheese, weighing 55½lbs, a Stilton cheese and some tea.

Then there was their new home to consider, which, having stood empty for many years, required completely refurbishing. On 29 January they visited Mr Elliot's and spent £112. 2s. 8d. on china, while 6 February found them at Mr Christie's buying pictures for £82. 8s. 6d. Ten days later they bought a second lot for £63, and further purchases of picture and prints from various dealers bought the sum spent up to £234. 17s. Their biggest single expense was on 'plate', bought from Mr Young on 20 February at a total cost of £303. 18s. In addition to these major acquisitions, they spent considerable sums on furniture, carpets, books, busts and a medicine chest, as well as paying visits to Mr Wood for a new chaise at £60, and Mr O'Keefe for a coach at £121. 15s.[21] Christopher also spent money on adding to his collections of coins and fossils. They returned to Sledmere on 5 March, where they no doubt imparted the good news to Parson and Mrs Sykes that Bessy was four months pregnant. They finally arrived back at Wheldrake on 20 March, Christopher having bought himself a new horse for the journey.

The next few months were spent settling into their new home. Correspondence between Christopher and his wine merchant, Sam Hall, shows that in true family tradition a love of fine wine ran in his blood and that stocking the cellar was a priority. He had evidently suggested to Hall, that he might come and personally supervise its laying down and must have given him some vague description of

Wheldrake. 'The notion I have of your place of abode from your description,' wrote Hall, 'is that it has been some old uninhabited mansion (at least by human kind) and which feeling the weighty hand of time call'd loudly for such assistance as I make no doubt you have given to it in yr. best manner.'[22] Christopher took delivery of a hundred dozen bottles of Champagne and five hogsheads at the end of April, and on 22 May received the following letter from Hall: 'My father has wrote to London for six dozen of the very best French Claret that can be had and it shall come with the Malmsey agreeable to your orders.' He apologised for not being able to come and oversee things himself, but told him that 'the wines that we sent you will be fine and fitt for Bottling by the time the bottles are become thoroughly dry (and if they were rinsed out with a little brandy it would be serviceable) and the sooner it is then done the better . . . you will please to direct your Buttler to lay them on their sides in a cool dry place of the cellar.'[23]

With the cellar organised and the furnishing complete, the house was ready to receive the new baby. Bessy was seven months pregnant when Christopher received a letter from her uncle, Joseph Stafford, expressing his family's delight at the impending birth. 'We are greatly rejoyced to hear you are likely to have an increase of your family soon,' he wrote, 'and most sincerely wish Mrs SYKES an happy Delivery & Luck in a Lad — according to yr. Cheshire phrase.'[24] His sentiments were timely, and on 20 August his niece was delivered of a son, whom they christened Mark. A guinea was paid to the Northenden bell-ringers to ring out the good news to the neighbourhood. A few weeks later, Joseph Denison wrote to say how delighted he and his wife were 'to hear the young gentleman is so well — our little Goods thank God are the same. Will is a perfect Parrott, & talks everything.' His own wife, he added, 'expects every day to follow Mrs SYKES'S example'.[25]

For Mrs Denison, however, whose good sense and sweet temper Christopher had so admired, it was not to be. A letter arrived in November from Denison's Clerk, Nicholas Dawes, bearing melancholy news. 'I am Extremely sorry to acquaint you that last Night about nine o'clock it pleased God to take away the Life of Mrs Denison after lying in. She was taken with a Slow fever, under which she laboured ten days, & tho' under the care of two eminent Physicians, their utmost endeavours proved ineffectual, so that it ended with a Mortification in her Bowels.'[26] Denison was heartbroken, 'incapable of writing'. When he did eventually put pen to paper, it was to his old friend Parson that he turned. 'I seem,' he said, 'to have many Afflictions to struggle with by the removal of those most near and dear to me.'[27] It was something that Parson knew about more than most.

Now that Christopher was settled, with a happy marriage and a son and heir, he turned his attention to what was to be the great work of his life: the improvement of Sledmere. Thomas Jeffreys's *Yorkshire Atlas*, published in 1771, gives one a rough idea of what the place then looked like, its appearance virtually unchanged since the alterations carried out by Uncle Richard. The house stood in front of a rectangular 'garden', with a few trees on either side and the Mere in the middle. To the east lay the Kitchen Garden with its glasshouses. South of the Mere, beyond the ha-ha, ran the main road from York to Bridlington, bisecting the U-shaped belt of trees known as The Avenue. The village was scattered mostly to the east of the house, but there were a few dwellings to the south-west. All around, the Wold land rose up to a height of more than five hundred feet.

In order to understand the full import of the work carried out by Christopher Sykes, which was to eventually earn him the sobriquet 'Reformer of the Wolds', it is necessary to understand the nature of the land as it then was. Farming as we know it today did not exist. To the north and south of the village lay a small number of large open arable fields. These were divided into long strips, 'ridge and furrow', which were owned by individual farmers. The land owned by a farmer was rarely in one place, his strips being widely distributed across the entire field system, and although he farmed this land himself, the management and regulation of the open fields as a whole were vested in the community and administered through the manorial court. A wide range of crops were grown, on a two- or three-course rotation, with one third of all land lying fallow at any one time; long-eared or sprat barley was grown on the better soils, with naked or wheat barley on the intermediate or less fertile soils. Summer and winter varieties of wheat, including buckwheat or French wheat, were also grown as was massledine, oats, clean rye, beans and peas.[28]

Beyond the village and its surrounding arable lands lay vast sheep walks which dominated the great expanse of bare upland that was the landscape, 'open, scarce a bush or tree . . . for several Miles'.[29] Daniel Defoe described the Wolds as being like 'the plains and downs . . . of Salisbury'.[30] Extensive rabbit warrens were also a characteristic feature of the area, one of the biggest being at Cowlam Farm, just outside Sledmere. This was described by the agriculturalist, William Marshall, writing in 1788, as being 'the largest upon these Wolds; and probably the most valuable warren in the Island. The . . . farm contains about nineteen hundred acres; and, generally speaking, it is all warren.'[31] Bounded by sod walls, they were an important part of the local economy, on a par with sheep. Each warren supported several thousand pairs of rabbits, yielding between 100,000 and 150,000 couple annually, whose skinned carcasses would be sold for meat in the industrial towns of the West Riding, as well as in local towns such as Hull, Beverley and York. The skins were dried and sold to furriers, whose main markets were the hat manufactories of London and Manchester.

This was all about to change, and the way it was transformed into the landscape that exists today was through enclosure. This was the replacement of the old open-field, strip-farming system, which was increasingly regarded as being outmoded and inefficient, with smaller fields both owned and controlled by one farmer. As the eighteenth century progressed, greater demands were being placed upon agriculture by a rapidly growing population, which rose from six million in 1741 to eight-point-nine million in 1801, and was to nearly double in the next half century. This created a powerful motive to improve productivity and in the minds of modern agricultural thinkers, amongst whom Christopher certainly numbered himself, enclosure was the way forward. It enabled landowners to improve their farming techniques, to consolidate their property into larger farms, and to add to its value by building farmhouses and outbuildings. Enclosed land also steadily rose in value, an important consideration since before 1800 each enclosure required the passing of an individual act of Parliament, making it an expensive business. A valuation carried out by Christopher's steward, Robert Dunn, in May, 1776, estimated that the land at Sledmere unenclosed was worth between 1s. 3d. and 20s. an acre, rising to 2s.–20s. on enclosure, and 3s. 6d.–20s. after fifteen years.[32]

Though family legend has always maintained that Christopher was the pioneer in this department, the truth is that he was carrying on a tradition that had been started by his Uncle Richard, when he took in hand the land which formed The Avenue, and later an area to its west, to form the Park. In Richard's lifetime he spent £40,000 on buying and enclosing land to consolidate the estate. 'I yesterday signed an Article of Agreement,' he had written to his brother Joseph in July, 1760, 'to pay £1,550 for £31 a year net Tythe rent of thirty-six Oxgangs at East Heslerton which is fifty years purchase, but if an inclosure take place may not be too dear.'[33] Christopher just did it on a larger scale. He began in 1771, when his account book recorded that he had spent £2,051 on 'Inclosing' at East Heslerton, and by 1775 he had instructed Robert Dunn to start on Sledmere. 'Mr Dunn has perhaps already informed you,' he wrote to one of his neighbours, Luke Lillingstone, in January, 1776, 'that I propose to enclose Sledmire',[34] explaining to him that 'In Sledmire . . . for some Years past there has not been above 500 Acres in Tillage . . . but upon the Inclosure the whole will be divided into three large and two smaller farms with not less than 1,500 or 1,600 Acres in Tillage.'[35] In his lifetime Christopher was to spend £180,000 on adding 18,000 acres to the estate, and on enclosing and improving the land.

Apart from two estates bought in the early 1770s, at Wetwang and Myton Carr, most of Christopher's major acquisitions took place in the 1780s, after his father's death. In the intervening years he concentrated his attention on laying out a new landscape at Sledmere. He had begun planting as early as 1771, when he spent £70. 15s. 7d. on trees, taking delivery of two consignments, one bought from Mr Dixon, the second, larger order from Mr Telford. This was the start of a programme which began on a relatively small scale, with about fifteen acres a year being planted, and became increasingly ambitious. Being young and modern with his finger on the pulse of everything new in the world of science and art he probably found his uncle's taste dull and outmoded. His earliest attempts at stamping his own ideas on the landscape can be seen in two drawings he made on a single sheet of paper which exists in the Library at Sledmere. The first is of *Mr Perfects Design of the Plantations*, which depicts the two belts of trees on either side of the Mere. The second shows 'The alterations of the Plantations'. On the east side, which runs next to the village street, the belt was to be 'fill'd up with Trees to cover the Houses', while its inside edge adjoining the Mere was given a ragged, more informal appearance. The belt to the west, adjoining the church, was to be cut into shapes, forming a series of circles and a diamond with, interweaving them, 'two little Serpentine Walks to Cross the plantation'.[36]

In 1775 Christopher decided to call in a professional to help him with his schemes: Thomas White, a landscape designer and nurseryman from West Retford near Gainsborough, who had previously worked for the celebrated Capability Brown on two major local projects at Sandbeck, South Yorkshire, and Temple Newsham, near Leeds. In April, 1776, he delivered to Christopher *A General Plan for the Improvement of the Grounds at Sledmere*, beautifully executed in watercolour on paper mounted on linen. This proposed the building of a new house to be sited directly in front of the existing stables, with the two buildings separated by lawns and a wooded area. It also showed the sites of three yet-to-be-designed farms, each of which would act as an 'eyecatcher' at the end of a vista. The plan covered a large area, with shelter belts proposed all round the boundaries and plantations topping the deep dales which are a feature of the Wolds. The most dramatic aspect of the new design was the sweeping away of Uncle Richard's entire Avenue, leaving the area directly to the south of the house almost totally devoid of trees, and the filling in of the Mere. Although planting had already started on the boundaries, and some of White's ideas were eventually to be incorporated into the final plan of the landscape, it is evident that Christopher was not entirely happy with the overall design. Though White continued for some years to supply him with trees, he was dropped the following year in favour of his more famous former employer.

On 18 September, 1777, Christopher recorded in his diary that 'the Great Brown came to Sledmere in the morning early'.[37] Lancelot Brown was the best-known landscape designer of the day, the successor to Kent, who died in 1748, and it is a measure of Christopher's ambition that he chose to employ him. He would certainly have come highly recommended by two Yorkshire neighbours, Edwin Lascelles at Harewood, and Sir William St Quintin at Scampston, both of whose parks he had recently transformed. Brown stayed for a day and although no details exist of exactly what passed between them on this visit, one must assume that he was shown around the grounds and that they discussed what part of the existing landscape was to be retained and incorporated into any new scheme. With the enclosure of Sledmere progressing at a pace, Christopher would have been especially keen to finalise the positioning of the three new farms, to be called Castle, Life Hill and Marramatte. Brown left early the following morning, 19 September, his client's mind thoroughly concentrated on the great task ahead.

Christopher was a 'hands on' gardener who had undoubtedly read Horace Walpole's essay 'On Modern Gardening', written in 1770, in which he had stated his belief that 'the possessor, if he has any taste, must be the best designer of his own improvements. He sees his situation in all seasons of the year, at all times of the day. He knows where beauty will not clash with convenience, and observes in his silent walks or accidental rides a thousand hints that must escape a person who in a few days sketches out a pretty picture, but has not had leisure to examine the details and relations of every part.'[38] He lost no time in getting started, and the very next week found him personally 'staking out' a series of new plantations. 'My method of planting,' he wrote, 'is in small holes made in the turf . . . The holes are made in the autumn at three feet asunder, and eight or ten inches over, returning the soil into the hole at the time of making it with the turf downwards.' A month later, on 30 October, he 'began to plant . . . having prepared several thousand holes'.[39] The next day he made a note in his pocket book of an order he had placed with Thomas White for a further 109,500 trees – '20,000 seedling Larches, 50,000 Scotch fir seedling, 5,000 Spruce 2y.0, 10,000 Spruce 1y.0, 1,500 Weymouth pine, 2,000 Silver fir, 10,000 Beech seedling, 1,000 Syca-more, and 10,000 seedling Birch of 1 or 2y.0'.[40]

One of the reasons for the success of Christopher's planting was that, as in all he did, he had immersed himself in the subject, learning everything that there was to know, and in the process becoming an expert in the chosen field. He understood that the most successful trees were those raised by the proprietor from seedling, taken from the bed exactly when they were required and planted immediately, so that they did not suffer from being out of the ground for too long. To this end he had two nurseries, one at Sledmere, the other at Wheldrake. An endpaper in the diary shows that his immediate requirements were 300,000 trees from White, 136,000 from John and George Telford, nurserymen from York, and 33,000 from William Shiells of Dalkeith, the majority of which would have been seedlings.

It was not only at Sledmere that Christopher had been planting. 'Mrs S. was taken ill at three,' reads the last entry in his pocket book for 1777, on 27 December, 'and delivered between four and five in the morning of a Girl Elizabeth.'[41] She was the fourth child born to Bessy since the arrival of Mark in August, 1771, all healthy, and making 'a pretty little flock'[42] as Joseph Denison referred to them in a letter to Parson. A second son, Tatton, named after his mother's family, had been born on 22 August, 1772, followed by another boy, Christopher, in October, 1774. Their first daughter, Decima Hester Beatrix, was born in December, 1775, and the new-born Elizabeth completed the family.

In spite of the fact that Christopher owned and ran Sledmere and that the family now numbered seven, Parson and Mrs Sykes remained ensconced there, while their son and daughter-in-law were still living at Wheldrake. 'As we have not met with a house to our satisfaction,' Christopher had written to his brother-in-law, William Egerton, in

December, 1775, 'we shall probably stay here.'[43] They appear to have lived fairly modestly with relatively few servants. There was Styan, the butler; William, Christopher's valet, who had been with him since his bachelor days; Charlotte, Bessy's personal maid; various 'servant women'; a housekeeper; a gardener, Richard Cooper; a coachman, and a full time nanny, Nurse Moore, who was to be the longest serving member of the household. At the various times of Bessy's pregnancies, the account book also shows payments to 'Nurses' and, in 1775, to a 'Wet Nurse'.

Christopher did not keep a detailed diary recounting the events of his life, but in a series of little pocket books, sometimes 'Goldsmith's Almanack' or perhaps 'The Ladies Own Memorandum Book, or Daily Pocket Journal', he briefly noted down his guests and dining companions, financial and estate matters, memoranda of servants, his travels, notes about gardening, etc., In the midst of which trivia are the occasional poignant reminders of more important personal matters. 'Mrs Sykes miscarried for the first time in her life after a months severe illness,'[44] ran the entry for 15 December, 1779, for example, while on 22 March, 1778, 'Little Tom Tatton, my Brother's Son died suddenly.'[45] Reading through some of the other entries for 1778, the first year of Elizabeth Sykes's life, one gets some idea of the domestic life of Christopher and Bessy.

There are few entries during the first six months, other than Christopher going back and forth to Sledmere. On 12 June, they set off on holiday, not to London or the Continent, but to the nearby east coast town of Bridlington, a popular resort for the newly fashionable pastime of sea bathing. 'Wife and Self dined at Sledmere,' he wrote. 'Got to Hilderthorpe at night. Servants dined at Wetwang.' Hilderthorpe, a coastal village to the south of Bridlington, was part of Christopher's estates and the site of the family's summer retreat, Flat Top Farm, since 1776. This was a three-storey house, built upon rising ground above Bridlington Bay and commanding magnificent views out to sea. The ground and top floors consisted of permanent accommodation for the tenant farmer, while the first floor, which had an octagonal salon and well-proportioned lodging rooms, was reserved for the occasional use of the family. It is important because it was almost certainly the first house designed by Christopher, being remarkably similar to other architectural drawings made by him in the Library at Sledmere.

On this occasion they stayed at Hilderthorpe for a month, and on 13 July, Christopher recorded 'I went to Sledmere to dinner. Wife went to Wheldrake.' Nineteen August found them in the midst of a house party. 'Wheldrake. Mr and Miss Sarrandes, Mr and Mrs Daniel, Miss Simpson, Miss Collings, Mr and Mrs Paul, Wife and self fished in the old River, dined, drank tea and danced upon the rugs.' A charming scene, repeated the following day. 'All the above drank tea and danced upon the grass.' On 31 August, Christopher rode over to Sledmere for dinner and 'sent Styan to wait for Mr Brown at Wetwang.' He did not turn up and finally arrived on 5 September. 'Mr Brown came this morning and we rode about, dined and lodged at Wetwang.' Brown left the next day. 'I returned home to dinner, met my Wife and Tatton,' noted Christopher. Ten days later the whole family visited Sledmere and also on 16 September 'Wife and Self went to Castle Howard. Dined there, drank tea at Eddlethorpe Grange and returned to Sledmere at night.' They stayed for a week and on 24 September 'Wife, self and children returned to Wheldrake at night.'

A curious letter written at this time from Christopher to an old Oxford tutor, the Revd William Cleaver, throws some light on the education of his children. Evidently the boys had a tutor at Wheldrake, who had been teaching them to read. He was, however, on the point of leaving, and in asking Cleaver to help him find a replacement, Christopher made it quite clear that he was unhappy with the way the children spoke, a sign that in the aristocratic society to which he aspired, local dialects were beginning to be frowned upon. 'The person who has had the instruction of my Children hitherto is going into another line of life,' he wrote on 15 September, 'indeed he is no loss as he has done them all the Good he is capable of which was to teach them to read English tho' but Ill. If you know of any Young Man you think fit to Succeed him, who can correct their Yorkshire tone and instruct them to *Your* Wishes (I am sure it will be to mine) I wish you would let me know to continue with them till you and he think they are fit for School.'[46] On 6 October, 1778, Christopher noted in his diary, 'Master Tatton and Christopher went to Mr Simpson to be under his care.' They were aged six and four respectively.

'The Great Brown's' return in September bore fruit when, two months later in November, he produced his 'Plan for the intended Alterations at Sledmere'. Christopher immediately preferred it to White's plan because, while new plantations encircled the Park to its south and west, the design incorporated much of the existing landscape, retaining all the southern portion of The Avenue and thinning out the section nearer to the house into a series of clumps. The Mere and the buildings around the house remained unaltered. So far as the positions of the three 'eyecatcher' farmsteads proposed by White were concerned, Brown was greatly helped by the fact these were already partly built.

'I do not at present see any probability of being freed from my engagements at an earlier period,' wrote Christopher in September, 1778 to a friend, 'by the constant attention I have paid to the Wolds having built fourteen dwelling houses with several Barns and Stables.' The most important of these new buildings were the three farms which would form the focus of the new vistas. The first of these appeared as an entry in his diary for 13 July, 1778, when he noted 'begun Castle'. Situated a mile or so to the south-east of the main house, and today my own home, Castle Farm was designed by John Carr of York, the best-known architect in the north of England. The design took the form of a Gothic gatehouse, with neo-classical wings – which were never completed. Work on it moved fast and on 3 September, two days before Brown's second visit to Sledmere, Christopher scribbled 'finished the Castle brickwork'.

The other two farms, Life Hill, to the south-west of the main house and Marramatte, to the north-west, were designed by Christopher himself, who drew up two sets of drawings for them, both working and presentation. These show him to have been a skilled draughtsman with a good architectural knowledge and a genuine ability to design. They were not just cribbed from one of the many pattern books available at the time, such as Thomas Lightoler's *The Gentleman and Farmers Architect*, but were his own ideas, cleverly combining the need for the houses to look beautiful while at the same time preserving their practical function as agricultural buildings. The charming pavilions at Life Hill, for example, which have pilasters on their gable ends and stand to the right and left of the farm house, are barns, and at Marramatte, the gable ends of the farm buildings also form pavilions, which have pilasters and oculi.

In the end neither White's nor Brown's schemes were adopted, though elements from both were used and they may have served as an inspiration, because Christopher's own ideas were on a far grander scale than anything either of them envisaged. They were more akin to those of the essayist Joseph Addison, who in 1710 had written 'Why may not a whole estate be thrown into a kind of garden by frequent plantations? A man might make a pretty landskip of his own possessions.'[47] Christopher's vision was indeed to turn his whole estate into a Park, to extend his woodlands and plantations so that they enhanced not only the surrounds of the house, but the entire agricultural landscape. He dreamed of creating a Paradise amongst the bleak hills of the Wolds. To this end, after he received Brown's plan, he indulged in a veritable orgy of planting, covering 130 acres in the 1778–1779 season, the largest area planted in the whole of the forty years it was to take to complete the landscape. His 'account of Trees planted at Sledmere', given to the local agriculture society, listed all the species used – 'forty Wild Cherry, sixty Mountain Ash, 300 Yews, 358 Silver Fir, 500 Weymouth Pine, 600 Birch, 1,540 Oak, 6,400 Holly, 12,000 Beech, 25,260 Spruce, 33,600 Ash, 42,122 Scotch Fir and 54,430 Larch'.[48] In recognition of his 'having planted the greatest quantity of Larch Trees', the secretary, William Ellis, wrote to tell him that 'you are entitled to make choice of any Book or set of Books not exceeding the price of Five Guineas'.[49]

When John Bigland toured Yorkshire at the end of the first decade of the nineteenth century, his description of Sledmere showed precisely how great a transformation of the landscape had taken place in the relatively short time that Christopher Sykes had lived there.

Sledmere is situated in a spacious vale, in the centre of the Yorkshire Wolds, and may be considered as the ornament of that bleak and hilly district. All the surrounding scenery displays the judicious taste of the late and present proprietors: the circumjacent hills are adorned with elegant farm houses covered with blue slate, and resembling villas erected for the purpose of rural retirement. The farms are in as high a state of cultivation as the soil will admit; and in the summer the waving crops in the fields, the houses of the tenantry elegantly constructed, and judiciously dispersed, the numerous and extensive plantations skirting the slopes of the hills, and the superb mansion with its ornamented grounds, in the centre of the vale, form a magnificent and luxuriant assemblage, little to be expected in a country like the Wolds; and to a stranger on his sudden approach, the coup d'oeil is singularly novel and striking.[50]

It was a fitting tribute to Christopher's great vision.

CHAPTER III

The Architect

In February, 1783, the month in which the American War of Independence finally drew to a close, Christopher received a letter from his brother-in-law, William. 'My Sister mentioned in her last',' he wrote, 'that you were looking for a House, I hope you have heard of one by this time that will be comfortable for you at the present, I can't help wishing very much that the Doctor wou'd give up Sledmere to you, but I conclude that is out of the question.'[1] If only for one reason, this was true: Parson was now an old man in his seventies and suffered from poor health. He had seen little of his son in the previous few years, who, as a result of the war, had taken up a commission as a Captain in Colonel Henry Maister's Regiment, the East Yorkshire Militia, though while away from home, Christopher had been kept informed as to his father's condition from regular letters sent to him by the Sledmere butler, John Hopper. Parson suffered constantly from pains in his chest, regular spasms and dreadful gout. 'He is very Low Spirited and Eats very little,'[2] Hopper wrote in April, 1782, though there were the occasional good days. 'I have the pleasure to acquaint you,' wrote Hopper on 15 August, 'that your Father got out an Airing last Saturday and has continued it every day since, he was at Church on Sunday.' In a memoir written by my grandfather, he recalled meeting, when he was a child, an old lady who remembered seeing Parson at church, 'a little old man with a powdered wig carried into Sledmere Church on his footman's back'.[3]

Parson did not recover from his illness, and his death the following year solved Christopher's housing problem. He survived long enough, however, to be the beneficiary of a great honour bestowed upon him by the King. Writing to Christopher early in February, 1783, Richard

Beaumont, his friend and fellow plantsman, told him that he had heard 'that a Baronet will shortly be created in the East Riding, so saith a Friend connected with the Rulers of the Nation'.[4] The Baronetcy to which he referred was to be offered to Christopher as a reward for his contribution to the reclamation of the Wolds. The high esteem in which he held his father is evident from the fact that he chose to turn down the title, insisting that it was conferred upon Parson instead. On 25 February, 1783, the Secretary of State for Foreign Affairs, the Rt Hon. Thomas Townshend, signed a patent on behalf of King George III: 'Our will & pleasure is that you prepare a Bill for our Royal Signature to pass our Great Seal containing the Grant of the Dignity of a Baronet of this our Kingdom of Great Britain unto our trusty and well beloved Mark Sykes, Doctor in Divinity, of Sledmire in our County of York.'[5] So Parson became the Revd Sir Mark Sykes, 1st Baronet of Sledmere.

Amongst the hundreds of letters of congratulation that came pouring in for both the new Baronet and his son was one from Uncle Joseph, who lamented that 'his poor state of Health will afford him so little enjoyment of this or of almost any earthly Comfort'.[6] They were prophetic words. On 9 September Christopher recorded in his diary, 'My father taken ill', and the following Sunday, 14 September, 'My Dear Father died at 4½ this morning. I got to Sledmere at 8½ not knowing of his illness till the night time at Hull Bank.' He was buried on 19 September. 'The Remains of my Dear Father,' noted Christopher, 'was taken from Sledmere at 8½ o'clock and was buried at Roos at 6 o'clock in the evening.'[7] His coffin was attended only by his servants, a stipulation he had made in his will. 'The very painful & lingering life which My Uncle led,' wrote Parson's nephew, Nicholas, to Christopher, 'may make his death be looked upon as a happy release by all his Friends.'[8]

By the end of 1783, Christopher, Bessy and the five children had moved into the big house, unfortunately for them in the middle of an exceptionally cold winter. In an age when most of us live in over-heated houses, it is easy to forget how uncomfortable it must have been to live in a large draughty house in periods of harsh and freezing weather. It was still a number of years before the advent of any kind of central heating, and the inhabitants had to rely on individual fires as their only source of warmth. 'I hope you all keep well & have plenty of Coals,' wrote Henry Maister to Christopher in January, 1784, 'for around a good fire is the only comfortable place',[9] though the truth is that most fireplaces usually produced more smoke than heat, and the only guaranteed way to keep warm was to wear more clothes. On 3 January, Christopher recorded 'a heavy storm of snow' in his diary, and throughout January and February there are regular entries for 'deep snow' and sometimes 'extremely deep snow'. Things finally began to improve on 22 February, when Christopher was able to write 'began this day to thaw'.[10]

No doubt inspired by the Arctic conditions they had been experiencing, Christopher also set about a new piece of building work at Sledmere, the creation of an ice-house. These buildings, which were *de rigueur* in most big houses of the day, were an advanced version of a 'snow-well' built for the Duke of York at St James's Palace in 1666. While that had been little more than a pit dug into the ground and thatched with straw, the new models were often architect-designed and vaulted in brick or stone.[11] They were situated close to the nearest large stretch of water – in the case of Sledmere, it would have been the Mere – so that during the winter the ice could be cut and placed in the ice-house, carefully insulated between layers of straw, for use the following summer, when it would have been used primarily for the refrigeration of food as well as for the occasional iced dessert. The design for the Sledmere ice-house came in the form of a working drawing, showing a detailed and carefully labelled section, sent to Christopher in February, 1784 by John Carr, the architect of Castle Farm. It was dug out in July and a sum of 12s. 6d. was entered in the house accounts the following January for 'filling Ice-House'.

Seventeen eighty-four may well have been a momentous year for Christopher and his family, their feet firmly perched upon the ladder of social ascendancy, but so it was for the outside world too. There was change in the air. The disastrous War of American Independence was over, and the ministry of the man who had presided over it, Lord North, had disintegrated. A new group of radical thinkers was beginning to influence politics, men like Joseph Priestley, Richard Price, Erasmus Darwin and Benjamin Franklin, who believed in the reformation of Parliament and in John Dunning's famous motion 'that the power of the Crown has increased, is increasing, and ought to be diminished'. They had found a voice in the short-lived Parliament of Lord Rockingham's Whig Party and had achieved a number of reforms before his sudden death in July, 1782, including the reorganisation and reduction of the Royal household, the disenfranchisement of revenue officers, and the debarring of government contractors from sitting as MPs.

The short reign of Rockingham's successor, Lord Shelburne, and the speedy collapse of the ministry which followed – an ill-judged coalition of two implacable enemies, the unpopular Lord North and the Whig, Charles James Fox – allowed King George III to invite a rising young star, William Pitt, to form a Government. Pitt, the second son of the Earl of Chatham, himself Prime Minister over a period of twelve years, made his maiden speech at the age of twenty-one, served in Lord Shelburne's Cabinet as Chancellor of the Exchequer aged twenty-three, and was only twenty-four when he became First Minister. Though this might seem an extraordinary feat to most people, it would not have surprised his family, whose nicknames for him – 'William the Great', when he was a small child, and 'the Young Senator', 'the Orator' and 'the Philosopher' when he was in his teens – suggest that they had a strong hunch he would go far.[12] When aged only seven, his mother had written to her husband, 'of William, I said nothing, but that was because he cannot be *extraordinary* for *him*'.[13]

Pitt was in the right place at the right time when oratory was becoming more and more a feature of debate. His maiden speech, made on 26 February, 1781, caused the assembled members to prick up their ears, especially since it was made off the cuff as a result of an unexpected call by a number of the opposition, eager to test out the so-called brilliance of Chatham's son. They were not disappointed. 'It impressed . . . from the judgment, the diction and the solemnity that pervaded and characterised it,' wrote Nathaniel Wraxall, who was present. 'The statesman, not the student, or the advocate, or the candidate for popular applause, characterised it . . . All men beheld in him at once a future Minister, and the members of the Opposition, overjoyed at such an accession of strength, vied with each other in their encomiums as well as in their predictions of his certain political elevation.'[14] Indeed Edmund Burke was so overcome with admiration that he is reported as having said 'he is not merely a chip off the old block, but the old block itself'.[15]

It was not long before Pitt had the ears of the House whenever he spoke, an honour rarely granted to new young members, and his name soon began to be known to a wider public beyond the benches of the Commons. As early as February, 1783, when he was still only twenty-three, he was the choice of a number of astute politicians to succeed Shelburne, who had resigned after two Government defeats. 'There is scarcely any other Political Character of consideration in the Country,' wrote Henry Dundas, 'to whom many people from Habits, from Connections, from former Professions, from Rivalships and from Antipathies will not have objections. But he is perfectly new ground . . .'[16] He actually was sent for by the King, but turned down the offer, on the grounds that if he was to come to power it was to be on his own terms. It was a brave and shrewd decision, for when the King asked him a second time the following December and he accepted, he was in an unassailable position. The news was received in the House of Commons with a shout of laughter. It was, after all,

> A sight to make surrounding nations stare;
> A Kingdom trusted to a school-boy's care.[17]

Any ambitious young man of position would have been swept up in the excitement of the moment, and in the general election of March, 1784 that put Pitt into office, a notorious affair that had gone on for forty days – 'forty days' poll, forty days' riot and forty days' confusion' as Pitt himself put it[18] – Christopher stood as MP for Beverley. His election was by no means a foregone conclusion since the rival candidate, Sir James Pennyman, had an enthusiastic following. 'Sir James came yesterday' wrote John Hopper, '. . . they all cry Sir James for ever as usual, and

the Bells Ringing with Every Demonstration of Joy at seeing him'.[19]
It is a measure of Christopher's own popularity that he was returned
with a majority of thirty-three, inspiring a local poet, John Bayley of
Middleton, to come up with a suitably unctuous set of lines:

> Whilst through the Streets loud Acclamations rung,
> And Sykes's Praises dwelt on every Tongue,
> 'Twas you whose Merits influenced each Voice,
> Unanimous to make so wise a choice.[20]

'I . . . heartily congratulate you on your Success,' wrote Henry
Maister, ' 'tho I lament the furor of the times which call'd you forth,
& only hope you may have no cause to regret the necessity of attending
the House which I am sure will not agree with your Constitution, if
the Hours in future are too as late as heretofore.'[21] He was sworn in
on 20 May, and in the early summer he was summoned to Downing
Street – '14 at table' he noted in his diary – where Pitt expressed his
gratitude both to him and to his fellow MP, William Wilberforce, for
the success of the important Yorkshire vote. Ironically it was the
defeated Fox who had said in the past 'Yorkshire and Middlesex
between them make up all England.'[22]

While Christopher voted, there were the first stirrings at Sledmere
of a move to improve the old house. On 29 June, 1784, 'Lady S. laid
foundation stone of offices in Court Yard,'[23] noted Christopher in his
diary. The work in question was the enlargement and modernisation
of the probably rather cramped domestic offices at the north side of
the house. The work was especially important as, according to a letter
written in September, 1784 by a Miss JC to her sister Nancy, Mrs
Marriott, Christopher and Bessy were already entertaining. She
attended a small family party, consisting of the Sykeses and their five
children, Mr and Mrs Egerton, Bessy's brother and sister-in-law, and
Richard Beaumont, Christopher's West Yorkshire neighbour, whom
she described as a *'pretty little upright Man of Brazen Nose* with a great
deal of Linnen about his Neck . . . a strange being indeed.' 'I thought
to captivate him,' she added, 'but he does not suit my taste.'

JC stayed the better part of a fortnight, and her letter gives a hint of what the atmosphere of the old house was like. ' 'Tis now a very good one of its Age,' she wrote, '& reminds me of the Highgate House below stairs – here's plenty of Books, Pictures good & Antiques, which keep one in constant amusement, besides Organ, Harpsichord, etc. etc.; which strange to tell I've exercised my small skill upon, before all the Party every day.' Though she said she had been 'taught to dread these Wolds', she found herself 'highly delighted & well may; nothing can be finer than the pure air here, only eighteen miles from Bridlington, the beautiful hill & dale of the country makes charming rides etc. Sir C has form'd & is forming great designs in the planting way which will beautify it prodigiously.' She also confirmed that 'the house is to be transformed some time'. Of her hosts she wrote, 'Sir C & Ly Sykes are both extremely obliging, indeed I don't know in what Family so nearly strangers to me, I cd. have been so agreeably placed for a visit . . . & not tire of it I assure you. Lady Sykes is very kind yet you must not expect any great polish in her, a resident in the country always, and without Education suitable to her great Fortune but she'll improve in Londres.'[24] She had, she added, 'very weak nerves', and 'dreads being presented at Court, w'ch you can pity her for: but the family must be elevated'.[25]

Now that her husband was in politics, presentation at Court was something that Bessy could not avoid, since the wife of an MP could not go out in Society or attend any Court functions unless she had been presented and Christopher wanted to be seen. He bought himself a smart London house, paying £3,700, the equivalent today of £185,000, for 9 Weymouth St, just south of Regent's Park and his diary for 1785 proudly opens with the words 'Sir Chris Sykes Bart. MP Weymouth St.' In accordance with his new status, he also bought himself a smart new coach, and had his coat of arms emblazoned on the doors. On 16 February, this gleaming new vehicle took the proud new member for Beverley and his beautiful wife to St James's Palace for the ceremony she so dreaded.

Any woman of a nervous disposition could be forgiven for feeling anxious about the approaching ritual, in spite of the fact that she would have been preparing for it for weeks. 'You would never believe,' wrote Fanny Burney, Assistant Keeper of the Wardrobe to Queen Charlotte, to her sister-in-law, 'the many things to be studied for appearing with a proper propriety before crowned heads.' She then gave a barely ironic list of 'directions for coughing, sneezing, or moving, before the King and Queen', none of which were permitted, finishing with the observation that 'if, by chance, a black pin runs into your head, you must not take it out . . . If, however, the agony is very great, you may, privately, bite the inside of your cheek, or of your lips, for a little relief; taking care to do it so cautiously as to make no apparent dent outwardly.'[26]

There would have been endless fittings for Bessy's presentation gown, which was hoop-skirted and elaborate and had to be worn with a train, as well as many expeditions out to buy the accessories required to wear with it, such as slippers, a fan, ostrich feathers and jewellery. Then she was forced to endure hours of deportment training so that she could approach the Sovereign elegantly, curtsy in a single flowing movement, without losing her balance or tripping on her gown, and then – the most nerve-racking part of the whole business – walk backwards out of the room, gathering up her train as she went, striving her utmost not to fall over it. Such practice was often carried out using a tablecloth as a simulated train. Bessy's presentation went without a hitch, and after it she patiently remained in London for three months while Christopher attended Parliament.

He soon had his first opportunity to prove his loyalty to the Prime Minister. Ever since he had first entered Parliament in 1781 Pitt had been a passionate advocate of parliamentary reform, believing that it was vitally necessary for the preservation of liberty. Amongst plans he had proposed were the checking of bribery at elections, the disenfranchising of corrupt constituencies, and the shortening of the duration of Parliament. On 18 April, 1785, he proposed a Bill that would extinguish thirty-six rotten boroughs and transfer the seventy-two seats therein to the larger counties and to London and Westminster. The House was full, with 450 members present, of which 422 voted in the division. Christopher and his fellow Yorkshiremen, the gentlemen and freeholders of a great county, were a powerful lobby and voted to a man with the Prime Minister, but he was defeated by 248 votes to 174. Memories were short. The movement for reform had been born in a time of crisis, now over, and with a recovery in trade and a resurgence of confidence, the issue was no longer a live one. Pitt's success in other areas had virtually killed it off and he did not try again. Perhaps Christopher became dejected by Pitt's unwillingness to pursue further the subject of parliamentary reform, but in the six years he represented Beverley he never once spoke in the House. More likely is the possibility that his heart was never really in politics at all, being firmly ensconced at Sledmere.

On 30 May 1785, the day he and Bessy returned to Yorkshire after his first vote in the House, Christopher was one week into his thirty-sixth year, and a very rich man. His landed income alone for that year was the equivalent of over £300,000 at today's values, and he had a corresponding sum in the bank of well over £4,000,000. It was money he was to put to good use in carrying out his ambitious plans. His first task in the preparation of the landscape he envisaged round the house was to clear away any buildings standing within its sightlines. These consisted of the few houses that remained from the old village, whose street had run in front of the house. Levelling work began in the summer of 1785 and continued over the next year. The inhabitants, who had no choice in the matter, were moved to new cottages, which had already been built elsewhere.

At the same time he was also planning a walled garden, a design for which he drew on the survey that had been commissioned by his Uncle Richard back in 1755. It was positioned to the east of that part of the old Avenue which was closest to the house, and was designed as an octagon, with tall brick walls enclosing it and hot houses against the north walls. The attention to detail in this design was typical of everything that Christopher did. Each door, for example, had its own reference identifying what type of lock it was to have and who should have a key, namely 'Labourer, Gardiner, and Master'. His final flourish was the design of a magnificent Orangery, nine bays in length with a semi-domed roof, sited immediately to the south-east of the house, between it and the walled garden. Though the Orangery has long since been demolished and the old wood-framed hothouses have been replaced by modern ones, this garden still survives, its beautiful brick walls, pale pink when they were built using bricks from the estate's own brickworks, now a deep rusty red. Some of them, which are of double thickness, have the remains of grates at their base, in which fires were lit to heat the walls through a series of inner pipes so that fruit could thrive on them.

With his plans for the garden and landscape well and truly in place, Christopher was at last ready to turn his attention to the house and bring to fruition the schemes he had been harbouring for many years. He was always sketching. His diaries and pocket books are full of hastily executed drawings, and undated designs and scribbles abound in the Library cupboards at Sledmere.

His passion for architecture was no secret to his friends, who were only too ready to turn to him for advice when they were planning to build. 'I have an alteration in view for the House at Tatton,' wrote his brother-in-law, William, in February, 1783, '. . . I shou'd be happy in your advice about my proceedings.'[27] For his West Yorkshire neighbour, Richard Beaumont, whose park at Whitley Beaumont had been laid out by Brown, he designed a pair of lodges to stand 'at the end of the Avenue where those stood built by my father'. In spite of Beaumont's enthusiasm for the project, Christopher himself appears to have been unhappy with the designs. 'The lodges are begun,' wrote Beaumont in September, 1783, 'but the cellar only of one is dug. It was my intention to build one this & another next year. If the weather continues bad I shall not finish either of them this Year . . . Tho' you disapprove of your Plan it is by no means disagreeable to me but if you will send me one more worthy of execution I shall be obliged to you. I intended the buildings to be exactly the size of those you sent me last Year . . . I have lost yr. Plan of those lodges & the gates & have only one copy of the lodges.'[28]

Because he was not a trained architect, Christopher was never in any doubt that he would require assistance on his Sledmere project. The first person to whom he turned was the architect of Castle Farm and the ice-house, John Carr, whose pedigree when it came to building large houses was matchless. A disciple of Robert and James Adam, he had worked on, amongst others, Harewood for Edwin Lascelles, Kirby Hall for Stephen Thompson, Constable Burton for Sir Marmaduke Wyvill, Temple Newsam for Lord Irwin and Kilnwick House for John Grimston, all Yorkshire houses of great importance. He had also built the stables at Wentworth Woodhouse for the Marquess of Rockingham and at Castle Howard for the Earl of Carlisle. At some point, possibly in 1786, though it is difficult to say this with certainty since none of the designs are dated and no reference to them appears in the Account Book, he came up with a plan for the principal, south, elevation of the new house, which was to be a very traditional seven-bay front with a central pediment supported by six Ionic columns. It was not chosen by Christopher, who would have considered it far too conventional and, perhaps, not nearly grand enough.

He next approached Samuel Wyatt, an architect whose practice was based in London, but who had undertaken two important commissions in Cheshire, one for Sir Thomas Broughton at Doddington Hall and the other for Sir Thomas Stanley at Hooton Hall. Christopher had met him through his in-laws, the Egertons of Tatton, with whom Wyatt had become acquainted while working on these projects and who were regular patrons of his. The first design he showed to Christopher was certainly imposing. It consisted of a seven-bay front with a shallow dome supported on columns – two single and two pairs – over the three central bays, all above arched ground-floor windows and a semi-circular ground-floor porch. It was rejected by Christopher, possibly because he found it too fussy.

True to form, and probably what he had in mind all along, Christopher now tried his own hand, producing a scheme which married elements of both the Carr and Wyatt designs, but introduced a note of striking simplicity. Keeping the scale of the elevation the same, he reduced the seven bays to three, using tripartite windows on both the first- and ground-floor levels, with the central dome replaced by a pediment supported on two pairs of columns. Considering that Christopher was an amateur competing with two of the most renowned architects of the day, he made a remarkable job of his design, and it was upon his drawings that the final scheme drawn up by Wyatt was based. Gone would be the old-fashioned house built by Uncle Richard. In its place would rise up an elegant country seat in the very latest neo-classical style, that would be a monument to the success and aspirations of its owner. The main rooms, off a central staircase hall, were to be a library, drawing room, music room and dining room on the ground floor, and a long gallery on the first floor.

Most patrons building on the scale that Christopher was doing would have employed a competent builder or carpenter as clerk of works to oversee the progress of the project. This was how many young men who went on to become successful architects began their careers. Carr, for example, had worked in this capacity for the financier,

Stephen Thompson, at Kirby Hall, and Wyatt for Lord Scarsdale at Kedleston. Characteristically, Christopher, as well as acting as executive architect, decided to be his own clerk of works, which brought an added cohesion to the whole scheme. It also meant that since he was the person corresponding with the various contractors, his preserved letters go a long way to telling the story of the building of the house.

The intention was to build two new cross-wings to the north and south of the 1750 house thus creating a new and much larger building on an H plan, the whole to be encased in Nottinghamshire stone. Work began in 1787. The stone proved problematical from the start, since it had to travel a great distance, and Christopher was to conduct a running battle with Mr Marson, the foreman of the stone quarry at Clumber, Nottinghamshire, from which it was dug. The grey lime-stone was then shipped up the River Trent to Hull, from where it was transported up the River Hull and the Driffield Canal to Driffield. It was then carried the last eight miles of its journey by wagon, a slow and arduous trip for the heavy horses who had to drag it uphill all the way from the flatlands of Driffield to the uplands of the Wolds. Obtaining it in the right sizes and quantities, at the right price and on time, provided him with many a headache. 'Till the last load or two,' he wrote to Marson in July, 1788, 'when our Vessel arrived at Stock-with, there was only one Boat load ready for her & she had to wait for another Boat returning from the Quarry. That the additional Expence has been on our side & hope you will allow me ½d. a foot the disadvantage. But seriously I believe all sides will be well satisfied if you could have one Load upon the Wharf & two Boats loaded against the Vessel gets to Stockwith, & the Captain or master can tell them within a Day or two at most when that will be.'[29]

He wrote another letter to Marson in August, complaining bitterly of his failure to deliver materials on time. It painted a vivid picture of the situation on site a year into the building work. 'The House wch. we are obliged to live in, having no other,' he wrote, '*is laid open on evry side*, & will be till the facia is put on, as my New Additions entirely surround my Old House. When you Read this wch. I wish you would do every Monday Morning & consider my Situation with a large family, you must not be of Human Materials if you do not Employ all Hands to get me stone for one Vessel not to wait an Hour & two Vessels if possible. I assure you upon my Word we have not stone here for fourteen days Work without turning away the Hands we have employed all Summer & without wch. we cannot live in my House this Winter.'[30]

The scene must have been one of chaos, with Uncle Richard's perfect, neat house opened up on all sides, new walls rising all around it beneath a forest of scaffolding, the air filled with a cacophony of noise – the shouts and curses of the workmen, the creaking and shrieking of the ropes and pulleys, the banging of tools, the rumbling of the arriving and departing wagons, and the neighing of horses. The family were tormented by dust and Christopher wrote that they were surrounded by 'hills of Rubish'.[31] To cap it all, Bessy's favourite dog, a Pomeranian bitch called Julia, was at death's door. 'How sorry I am to hear of her dangerous state,' wrote her son's tutor John Simpson to Christopher in October, 'I am afraid Lady Sykes will take it too much to heart. I wish she wou'd never have another favourite dog. It is a Dog's life to have to mourn for the loss of them every six or seven years.'[32] The problems with the quarry dragged on. 'I entreat you will use every effort to send us immediately some large Stones,' Christopher wrote to Marson on 4 October, 'which we wrote for so long ago & three Col[umns]: we cannot conclude our Work without them this Winter, and shall be all at a standstill in a Week's Time.'[33]

The outside walls appear to have been up by April, 1789, which was a crucial year in Christopher's life, in that it was when he made his decision to give up politics, sell his London house, and devote all his time to Sledmere. This is not so surprising when one considers how much time and energy he was giving over to his great project, leaving little room in his life for the machinations of the political world. He also liked to be at the helm and could never have been happy as a small cog in a large wheel. Bessy hated the political and court life, and this too may have been a factor in his decision. He broke the news to his constituency at the beginning of June, writing to his agent, Mr Lockwood, 'I have given up every thought of Standing again for Beverley. When I came the last Time it was done on a sudden, & I find a steady attendance at the House of Commons not consistent with my health, or consonant to my feelings & mode of Life.'[34]

In anticipation of the completion of all the stonework by the end of the year, Christopher now embarked on the next stage of the work on the new house, which was to consider the interior decoration. While helping out a neighbour, Sir Thomas Frankland, with designs for the improvement of his house, Thirkleby Park, near Thirsk, he had been introduced to the work of Joseph Rose, one of Robert Adam's leading decorators, whose work included the ceilings of the Gallery at Harewood, the Library at Kenwood, the stuccoes of the Hall at Syon and the ceiling of the Great Parlour at Kedleston. 'I am building a large House,' he wrote to Rose on 26 July, '& thro the Recommendation of Sir Thos. Frankland, & your General fame wish you to undertake the plaistering . . . I intend to finish very slowly as I wish the Work to be well done neat & Simple rather in the Old than New Stile nothing Rich or Gaudy, but suiting to plain Country Gentn.'[35] He asked him to come as soon as possible, and in a further letter expressed his wish that '*all* the Men you employ here will not be sent from London as I have a particular pleasure in employing Persons in my Neighbourhood when it can be done consistently with the Work being well executed, & they are usually well acquainted with the Nature of the Materials'.[36]

Sir Thomas Frankland could not have made a better recommendation than Rose whose ideas turned out to be exactly what Christopher had been looking for. He was thrilled with the first set of drawings. 'I perfectly agree with you in your Ideas of the Stile in wch. my House ought to be finished,' he wrote excitedly at the beginning of October, '& I would have but few Ornamts. But what decorations are introduced I would have them singular, bold and Striking & only where propriety & good Taste required them.' The delivery from London of an order of fixtures and fittings the following week might have suggested that work was now progressing at a pace. 'On Saturday Night the Doors arrived here,' Christopher confirmed to John Andrew of Aire Street on 12 October, 'and when we opened them this Day they had got some little wet but will be no worse, I think them very handsome Doors.' Not so. There was, inevitably, a sting in the tail; 'the Hinges also come, but you have forgot to send the Screws'.[37]

Errors such as this, small though they may have been, were an irritation to Christopher and his family who had been steadily retreating into more and more cramped conditions, virtually confined to the top floor of the old house. Here they survived until 1 February, 1790, when, at five in the morning, they set out for London. They were to spend as much of the year as possible in town, sheltering from the dust and the discomfort, and taking advantage of the fact that the house in Weymouth Street still remained unsold.

When the family finally returned to Sledmere, in the winter of 1790, they found the situation there greatly improved, with most of the exterior completed. This allowed Christopher to turn his attention to thoughts of the interiors, beginning with what was to be the most important room in the house, the Gallery, which had made its initial appearance on the design submitted by Samuel Wyatt in 1787. Though no drawings for it have survived, it is likely that Wyatt must have executed some, and it was these, or adaptations of them by Christopher, that Rose used as the basis for his ideas. 'Both your last letters have much pleased me,' he wrote on 2 April, 1791 'your first in giving me an account of the Gallery and saying that *you was much pleased with it* – I think it will be one of the finest rooms in the Kingdom.'[38] He did not exaggerate, for to this day the room has few rivals in grandeur, even in houses twice the size. Two storeys high and running the entire length of the south front of the house, a distance of 120 feet, it is divided into three great cross-vaulted compartments, inspired by such Roman buildings as the Baths of Diocletian and Caracalla, soaring upwards into the roof space. Though Wyatt undoubtedly intended it to be a room for the display of pictures, for congregation and for occasional use as a ballroom and it was always referred to by Rose as 'the Gallery', at some point the idea took hold in Christopher's mind that it should become a Library.

The rooms which followed, in particular the Music Room and the

Drawing Room, suggest that, about this time, Christopher appears to have modified the notion of himself as the 'plain country gentleman' who wanted things done 'neat & simple', a description which could in no way be applied to the Drawing Room, an exquisite creation of which Rose was especially proud. 'I must own that I think it the best design I ever made,'[39] he wrote on 31 May, 1792, and with its intricately designed ceiling, containing motifs depicting Greek religious rites, with complex patterns coloured in blues, terracotta and light pinks, and its gilded highlights, the room showed Rose in his most ornamental mood. He was nervous, however, that Christopher would find it too elaborate. 'I am afraid you will send it back again,' he continued gingerly, 'you will tell me that it is *far too fine* for your house, and too expensive and yet when I think of your Gallery, the proportion will bear me out.' He excused the finery by saying that 'the design is made for *Lady Sykes room*.'[40]

'I never saw any place so much improved as Sledmere,' wrote Christopher's nephew, William Tatton, to his father, during a ten-day stay in May, 1792. 'I think the Gallery as fine a room as I ever saw. They have not yet finished the Sealing and I suppose it will be nearly two years before they will be able to make any more of that room.'[41] A year later, apart from the floor of the Gallery, all the major building work was complete, and Rose's time was taken up with painting and decorating. At the end of May, Rose, whose relationship with his client had grown to a stage where he was also acting as his agent in London, had sent Christopher 'a great number of patterns of papers . . . many of them very pretty' from shops in Swallow Street and Ludgate Hill.[42] This was the first mention of wallpaper in their correspondence and he returned to the subject now. 'Mrs Rose has been about your papers to Ludgate Hill and chosen the borders . . . if the papers are to be glaz'd upon an average they will cost three halfpence more.'[43]

Though John Houghton, a contemporary of Evelyn and Pepys, had written as early as 1699 that 'a great deal of Paper is nowadays so printed to be pasted upon walls to serve instead of Hangings',[44] wallpaper did not truly become fashionable till the 1730s when improvements in manufacturing brought down the price. 'I am told there is a new sort of Paper now,' a neighbour of Christopher's, Nathaniel Maister, had written to his friend, Thomas Grimston, in 1764, 'made for hanging rooms with, which is very handsome, indeed from the price it ought to be so, for I think it is 2s. 6d. a yard. Have you seen any of it?' Christopher's paper was ready to be shipped on 4 September. 'I have not been so fortunate as to see any room fitted up with the furniture and the paper having a border of the same pattern,' wrote Rose. 'I should imagine it would look very pretty . . . if you please I will make further inquiries about it.'[45] He had soon found a Mr Sagar, a former upholsterer turned wallpaper-hanger, to 'come over to Sledmere & hang as many Rooms as are wanted to be hung at 7d. a Sheet, borders included, everything to be found for him to hang the Rooms with.'[46]

Rose also took it upon himself to furnish Christopher with everything he needed for his new home. It was a job he was only too happy to do, particularly since he knew his employer to be a prompt payer. 'I am exceedingly obliged to you for your offer of money,' he wrote in June, 1793, 'but I am not in want of any at present, and I am fully persuaded I never should be, if all my employers paid as you do: *or only one half of them.*' Rose organised the ironwork for the staircase, mirrors for all the rooms and supervised numerous other orders, such as a 'lamp for the Drawing Room ceiling', 'handles for the Vazes in the Hall', the 'Altar and Grate' for the hall fireplace, and 'sham stoves' to heat the outer hall. Something else arrived for the house in the middle of August, something for which the Sykeses had waited seven years and which was one of the most important purchases Christopher ever made. 'By Sir Christopher Sykes's directions,' noted William Saunders of Cavendish Square, London, on 2 August, 'I pack'd up in a packing case upwards of nine feet long, a picture, & with it a small Box – sent them to the White Horse, Cripplegate, directed to you – the Waggon left London Yesterday (Thursday) Morning, by that you will know when to expect them.'[47] The small box contained a white satin dress, the packing case 'a large whole length picture'. It was to turn out to be one of the greatest eighteenth-century portraits ever painted.

'Painted by Mr Romney,' stated the account, dated 16 May, 1793, 'a large whole length picture of Sir Christopher and Lady Sykes. £168.'[48] The picture, so carefully packed up by the framer, William Saunders, was a full-length portrait of Christopher and Bessy by George Romney that had been started in 1786. This painting, which today is regarded as being one of Romney's finest works, was commissioned by Christopher when he first became an MP, as an expression of his status. Twelve sittings for this painting were recorded in 1786 and the picture was then left unfinished in Romney's studio for several years. The fact that it took so long to complete meant that by the time it was delivered it had evolved into something much more than just a straightforward portrait of a country gentleman.

Here stands an elegant slim young man, wearing a scarlet coat and black breeches. With a long, straight nose and high forehead, he is tall and brimming with confidence. In his right hand he holds a pair of spectacles, in his left a plan of some kind, both of which suggest the seriousness that becomes a man of his station. If he were on his own, one might describe him as haughty, but he is saved from this by the charming and softening nature of his beautiful red-haired wife, Bessy. Wearing a long white silk dress, with a string of pearls flung almost casually across her right shoulder, she leads him out of some Ionic portico into a landscape which reflects his accomplishments; those in architecture represented by a distant 'eyecatcher', probably Life Hill Farm; in agriculture by the acres of plantations and enclosed fields which stretch out before him. Her hair, strung with pearls, catches the wind and at her feet a brown and white spaniel stands adoringly. She is gazing at her husband with a look of both love and admiration. Often called *The Evening Walk* – in comparison to Gainsborough's famous painting of Mr and Mrs William Hallett, *The Morning Walk* – it is a portrait of the greatest charm.

More important, however, is the fact that it represents Sir Christopher Sykes as he saw himself, a man who was at the very pinnacle of his achievements, who had risen from the ranks of the merchant class to become the epitome of the aristocratic landowner. In the general scheme of things it could not possibly have come at a more appropriate time. His land holdings were approaching their peak. He bought eight estates in the years 1792 and 1793, spending on them in excess of £52,000, the largest sum he had ever spent in such a short period. This brought the rental income he received annually from his estates up to £12,004. 8s. ¾d., which was a remarkable increase on the £1,960. 11s. 6d. he had started with in 1771.

The spaniel which Romney painted standing at the feet of its owners is a sporting dog, lending the suggestion, not incorrectly, that the subject was a lover of field sports. Christopher considered 'the pleasures of the chase' to be 'really useful and beneficial to Society'. He laid out his reasons for this in a letter to his close friend Thomas Grimston. 'They give opportunities of wearing off Shinesses, dispelling temporary differences, forming new friendships and cementing old, and draw the Gentlemen of the Country into one closer bond of Society.'[49] His account book shows that he was a regular subscriber to a number of hunts throughout his life, while his diaries record several occasions when he rode out with hounds, his last outing having been in November, 1785, when he 'hunted with Sir J Legard'.[50]

In spite of this, it was well known in the neighbourhood that hunting was not allowed at Sledmere. The reason for this was that he did not want his young plantations trampled to pieces. His neighbours were happy to respect his wishes. 'You have objections, which no one has a right to controvert or even discuss,' Lord Carlisle had written to him in October, 1788 from his nearby seat at Castle Howard. 'You may depend upon my hounds not approaching in quest of their game any covers from which it is your inclination to exclude them.' This rule did not apply, however, to other parts of his estate where hounds were free to go as they pleased. 'I thankfully receive the permission to go upon your other estates,' wrote Carlisle, 'with the obliging offer of making covers, & accommodations upon them.'[51]

The final element in the Romney portrait, represented by the ruined Temple and the distant view of Life Hill, was architecture. It was timely since the arrival of the painting signified the virtual completion of the house. Rose was critical of the picture, 'indeed I cannot see any likeness to Lady Sykes,' he said dismissively,[52] and there was a long-running argument as to where to hang it. Neither Rose nor his wife wanted it to hang in the Drawing Room. 'Mrs R says the Picture *must not* hang over the Chimney,' he had told Christopher in August, 1792, 'and she is sure that Lady Sykes will not agree to it.'[53] He even suggested that 'Lady Sykes . . . shall scold when she sees you.'[54] In the end it was hung in the Dining Room, where it still hangs to this day.

It seems that by the end of August, 1793, Christopher, although still telling people that 'my House is far from finished', was ready to receive a few guests outside the family. 'How happy it would make Lady Sykes and myself,' he wrote to the Duke of Leeds, on hearing that he was to visit Beverley, 'if my Lady Duchess and your Grace would do us the Favor to come upon the Wolds . . . we have Beds sufficient to accommodate your Grace, and any Friends you may do us the Honor to bring with you.'[55] By the time they visited, in October, with the exception of the Drawing Room and the Gallery, they would have found most of the main rooms painted and papered. Christopher having spent the princely sum of £1,384. 17s. 5d. in 1792 and 1793 on furniture, there was also presumably no lack of places to sit.

There was still much work to be done on the Gallery, including the laying of the floor, but so impressed by it were all those who saw it that Christopher decided to commission a picture of it to send out to all his friends. The man he chose to do this was Thomas Malton, an architectural draughtsman and occasional scene painter who had recently published with some success *A Picturesque Tour Through the Cities of London and Westminster*. Malton's finished drawing, a watercolour, which arrived early in 1795, was exquisite. It showed the room empty except for a desk, thereby considerably enhancing its size, and the feeling of space was further magnified by the use of perspective, achieved by leading the eye towards the window at the far end and out of it to the church tower. Three minute figures, one seated at the desk, the others lolling in an alcove, completed the impression of vastness. The plate read 'The Library at Sledmere, the Seat of Sir Christopher Sykes Bart, in the East Riding of Yorkshire', and in the bottom left-hand corner an inscription gave credit where it was most due: 'Designed and executed by Josh. Rose in 1794.' Two hundred black and white impressions were made from it which must have greatly stirred the imaginations of all those who received them. The architectural historian, Christopher Hussey, wrote of it in 1949, 'architecturally designed libraries are a feature of several of Adam's country houses, most notably Kenwood. But this one surpasses them all in majesty of conception, suggesting rather the library of a college or learned and wealthy society; indeed in the space allotted to it, in the amount of shelf room, and in the beauty of its decoration it is surely the climax of the Georgian conception of the library as the heart and soul of the country house.'[56]

So the Gallery officially became the Library. The bookshelves ran down both sides from the floor to beneath the vaulting, with semicircular ones at each end on either side of the windows. Two great mirrors, designed by Wyatt, hung on the north wall while the floor was covered with a fine worsted carpet which stretched the entire length of the room and had a design which matched that of the ceiling. This was an entirely homespun affair, having been woven at a carpet factory run by Mr Christopher Bainton on one of Christopher's estates at Wansford. Today it only exists in the Malton watercolour, since at the time of the fire it was being stored in the attics and was subsequently amongst the few contents of the house that were destroyed.

Thomas Malton also painted a watercolour of the exterior of the house, which is the only existing picture showing the grounds as they were in 1795. On the right of the picture, the landscape to the east of the house is heavily planted with large shrubs and maturing trees, and the ground slopes down to Christopher's beautiful Orangery, with its rows of tall windows. In the middle a roughly cut lawn rises on a gentle incline right up the front door, which is reached by five steps, and where a number of people are congregating. To the left of the house a number of deer are gathered beneath a mature tree, observed by a woman and child, while in the foreground a couple are enjoying a leisurely stroll. It represents a romantic idyll, and is the first recorded view of the final realisation of a great project.

While the peaceful mood of the scene suggests the best of times, in the outside world there were clouds gathering which were soon to take Christopher away from his beloved Sledmere. Since 1793, England had been at war with France, and there had been few successes for her in the conflict. As Napoleon Bonaparte rose inexorably to power, Prime Minister Pitt and his colleagues could only look on with growing horror. One by one Britain's allies on the Continent either made peace with or were defeated by the French, culminating with the collapse of Austria in 1797, which left England effectively fighting alone against this now all-powerful enemy. When Pitt himself made an attempt to reach a settlement with France, he was treated with the utmost contempt by the Directory, which had governed the country since the end of the Terror. They set terms that they knew would be impossible for Pitt to meet and immediately set about mobilising the combined French, Spanish and Dutch fleets to sail against Britain. Napoleon, triumphant after his success in conquering Italy, was appointed 'Commander-in-Chief' of the forces for the invasion of England, the Army of England.

On 22 January, 1798, Henry Dundas, Principal Secretary of State for War, sent Christopher the following letter. 'Sir, Living in this distant part of England,' he wrote, 'I request you will excuse me troubling you to inform me if there is any plan to be given to the Country Gentlemen for having their Tenants and Neighbours enrolled for the use of their Waggons or their personal service either on Foot or Horseback at or near their Homes or whether anything of this kind is in Contemplation . . . and if not whether we . . . are justified in assembling those who are willing either with or without arms . . .'[57]

Dundas had in fact anticipated exactly what Christopher had in mind, who, before he ever read this letter, had written to the Duke of Leeds telling him that 'I have lately thought that something should be done towards being prepared for defending ourselves against the French our infernal Enemies.' He had appealed to the Duke to 'make the proper Application to know if arms and Ammunition will be allowed to any Body of Horse or foot appointed for Defence of our own Coast & neighbourhood only, under myself & other neighbouring gentlemen. The Officers to be answerable for the Arms when called upon. The Men and Officers requiring no Pay except for Sergeants to teach them the Exercise & Evolutions. By Arms I mean a Sabre & pair of Pistols in Holsters for the Horse & Muskets with Bayonets (perhaps if one half had pikes) for the Foot.'[58]

Christopher concluded his letter to the Duke by saying he was certain that if he was allowed to pursue his scheme, 'I have Reason to believe I shall be able to assemble a Number of Persons in this Neighbourhood.' The result was the formation of the Yorkshire Wolds Gentlemen and Yeomanry Cavalry, which raised forty-five men as volunteers from sixteen parishes adjacent to Sledmere. On 22 February his friend Thomas Grimston from Kilnwick, who had his own troop, was writing to tell him that Sergeant Robert Wilson, one of the Sergeants in the Militia, wished 'to refresh his Memory by overlooking now & then the Regulations laid down for ye Sword Exercise,' and hence he had taken the liberty of ordering from the York bookseller, Mr Todd, 'a Book of the Sword Exercise'.

Ten days later Grimston was offering him 'ye Sabres which have been used by my Troops', so long as he could keep back four 'in order to be used for the Attack & defence'. 'There will still remain fifty,' he assured him, 'which if you wish for you may have immediately', though he added the proviso 'that in case my troop shd. be embodied or be called out for any Service before I get new Swords that you will lend me the old ones in the interim'. They would cost him 19s. each; 'Christopher's account book shows that he spent altogether £678. 18s. 9d. on equipping his cavalry. Many of the muskets, bayonets and other arms that he acquired still decorate the walls of the Entrance Hall at Sledmere.

So seriously did Christopher take his role as Captain of the Militia that at one point he was considering equipping them with cannon. His neighbour Lord Mulgrave, unlike Christopher an experienced soldier, soon set him right about this misguided plan. 'With respect to the advantages which you might derive, in the event of actual service before an enemy, from the addition of cannon to your corps, I entertain strong doubts,' he wrote on 19 June, 1798. 'Large corps of Cavalry, forming the Wing of an army or detached to a distance & obliged to maintain themselves in their Post, find great advantage from a small proportion of light artillery, well trained and under the command of skilful Artillery officers. But a small corps, acting as light troops would find themselves much embarrassed in their movements, would lose much of that most essential quality of rapidity, and would in many instances expose themselves to the sacrifice of many men, or to the loss of their guns if the Enemy should encounter them with a superior body of Cavalry.'[59]

On 19 July, Christopher, who had organised his troop with the same efficiency and pride that he had set about the rebuilding of Sledmere, received his official orders from the King. 'To Our Trusty & Wellbeloved Sir Christopher SYKES Bt. Greeting,' they began, and followed on 'We, reposing especial Trust and Confidence in Your Loyalty, Courage and good Conduct, do, by these Presents, constitute and appoint you to be Captain of the Yorkshire Wolds Gentlemen and Yeomanry but not to take rank in Our Army except during the Time of the said Corps being called out into actual Service.'[60] The call never came. On 1 August, 1798, Admiral Nelson and the British Navy, described by Pitt as the 'saviours of Mankind', successfully annihilated the French fleet at the Battle of the Nile, thereby ending Napoleon's dreams of an invasion. The Yorkshire force was soon disbanded.

The last year of the eighteenth century saw Christopher much on the move, apparently in search of a cure for Bessy's failing health. 'I am truly sorry for the indisposition of Lady Sykes,' Rose had written to Christopher in May, 1798, 'and I hope the Machine, which I have ordered from Mr LOWNDES will be of infinite use, indeed I think it a very ingenious machine.' The contraption he referred to was an exercise machine, and he was quick to assure his employer that he would not be recommending something that he had not tried himself. 'After Mr LOWNDES had showed me utility of it, I got into it, and find that it will be very strong exercise.' Mr Lowndes, he continued, 'has promised to inform you of all the situations for the different parts of the body, it will be particularly strong if you turn the machine yourself, I have ordered the Pedometer as I think it may be of great use, as by it you may know how many miles you have supposed to go.' He concluded by telling Christopher that 'from the simplicity of the construction of the device I think it is impossible to be ever out of order', though he did admit, hinting at the truly Heath Robinson nature of the machine, 'only you may want a new string now and then'.[61]

Though there is no mention of the exact nature of what was wrong with her, other than that she suffered from 'weak nerves', there is a strong likelihood that she may have been victim to one of the many illnesses which are now known to have been caused by lead poisoning, such as disease of the kidneys, recurring headaches, lassitude, and indeed problems of the nerves, all due to the then common use of the metal in everyday things such as water pipes, earthenware, cooking pots, pewter plates and tankards, cosmetics, hair dyes and medicines. Unsurprisingly, Mr Lowndes's apparatus did little for Bessy's condition, and the bitter cold month of January, 1799 found her and Christopher consulting a Dr Hall in London, staying with some of the family at a house they had rented in Lisson Grove.

At first her condition appeared to be improving. 'I am happy to say my Mother is much better,' wrote their son Christopher to his brother Tatton, 'and in a very fair way of Recovery.' Though it was at a cost. 'This man puts her to a great deal of pain,' he continued, '& I have to go to him every Morn. above three miles off. In short for what she undergoes with him, she deserves her health. From his account the Complaint has been long coming on, & will be long in getting the better of it.'[62] In February, an Irish friend, the Hon. William Skeffington, wrote to inquire after her health. 'I have felt much for Lady Sykes during the recent severe weather,' he told her husband, 'I am very impatient to hear that it has not thrown her back & flatter myself your next will give a good acct. of her recovering with Dr Hall.'[63]

June found the Sykeses in Bath, with Bessy apparently no better. 'I was happy to find . . . that you had arrived safe,' wrote George Britton to Christopher, 'and found Lady Sykes not worse than might be expected from her late Relapse; I hope the Change of Air, Journey and Benefits of the Bath Waters will be of infinite service.'[64] By far the most popular and fashionable form of treatment of the day was 'taking the waters' at one of the many spa towns, such as Harrogate, Bath and Weymouth. This consisted of both drinking the mineral waters and taking prolonged baths in them. Recent studies have shown that there was indeed great benefit to be gained from doing this, particularly for those people who suffered from diseases caused by lead poisoning: full immersion of the body in water for several hours increases the excretion of urine from the body, and out with it goes a significant amount of lead. Drinking a large quantity of the waters has the same effect. They were, proclaimed an eighteenth-century postcard, 'wonderful and *most* EXCELLENT agaynst all *diseases* of the body proceeding of a MOIST CAUSE as Rhumes, Agues, Lethargies, *Apoplexies*, The Scratch, *Inflammation of the Fits*, hectic flushes, Pockes, deafness, *forgetfulness*, shakings and WEAKNESS of any Member – Approved by authoritie, confirmed by Reason and daily tried by experience.'[65]

While Christopher and Bessy were benefiting from their daily immersions, George Britton, who had succeeded to the post of his Steward, after the death of the faithful Robert Dunn in January, 1795, conducted a regular correspondence, keeping them informed about everything which went on at Sledmere in their absence, and answering Christopher's endless inquiries. On 2 June it was a piece of ornithological news: 'I have occasion to write till near 12 o'clock two nights,' he told them, 'at which late hours I heard the two Nightingales distinct. After opening the Window they filled my Room with Melody, their different Notes exceeded everything.' On 9 June he described the disastrous unpacking of a new carriage: 'Truslove went to unpack it and set it up & Mrs Rousby brought it here. Truslove informs me that it was very ill packed. The rats while on shipboard have eaten the greater part of the leather trunk behind . . .' A fortnight later he gave an account of how the garden was looking. 'The Laburnums are just showing the Flower Bud, the Apple Trees in full Blossom, so are Strawberries, the former in abundance, the White Thorn not out yet, every Hedge and Tree will be full, one may just perceive from the House a whitish cast from the tops of the single trees in the Lawn, old Ash not yet in full leaf.' By the end of the month he was able to write 'I am very glad to hear that Lady Sykes continues gathering strength', adding rather wistfully 'I wish you all had a Month of Sledmere Air.'[66]

After Bath they went to Weymouth, the most fashionable of all the resorts, being the favoured haunt of the King and Queen. 'I suppose you are now so great with Royalty & Royal Parties,' William Skeffington teased Christopher, 'that you could hardly enjoy the humble Society of the family', though he added 'I most sincerely hope Lady Sykes will receive benefit from Sea Bathing.'[67] One blessing of this particular stay was that the weather was warm, which George Britton hoped would 'speed her Ladyship's recovery'. In the meantime he continued his reports from home. 'We have had three or four charming Hay days in the course of last Week which have enabled us to . . . get into stack in very good condition.' 'Currants are very plentiful,' he wrote of the garden. 'The servants took at the same time two fine melons and a small Pine.' In the autumn they returned to Bath for more of the waters. 'I'm sorry to find by your two last letters that your colds seem to hang on,' Britton wrote to them there, adding 'the Change of Weather will I hope soon remove them'.[68]

There are continuous anxious references to Bessy's health in Christopher's correspondence over the next two years, and in 1801 he fell ill himself. The first indication that all was not well came in a letter sent by George Britton to Christopher while he was en route to the Hotwell Spa at Bristol, whose mineral waters had a reputation as a cure for diverse ailments such as kidney complaints, 'hot livers' and 'feeble brains'.[69] 'Your Health was particularly enquired after by all the Gentlemen at Driffield,' he wrote on 30 August. 'I hope you are approaching near to Bristol when you will then be relieved from Fatigue of Travel and I trust in a little time you will be gathering strength so as to bring about a speedy Recovery.' A few days later they had still not reached their destination and Britton was writing 'we are all sorry to find that your travel was slow and irksome', adding ominously 'I was very sorry to find that upon the whole you had gathered little strength.'

By 13 September the party 'had all reached Clifton safe and met with a comfortable situation'. But all was not well. 'I am equally sorry to find,' Britton told Christopher, 'that the State of your Health appears not in any shape to improve, God grant a Change for the better.' His letter was then filled with the usual account of the day-to-day goings on at his beloved Sledmere. Richard Beaumont had sent 'a small Box containing a Gate Sneck . . . the Kind is very simple and may be of use for Hand Gates, the one sent is to be let into stone but with a little Alteration may be made do for Wood'. The gardeners would 'attend to the new planted trees in time, Cole to the new paled trees agreeable to your directions. I cannot see that the Deer or Horses have disturbed the trees in the Park since you left Sledmere.' The hay stacks had all been 'thatched without a Wisp of Hay damaged', but there were 'only five Bunches of the Raisin Grape, three of which are spoiled by Mildew occasioned by the steam or Vapour rising from the Tank in the Vinery'. There had been 'a fine week of Harvest Weather . . . I have got our Clover Stubble eaten with sheep and have begun to plow the same and from the appearance of the land shall be tempted to sow the same with a hardy kind of Red Wheat.'[70]

All this information was doubtless passed on to Christopher in answer to worries he had expressed over estate matters, and shows that even when he was supposedly resting at a spa, he was incapable of relaxing. Britton concluded his news as follows: 'I think I have nothing more particular at this time to name – I remain with my ardent Wishes for your Recovery. Your obedient humble servant, Geo. Britton.' It was the last letter he was ever to write to Christopher, who died four days later on 17 September aged fifty-two. No account exists of the manner of his death, but it is tempting to speculate that he died with Britton's letter in his hand and Sledmere on his mind. What killed him is a mystery, though it was probably heart failure due to chronic fatigue brought on by a lifetime of overwork. 'He has left an excellent character in every relation of life, whether public or private, and was, in every sense, an *enlightened country gentleman*.' So ran his obituary in the *The Gentleman's Magazine*, continuing 'His early rising and great activity, both of body and mind, prompted the conduct of every plan of amending the state of the country, whether by drainage or inclosure, building or navigation: and his improvements extended themselves over a surface of nearly 100 miles. The Wolds of Yorkshire will be his lasting monument.'

But Sledmere itself was to be his chief monument. Eight years after his death, a Hull merchant, Theopilus Hill, making an autumn tour through Yorkshire by chaise, visited it and wrote an account of his impressions. When Hill and his friends had finished their tour of the house, they roamed the grounds, taking in all of the 'numerous and extensive' plantations. They were amused by 'a Pyramidical Monument of stone, with an inscription to the memory of some favourite dogs', and visited the Orangery, which had 'the largest and finest fruit we ever saw'. A gardener gave them a tour of the Walled Garden.

> The Gardens are about two-and-a-half acres with Hothouses etc: in the latter we found many fig trees, and were informed they produced abundant fruit, which ripened well; the family are partial to this fruit. We found some very good apple trees, which the Gardener highly extolled for bearing large fruit and in all seasons: he said he knew not where Sir Christopher had got them from, but they had now acquired the name of Sledmere Apples. We also observed against a wall, a species of shrub, which the Gardener said was between a raspberry and a bramble, and bore fruit till Christmas: we tasted some of the fruit, and found it to be of good flavour.

Hill concluded his memoir with a eulogy to the creator of this paradise.

> The House has been built twenty-two years, and the Plantations were made about eighteen years ago, by the late Sir Christopher Sykes; whose improvements are a lasting honour to his memory. He changed a naked and barren tract into a fertile, woody, and cultivated region; and his successor is treading in his steps; many other useful and ornamental additions being now in contemplation.[71]

CHAPTER IV

The Collector

On 19 February, 1784, a day on which exceptionally deep snow lay round about, Christopher noted in his diary, 'Mr Simpson and the boys left us.' They were heading for York by coach, and the journey proved an eventful one. 'We set off for York, got to Weighton in ye coach with much danger and difficulty,'[1] reported Simpson, though they finally reached their destination on the evening of 21 February. The Mr Simpson who took Christopher's sons away with him was the Revd John Simpson. He had been their tutor since October, 1778 when he had been recommended for the post by the Revd William Cleaver, Christopher's former tutor at Oxford. He was paid a salary of £120 a year and was evidently regarded as a friend by his employer, who lent him money on a regular basis and occasionally took him as a companion on trips to London. On 2 January, 1782, for example, they had both 'supped' with Dr Johnson, while on 4 January they 'dined' with Mr Brown.[2] The boys were now coming up to the ages of thirteen, twelve and ten respectively and it was time for Christopher to consider the next step in their education. He decided to send Mark and Tatton to Westminster, where his Uncle Richard's friend Henry Pelham and his brother the Duke of Newcastle, both Prime Ministers, had been pupils. The youngest boy, Christopher, was to remain under Mr Simpson.

'I am exceedingly rejoiced you have determined to send your two Eldest Boys to Westminster,' wrote Henry Maister in February, 1784, delighted that the boys were going to a school frequented by the sons of other Yorkshire gentry. 'I went yesterday to Mrs CLAPHAMS, the House the HOTHAMS & HUDSONS are at, & which by all Accts. is the best in the place . . . she will have room for your two young

Men, should you come up with them. I am sure you will like their Dame as they call her.' He concluded his letter with an account of her terms: '£25 p.a. for Board and Washing, two Guineas for Fire and candle, two Guineas for Servants, eight shillings for Mending Linen and Cleaning Shoes, five Guineas Entrance Fees, two Guineas to the Masters, and an extra four Guineas a quarter for the use of a Single Bed'. In addition 'each Young Gentleman to bring one Doz. Of Towels and one Table Spoon'.[3]

Mark and Tatton went up to Westminster, to board in 'Mother' Clapham's house, in June, 1784. The Headmaster was Samuel Smith, a man described by one of his pupils, the dramatist George Colman, as being 'very dull and good-natured'.[4] Under his regime, the boys enjoyed a freedom that would be considered unthinkable today and the general atmosphere of the school appears to have verged upon almost constant anarchy. Bullying was rife. Frederick Reynolds, a contemporary of Colman's, who a few years previously had attended the same house as the Sykes boys, described the treatment of new boys in his memoirs. On the very eve of his arrival, to shouts of 'New boy! New boy!', he was set upon by 'a vast number of boys' who subjected him to every manner of indignity. 'After enduring an inundation of ink from every squirt in the room,' he recorded, 'till I, and my fine clothes, were of an universal blackness; after performing various aerial evolutions in my ascents from a blanket managed by some dozens pairs of hands insensible of fatigue in the perpetration of mischief; and after suffering the several torments of every remaining species of manual wit, I was at length permitted to crawl into my bed. There I lay, comforting myself with the assurance that torture had done its worst, till I gradually sobbed myself into a sound sleep.'[5] Reynolds's Welsh roommate was so tormented by bullies that he tried suicide by hanging himself from the bedpost, an attempt which failed when Reynolds returned to the room unexpectedly and cut him down. The boy's reaction to his rescuer, when he had fully recovered, was to knock him to the ground. 'There, take that,' he cried with much apathy, 'and the next time I choose to hang myself, you will know better than to prevent me.'[6]

There were instances of violence and rebellion against which the goings on in most of today's inner-city schools pale in comparison. The *Annual Register* for 1779, for example, gave an account of the trial of 'Messrs. Kelly, Lindsay, Carter, Hill, Durrell, and another six Westminster schoolboys . . . for an assault of a man in Dean's Yard in January last, when they beat and wounded him in a most shocking manner, and after that, Kelly, with a drawn knife in his hand, said, "If you don't kneel down and ask pardon, I will rip you up." '[7] In 1786, there was a rebellion at Westminster, led by Sir Francis Burdett. Though this may have been inspired by similar events at Eton College three years previously, when the boys had broken every window in the school, smashed up the Headmaster's chambers and burnt chunks off the flogging block, it was ended swiftly when Headmaster Smith decided to exert his authority. He confronted Sir Francis and, when he refused to give ground, felled him with a blow from a thick stick.[8] He was subsequently expelled.

Though there is no record of what Christopher's attitude was to the lax regime that existed at Westminster, the fact that his sons only remained there a year suggests that it did not please him. They both left in August, 1785, and, through his Egerton in-laws, he organised for them to attend a school run by the Bishop of Chester, until they were to go up to Brasenose College, Oxford. On their return home, the scene they found at Sledmere, where they were reunited with their family for the summer holidays, was one of chaos. The place was a building site, with work on the new servants' wing at the back of the house being in full swing, and the levelling of the remains of the old village going on at the front. Even the gardens were a mess, with work on the new walled garden and the construction of hot houses going on apace. It was, however, a delightful change from the horrors of public school, and they were happy to see their siblings.

Of the younger children, Christopher, as befitted the third son of a gentleman, was destined for the clergy and attended the Revd Goodinge's school in Leeds. The two girls, Decima and Elizabeth, remained at home with a governess. They were described by John

Simpson after they had paid a visit to him at his parish in Roos as being 'such good children that they must excite affection and regard for them wherever they go'.[9] Mark and Tatton matriculated from Oxford together in May, 1788. A letter written to their father in September, 1788, from the Bishop of Chester, reflects Christopher's concern that they should be kept away from university low life. 'I consider the Winter months,' he wrote, 'as much more useful with a private Tutor in College, and less dangerous, as giving less occasion to schemes & parties, than those of the Summer, and should think it better to take them away at Ladyday than now, as I have always found more difficulties with young men in the two Summer Terms.' He recommended a Mr Morris. 'Whilst [he] keeps them to their studies in the Evening from six to nine, they can never be more safe from drinking than under that engagement constantly kept up.'[10]

Tatton spent only six terms at Oxford, taking up a post in February, 1790 as an articled Clerk to Atkinson and Farrer, attorneys of Lincoln's Inn Fields, with a view to studying for the Bar, a suitable job for a second son. He travelled to London at the end of January and took lodgings with a Mrs Lockall in Lambs Conduit Street. Scarcely had he arrived there than a letter was delivered from his mother announcing her intention to visit him. His hopes of independence were shaken. 'Your Mother and Sister unite in wishing to see you *this week*,' she wrote, continuing 'be *assured* it would be a true comfort to me to have that happiness.' She made her affection for him obvious. 'Absence never can erase the Love I have,' she told him, 'for God only knows when & *where* we may be permitted to meet again, therefore embrace if not very inconvenient our present meeting.' There was also an element of the kind of nagging that any son of seventeen might expect from his mother, when living away from home. 'If you have not sent the Shrimps to Mrs Ardens at the Leases near Northallerton, let them go as soon as you can, & . . . also pay Mr Scotcherd eight Shillings for two pound of Cocoa he sent me to Bridlington.'[11]

Though Tatton's account book for that first year in London is full of mundane entries for such items as 'Hairdressing', 'Washerwoman', 'Fruit', 'Breakfast' and 'Tarts,' in amongst them are recorded other payments which give an indication of the kind of life he was leading. London was an extraordinary city, a wonder to those who visited it. From the very outskirts they were struck by its hustle and bustle. 'The road from Greenwich to London,' wrote the Prussian traveller, Carl Philipp Moritz in 1782, 'is actually busier, and far more alive, than the most frequented streets in Berlin; at every step we met people on horseback, in carriages, and foot-passengers.'[12] The city thronged with people going about their business at a pace. Briskly walking pedestrians, street-sellers shouting their wares, and trotting sedan-chairmen weaved their way through the streets, each trying to avoid the other as well as the hooves of horses pulling numerous carriages at breakneck speed. 'The hackney-coachmen make their horses smoke,' complains Smollett's Matt Bramble, 'and the pavement shakes under them; and I have actually seen a waggon pass through Piccadilly at the hand-gallop.'[13] Even the river was a crowded thoroughfare. 'On the Thames itself,' noted Moritz, 'are countless swarms of little boats passing and repassing, many with one mast and one sail, and many with none, in which persons of all ranks are carried over. Thus, there is hardly less stir and bustle on this river, than there is in some of its own London's crowded streets.'[14]

There were even the equivalent of today's fast-food outlets. The historian Robert Southey, a pupil at Westminster not long after the Sykes brothers, described visiting a pastrycook's shop one bitterly cold winter's morning and inquiring of the proprietress as to why she and her fellow tradesmen kept their windows open during such severe weather. 'She told me,' he recalled, 'that were she to close it, her receipts would be lessened forty or fifty shillings a day – so many were the persons who took up buns or biscuits as they passed by and threw their pence in, not allowing themselves time to enter. Was there ever so indefatigable a people!' It was no doubt at just such a place that young Tatton would have bought his tarts.

While Tatton worked in the solicitor's office in Lincoln's Inn Fields during the day, after hours he busied himself exploring all the varied pleasures that London had to offer a seventeen-year-old boy. On 9 March, for example, only a short time after he had taken up his new post, he paid 3s. for 'Seeing the Wild Beasts at Exeter Change'. Menageries were at the time a popular diversion for people from all walks of life, most of whom would only have seen wild animals in pictures. The most famous was the one in the Tower of London, where lions and occasionally other species had been kept for the King since medieval times. Visiting it in April, 1787, Thomas Pennant saw 'a leopard of a quite unknown species, brought from Bengal. It was wholly black, but the hair was marked on the back, sides, and neck with round clusters of small spots, of a glossy and most intense black . . . Here were also two tigers.'[15]

The Exeter Change in the Strand was the eighteenth-century equivalent of a shopping mall, with various shops lining the walks around a central staircase. It was on four floors, and one of the rooms on the upper floor, the walls of which were painted with appropriate jungle scenery, was traditionally let to a menagerie. Tatton saw an entertainment called Pidman's Exhibition of Wild Beasts, which consisted of a variety show followed by a viewing of various helpless animals kept in cages. Byron visited the Exeter Change in 1812. 'Such a conversazione!' he remarked in his journal. 'There was a "hippopotamus", like Lord Liverpool in the face; and the "Ursine Sloth" hath the very voice and manner of my valet – but the tiger talked too much. The elephant took and gave me my money again; took off my hat; opened a door; *trunked* a whip; and behaved so well that I wish he was my butler.'[16] Unfortunately, Tatton's evening was slightly marred. 'Lost out of my pocket 5s.,' he noted, though in later entries, when he was more experienced, he wrote simply 'Had my pocket picked.'

Other entertainments he appears to have particularly enjoyed included frequent trips to the theatre. 'At the Lyceum. 1s. 6d.,' he wrote on 13 March, where he would have been treated to a performance of *The Wags*, by Charles Dibdin, a pot-pourri of anecdotes and gossip, interspersed with sea songs. After the show, he then took a 'coach to the Playhouse. 2s. 6d.', either the Drury Lane Theatre or the Haymarket, to watch a play by Sheridan. He went to 'Merlin's Museum' on 17 March, Westminster Abbey on 13 April, and on

3 May, 'took a Coach to a rout', one of those evening rendezvous in public rooms, where people drank tea and walked up and down gossiping. In June he paid his shilling to visit the celebrated Vauxhall Gardens on the south bank of the Thames. On any night in these elaborate pleasure gardens, laid out with walks, statues and tableaux, he could listen to one of several orchestras, watch dazzling fireworks, dance if he wished to, and take supper in a gaily painted alcove.

When he was not being a tourist, Tatton spent some of his spare time 'at Johnson's School', and 'the Boxing School'. Owing to the patronage of the sport by the Prince of Wales and his cronies, prize fighting had begun to attract the attention of men of substance and respectability. Fighters sprung up who were more sophisticated than the thugs who had represented the sport in fairground boxing booths, and who brought with them a more elegant and scientific technique. One of these men was Tom Johnson, whose most famous fight was with a seventeen stone, six foot two inches giant from Birmingham called Isaac Perrins, who had issued a challenge to fight anyone for £500. The fight, which took place in October, 1789, ended in victory for Johnson, who was three stone lighter than his opponent, though it took him one-and-a-quarter hours and sixty-five rounds to achieve it. His backer, a Mr Bullock, won £20,000 on the contest, and gave Johnson £1,000, part of which he used to set up his own boxing school. Such establishments became popular with the young gentlemen of the day, and the lessons would have given confidence to Tatton who, though tall, was of a somewhat skinny physique and had a rather thin, squeaky voice.

The man who was to teach Tatton the most valuable lessons was 'Gentleman' John Jackson, a man of almost perfect physique, who was said to be 'the best-made man of a generation of very well-made men'.[17] Though he only fought in the ring three times, on the last occasion beating the reigning champion, Dan Mendoza, in ten minutes, he made a deep and lasting impression on all who saw him. 'His style of boxing,' wrote Lord Knebworth, a historian of the sport, 'was elegant and easy, and he was particularly light and quick on his feet. His judgement of distance, so important in boxing, was unsurpassed, and his blows, which were terrific in their force, were delivered so fast that they were said to be perceptible in their effect alone.'[18] He too set up a school in rooms at 13 Old Bond Street, and it was here that Tatton attended. The Revd M. Morris, who knew the Sykes family well in later years, told a story in his *Reminiscences*, of how the young Tatton 'once got his father to go to London to see a great fight on some sort of stage. On reaching the appointed spot the father, to his surprise, saw his son appear as one of the combatants, whereupon he instantly took his departure.'[19]

In August Tatton set out on a visit to Sledmere. 'Took a place in the York Coach,' he noted on 19 August. He paid a down payment of £1. 5s., which represented half of the fare. He paid the other half when he left two days later. Long before dawn, a hackney coach, price 2s., collected him and his trunk from his lodgings and took him to the White Horse Inn, Fetter Lane, in time to catch the 5.00 a.m. York Highflyer. He would also have had the choice of either the Royal Mail, which left from the Bull and Mouth Inn, St Martins-le-Grand, or the Mercury, from the Saracen's Head, Snow Hill. Thirty years previously, such a trip, a distance of 200 miles up the Great North Road, would have taken three days in the summer and four in winter. The coach boarded by Tatton did the same journey in thirty-one hours.[20]

The time the journey took reflected the advances in the state of England's roads, which had taken place in the latter half of the eighteenth century. 'The great improvements which, within the memory of man, have been made in the turnpike roads throughout this kingdom,' wrote a contributor to the *Gentleman's Magazine* in 1792, 'would be incredible did we not actually perceive them.' When Faujas de Saint Fond, the noted French traveller, set out on his journey to the Hebrides in 1784, he travelled up the Great North Road. 'From London to Barnet, twelve miles,' he noted in his journal, '– a superb road, covered with carriages, and with people on horseback and on foot, who were returning, in a fine moonlight evening, to London, from the country houses and neighbouring villages, where they go to recreate themselves during Sunday.' He passed through Hatfield,

Stevenage, Dugden and Stilton, where he commented, 'Nothing can surpass the beauty and convenience of the road during these sixty-three miles; it resembles the avenue of a magnificent garden.' Saint Fond also noticed that 'at Stilton, one begins to observe, on the sides of the road, large heaps of stones destined to repair it'.[21]

The Highflyer took the same route. After Stilton, with a change of horses at staging posts some twelve to fifteen miles apart, and an average speed of seven miles an hour, the main stops were at Stamford, Newark, Doncaster, Ferrybridge, Tadcaster, and finally York. Here Tatton was deposited at the York Tavern at around midday on 22 August, his eighteenth birthday. He chose to lodge in the city for the night, and on the following day he visited the hairdresser. Then he picked up a horse and rode over to Sledmere. He didn't stay long. Driven away by the piles of rubble everywhere, the scaffolding all over the house, and the constant noise of the workmen, he decided that some sea air would do him good and went instead to Scarborough, still a fashionable spa, where he took lodgings for a month and passed his time sea-bathing, riding, coffee-housing and visiting the play at the theatre on Tanner Street. Altogether he spent ten weeks in Yorkshire, before returning to London at the beginning of November and back to the offices of Atkinson and Farrer. He was soon visiting his old haunts and 13 November found him back at the boxing school.

Apart from his love of boxing, there is one other clue as to the path that Tatton's life was to take, and it is to be found on the inside cover of the book in which he wrote his accounts. In small neat handwriting he wrote, 'My bay Mare covered by Astonishment in May 1790. Astonishment was bred by the late Sir John Lister Kay and sold by him to Col Ratcliffe. Astonishment was got by Highflyer, his Dam (which was also the dam of Phenomenon) by Eclipse, his Grandam by Engineer . . .' For a seventeen-year-old this demonstrates a precocious interest in breeding, for Astonishment, the stallion which had covered Tatton's bay mare, had a startling pedigree. His father, Highflyer, had sired the winners of 470 races, including three Derbys and four St Legers, and had made so much money for his owner, Mr Richard Tattersall, that he was able to build himself a mansion near Ely, which he named Highflyer Hall. Astonishment's mother was a daughter of Eclipse, said to have been 'the fleetest horse that ever ran in England'.[22]

Tatton's heart was not in the Bar. While he sat in the office, hunched over documents and occasionally scratching away with his quill pen, he was dreaming of horses and the Turf. According to the sporting journalist, Henry Hall Dixon, better known as 'The Druid', Tatton astonished his fellow clerks by walking from London to Epsom in June, 1791, to see the Duke of Bedford's Eager win the Derby, leaving his lodgings at four in the morning and returning the same night at eleven. Why he chose to go on foot is a mystery, since his accounts show that he kept a horse in town, stabled at Joseph Denison's house. The following year he rode down to watch the race won by Lord Grosvenor's John Bull, and stayed on to see the Oaks taken by Lord Clermont's Volante, another progeny of Highflyer. Three weeks later, an entry in his account book for 12 June reads 'Expences at Ascott Races two days. £2. 2s.'. He was hooked.

Having acquired a rudimentary knowledge of the Law, but shown no aptitude for the Bar, Tatton was summoned by his father back to Sledmere at the end of 1792 and set to work in the East Riding Bank. He lodged with a Mrs Martin in Dagger Lane, Hull. Evidently he did not forget his fellow clerks back in London, for one of the friends he had made amongst them, Thomas Byron, wrote to him on 5 December thanking him for a gift of hares which he had sent them. 'I assure you I never tasted better,' he told him, going on to say how glad he was 'you like your new Situation so well; something more agreeable I think than an Attorneys Clerk'.[23] True to form, Tatton caused raised eyebrows on his first Saturday at the bank by walking the thirty-two miles home to Sledmere at the end of the day's business, in order to spend Sunday there, and walking back again in time for work on Monday morning. Already, at the age of twenty, legends were beginning to grow up around him.

Tatton's diary for 1793 suggests that his life in Hull was mostly taken up with life at the bank, visits to his father at Sledmere, where he occasionally helped with the accounts, hunting and riding. He also made frequent visits to his grandmother, Decima, Lady Sykes, who lived in Beverley and whose health was failing. On Friday, 15 February, he received unwelcome news: 'A Messenger came from Beverley with the sad news of my Grandmother's being seized with the Palsy. My Father and I came over.' Apart from the odd rally round she never recovered and his entry for 9 March reads '4 o'clock this morning my Grandmother died. My father came down from London.'

Before he died, Parson had left a touching eulogy to her, entitled 'My Wife's Character'.

> She was lovely and amiable in her Person
> Courteous and affable in her Behaviour
> Lively and cheerful in conversation
> Of a sweet and engaging temper
> Of an open and ingenuous mind
> In her Judgement of others candid
> Zealous & sincere in the discharge of all conjugal duties
> In the care of her children tender and affectionate
> To her Servants kind & indulgent etc. etc.

It was written from the heart and he accepted its shortcomings. 'This Character not being in Rhime,' he wrote, 'nor Poetical, & perhaps too long for the Present Taste, may be improper for an Epitaph; yet I choose to leave it, as a Testimony of my affection & love for, & the High Opinion I had of her. And I sincerely believe the whole to be strictly & fully true.'[24]

Tatton made no mention of his grandmother's funeral in his diary, entries in which show that, outside working at the bank, he was becoming more and more tied up with his horses. 'My brown mare foaled a Filly,' he wrote on 26 March, and noted excitedly the details of its sire, Guido: 'a bright bay Horse, full fifteen hands, one inch high with a deal of Bone, remarkably temperate and quiet to ride & leaps well; was bred by the Duke of Queensbury. Guido at four years old won the Revolution Stakes of 200 guineas each at Newmarket beating eight others . . . Guido twice beat the famous mare Dido.' As the year wore on more foals were born, physick was administered on a regular basis, and in the summer months, when fashionable society was gathering in the spas, taking the waters and attending assemblies and balls, the only balls mentioned by Tatton were those of a medicinal nature, such as on 18 July, when he began his mare on a course of 'Taplin's Cordial Balls and a Mash Morning and Night', or on 11 August when 'my Mare had a Ball. I went and dined at Welton. My Mother, brother and Sisters were there. Returned at Night.'

All the while that Tatton was serving his apprenticeships, Mark, who was being groomed to inherit everything his father had created, remained at Oxford to round off his education. According to a letter written to Christopher in June, 1790 by his then tutor at Brasenose, the Revd George Harper, in which he spoke of Mark's desire 'to gain your esteem and confidence', he came close to being a perfect student. He was attentive to lectures 'during the whole of Lent & the first part of the Easter Terms', mixed with a group of 'respectable and ingenious men', and could now, wrote Harper, 'number among his intimate acquaintance some of the most valuable persons in this place'. However, what prevented him from giving 'an absolute and unqualified approbation of his conduct' was the fact that 'there still remains on his mind a boyish improvidence . . .'[25]

The Revd Harper appears to have been somewhat naive in his approval of Mark's set, for the one thing that they appear to have been most ingenious about was in parting their rich young friend from his money. Christopher was obliged to engage a new private tutor for Mark and to send them both into the country to study in a rented cottage. 'I cannot conceive how he contrived to spend so much money in the University,' wrote George Halme to his employer, on 30 September, 1790. 'He did not appear extravagant when I was in College, but in Oxford, though one hardly expects it amongst Gentlemen, there are numbers ready to take advantage of generosity and inattention: a few of that description, I suspect, assisted him spending his money and his time.' In the new situation in which Mark found himself, living in a country village, 'his pocket expenses cannot be very great,' Halme assured Christopher, 'as there are no temptations to spend his time which is not spent in his own improvement'.[26]

Mark managed to rein in his extravagance during the rest of his father's lifetime and after he left Oxford he did everything he could to gain his approval. He became engaged to a local heiress, Henrietta Masterman, the only daughter of Henry Masterman of Settrington Hall, near Malton. Orphaned when she was only five years old, Henrietta was heir to the Settrington Estate, which included two houses: an Elizabethan manor house, enlarged about 1703, and a new rather austere neo-classical mansion, still partly under construction, which was intended to replace it. She was five years older than Mark, and, being a close neighbour, had known him for some time. She was well educated, spoke and wrote French, and wrote novels in her spare time. It was a love match and one the family warmly approved of. 'I can assure you we are all extremely anxious to hear how you go on,' his younger sister Decima wrote to him in June, 1795, '& I hope you will relieve us from our anxiety as soon as it is in your power.'

Decima, who was herself on the point of marrying a neighbour, John Robinson Foulis, the second son of Sir William Foulis of Ingleby Manor, York, was evidently alone at Sledmere with her parents, and the strain of sitting around for days on end with very little to do was beginning to show. 'I long to see you again either *married* or *unmarried*,' she told him, 'as at present we are left entirely to ourselves & as you know well to our *devout conversations* which are *still* very *numerous*. I have nothing more to say of any consequence & will only add the anxious wishes for your *lasting happiness*.'[27] Mark and Henrietta were married on 11 November, in the church of Holy Trinity, Micklegate, York, where Henrietta had herself been baptised in October, 1766.

On the following day, 12 November, 'the morrow of St Martin', Mark, aged twenty-four, was nominated as High Sheriff of Yorkshire. It was a prestigious post and Christopher was so delighted that he agreed to pay for the considerable expenses that were involved. The cost of fitting out the sheriff and his retinue alone came to £355, which included £80 for horses, £35 for a coach, £19. 11s. for a banner, £68. 18s. to his tailor, £80. 18s. for silks & velvets etc, £26. 18s. for lace, £18. 18s. to the shoemaker, £9. 12s. to the hosier and

£15. 12s. for buckles. By the end of the year, the total costs had amounted to the huge sum of £1,077. 17s. 6d.[28]

After the wedding Mark and Henrietta went to live at Settrington, and in September of the following year, as co-heir to his wife's property, he adopted the name of Masterman to run before Sykes. Since Settrington was only ten miles from Sledmere, there was much toing and froing between the two houses. 'Lady Sykes with Mrs Sedgewick, Miss Charlotte the lovely, & Mrs Crockay, your little Flirt, dined with us on Thursday,' wrote Henrietta to Tatton, soon after her marriage. 'Chr. also and Miss Crofts; & on Saturday she took her whole phalanx of Ladies, the above, Miss Langfords and my Sister to Heslerton.' Henrietta seems to have struck up a particularly close relationship with Tatton, of all Mark's siblings. 'Fie on the lame Horse or the lazy Master, My dear Tatton,' she wrote to him in the same letter, referring to an occasion when she and Mark had ridden over to Sledmere to see him and he had failed to appear, 'for you have between you grievously disappointed all here especially My Saint and I who came over Saturday evening with a fair Wind and light Sailing to meet you. I in particular was in such a Merry way at the thought of so soon shaking hands with you . . .' If his horse, 'the unworthy Beast', went lame again, she continued, then rather than be disappointed once more, she would send over her own mount, 'my Old Brilliant', to fetch him. 'She will canter you over, sail foremost, from Dagger Lane in a tangent.'

It appears from this letter that she and Tatton may have formed some kind of sentimental friendship, for she refers to him as her 'Pet' and thanks him for a ring he sent her, set with a lock of his hair, which she is now wearing. 'It shall never be taken from thence till the Wearer of it be dead,' she assures him, continuing 'This promise, slightly as it be made, I hold as sacred as the Friendship I long ago gave you without Reserve.' She returns the compliment, sending him 'Another, sett in the very same manner', which she begs him to wear 'until the hair of some Lady yet in the clouds, & justly preferred, has a stronger claim to its place.' She finishes her letter by telling him that his sister, Elizabeth, wants his opinion on a horse. 'Elizabeth, with her love, bids me tell you she has got a new horse, *with a long tail*, but will neither pass her opinion, nor mount it till you have been here.'[29] Tatton's close friendship with the Masterman Sykeses is further borne out by the fact that when they were painted by Sir Thomas Lawrence in 1805, he was included in the portrait.

On the death of Mark's father, in September, 1801, the Masterman Sykes's moved from Settrington into the newly completed Sledmere, though they kept the former as a second residence. The 'improvidence' which Mark had shown as a young man, and which he had so carefully reined in during his father's last years, was now let loose. He inherited an estate that, in spite of the considerable annual income brought in from rents, was saddled with debts of over £30,000. This was because, to Christopher, rising incomes were an excuse to spend more on his land and increase investment. He saw the debt as a temporary necessity. Mark, however, did not share his father's interest in agriculture. His interests were sport and books. Unfortunately for Sledmere, he was also a prolific gambler.

Within a few months of inheriting the estate he had saddled it with a debt that came close to being ruinous. Mark lived in an age when eccentric wagers between gentlemen were a common occurrence. No incident was too trivial to bet upon; the colour of a horse, the next day's weather, the distance a man might walk, the impending birth of a child were all topics that might be the subject of a bet. A favourite speculation was on how long a man might live and the old betting book at White's Club is full of such wagers. On 8 October, 1746, for example, Lord Montfort bet Mr Greville 100 guineas that Mr Nash would still be alive on the same day in four years' time, while on 4 November, 1754, 'Lord Montfort wagers Sir John Bland one hundred guineas that Mr Nash outlives Mr Cibber.'[30] In a similar tome at Brooks's Club, one member bet another 500 guineas to ten that none of the Cabinet would be beheaded within the following three years.[31]

As the new landlord, Mark made it his duty during the first few months of his arriving at Sledmere to entertain his neighbours and tenants to supper. Among these were the various members of the clergy whose parishes lay within the estate's boundaries. On 31 May, 1802, it was the turn of the Revd James Gilbert, rector of the adjoining village of Kirby Grindalythe, and during the course of the evening a heated debate took place on a subject which was on everyone's mind at the time, namely the threat posed to Britain by Napoleon Bonaparte, the terror of Europe. A majority of the guests present, including the Revd Gilbert, took the view that in spite of the recent signing between the English and the French of the Treaty of Amiens it was only a matter of time before France attempted an invasion of England. Mark had a quite different theory. In his opinion, Bonaparte's position was less secure than it looked because 'the very atmosphere that [he] breathed was fraught with treason', and even if he were to escape death in the hazardous pursuit of his ambitions then he would be killed by an assassin.

At this point in the proceedings, Gilbert stood up, no doubt less than steadily after the imbibing of large quantities of port, and in no uncertain terms expressed his belief that his host was wrong and that Bonaparte would in all likelihood live to see the achievement of his plans. So strong was his conviction on this point that he would lay a wager on it, there and then, of 100 guineas, on the condition that Sir Mark would agree to pay him one guinea a day for every day that Napoleon lived. 'Done!' cried Mark, in the excitement of the moment. Though the other guests present showed their disapproval of the proceedings with cries of 'No, no, no wager!' neither their host nor the rector chose to listen to them. The die was cast.[32]

As it happened, Mark's belief that Napoleon would be assassinated was not some foolish fancy. There had already been two attempts on his life, the second of which had come dangerously close to succeeding. The first, which took place in Paris on 10 October, 1800 and involved the Adjutant-General, Arena, and a Roman sculptor called Ceracchi, was a plot to knife him in his box at the opera while he was attending the first performance of Salieri's *Les Horaces*. It was foiled by the arrest of the conspirators during the production. On Christmas Eve, he had a much closer brush with death when, en route to watch Haydn's *Creation*, a bomb, ignited by three Breton royalists, Limoëlan,

Saint-Réjant and Carbon, exploded in the Rue Saint-Nicaise as his coach passed close by. The windows of the coach were all smashed but miraculously Napoleon escaped without injury, though nine people were killed and twenty-six injured in the blast.

On the morning of 1 June, the day after the wager was laid, the Revd Gilbert, evidently a wealthy as well as an honest parson, sent his patron the princely sum of 100 guineas. On 8 September, with no sign of Bonaparte succumbing to an assassin, Mark returned the money and began the slow process of paying his part of the wager, seven guineas per week. The days rolled by, and as the warlike activities of the French increased and they consolidated and extended their domination of Europe in Holland, Switzerland and Italy, it became apparent that the so-called peace was nothing more than an uneasy truce. In May, 1803 the British declared war on France and with the threat of invasion once again raising its ugly head the government began the mustering of troops up and down the eastern maritime counties. The East Riding coast, though a considerable distance from the main body of French troops at Boulogne, was so perfect a potential landing place that there was a strong possibility the enemy might try their luck there. Up and down East Yorkshire, disbanded units of militia were reformed, including the Yorkshire Wolds Gentlemen and Yeomanry Cavalry, formerly commanded by Sir Christopher Sykes. Mark was its new commander and he raised 300 men, equipping them with a smart uniform of scarlet, with green facings.

Week after week Mark dispatched his seven guineas to the Rectory at Kirby Grindalythe. The months rolled into years. In March, 1804, Mark must have experienced a twinge of disappointment when news broke of the foiling of another assassination attempt on Napoleon, this time financed by the British and intended to have been carried out by Georges Cadoual, a Breton royalist who ran a training camp for guerrillas in Romsey and who, it turned out, had also masterminded the Christmas Eve bomb plot. He and his fellow conspirators, dressed as hussars, were to have stabbed the First Consul to death during a military parade on the Place du Carrousel. Police intelligence, however, got the better of them, and Cadoual was arrested on 9 March.

On 2 December, 1804, Napoleon crowned himself Emperor of France in front of a congregation of 8,000 in the cathedral of Notre Dame. For Mark, this supreme act of arrogance was the last straw and he lost faith in his hopes of a successful assassination. He also felt that the Rector's investment of 100 guineas, which by Christmas Eve, 1804, had brought in £601 13s., had reaped a handsome enough profit. Enough was enough, he decided, and let it be known that after Christmas Day, he would pay not a penny more. From this point on relations between the Squire and the Rector cooled to the point where all communication ceased. All that is known of the subsequent proceedings is that in 1811, after several years of watching his annuity run on unpaid, the Revd James Gilbert decided to take the case to court and issued a writ against his patron for the recovery of the £2,296 which he claimed was due to him under the terms of the wager. The case was tried at the York Assizes, before Mr Baron Thompson, and the jury sided with the landlord in preference to the parson, on the grounds that the bet was not a serious engagement at the time it was made.

Furious that the verdict had been returned in favour of Sir Mark, Gilbert applied to the King's Bench to have this decision set aside. The case was tried on 23 March, 1812, before the Lord Chief Justice of the King's Bench, Lord Ellenborough, who as a young man had acted as leading Counsel in the defence of Warren Hastings. After due consideration, the judges decided that there should be no new trial and that the original verdict should stand. The reasoning behind this decision was that 'the wager was calculated to induce mischievous consequences to the public, inasmuch as it would tend on the one hand to make Sir Mark Sykes plot the assassination of the potentate, and on the other to induce the Revd Gilbert to do all he could to shield the King's enemy . . .'[33] So Gilbert went home with his tail between his legs, having lost all his winnings in the costs of trying to gain more, and Sir Mark Masterman Sykes was finally relieved from his honourable obligation and the huge burden it nearly imposed upon the estate. Neither man, to be sure, came out smelling of roses. Thereafter, until the day of his death, it was said that Sir Mark was filled with an intense dislike of parsons, especially those of the sporting variety.

Mark shared Tatton's love of horses, and with his help began to form a stud at Sledmere. There was already one large walled paddock to the north-west of the house, adjacent to the stables, where Sir Christopher had kept his hacks and carriage horses. Mark added three more to the north of this. A small rectangular book, with a cover of marbled paper and leather-bound spine and edges bearing the legend on the spine 'CATALOGUE OF PRINTS. VOL 1.' and the date 1801, actually contains a list of his first horses. There was 'the Thixendale Mare got by Turk', 'the Old Ch. Mare bought of Mr Bell of Roos 1794. Got by a Son of Mr Sam Waters's Alexander', 'the Large Bay Cropt Mare Got by Bay Richmond', and 'Stella. Got by Phenomenon and bought by me of Mrs Goodricke, October, 1801.' His first foal, a brown colt, was from the Thixendale Mare, sired by 'My Brother's Old Brown Horse'. 'Given to my wife,' he noted.

From such modest beginnings, there began a racing empire which would make the name of Sledmere famous throughout the world. Tatton left the bank and moved to a house in Westow, a village on the Sledmere estate, from where he used his great knowledge of bloodstock to help his older brother buy and breed racehorses. According to The Druid, by 1804 there were four or five brood mares at Sledmere, 'among them the sisters Miss Teazle Hornpipe and Miss Hornpipe Teazle . . . Both of them were sent to Sancho, and they returned in foal with Prime Minister and President. The former beat Tramp, after a most desperate finish in the Four-year-old Subscription at York, and the latter was a little brown horse, who passed into Sir Tatton's hands, and was given by him to an earthstopper.'[34] The brothers hired a Malton trainer, George Searle, to train exclusively for them, and engaged as their jockey, at £100 a year, Sam Chifney, famous for his 'mighty rushes' in the last furlong. He had a lazy streak, however, and, after turning up late at a meeting once too often, was eventually replaced by another, more reliable jockey, John Jackson.

Amongst the first race meetings attended by Sledmere horses, was the St Leger meeting at Doncaster in 1804. Though Sir Bertrand, a brown colt and Mark's entry in the big race, failed to win, Sir Pertinax, his bay gelding, won a sweepstake with his brother Tatton in the saddle, a success he repeated the following year, also at Doncaster, on Pegasus, another Sledmere mount. Tatton was soon riding regularly at all the northern meetings, not only on Sledmere horses but on those of many other prominent owners. By 1809 there were few racecourses in the north where the Sykes colours, the 'Mazarine blue' of Sir Mark Masterman and the 'orange body and purple sleeves and cap' of Mr Tatton, were not a familiar sight. Equally familiar were the names of Mark's colts. As well as Sir Bertrand and Sir Pertinax, there were Sir Reginald, Sir Petronel, Sir Sacripant, and Sir Scudamore, all inspired by imaginary Knights of the Round Table.

As well as creating the stud Mark also ran a costly pack of hounds, the Middleton, which he had bought from the first Lord Feversham in 1804 and ran at his own expense. 'It was finally arranged at Beverley races last week,' he wrote to his neighbour, Lord Middleton, in June, 1806, 'that Mr Watt & myself with the permission of the Gentlemen of the Country, should hunt for Five Years Certain, the country which I have hitherto hunted; & I hope that your Lordship will give us the use of your Covers as usual. The Hounds are to be kept at Eddlethorpe Grange, & Digby *Legard* has agreed to farm them at £3,000 a year . . .'[35] Each hound had a distinctive S branded on its rear left flank, the hunt coats had light blue collars with a silver fox and 'Sykes Goneaway!' on the buttons, and all Mark's men had fine mounts of his own breeding. The huntsman and first whip were old Will Carter and his son Tom, who came from a long line of hunt servants.

The fact that Mark lavished so much money on hunting, a diversion he had informed his father 'he did not care for', is indicative of his desire to throw himself into all aspects of county life. Although he did not follow in his father's footsteps and stand as MP for Beverley he did fight a very severe and expensive contest in 1807 for the seat of York, which he won, doubtless partly owing to his treating 'plumpers, consisting of upwards of 350 in the city and vicinity, with a hare each. They are ticketed off with the date when killed, tied with a blue ribbon, on one side of the ticket is marked "No Popery".'[36] His victory necessitated him buying a house in London, 21 St James's Place, which stood on part of the garden of the former Cleveland House. It was a large establishment with stabling for eight horses in Mason's Yard, as well as two double coach houses attached, with lodgings above them for the coachmen.

If details of Mark's spending are rather sketchy it is clear that he lived a lavish lifestyle. His greatest extravagances, however, were reserved for his passion for collecting, both pictures and sculpture, but in particular books. In answering a query about him to Lady Holland, a fellow book-collector, Thomas Grenville, told her that all he knew of him was that he was 'often rich and obstinate enough to outbid me at a book auction . . . but he also deals largely in hounds, and in running-horses, in prints, in pictures, in trees and in turnips'.[37]

As early as 16 May, 1801, he paid 1,550 guineas for one of the most important pictures from the celebrated William Young Ottley collection of Italian Old Masters, the sale of which was being held at Christies. This was Salvator Rosa's *Landscape with Mercury and the Dishonest Woodman*, which now hangs in the National Gallery. At the same sale, he also paid 1,000 guineas for Nicolas Poussin's *Noah's Sacrifice after He Quitted the Ark*, thought to be one of his best Italian pictures, and 580 guineas for a fine head and hands of St Peter by Guido Reni. Ottley, who was renowned as an art historian, as well as a collector, was consulted by Mark some years later, in August, 1808, on the provenance of a painting by Guercino that he wished to buy. 'It formerly was in the collection of *Charles Jennings Esq of Ormond St.*,' Ottley informed him, 'and is mentioned in the *Catalogue* of that Gentleman's pictures in a work entitled *London & its Environs* published by Dodsley in 1761. It is there titled *St Jerome with an Angel Blowing a Trumpet*. Where this picture immediately afterwards went I cannot discover but it was said to have been sold with several other fine pictures a few years ago & to have then belonged to the Baroness How. That it is a Cabinet Picture of Guercino in his very finest manner is unquestionable . . .'[38]

That Mark filled Sledmere with works of art is borne out by a description of the house, made on 14 October, 1809, by Theopilus Hill, a Hull merchant making a tour through Yorkshire by chaise. As was the custom in those days, when the family was absent from home, he and his friends were shown around by the housekeeper. Though singularly unimpressed by the exterior, considering the front of the house to be 'neither large nor handsome enough to convey an adequate idea of the Building', he found the interior 'elegant and beautiful beyond all our conceptions'. He recorded how almost every room in the house was 'adorned with pictures, busts and elegant furniture and trinkets', and was impressed by the spacious staircases and the passages lined with sculpture and hung with paintings. The Drawing Room he found 'magnificent', while his greatest praise was reserved for the Library which he described as being 'fitted up in a superb style of modern elegance, superior in beauty to any thing I remember to have witnessed even at Oxford or Cambridge. The books are very numerous and arranged in several different bookcases; the side columns of the doors being painted to appear like a dark marble.'[39]

What Hill failed to comment upon was the actual contents of the Library, a unique collection of printed and illuminated books. In building up this collection, Mark was following in the footsteps of his father, who had made a small collection of rare and unusual religious books, many of which he had bought from a book dealer in Hull called John King. On 8 January, 1799, for example, King had written to Christopher 'I having accidently met with a Copy of the original edition of Servetus on the Trinity, and knowing your partiality for Literary curiosities, I am induced to make you an offer of it. The Duke of Grafton gave for a copy at Mr Paris's sale upwards of twenty pounds & its rarity is such that in the life of Servetus, only four copies are mentioned as known to exist.'[40] When the copy arrived three days later, King included a recipe for removing stains from ancient paper which, he claimed, 'is nearly as scarce as the Book itself, viz. 'Origene-ated Muriatic Acid' with which wash any stained Print or Book, and it will erase the stain, without injury to the Ink or Paper'.

Many of Mark's books were bought for him by his friend and self-confessed 'bibliomaniac', the Revd Thomas Frognall Dibdin. In his book *The Bibliographical Decameron*, which he used to refer to as his 'record of BOOK-MADNESS', he described attending the sale in 1811 of the library of the late Duke of Roxburghe, at his house on the north side of St James's Square. 'I will unfeignedly confess myself to be the greatest sinner,' he wrote. 'I gave £81 for *Hawe's Pastime of Pleasure,* 1517, 4to; £65 for the *Castell of Pleasure*; £60 for the *Love and Complayntes between Mars and Venus*; and £54 for *La Conusance d'Amours* (an English poem)!!' Again, a further record of unparalleled bibliomaniacism: '£30 for a Booke in English Metre called *Dives Pragmaticus* – very preatie for children to rede!!! and £51 for two little quarto pieces of *Spenser's Poems.* With these tiny tomes I marched away – holding them between my finger and thumb, and "making homeward" with a sort of nervous precipitation.' Not one of these 'rare bijoux' was for himself, he continued. 'I neither breakfasted, dined, nor supped off any of them.' He had bought them all for 'my friend Sir M. M. Sykes'.[41]

Dibdin left a marvellous description of the Library, after spending ten days as a guest at Sledmere in the early summer of 1815. Though he considered the room to be 'one of the finest in the Kingdom', he thought it 'perhaps rather too splendidly "got up" for the purpose to which it is converted'. However, he waxed lyrical about 'all the *Editiones Principes* of Sir Mark . . . his *History* and *Topography*, and *Voyages*, and *Travels*, mostly upon large paper, in beautiful condition and appropriate bindings: while below stairs, in Sir Mark's own particular department – and by the side of a bookcase which contains some of the very rarest OLD ENGLISH POETRY in our language – are to be found his beautiful *Hollars*, and matchless *Faithornes* . . . T'was during a morning of heavy and incessant rain that I sat myself down to the long wished for occupation of examining leisurely and minutely these said "matchless Faithornes": and a most delectable entertainment did such occupation afford me.'[42]

So far as Dibdin was concerned, however, 'the *cream of the Collection* . . . was the VELLUM LIVY of 1469. What insects of varied hues spread their dazzling wings to alight upon this tempting dish of cream!' The book in question was extraordinarily rare, the only copy of the first edition of Livy, from the press of Sweynheym and Pannartz, known to exist on Vellum and as such it had been hard fought over when it had come up for sale in April, 1815. It had belonged to a well-known bibliophile, James Edwardes, the sale of whose collection lasted for five days and the Livy had come up on the second day. 'Even now I see Mr Evans, aloft in his chair of state, with *this very Livy* before him, upon which his hammer rested,' recalled Dibdin.

> He seemed to exult in the coming storm of competition. The Duke of Devonshire appeared in person to the right of Mr Evans; and, bidding for him, I took my station calmly at the bottom of the table, facing the vendor of the tome. His Grace was present in order to take up the bidding, if he should feel so disposed – and if the sum agreed upon between ourselves should be insufficient to secure it. That sum was firmly fixed by his Grace at £750; and after bidding to that extent, I turned from the table and mingled with the comba-tants to witness the result. His Grace however remained inflexibly silent; not a word escaped him; but a voice, issuing from a quarter which I have never been able exactly to ascertain, kept up the bidding, against Mr Arthur Arch (who was the Esquire for the Knight ycleped Sir M. M. Sykes Bart on the occasion) till it reached the sum of £903 – when 'the unknown' gave in – and Sir Mark by means of his esquire, became victor. I will frankly own that he evinced undaunted mettle in screwing his courage to its 'sticking place'; that he was prepared to make still greater sacrifices; and that, on my communicat-ing to him the issue of the battle, he gloried in the victory he had achieved, in a manner which renders him ever worthy of a foremost place in the first rank of bibliomaniacs! The vellum Livy slept within his mahogany bookcase on the self-same night of the day upon which it had been obtained.[43]

It sleeps today in the British Museum.

Curiously enough no mention is made by Dibdin of one of the most famous books in Mark's library, a copy on paper of the Gutenberg Bible. Produced in Germany by Johannes Gutenberg, and known alternately as the 42-line Bible for the number of lines of type in a column, or the Mazarin Bible, after the seventeenth-century French Cardinal who owned a fine copy, this was the first book known to have been printed using metal plates. It was rare enough then, only about 200 copies having been made. Today forty-eight survive, twelve on vellum and thirty-six on paper, and they are regarded as amongst the most valuable books in the world. A few years ago I visited the Pierpont Morgan Library in New York, where Mark's copy now resides. After the initial joshing from the Curators, along the lines of 'Mr Sykes has come to pick up his Bible!' followed by 'OK! Wrap 'em up, Charlie!', the cherished Gutenberg was brought in. There are two volumes, each housed in a special case bearing the bookplate of Sir Mark Masterman Sykes. Gingerly, the Curator, Charles Ryskamp, took one out for me to look at. It was a heart-stopping moment. I looked with astonishment at the perfect, crisp type, modelled on the handwriting of the period, so that the printed volume might resemble a manuscript as close as possible, and understood for the first time how print can be just as beautiful as illumination. I was amazed at the mint condition of the volumes, and felt a great sense of pride at my ancestor's good taste.

Henrietta Sykes had a different taste in books. On the flyleaf of her diary for 1813, kept in The London Fashionable and Polite Repository, she wrote a list of '*Good* Novels' she had recently read. While titles such as *The Placid Man, or Memoirs of Sir Charles Beville*, *The Wanderings of Warwick* and *Anecdotes of the Delborough Family* suggest a fondness for historical novels, the more lurid *Fanny, or the Demented Daughter*, *Hermione, or the Orphan Daughters* and *Victim of Passion* reveal she also had a taste for the then fashionable Gothic. She certainly admired the works of Clara Reeves, whose *School for Widows* was included in her list, and who had enjoyed great success with *The Old English Baron – A Gothic Story* which was a rather pale imitation of Horace Walpole's *The Castle of Otranto*. Henrietta also painstakingly copied out into manuscript books the work of other authors she liked, such as *Margiana, or Widdrington Towers* by her namesake, Mrs S. Sykes, and translated from the French the eccentrically titled *Journey Round My Room* by Xavier de Maistre.

At some point she tried her hand at writing a novel herself, which she called *The Yorkshire Baronet*. In two volumes, it was written out in red leather-bound manuscript books in the neatest handwriting and with remarkably few mistakes or alterations. I wish I could say ('dear reader', as she would put it) that it was a beautifully written page-turner, and lament that it had never seen the light of day, but the truth is that it is long-winded and filled with edifying morality, fine sentiment and stilted dialogue.

It begins,

> Every period of Life has its privileges; & the World allows the exercise of them while they are restrained within their due bounds. We not only bear with, but even listen with indulgence to the noisiness of Infancy, the thoughtlessness of Youth, & the talkativeness of Age. I am about to introduce a garrulous old man to my reader's acquaintance; In return for the patience with which he may attend to me, I will engage to exert my best endeavours to entertain him; & it will perhaps be in his own power to improve also by the benefit of my experience.
>
> The Narrative I am going to relate will enforce a commonplace Moral, but one that cannot be too tenaciously held in view: Namely, that how strongly soever present circumstances may tempt thereto, a serious deviation from Truth & Honour can never fail to produce harmful consequences to the Deviator.
>
> I am now, my indulgent friend, (& if you do not feel within yourself a friendly disposition towards me, I beg you will not read another of my pages) I am now just entering into my grand climacteric . . .[44]

At which point the friendly disposition of any dear reader worth their salt is likely to evaporate.

Any thoughts Henrietta may have had about a literary career were sadly cut short. Her diary for 1813, written in French, starts happily enough with an account of New Year's Eve at Sledmere in the company of various Yorkshire neighbours – 'ceux de Heslerton, de Westow, de Croom et de Foxholes' – and a sprinkling of French aristocracy – 'Les Villedeuils, le Comte de Narbonne et son frère le Prince, et le Comte de St Antonio. Aprés souper de la fin de l'année,' she wrote, 'nous sommes trés gaies et nous dansons commes des fous.' Over the next few days the men went hunting, and Henrietta too was out on her horse, usually travelling between Sledmere and Settrington. On 1 February, she noted that while out riding she got 'bien mouillé', and caught a chill. Mark left for London on 6 February. On 19 February, Dr Simpson called and on the following morning 'Cobb vient me saigner la poitrine.'[45] After this bleeding of the chest, accomplished by the application of leeches, Henrietta's health seemed to deteriorate. 'Bien malade à corps'[46] she wrote on 8 March, and on 13 March 'Je ne me porte pas bien . . .'[47] She began to be afflicted with terrible headaches. 'Un mal a tête affreux,'[48] she recorded on 16 March, and three days later she was 'très mal avec une Nausée tout le jour'.[49] The tenth of April was a happy day: 'jour superbe',[50] she recorded. 'Ma tête mieux. Beaucoups dehors. Retour de Mark.'[51] But it was the last entry in her diary. She died, a little over three months later, on 26 July.

Henrietta's will, dated 21 July, 1813, with its charming opening sentence, unequivocally shows that she had married for love. 'If I do not recover from my present illness,' she wrote, 'I pray God to bless you my dearest Mark, and to render your future life happy, as you have by your kindness to me deserved all my good wishes, and as my affection and friendship for you are most sincere.' She reaffirmed her affection for Tatton, leaving him 'my Bay Mare by Beningborough, which was originally a present to me from himself', and also remembered his youngest brother, Christopher, 'for whom I have as much regard as if he was my own brother'. He was to inherit 'any of my other horses which you do not particularly wish to retain yourself comprehending the brood mare Lady Rachell, her year old filly, her colt foal, the Old Chestnut Mare, Grey Horse, the Spanish Horse given me by Mrs Boroes, and the White Pony'.

Amongst her other bequests were 'two Miniature Pictures in my writing desk at Sledmere, one of you, the other of myself'. These she wished to leave to a Miss Egerton, along with 'the carpet bordering canvas work for the staircase at Settrington which I have now in hand in case she wishes to finish it for you'.[52] The thirty-year-old Miss Egerton was Mark's sister-in-law and cousin, Mary Elizabeth Egerton, whose brother Wilbraham was married to Elizabeth Sykes, the youngest of Mark's siblings. It was as if Henrietta was dropping a hint to Mark as to where she believed his future lay in the event of a death she knew was imminent. He did not miss it. On 2 August, 1814, one year after Henrietta died, Mark took Mary Egerton as his second wife.

Though Henrietta had failed to bear Mark any children, it is clear from the terms of a will which he drew up on 21 May, 1819, that he had every hope that Mary would provide him with a family. 'I hereby give and devise my Mansion House in St James's Place,' he wrote, 'unto any son I may have at my death . . . but in case I shall not have any son . . . unto any Daughter I may leave.'[53] Sadly this was not to be, and when he died on 16 February, 1823, after a long illness, he did so childless, paving the way for his younger brother Tatton to succeed him. The obituarist of the *York Chronicle* marked his passing with the usual account of the 'high estimation in which Sir Mark was justly and universally held, particularly by every description of inhabitants in this city and neighbourhood'. However, he continued,

It was in private life that his character shone with the greatest lustre; blessed with a princely fortune, he had the means as well as the inclination to benefit his fellow creatures: to him the distressed never appeared in vain, his purse was always open to the calls of humanity; his benevolence was always exercised with the greatest delicacy, always appearing fearful of hurting the feelings of the objects of his bounty.[54]

CHAPTER V

The Squire

In his will, Mark showed himself to be a great benefactor to his family. He left the generous sum of £1,000 to each of his five nieces, Henrietta Pelham, Sophia Dixon, Emma Mainwaring, Frances Tatton and Louisa Turner; £1,000 to his each of his godchildren, Thomas Tatton, Charles Bower Martin, Mark Otley, Mark Henry Lockwood, and Lucy Sykes, his brother Christopher's daughter; and the princely amount of £5,000 to Charles Hotham, 'the younger son of my friend George Hotham Esq'. As he had been extravagant in life, so he was in death. On paper things didn't look too bad. He had assets of £100,000. Unfortunately his debts outstripped them, so the reality was that the value of the estate was nil. Tatton found himself faced with a crisis.

Tatton was fifty-one when he inherited Sledmere. He was newly married, to a West Yorkshire girl, Mary-Anne Foulis, and he had already acquired a formidable reputation as a tough and hard-living country squire. Since the exploits on foot that had so amazed his fellow workers in London and Hull when he was a young man, other tales of endurance had matched them. Scarcely had he come of age, in 1793, than he performed a feat which became a legend throughout the north of England. He had as keen an eye for a good sheep as he did for a horse, and one of his ambitions was to own a flock of pure Bakewells, the big and delicately-boned pure-bred Leicester sheep that were noted for their quality fleece and fatty forequarters. He had set his heart on buying them from one of the great breeders of Leicesters, a Mr Sanday of Holme Pierrepoint, Nottinghamshire, and duly rode off to look at them.

After selecting ten young ewes at twenty guineas each, he drove them home to his farm at Barton, near Malton, alone and on foot, a journey that took three days, which would have been a considerable achievement for an experienced shepherd, let alone an inexperienced young gentleman. Nothing, however, could have dissuaded him. 'Never was a man more proud of anything than I was of my ten gimmers,'[1] he used to say. These became the foundation of a flock which was celebrated for its excellence, and whose numbers ran into hundreds. Their purchase also showed sound business sense, since good Leicesters were valuable stock and the annual letting of rams was lucrative. 'Leicester sheep were his delight,' wrote the Druid, 'and he would keep at least twenty score of ewes. He let from 100 to 110 rams annually to ram breeders and tenants.'[2]

Driving his own stock to and from market became a regular pastime for Tatton, and it amused him that in the rough garb he used to wear on such expeditions he would often be mistaken for a drover. In such circumstances he did little to disabuse those who accosted him, even if it meant trouble. After bouts with 'Gentleman' Jackson he could, after all, look after himself. 'Thormanby', pseudonym of the sporting writer William Willmott Dixon, told the following tale.

Once, when Sir Tatton was out on one of his sheep-buying expeditions, he ordered a pitcher of ale at the bar of an inn. There were a couple of big, truculent drovers lounging in the tap room, and one of them coolly took up the pitcher and drank the ale. Sir Tatton said not a word, but in his mild, quiet voice ordered another; it was placed before him, but before he could put his lips to it the second drover, with a laugh and a coarse oath, laid hands on the pitcher and tossed off the contents. Still Sir Tatton took no notice, but called for a third supply, and when he had quaffed it, quietly buttoned up his coat and turning to the first drover told him to stand up if he was a man. The big, brawny fellow, nothing loth, stood up and very soon found that he had caught a Tartar. In five minutes, bruised, bleeding and utterly licked, he was sitting ignominiously on a bench mopping his gory visage. Then Sir Tatton turned to the second drover, the bigger of the two, and asked him to come on, which he promptly did, for he was quite as much enraged as surprised at the discomfiture of his mate. But he, too, miscalculated the strength of that slender, well-knit, sinewy frame and was soon glad to cry 'enough' after the worst hiding he had ever had in his life.[3]

On another occasion, he accosted a drover who was driving some beasts along the road to Sledmere and asked him where he was taking them. Hearing that they were for 'Sir Tatton', he agreed to help the man in return for half his fee. When they arrived in the village, Tatton slipped away and instructed his bailiff to pay the man a sovereign. After waiting a while till the man had been paid and was on his way, he caught up with him again and asked him what he had received for his work. The drover replied that he had been paid a shilling, ensuring that he was never employed at Sledmere.[4]

Tatton's great feats of horsemanship were also the stuff of legend, even in an age when such exploits were quite commonplace. The difference, however, between his and those of, say, his friend and contemporary, Squire George Osbaldeston, who was constantly making wagers and matches to prove his powers of endurance, was that Tatton did not see them as 'achievements'. They were part of the routine, pleasure and habit of his life. His diary for 1 March 1797, for example, records how he set out for London at nine o'clock in the morning, returning at ten o'clock in the evening on 3 March, a distance of over 400 miles achieved in three days. 'As a gentleman jockey,' wrote his contemporary, the sporting journalist, Charles James Apperley a.k.a. 'Nimrod', 'Sir Tatton has long been in repute. He is very powerful in the saddle, and never loses his head.'[5] He was hooked on the sport from the moment he won his maiden race on his brother Mark's Sir Pertinax at Beverley and thereafter would travel any distance without a moment's thought to ride a race for a friend. 'If asked to go a hundred miles to ride a race, he puts a clean shirt in his pocket, his racing jacket under his waistcoat, a pair of overalls above his leathers, and, jumping upon some thoroughbred tit, arrives there the next day by the time of starting, and, when the race is over, canters his thoroughbred back home.'[6]

In May 1808, the *Sporting Magazine* reported that 'Durham Races were attended by the most numerous and fashionable company ever known at that place. The Lambton Hunt Stakes and several Hunters' Stakes and Matches ridden by gentlemen, afforded great amusement. Mr Tatton Sykes, as usual, was allowed to be the best rider. He rode the winner of the Hunters' Stakes at Skipton on Thursday, and rode a distance of near ninety miles to ride at Durham the next day.'[7] Another time he rode sixty-three miles in the morning for a mount in the Macaroni Stakes at Pontefract, came second, slept the night at Doncaster and rode all the way to Lincoln the following day to take part in a four-mile race. 'I cannot exactly determine the value Sir Tatton puts upon riding a winning race for a friend,' wrote Nimrod, 'but if I am to judge from what escaped him after winning the Bosworth, with Gosoon, at Lichfield, all the pleasures we are taught to anticipate from the realms above fall far short of the mark.'[8]

When the Welter Stakes was the greatest race in Scotland Tatton rode twice to Aberdeen, on the first occasion in 1817 to ride without success for the Marquis of Huntly on Kutusoff, which he said was the best horse he had ever ridden, and on the second occasion in 1822 to win on Sir David Moncrieff's Harlequin. Each time, without stopping to dine, he rode back forty miles to sleep the night at Brechin and then made a six days' ride to Doncaster to watch the St Leger. The journey of 720 miles was done, according to the Druid, 'principally in the forenoon, on a little blood mare, and with the exception of a slight stiffness she seemed no worse'.[9] He did once, as a young man, suffer a near fatal fall while crossing the bridge at York, his life being saved on that occasion by some cork-cutters who were witnesses to the event and who promptly put in his neck. Without their effort, commented the Druid, 'that greatest and most versatile of all sporting careers would have been quenched very early'.[10]

The entries in Tatton's diaries are brief and to the point, usually no more than a sentence to remind him of what he had done on a particular day. Very little of it is personal, though he did record his father's death on 17 September 1801, with the entry 'My Father died this day.' There is no mention of the death of his mother on 27 July 1803. Most of it merely affirms that he was becoming increasingly involved in country life. He dug ditches and trimmed hedges, he planted cabbages and potatoes, he bought and sold sheep, he hunted and shot, he rode races, and he continued to breed horses. In August, 1815, there are three rather peculiar entries. On 10 August, 'Two men began to break bones.' On 12 August there were 'three men breaking bones'. Finally the entry for 19 August reads, 'finished breaking bones, have got in all from Carter. 10 tons 56 stones.'

There was method in this madness. It had come to Tatton's notice that on the ground where hounds or his shooting dogs gnawed their bones, the grass grew richer and in greater profusion. He therefore decided to carry out an experiment, and had a number of men break up bones with large hammers. The walnut-size pieces of bone that were harvested from this procedure were then spread over soil in which crops of wheat or turnips had been planted. Many of his neighbours laughed at him for such a whim but the crops flourished like never before. In fact the results were so successful that Tatton went on to design a special machine for crushing bones into a fine powder. Whether or not he already understood the importance of phosphates to the fertility of soil or whether it was just the result of good observation, he had discovered the use of bone meal as a fertiliser.

On 3 January, 1815, Tatton 'hunted at Ingleby'. Ingleby Manor in West Yorkshire was the home of Sir William Foulis, whose Uncle, John Robinson, was married to Tatton's sister, Decima. It was a successful day as he managed to sell Sir William a horse – 'my Sancho colt out of Leicester Lass'. The price was 130 guineas, a further twenty to be paid when he won his first race. According to the Revd Morris, Tatton had his eye on Sir William's daughter, Mary-Anne, as a possible wife for his nephew and Decima's younger son, Mark. In wishing to engineer such a match, Tatton was thinking of Sledmere's long-term prosperity: since there was no direct male heir to Sledmere, his younger brother Christopher having only daughters, the estate was entailed on the male issue of his sisters. When the young man declined the suggestion, however, Tatton, up till then a lifelong bachelor, cast aside his inhibitions about marriage and, in the interests of the future, made the decision to court her himself.

In his pursuit of her he was meticulous. He began by giving her a present. 'Dear Sir,' she wrote to him early in 1819, after they had met out hunting, 'As you were so kind as to promise the brush for me on Wednesday, I take the liberty of sending John for it, lest you should have the trouble of sending it here.'[11] He then invited her to lunch with him 'at Bachelor Hall on Tuesday', an offer she felt obliged to turn down, feeling it was a little premature. Her next letter to Tatton began 'My Dear Sir', the 'my' suggesting that their relations were warming up, though she was still cautious about accepting any offers that might be seen in the wrong light, telling him 'I can assure you that I feel fully sensible of your very great kindness and attention in offering me the use of one of your horses; but however reluctant I may be to decline a favour at your hands . . . I'm sure you will agree with me that I am right in not risking to do anything which may invite the attention of the public, or give rise to their questions upon my conduct . . .'[12]

Tatton's behaviour can only have been exemplary, since in her next letter, which begins 'My Dear Tatton', Mary-Anne tells him, 'As you wish I shall in future address you by this familiar name, which will ever remind me of our mutual engagements to exchange the distant and *proper* formalities of *Friendship* for the more warm and heartfelt attentions of *Love*.' She puts his mind at rest over the attentions of two possible rivals, George Tracy and Robert Hildyard, assuring him that they 'never once made any impression upon my heart', and tells him that her affection for him 'is not the mere impulse of the moment but founded upon the great esteem and regard in which I have always held your character'. She finishes the letter by telling him, 'I look forward with confidence to that period in which I can call you my own.'

Tatton's courtship, which appears to have taken place almost solely on the hunting field, progressed steadily over the next two years, though Mary-Anne appears to have had to put up with a certain amount of snide comments and jealousy from other female members of the hunt. Tatton would, after all, have been regarded as quite a catch. 'I firmly believe there are more ill natured things said thro' *Envy* than any other course,' she told him in one letter, while in another she expressed her hope that 'the time will come when I may have a Hunt with you without any scandalous reports'. In January, 1822, she told him 'I hope we shall have many pleasant and happy rides together, and I may with truth say the more I see of you the more I feel satisfied with my decision in your favour. I think our ideas in things of real consequence are very similar, and the most sincere wish of my heart is that we may live many, many happy years together in this world, and finally meet together in Heaven to live for ever and ever . . .'[13] They were married on 19 January, 1822. For Tatton, his wedding day was just another day, and the romantic entry in his diary on that date reads simply 'paid Dobson and all to this day'. Two days later it was back to hunting. 'Settrington Beacon. Killed one fox.'

For the first two years of his married life, Tatton lived at Westow, where he occupied a large farm, with paddocks for breeding race-horses. Early in 1824, the year after Mark's death, he moved into the big house, and from that moment on he devoted himself to Sledmere. He immediately had a difficult decision to make. A large sum of money had to be raised to pay off the considerable debt with which the estate was encumbered. He did not wish to sell any land since this was the main source of the family's income and he was reluctant to part with his horses or hounds, which represented his favourite pas-times. This left his brother's works of art and his books. Though he had no trouble coming to a decision about the former, which com-prised Italian paintings, sculpture, medals and coins, and a collection of some 50,000 prints believed to be 'the rarest and best selected assemblage, particularly of portraits, of any private collection in the kingdom',[14] he had greater difficulty when it came to the latter, know-ing the passion Mark had felt for them. It is said that when the day came on which the decision had finally to be made, he went and stood alone outside the door of the Library.

In the event, they all went. The sales, which took place over a period of two months in the summer of 1824, the library itself being sold between 11 May and 24 May, caused a sensation, and buyers came from all over the world. 'We understand the Revd H. J. Todd is now busily employed in preparing the catalogue,' commented the

Gentleman's Magazine, in November, 1823, 'and furnishing it with Bibliographical notices. Sir Mark's Library is one of the finest collections for a private individual, of any in the kingdom, and is particularly rich in Classics, large paper copies, and first editions . . . We understand an offer of £1,200 has been made from Paris, from the French King's Library, for his *unique* copy upon *vellum* of the first edition of Livy.'[15] Alongside the lot number for the Gutenberg Bible, which was to sell for a mere £199, the Revd Todd had noted, 'I have never seen a finer copy than this.' The coins fetched £1,462, the pictures and bronzes, £5,901, and the books £36,436. Mark may have been turning over in his grave, but the estate was preserved and, as his old friend and fellow bibliomaniac, Thomas Dibdin, reflected, 'Never did the owner of such treasures so thoroughly enjoy them! Never was one more keen in their acquisition! Sweynheym and Pannartz, and Hollar, were the gods of his idolatory!'[16] The sale of the Library did not get the tiniest mention in Tatton's diaries. On 11 May the entry is blank. On 24 May it reads 'York Races'.

Whatever preconceived ideas Mary-Anne Foulis may have had about what life with Tatton would be like, one cannot help but wonder as to how she coped with the rigorous routine which he adopted soon after moving from their modest home in Westow into the big house, and which he kept up every day of his life until his death. Winter and summer, he rose at five, shaved himself with cold water and washed his head. Then, having donned his dressing-gown, slippers and breeches, he would make his way to the Library and walk up and down, up and down, the candlelight in winter casting his ghostly shadow on the walls. He kept his pockets filled with coins and each time he completed the return journey, he would deposit one of them on a table at one end, thus calculating exactly how many times he had walked the 240 feet it comprised. He often covered three or four miles in this way.

When the walk was over, he put on his riding clothes and went downstairs, passing through the entrance hall which he had hung with agricultural implements, and met his groom, Jacob Snarry, who was waiting with his favourite mount. He rode hard for an hour or so, and was always back for an eight o'clock breakfast. This never varied; a basin of new milk from the dairy and an apple or gooseberry tart, accompanied by lumps of mutton fat, and occasionally supplemented by a glass of stout and cream. He never ate bread and only very rarely drank tea. As soon as he had breakfasted, he was outdoors again, touring the paddocks with Snarry or looking over his sheep with the shepherd. He could not bear to waste a single second of his day, and would put his hand to any task that was going. He loved hedge-slashing, for example, and one of his huntsmen, Jack Shirley, loved to tell how he had once come across an 'old gentleman' cutting the hedges outside the kennels at Eddlethorpe and had complimented him upon his excellent work before realising that it was his master. Ditch-digging and pond-making were other tasks he relished or, a particular favourite, breaking up stones for the roads. 'Sir Tatton was also fond of road-making,' wrote the Druid, 'and he would take a turn with the turnip-hoers if there was nothing special going on at the paddocks that morning.'[17]

He had little time for lunch, and for many years ate only breakfast and dinner, always taken at six, with nothing in between save the occasional glass of wine or a tankard of Sledmere's home-brewed 'Old October' ale. This was a highly hopped strong ale, bright, bitter and medium to pale in colour, and renowned throughout the North of England both for its strength and for the liberality with which it was dispensed.[18] The ale was intended for keeping at least a year before drinking. It was so called because October, when the weather was cool and the new season's malt was still fresh, was considered by most brewers to be the best brewing month. Tatton's diet explains how he kept his figure. He was over six feet in height, and never weighed more than twelve stone. 'In physique Sir Tatton was a good specimen of a fine, straight, upstanding Englishman,' wrote Thormanby. 'He was wiry, muscular, sinewy, without that beef and brawn which the English squire usually puts on after he passes his thirtieth year.'[19]

So far as food in general was concerned, he liked nothing better than a really fat shoulder of mutton and had no taste for eggs or puddings. The daughter of a servant at Sledmere in those days cast some light on another favoured dish, when she told the Druid the following story. 'Once when Lady Sykes and family were going to London', she recalled, 'her Ladyship told the housekeeper to be sure and ask Sir Tatton every morning what he would have for lunch. The same morning he said, "same as I had yesterday", so after finding out what Sir Tatton had eaten she sent up the same dish. Next morning the reply to the query was the same – "same as I had yesterday". This went on for nine days, and the favoured dish was broad beans, bacon and new potatoes.'[20]

During the hunting season Tatton was in the saddle from dawn till dusk, three or four days a week. The hunt kennels were at Eddlethorpe, close to his former home at Westow, which necessitated a fifteen mile ride each morning to meet up with hounds and his huntsman, Tom Carter. Tatton ran his Hunt beautifully, with his servants mounted on the very best thoroughbreds, a favourite maxim of his being, 'give your servants good horses and they won't abuse them',[21] but it was run entirely for his own pleasure, and at his own pace. Curiously enough this was one area in which he did not push himself, looking upon the sport as a form of relaxation. Nimrod, who joined the Hunt on Friday, 10 November 1826, at Castle Howard, commented, 'Sport here with a pack of foxhounds is never, I should think, looked for, therefore no disappointment can arise.'[22]

Some found this dull. 'Fiery sportsmen who loved a good rattling gallop called him slow and pottering,' wrote Thormanby, 'and I can well conceive that men accustomed to brilliant runs over the Leicestershire pastures would have found hunting with Sir Tatton's but dull sport. It was a nobleman of this class who once provoked from Sir Tatton one of the very few retorts bordering upon rudeness ever known to pass his lips. The nobleman in question spoke out his mind pretty freely to Sir Tatton on the slowness of his hounds, and wound up by saying "Next time, by Jove, I'll come out on a donkey." "Do, do," exclaimed Sir Tatton in his high-pitched voice, "and then there'll be a pair of you!"' The Druid confirms that Tatton was 'a quiet rider',[23] which is perhaps the reason why he thought nothing of riding forty miles home at the end of a long run.

If Tatton's regime kept him fit, it also kept him extremely fertile. Mary-Anne bore him eight children, two boys and six girls; Christopher, Mary Elizabeth, Katherine Lucy, Sophia Frances, Elizabeth Beatrice, Louisa Anne and Emma Julia, and the first-born, Tatton, who came into the world on 13 March 1826. The latter's son, Mark, was to be my grandfather, and he handed down to one of his sons, my uncle Christopher, various stories on the subject of his father's upbringing, which were received as it were 'from the horse's mouth'. If these are anything to go by, there must have been times in all of their lives when these eight siblings wished they had never seen the light of day. In spite of having been referred to in letters as being 'gentle' by his sister-in-law, Henrietta, and 'kind' by his future wife, Mary-Anne, Tatton's ideas on the upbringing of children were as rigorous as his daily regime.

In Samuel Butler's autobiographical novel, *The Way of All Flesh*, the Revd Theobald Pontifex and his wife Christina, characters closely based on his own parents, derive their ideas on how to bring up children from a manual, the first precept of which is 'Break your child's will early, or he will break yours later on.' This principle, better suited to a horse or dog, was followed exactly by Tatton who imposed it upon his own offspring in no uncertain terms. They were expected and forced to live by the very same rules that he did. They had to rise at dawn in winter and summer, were allowed no hot water, and had to live in the most spartan of conditions. Play was unheard of and they were frequently beaten. For the boys, the horrors of public school were almost a relief. There is a story that on one return home for the holidays, savage beatings were administered because a toothbrush, considered 'an unmanly frippery', was found amongst their luggage. It had been given to Tatton by his fagmaster at Harrow, William Gregory.[24] Poor Tatton was often singled out for particularly harsh treatment because he was the eldest and also the weaker of the two boys, and was once seen being chased barefoot and screaming down the drive by his father, who was armed with a whip. Even as a young man, his father would find any excuse to belittle him. 'What! Do you put a clean shirt on every day?' he once barked at him. 'Certainly I do,' replied Tatton. 'Well! You must be a very dirty fellow!' commented his father. 'Two a week are enough for me.'[25]

The girls fared little better, their sex gaining them only the smallest of special privileges. 'I must tell you that last Saturday,' wrote Emma excitedly to her brother, Christopher, when she was in her teens, 'I asked Mama if I might have a fire in my room once a week which request was granted: & I have one every Saturday night.'[26] A daughter in particular was at the mercy of her father's whims. The Revd Mr Morris tells how a certain Archdeacon once wished to marry one of them, but the daughter in question, Mary, was too frightened to ask her father's permission, for fear of the consequences if she caused him displeasure. She therefore persuaded her brother, Christopher, to present her case. His father listened to the request in stony silence, and then remarked 'Who told her she wanted marrying?' That was the end of the matter and she was condemned to spinsterhood.[27] Another daughter, Louisa Anne, died young, in December 1847, apparently having caught pneumonia after being locked out of the house one winter's night because of some misdemeanour. Two of the girls, Katherine Lucy and Sophia Frances, did manage to escape fairly quickly, perhaps because they married into titled families, but the other two, Elizabeth Beatrice and Emma Julia, had longer to wait and had to remain at home.

In her letters to Tatton during their courtship, Mary-Anne had expressed her belief that their ideas in matters of 'real consequence' were very similar. Whether or not she shared his ideas about the upbringing of children, the reality is that, even if she had not, she had little choice in the matter for at that period, however vicious or irresponsible a father might be, a mother had no rights whatever over her offspring. A married woman belonged to the category classed as 'criminals, idiots, women and minors'.[28] Powerless to intervene, Mary-Anne devoted herself instead to the welfare of others. She pioneered the establishment of Dame Schools, small private schools for the education of working-class children, in a number of villages on the estate and placed intelligent men or trained tutors in others, all at her expense and long before the state saw this as their responsibility. She dispensed boundless charity. 'Twice every week,' wrote the Revd Morris, 'Lady Sykes and her daughter would drive with postilions in scarlet and white liveries to some of the villages on the estate to see how the people fared, especially the sick and aged, and to supply them with anything they might need.'[29] She also directed her attentions to the pleasures of gardening, cultivating plants in Sir Christopher's great Orangery, and in the numerous hothouses in the walled garden.

Sophia Frances, the third of Tatton's six daughters, was a talented artist and in 1847 completed a series of watercolours of three of the main rooms at Sledmere, which show exactly how they were furnished and lived in at a time when the children were in their teens. The drawing room at this date was considered very much the feminine room of a house and Rose's beautiful room, with its fine ceiling and sophisticated decoration, was no exception. Three of Sophia's sisters are to be seen inhabiting it, engaged in various pursuits. Light streams through the windows as they embroider, sew and arrange flowers, while shawls tossed carelessly across tables give a delightful informality to the scene. The floor is covered by a large Turkey carpet, John Robbins's suite of white and gold furniture lines the walls and is scattered about the room, there are various tables to work at, a suite of plain rout chairs in between the windows, and the walls are lined with pictures including, at the far end of the room, Sir Thomas Lawrence's full-length portrait of Sir Mark Masterman, his wife Henrietta and the young Tatton. Altogether an air of comfort pervades.

The dining room was considered the masculine room of the house and this shows in the décor, with its dark red carpet, heavy velvet red curtains, comfortable leather-seated dining chairs, and the walls hung with family portraits, including at the south end the great Romney of Sir Christopher and his wife. Propped up on the side tables between the windows are two horse paintings. Tatton must have been out hunting when Sophia came to paint this room for rather than it being peopled with his sporting cronies seated at a groaning table, the scene is a peaceful one. The long table is covered by a heavy green cloth, and decorated with a single vase of flowers, while at the near end sits a young woman, presumably one of the sisters, working at her embroidery, some of which is on the corner of the table. A small, unidentified child sits at her feet playing with a doll.

The final watercolour shows the Music Room with another sister in a yellow silk dress sitting at a writing table. Bookshelves line one wall, while against the end wall stands a large organ, with cabinets on either side of it with china vases on top of them. A harp stands close to the windows. Small tables are scattered about, some bearing china bowls and vases, others books, and as well as a number of chairs, there is a comfortable chaise-longue. It is a room for retiring in as well as for listening to music. It is a pity that Sophia's attempts to capture the interior of the house ended here and that she did not turn her talents to the Library or to some of the more informal rooms such as her father's sitting room, which, according to the Druid, was lined with paintings and prints of famous sportsmen.

A series of letters from Elizabeth Sykes written in the autumn of 1848 to Christopher, who was then in his first year at Cambridge, recorded the progress of various decorative schemes which were then being carried out in the house by the firm of Dowbiggin, which had recently been employed by the Queen on the refurbishment of Osborne House on the Isle of Wight. It seems that now that the children were growing up, they were to have their own suite of rooms. 'My dear Christy,' she wrote on 29 September, 'the furniture is getting on rapidly – the table, sofa and chairs for the Green Drawing Room have come. The table is most beautiful.' Somewhat cheekily, she continued, 'I hope you have no particular regard for a pair of drawers that were in your room, for as they were the only ones that matched with another, they are now put in my room. One drawer is locked and you have the key. It has long been a subject of curiosity with many housemaids what you keep in it.'[30] It is a testament to her brother's good nature that he allowed such an intrusive act to pass without comment.

'Our little bedrooms are lovely,' she told him, with barely suppressed excitement. 'Your room is completed. And looks very nice. The carpet is very pretty. The Upholsterer admires it *much*.'[31] They had ordered 'plain and simple' furniture for their Sitting Room, which had been papered and looked 'very pretty'. It also had new curtains, which she reported were 'very handsome indeed'. Their mother had drawn the line, however, at a new mirror for the Green Drawing Room on the grounds of its cost, £20. 'Satinwood and Gold,' she sighed, 'it would have been very splendid.' There was new furniture for Elizabeth's room, Emma's schoolroom was being repapered, and the Billiard Room was 'much improved with its swags and tails'.[32]

Along with the redecoration, there were other changes under way. Mary-Anne had evidently decided that now that the children were approaching marriageable age and would soon be entering society, the household should reflect their status. Hopefully, there would soon be suitors to impress and whatever might have satisfied Tatton's simple tastes would not necessarily impress a sophisticated young gentleman from London. She wanted a new cook, for example, who could prepare more refined dishes than mutton and boiled bacon. Her sister-in-law, Mrs Egerton, recommended a new housekeeper, who was said to be clever and was fresh from training at Gunters, the celebrated tea shop in London's Berkeley Square, where she had learned preserving confectionery. Then each of the girls – except for the youngest, Emma, who was still under the care of her governess, Miss Eden – was to have her own ladies' maid. The number of men servants was also increased. 'The new footman appears to be a very nice servant,' reported Elizabeth, excitedly. 'He is rather too red, but he is very nice looking and matches Edward very well in height.'[33] When the 1851 census was published, there were eighteen indoor servants living at Sledmere.

At the beginning of the Season, Mary-Anne set off for London, where she presided over a glittering social circle at 13 Carlton House Terrace, a grand townhouse leased from Lord Grey. The house became famous for its fashionable receptions, often attended by the Duke of Wellington, then at the height of his popularity. On the very few occasions that Tatton showed his face at these events, usually arriving fresh off his horse and booted and spurred, he showed deference to his wife, recognising his limitations in her domain, and allowed himself to be stowed away out of sight. These rare visits to town took place only out of the utmost necessity, such as the one he made in 1848 when he went to have his portrait painted by Sir Francis Grant. Mounted on a favourite black mare and accompanied by his faithful manservant, Tom Grayson, who carried a bundle of shirts and white neckcloths for his master, they rode about forty miles a day, stopping the night at various inns. They travelled, according to the Revd Morris, 'at a fadge – a sort of jog trot all day; for, as Sir Tatton said, "Give 'em time, and they can go for ever." '[34] The result, presented to him by the members of the Hunt on his retirement as Master of Foxhounds in 1853, shows a fine tall figure sitting astride his horse, handsome, slightly arrogant, holding a top hat in his right hand and a walking stick in his left, and wearing the uniform that distinguished him from other men right up to the day of his death, the long high-collared coat of the Regency, chokers, frills and mahogany-topped boots. In the age of peg-top trousers, he must indeed have looked eccentric.

Tatton had little time for society, though, relishing instead the company of country people, amongst even the lowliest of whom he had acquired legendary status. 'No one,' wrote Thormanby, 'not even the most villainous looking of tramps, was ever known to leave that hospitable roof without at least a substantial "crust" and a pint of that "generous malt" over which every wandering beggar in the Kingdom had smacked his lips in ecstasy.'[35] There was only one group of men to whom Tatton took an exception and those were parsons, an aversion no doubt brought on by the former behaviour of the Revd Gilbert towards his brother. It being in his power to do so, he thus would not allow the vicar of Sledmere to reside in the village, but kept him four miles distant in Kirby Grindalythe. The story was told that when on one occasion a certain parson was thrown from his horse on the hunting field, Tatton shouted out to those who went to his aid, 'let him be, let him be. He won't be wanted till Sunday!'

Otherwise, gentlemen and servants, hunting squires and huntsmen, trainers, jockeys and farmers, were welcomed to Sledmere. So many people passed through, in fact, that the atmosphere of the village was described by one of Tatton's grooms as having often been like a horse fair and scarcely a day went by without his entertaining a few of these visitors to lunch. 'I often used t'wonder,' he mused, ''ow they managed in t'kitchen to provide for all the folks what landed up. Of course Sir Tatton had his own sheep killed on t'spot, and they always had plenty o' mutton hangin', and plenty o' poultry.'[36] Since he rarely partook of this meal himself, it was his pleasure to officiate as butler to his friends, dispensing liberal quantities of the home-brewed Old October ale.

'The soul of hospitality,' wrote one guest, W. H. Langley, 'Sir Tatton personally attended upon his friends at luncheon ... Whilst discussing the merits of the respective animals they were anxious to purchase, Sir Tatton pursued his invariable custom of refilling the glasses of his guests whilst walking round the table, until at length the potent effects of the famous "tap" quite overcame them.'[37] Count d'Hedonville, a prominent member of the French Jockey Club, who once lunched at Sledmere, forever after used to refer to 'that damned strong ale!' 'The Egyptians are the reputed inventors of ale,' wrote the correspondent of *Baily's Magazine* in January, 1861, 'but it is believed in the East Riding, that the invention originated at Sledmere.'[38] There was certainly no shortage of it in the Sledmere cellars, which housed twenty-four hogsheads and twenty double hogsheads, together capable of storing nearly four and a half thousand gallons.

The egalitarian streak, which made Tatton so popular, is perhaps best illustrated by the fact that when he made his annual pilgrimage to see the St Leger at Doncaster, a race he watched seventy-six years running, with only one break due to illness, he lodged for forty of those years with a cow-keeper in Sheffield Lane, whom he had first met when he arrived late one night and who had offered him a bed knowing there was not one to be had at any inn in the town. When he attended the races at York, he always stayed at the Black Swan in Coney Street, an inn from one of whose windows Lord Glasgow had once thrown a waiter, with the cry of 'Put him down in the bill.' It was run by a Mr and Mrs Hussey, former servants of Tatton's, who annually kept him the same bed and sitting room. On one occasion, he turned up later than usual to find his rooms let to someone else. Though Mrs Hussey was apologetic in the extreme and promised to provide him with quite as good if not better accommodation, he merely exclaimed, 'Mrs Hussey, you're a hussy!' and rode off back to Sledmere. His rooms were never again let to another.[39]

By the middle of the nineteenth century, Tatton had been breeding horses for over fifty years and it showed. Quantity had begun to exceed quality and the situation was exacerbated by the fact that he could never bear to get rid of the fillies. He loved them all. Year by year his regiment of brood mares grew larger until there was scarcely an acre of grassland that was not grazed by bloodstock. 'The park vista, from the front door to the Castle Field woods,' wrote the Druid, 'presented an ever varying group of mares and foals' and he went on to describe 'the well-known figure on the black, and latterly the dark chestnut, and Snarry, in his snow-white jacket, as interpreter to a small troop of friends on foot or horseback, who have "come to look round". Now they would be scanning a short-legged chestnut Hampton, or a bigger white-legged one by Phyrrus, such as only the King of Italy could tempt from those pastures; then a brown thick-set Caster; a smart chestnut, whose dark mahogany hue and tail-crest "testify of Daniel"; and bays and browns by Sleight-of-Hand, of which Snarry observes, in an almost defiant tone, "We can challenge any stud in England with our Sleight-of-Hand mares!" '[40]

So they could, with no less than forty-six mares by that stallion alone entered in the Stud Book, hardly one of which even had a name. They must have been about as indistinguishable from one another as his sheep. 'There were too many of them,' wrote the Druid, 'and hence no stud lived so hard out of doors. When grass was very scarce they had hay, varied at times by oats and chopped straw . . . Instead of reducing, Sir Tatton kept increasing his stock of brood mares; and unaccountable as it may seem, while he had some 320 head of horse stock, including hacks, in his stables and his paddocks, he would never keep a pair of carriage horses, but hired post horses from Malton, and latterly the Sledmere Inn.'[41]

Amongst the dross, however, there were some very fine animals bred by Tatton, including The Lawyer, Gaspard, Elcho, Dalby and Lecturer, and though he never bred a winner of his beloved St Leger, he used to say that at least he got closer to the Derby each time, with Grey Momus, who came third to Phosphorous in 1837, and Black Tommy, who ran second to Blink Bonny's in 1857. He also bought the great stallion Fandango, bred by the Marquess of Zetland and winner of numerous races, bidding 3,000 guineas for him at the Doncaster Sales. On that occasion he was so anxious to complete his purchase that he bid a further 100 guineas against himself. When this was pointed out to him by the auctioneer, Mr Richard Tattersall, he merely pulled out his watch and said 'Knock him down, Mr Tattersall. Knock him down. We want to go to the races.'[42]

Tatton was eighty-nine years old when he bought Fandango in September, 1861, and the word was out that he hoped to reach 100. This would have surprised no one since he had been a legend for so long as to have acquired immortal status. All over England, when his name was mentioned, the old stories would be told, of his quaint manner of dress, of his sheep-droving and horse-riding exploits, of his pugilistic prowess, of his having missed only one St Leger since he was fourteen, of his love of stone-breaking and ditch-digging, and how he had done all these things living on a diet of ale and apple pie. '"How's Sir Tatton looking?" was one of the first questions asked as each York and Doncaster meeting came round,' wrote the Druid. 'Strangers might well descend from the Grand Stand as soon as he had been pointed out to them at his wonted place by the rails, and make a series of mysterious gyrations round him, in order to do full justice to the assurance, "You'll never see such a man again."'[43]

It was not to be. His health had in fact been failing him for some time. On 13 February, 1855, Christopher had written in his diary, 'My Father had no sooner sat down to dinner than he was subject to a violent shivering fit; he wandered in his talk, all dinner time and ate nothing. Mary was dreadfully alarmed and we had a very silent dinner . . . I never remember before seeing him look ill; he was quite transformed into a tottering old man.'[44] On 1 April of the following year, after relating how during dinner Tatton had pulled out a tooth, saying it had long annoyed him, but had done good service of eighty years, he wrote, 'I fear old age has at last overtaken my Father; talking to him this evening his memory appeared to be failing; indeed I have noticed many little symptoms.'[45] He then suffered two blows which further weakened him. The first was the loss of his wife, who died on 1 February, 1861, her passing greatly mourned in the neighbourhood. 'The poor and afflicted,' wrote the correspondent of the *Driffield Times*, 'have sustained in her death an irreparable loss . . . Like an angel of mercy she visited the abodes of wretchedness and want, relieving the distressed and dispensing joy and gladness wherever she went. It has seldom fallen to the lot of anyone to depart this life amid such deep and widespread sorrow and regret.'[46]

In spite of the elevated position she had held in London circles, she had stipulated that her funeral was to be a simple one. The coffin was borne by twelve labourers, and was preceded by a choir made up of the schoolmasters from her village schools. The hymns sung in the church were the same as would be sung at the funeral of an ordinary villager, and she was interred in a plain brick grave. The only note of real formality was that all the farm labourers employed at Sledmere, all the widows, the schoolchildren, the schoolmasters and all the other employees were all presented with a full suit of black. It was noted that 'the venerable Baronet . . . though eighty-eight years of age, is still hale and hearty, his silvery hair alone betokening that advent of age which his erect form and upright gait would seem to deny'.[47] Invincible though he may have seemed, however, the following year, Tatton too was struck down by illness. In spite of his advanced age, he had been at his familiar task of breaking stones in some woodland at Sledmere, stripped to his shirt sleeves, and, while taking a rest, had fallen asleep under a tree. He woke chilled to the bone. From that time on he was never the same, and spent less and less time outside, preferring to sit reading in his study. He attended the St Leger meeting as usual, his seventy-sixth, but it was noticed that he was not quite himself and that instead of standing at the ringside all day, he spent much of the time seated.

In early March, 1863, the scarcely believable rumour began to be whispered all over Yorkshire that 'Sir Tatton is dying.' It had a solid foundation. The previous November he had been shaken by a bad attack of bronchitis, and it was considered a bad sign that rather than go out among his mares and foals, he preferred to sit in front of the fire and be read to. The bronchitis was followed in February by an attack of gout, a disease that he had up till then avoided, despite the family's predilection for it. There was still enough fire in him to make jokes about it. When the dropsy set in, however, he was a defeated man, and not even the administrations of three doctors, Mr Clements, the surgeon from Wetwang, Dr Swaine of York and Dr Bence-Jones of London could help him. After lying almost insensible for five days, from Tuesday to Saturday, he died on 21 March. He was ninety years and seven months old.

Tatton's funeral, which took place on 27 March, 1863, was attended by nearly 3,000 people of all classes from the East and North Ridings of Yorkshire, as well as by sportsmen from across England. It was a demonstration of the 'reverence . . . akin to idolatry'[48] in which he was held. Amongst the crowds was the Druid, who wrote,

> The day was clear but cold, and Sledmere, with the troops of deer moving in the distance, and the brood mares and foals throwing up their heads and trotting round the park, and then stopping to gaze at the multitude which had invaded their solitudes, never looked more beautiful. Two years later, on 17 May, 1865, the foundation stone was laid of a memorial to Tatton, its cost of £1,916. 16s. 4d. paid for by subscription from his friends and tenants 'in testimony of his excellent qualities and sterling virtues'.[49]

The architect, John Gibbs of Oxford, designed a pure Gothic tower, 120 feet high, with a winding staircase inside it up to an observation chamber, and placed it on the summit of Garton Hill to the south of Sledmere, from where it still commands an extensive view of the Wolds. On its base are panels carved in relief, one showing a pastoral scene with a farm on a hillside and sheep in the fields, while another depicts 'T'aud Squire' himself, mounted on his horse, his tall hat in his hand. In a cavity in the foundation stone was placed a sealed bottle, containing the inscription written on parchment:

The birthplace of Sledmere.

Richard Sykes, the builder of Sledmere.

Plan of the house, 1751.

The Reverend Sir Mark 'Parson' Sykes, 1st Baronet.

Maria 'Polly' Sykes

Elizabeth Tatton,
affectionately known as 'Bessy'.

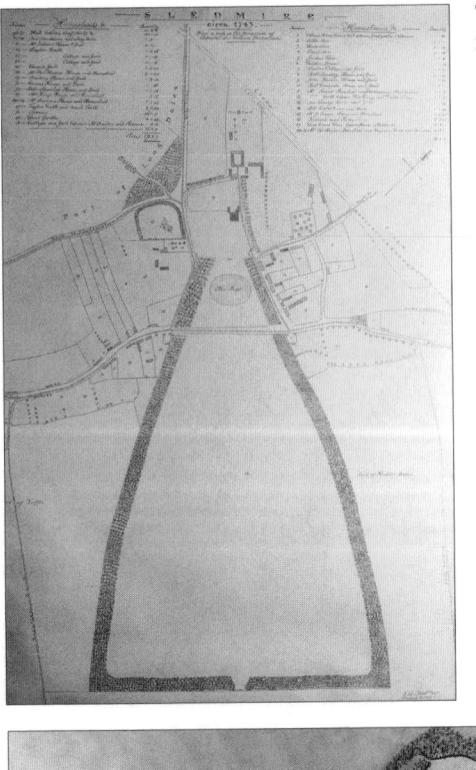

The landscape of
Sledmere, 1755.

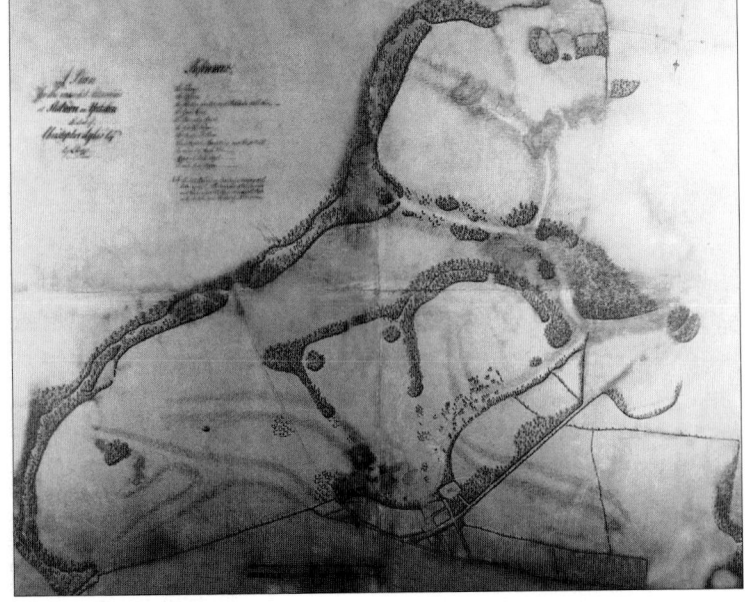

Capability Brown's 'Plan for the Intended Alterations at Sledmere'.

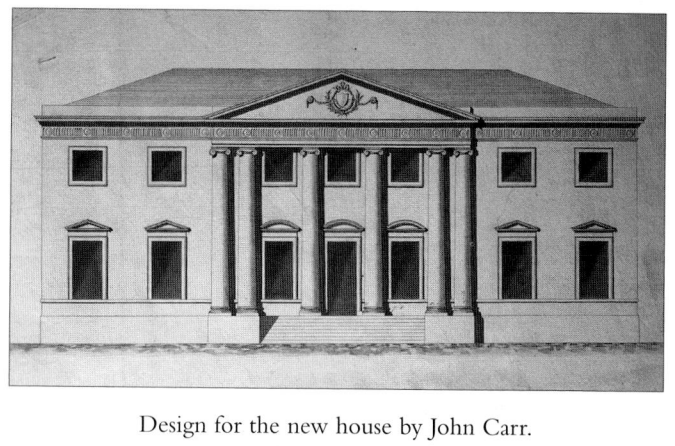

Design for the new house by John Carr.

Design for the new house by Samuel Wyatt.

Christopher Sykes's own design for the new house.

Joseph Rose, designer of
most of the interiors
of the new house.

The Library,
photographed
by the author.

Sophia Sykes's watercolour of the Drawing Room.

View of the house from the south.

Romney's portrait of Sir Christopher and Lady Sykes.

THE MEMORY OF THE JUST IS BLESSED.
A memorial, of which this is the foundation stone, was erected to the
memory of the late Sir Tatton Sykes, 4th Baronet, by his tenantry
and numerous friends, in testimony of his worth and the esteem in
which he was held by all who had the privilege of knowing his many
virtues in all the relations of life as parent, friend or landlord. To his
tenants he was a liberal landlord, and to the poor a kind and
considerate friend.

But the epitaph he would have been most proud of would surely have
been that written in his obituary in the *Illustrated London News*, a
fortnight after his death, which began, 'We once heard a Yorkshireman
asked what were the three things most worth seeing in his county?
His reply was, "York Minster, Fountains Abbey and Sir Tatton".'[50]

CHAPTER VI

The Eccentric

'Aye, whya, there may be many mair Sir Tatton Sykeses,' said the faithful groom, Jacob Snarry, on hearing of his master's death, 'the more the better, but ther'll nivver be another Sir Tatton.'[1] He was certainly right in respect of Sir Tatton Sykes II, who was as far removed from being the bluff country squire as it was possible to be. His childhood had put an end to that. A sickly boy, he was bullied and despised by his father who saw in him none of the qualities he admired in men and who was only too ready to tell his sporting cronies, in the rough Yorkshire accent he liked to adopt when in their company, that ''Ee's good fur n'owt!'[2] Neglected by his mother, who chose not to cross her husband in the matter of his upbringing and who immersed herself in gardening, good works and Society, he turned to religion as his solace. He could not wait to get away from Sledmere and from England, and as soon as he left Oxford, he fled abroad to look at churches and architecture. When the news of his father's death reached him, he was travelling in Egypt. 'Oh indeed! Oh indeed!' was all he could manage to mutter.[3]

A painfully shy young man, Tatton had no interest in society or in the field sports which his contemporaries would have enjoyed, and the neglect of his mother had left him with an innate dislike and distrust of women. He valued solitude and so was never happier than when travelling alone to some distant place. The world was opening up more than ever and for Tatton, a very rich young man, the prospects were exciting. When he was twelve years old, in April, 1838, he must have heard with great excitement the stirring accounts of the race between the *Sirius*, a small paddle steamer of 703 tons, and Brunel's mighty *Great Western*, 1,340 tons in weight, to be the first ship to cross the Atlantic entirely under the power of steam. The voyage was accomplished in fifteen and a half days, the fastest crossing ever from England to America. What dreams this must have given him of the speed with which it would soon be possible to visit strange and exotic lands.

The most common accounts he might have read of distant travel are likely to have been descriptions of journeys undertaken in the previous fifty years to India, a popular destination for adventurous travellers owing to the considerable amount of trade carried on there by the East India Company. Tatton made several trips to India during his lifetime and the first would have been made on one of the sailing ships known as Indiamen. These were generally regarded as being the finest merchant ships in the world, built strong and fit for the long and strenuous journeys they had to make, and to protect the very valuable cargoes they carried. Averaging about 1,000 tons, they carried 100 crew and had room for forty cabin passengers. The latter booked their passages direct from the captain, and paid according to the size and situation of their cabin. This could be expensive. When William Hickey, for example, applied for a cabin on the Nassau, sailing back to England from Calcutta in 1779, he was quoted the sum of 5,000 sicca rupees, or the equivalent in sterling of £583. 6s. 8d.[4]

Tatton would have paid extra for food. Provisions and water, over 20,000 gallons of it, were laid on for six months, and the former included a large number of live animals to provide fresh meat. Robert Ramsay, a cadet aboard the Lady Campbell in 1825, described them taking on board fifty sheep, thirty pigs, three dozen rabbits, five dozen ducks, three dozen geese and turkeys, and five or six dozen chickens. They also carried two cows with their calves for fresh milk, and some captains even grew salad vegetables in tubs on the poop deck. The journey took four or five months, and could take even longer if the passage was a bad one. Patience and fortitude were required to get through it. The former was necessary to endure being cooped up for weeks on end in a small space with strangers without falling prey to quarrels, the latter to survive the often horrendous conditions.

These included appalling smells, particularly once they reached the tropics when, there being no ventilation, 'foul air could be seen rising through the hatches as if it were steam from a boiler',[5] and constantly leaking seams owing to the shrinking effects of the sun. 'The rain was very annoying during dinner,' wrote Robert Ramsay in his journal of 21 May, 1826; 'it came from the deck in the form of a shower-bath through numerous invisible cracks. Mr Shepherd at our side-table sat all the time with an umbrella over him.'[6] Then there was the weather, which could be particularly bad round the Cape of Good Hope. 'Early in the morning,' Ramsay recorded on 29 May, 'the inmates of four of the poop cabins were literally washed out of their beds by a sea which struck the vessel on the windward quarter, knocked in the windows and burst open the doors. It was most amusing for us to see the gentlemen running about the poop steerage with hardly anything on them, lugging out trunks, boxes, etc. The ladies within must have been in a fine mess . . .'[7] On subsequent journeys to India, Tatton took one of the steamship routes, such as the Peninsular and Orient Line, which carried the mail. This involved one steamer carrying the passengers to the port of Alexandria in Egypt, thence they travelled overland across the Isthmus of Suez, where another steamer waited to take them down the Red Sea to India. It was a much shorter route than via the Cape, which was the way the Indiamen went.

By comparison, travel to China, another of Tatton's ports of call, was a much more civilised affair. He would have sailed on one of the American tea clippers, magnificent ships averaging over 2,000 tons, with permanent well-appointed cabins and saloons aft, and which travelled at great speed. The first part of the journey was from Liverpool to Boston, before they raced on to San Francisco round Cape Horn, often covering over 350 miles a day. From 'Frisco, they crossed the Pacific to China, where they could command a greatly inflated freight rate because of their speed, which was so valuable in getting the first of the season's tea crop on to the European market while the price was at its highest. Tatton also visited Europe, Russia, the Levant, Mexico and Japan, making him at thirty-seven, the age he was when his father died, one of the most travelled men of his generation.

Unfortunately, other than one unspeakably dull account of a trip to Italy, he kept no journal of these early journeys, though a few years ago I did find some souvenirs of his travels. Whilst whiling away a rainy afternoon conducting one of many ongoing explorations of the Sledmere attics, I prised open one of the numerous old trunks lying around up there and discovered, hidden amongst piles of old clothes and books, a number of ancient looking lantern slides. They were mostly of rather dull landscapes and cityscapes, some of mountains, others of ships, the most interesting being a scene of a number of people walking about in a snowscape, beneath what looks like a huge frozen waterfall. Their obviously Victorian mode of dress led me to surmise that Tatton had brought these slides back from his travels in order to entertain his sisters with them during the long evenings at Sledmere.

On hearing of the death of his father, Tatton returned home and within a few months he began to make a clean sweep of things. He started with the stud, instructing Messrs Tattersall of Doncaster to sell the lot and on 10 September, 1863, there began what was described in the newspapers as 'the most remarkable sale of bloodstock which ever took place in this or any other country'.[8] The sale went on for three days, and breeders, owners and trainers came not only from all corners of the United Kingdom, but from all over the world, prominent amongst whom were customers from Austria, Hungary, Spain, Russia, Prussia, France, Italy and Germany. One of the principal buyers was an Australian, a Mr Chirnside, who returned to Melbourne with eight mares and foals, eleven yearlings, twenty-one young mares, one young stallion and six hunters. Tatton did keep one horse back, a two-year-old chestnut filly called Wensleydale, whose bloodlines went back to one of old Tatton's best colts, Grey Momus, winner of the 1838 2,000 Guineas. From her he intended to start breeding for a new stud, with an eye for quality rather than quantity. Altogether 313 head were dispersed in this sale, raising the sum of 24,171 guineas. One aspect of the new regime which was immediately noticed was the distinct lack of welcome, as the reporter from the local paper remarked somewhat acidly, 'Alas! For the old Sledmere hospitality, there was not a chop or crust to be had unless you paid for it.' It was a sign of things to come.

Tatton next turned his attention to the gardens, which he set about destroying with relish. Sir Christopher's beautiful Orangery, depicted in the Thomas Malton watercolour, was demolished; all the hothouses in the walled garden were dismantled, and, giving the excuse that the grass needed turning to make it grow better, the lawns were dug up right to the very walls of the house. He developed an obsessive hatred of flowers, which was eccentric to say the least. He considered them, he used to say, to be 'nasty, untidy things', and to anybody who tried to argue that they might improve the landscape, he would say, 'No! No! No! I like to see the ground raked over, raked over, raked over!' characteristically repeating the words over and over again. He categorically forbade their cultivation in the village, whose inhabitants were told, 'if you wish to grow flowers, grow cauliflowers!' and if, on his regular tours of inspection, he found these orders had been ignored he would take his walking stick to the offending plants and slash their heads off. Not all his tenants took this lying down. One man who surprised him in the act of flower-bashing told him 'Whya, Sir Tatton, if you tak t'flooers, you'll a'e ti tak mah au'd woman an' all!'[9]

Another peculiar trait of his character was that he hated to see the villagers using their front doors. He thus insisted that existing front doors were kept bolted and locked at all times, whilst any new cottages were to be built with false ones. There were various theories put about to explain this eccentricity, among them that he nursed a hatred of seeing women gossiping on their front steps, while another suggested that he disliked seeing children running about in the village street and wished to see them restricted to their back yards. The latter is certainly borne out by the account of a contemporary, who told of how 'on one of my visits, some building was going on – I think it was the school. As children will, they loved to play about amongst the bricks, etc. Sir Tatton said to the foreman: "Now if those children come bothering round I'll turn all their parents out of their cottages."'[10]

The same source, however, also wrote of how he could be kind and thoughtful to those in need, citing the case of a sick labourer who needed periodical specialist operations. Tatton evidently made sure that this man was always sent, at his expense, to one of the best doctors in London and arranged everything possible for his comfort and welfare. Such generosity may well have been inspired by his obsession with his own health, for it is no exaggeration to say that he was a hopeless hypochondriac. When once dithering about whether or not to set out on a journey to America, he told his brother Christopher, 'You see I have such a very delicate stomach, that is the thing.'[11] In later years he was to tell anyone who would listen that he attributed his long life to his respectful treatment of his stomach. This meant virtually living on a daily diet of milk puddings. He even employed a special cook to travel with him, an expert in these concoctions, so that, in whatever part of the world he was, he would never be without them.

The belief was also sacred to him that the best recipe for a healthy body was to keep it at a constant temperature, and he devised a novel method for achieving this. 'On two chairs outside his special den,' wrote one of the vicars of Sledmere, 'were arranged different coats. On one there were heavy overcoats, on the other four covert coats, all of different colours and each was a perfect fit, made to go one over the other, and allowing for size. He sometimes wore six coats. I have seen him in church gradually strip off four covert coats and Ulster, and he still had a coat on.'[12] He would begin the day wearing a number of coats, and as his body warmed up he would remove one coat and discard it. If he was out for a walk, the coats were just thrown on the ground. When I was a child, I remember well being told by the retired gamekeeper, Arthur Sygrove, that, when he was a schoolboy in the village, he and his friends used to follow Sir Tatton when he was out walking, because they knew that if they retrieved his discarded coats and took them back to the house, the butler would give them each a shilling.

Occasionally, in addition to the coats, Tatton would wear two pairs of trousers and when he once got too hot while travelling on a train, he simply removed his shoes and socks and stuck his feet out of the window. Needless to say, his original mode of dress was wont to cause a few raised eyebrows. When he made a rare visit to Ascot Races, to watch his horse Doncaster run in the Ascot Cup, his brother Christopher was mortally embarrassed when the Prince of Wales, in whose company he happened to be, turned to him and said, 'Who on earth is that extraordinary fellow over there? Why on earth do they allow people to come into the Enclosure dressed in such ridiculous clothes?'

Though Tatton enjoyed racing, and was regularly seen on racecourses all over the country, it was the breeding of bloodstock which was his passion. Having dispersed of his father's stud and kept the one filly, Wensleydale, to be his first brood mare, he bought two fillies, Miss Agnes and Little Agnes, from the famous jockey turned trainer, John Osborne, and to these he then added one more, 'the speedy lop-eared Marigold, by Tedington'.[13] 'It is a strange contrast to old times,' commented the Druid, 'when three or four stacks with eight or nine foals haltered to each, so that they might learn to lead, were the object of a morning's walk.'[14] The mares were carefully chosen, however, and the new order soon began to bear fruit, with Wensleydale producing two winners in the first three seasons, and the Agneses four. In the second season of his running the stud, however, Tatton missed an opportunity that he was to regret for ever. After sending his mare, Miss Agnes, to be covered by The Cure, she produced a rather small and weedy-looking foal, with a clubfoot and faulty forelegs, which was named Polly Agnes. He considered her to be such an eyesore that he told his old stud groom, Jacob Snarry, that he should either have the animal destroyed or give it away to somebody. Surprised though amused when Snarry told him that he would keep her himself, Tatton made the condition that she had to leave Sledmere. She was sent to Snarry's son, James, who had a farm near Malton, and he, thinking she might make a useful brood mare, sent her to be covered by Macaroni. The result of this mating was 'a lop-eared, ragged-hipped filly'[15] which they called Lily Agnes, who turned out to be endowed with great ability. She won no fewer than twenty-one races and was eventually sold to the Duke of Westminster. On her third mating, with the Duke's famous stallion Bend Or, she produced Ormonde, unbeaten in all his races and eventual winner of the English Triple Crown, a colt many consider to have been the greatest racehorse ever foaled.

Tatton moved slowly and cautiously in the build up of his stud, determined that every mare he chose should have such individual character, quality and merit as to raise her above the average. Price was a secondary consideration. It was not long before his methods began to show spectacular success. As early as 1870, he had bred Doncaster, who was destined to go down in turf history as the winner of the Derby in 1873, second in the St Leger of that year, winner of both the Goodwood and Ascot Cups, before becoming a successful stallion for the Duke of Westminster. Other notable horses he was to breed included Spearmint, winner of both the Derby and the Grand prix de Paris, and sire of several Derby and St Leger winners; Mimi, winner of the 1,000 Guineas and the Oaks; Disraeli, winner of the 2,000 Guineas and second in the Derby, not to mention many others all of whom contributed to making Sledmere a Mecca for the horse-racing world. Wherever Tatton was while travelling he kept in touch with what was going on at the stud. 'I send a wire from here without waiting until I arrive at Jerusalem,' he wired to his agent from Syria, in March, 1874. 'Marigold must go to King Tom about ten days before foaling.'

The other passion in Tatton's life grew out of his early travels, when he had been impressed by the religious fervour he had encountered amongst the large number of pilgrims to the Holy Cities. The considerable quantity of crosses and memorials which had been erected along the roads as reminders of these journeys had made a deep and lasting impression upon him and he had returned home determined that some similar demonstration of the people's faith should be made in the East Riding. He therefore decided that he would use some of his immense wealth to build churches where none stood and to rebuild or restore others. The architect he initially employed for this task was John Loughborough Pearson, a former pupil of Salvin, who in 1843 had set up his own practice specialising in church architecture. While his father was still alive, Tatton's ambitions were out of necessity reasonably modest and the work carried out by Pearson in the late 1850s was restricted to the restoration of three churches, those of Garton, Kirkburn and Bishop Wilton, and the building of one new one at

Hilston. After the old Squire's death, however, he was free to begin in earnest the work for which he would become famous.

He now took up with George Edmund Street, future designer of the Law Courts. A former assistant to Sir George Gilbert Scott, Street had a thriving church-building practice, and was regarded as one of the great champions of the Gothic style. Their first project, completed in 1868, was the building of a church at Wansford, followed in 1870 by another at Thixendale, and in 1871 by the complete rebuilding of the church at Fimber. In all, over the next few years, he built or rebuilt six churches, restored four more, built four large new parsonages and a similar number of schools. Altogether in his lifetime Tatton was to spend at least one and a half million pounds, in his own words 'probably more', on building and restoring seventeen churches. Today, if you look hard enough, you can still find a small plaster bust of him displayed somewhere in every single one of them. They have turned out to be, as the Archbishop of York foretold, at the dedication ceremony of the restoration of the ancient church of St Hilda's, Sherburn-in-the-Forest, 'among the wolds and plains of this part of Yorkshire, a memorial which time itself will not be able to efface'.[16]

A deeply religious, introverted, misogynistic and middle-aged eccentric could hardly be looked upon as the ideal husband yet, in 1874, those who knew Tatton were astonished to read of his engagement to be married to a woman thirty years his junior. 'Imagine my surprise,' wrote Tatton's brother Christopher to their sister Mary in July, 1874, 'when late this afternoon Tatton arrived in the middle of the Royal Enclosure talking to Miss Jessie; so altered in appearance, dress and manner I could not believe my eyes. They stood together talking and leaning on the rails – I cannot tell you how different he looked to anything I ever saw; he must have at last met a person he likes . . . It seems like a dream.'

The bride to be was the eighteen-year-old Miss Christina Anne Jessica Cavendish-Bentinck, daughter of George 'Little Ben'[17] Cavendish-Bentinck, Tory MP for Whitehaven, and a granddaughter of the fourth Duke of Portland. Though Jessie, as she was known, was no beauty, having too square a jaw, she was certainly handsome, with large, dark eyes, a sensual mouth and curly hair which she wore up. She was highly intelligent and had opinions, which at once set her apart from the average upper-class girl. Her father, to whom she was close, encouraged her to express her views and with him she was able to talk politics as well as discuss his other passion, horse-racing. She loved art, for which she had a talent and which she went to Paris to study when she was sixteen, and her hero was John Ruskin, with whom she had met and become infatuated while travelling with her family in Italy in 1869. The introduction came from Rawdon Brown, the leading English scholar in Venice and a close friend of the Bentinck family. She shared Ruskin's romantic view of the past and was later to write that when she read *The Stones of Venice*, she experienced 'an emotion and pleasure as great as I ever felt'. He barely noticed her. 'Y[esterday] the Bentincks at lunch,' ran the entry in his diary for 16 September. 'Today hard at work on water plants and Lucian.'[18] Just over a year later, doubtless on her daughter's behalf, Jessie's mother tried again to strike up a friendship with Ruskin when she spied him in Oxford outside the hall where he was about to deliver a lecture. 'Ugly woman – Mrs Bentinck – pounced out of a barouche on me,' he wrote to Joan Agnew on 7 December, 1870. ' – had to be civil – & take her into the lecture.'[19]

The 'ugly woman' was Prudence Penelope Cavendish-Bentinck, a formidable woman of Irish descent, who went by the nickname of 'Britannia'. Photographs show her to have been large and proud-looking, and she certainly held very firm views as to the behaviour of daughters, whom she expected to be as obedient to their mothers as they should later be to their husbands. She believed strongly in the old order and did her best to instil into her girls a set of rules designed to protect society. These included the axioms that the private lives of the upper classes should never come under too much scrutiny, that they should accept without question the behaviour of rich and power-ful men, who were the victims of so many temptations, and that women should remain pure. Though her younger and prettier sister, Venetia, was only too happy to go along with all this, Jessie herself was far too strong willed to blindly accept her mother's views and the two found themselves constantly at loggerheads.

Jessie had had no shortage of admirers, who loved her for her sharp mind and her wayward spirit. One such worshipper, Thomas Gibson Bowles, future MP and founder of *Vanity Fair* magazine, admitted to having 'cried like a baby' when she told him that she could not return his adoration. He was arrogant enough to see this as a weakness in her character, and consoled himself that she was not the woman he thought she had been. 'After all,' he wrote to her in March, 1873, 'she *is* nothing more than that ordinary weak little girl she seems to others to be. *My* Jessie has never existed. *She* was a very different kind of woman to all others – that was why I loved her so passionately – this is a woman very like all others. How comic to think I have made such a fool of myself as to worship a shadow!' He told her, in a rather bitter letter that, now he had seen the light as to her true character, he no longer loved her. 'But,' he continued, 'I shall never love anybody else, for I have spent all the love I had to give on my heroine of romance and having buried her, there is an end of it.' He ended his letter by telling her not to hurry to get married. 'There is a considerable choice of fairly good men,' he told her, '& I shouldn't like to see you throw yourself away.'[20]

Britannia, however, was determined to net her daughter a rich and influential husband. The story goes that the Bentincks were travelling through Europe in the spring of 1874 when, as they were passing through Bavaria, Jessie became mysteriously separated from the party. Faced with the unwelcome prospect of spending the night alone, she had been obliged to turn for help to the middle-aged bachelor they had just befriended, Sir Tatton Sykes. He, quite correctly, made sure that she was looked after and, the following morning, escorted her to the station to catch the train to join up with her family. However, when she finally met up with them, her mother feigned horror at the very thought of her daughter having been left unchaperoned overnight in the company of a man they barely knew. As soon as she was back in London, Britannia summoned the hapless Tatton to the family house at 3 Grafton Street and accused him of compromising her daughter. It was a shrewd move, for Tatton, to whom the idea of any kind of scandal was anathema, agreed at once to an engagement, to be followed by the earliest possible wedding.

Though Jessie would have had a choice in the matter she decided to bow to her mother's wishes, ignoring both Bowles's warning against her rushing into marriage and any misgivings she may have had about the age difference, she being eighteen and Tatton forty-eight. She was motivated in her decision by two things. First of all she longed to be free from her overbearing mother and marriage was in those days the only way a daughter could get away from home. Secondly she told Rawdon Brown that she was marrying Tatton 'out of affection based on esteem and respect'.[21] He told her in return that her prospects were 'the brightest that any married woman can desire'. No doubt she also took seriously her mother's assurance that 'once you are married you will be able to do anything you like with him'.[22] It proved to be the greatest mistake of her life and one she might never have made had anybody told her about Tatton's previous foray into the marriage market.

In spite of his attitude to women, Tatton understood only too well that marriage was a necessity in order to produce an heir and in 1856 he had shown an interest in Lady Gertrude Talbot, a daughter of the eighteenth Earl of Shrewsbury. 'I think Tatton will think he has indeed been clever if he carries off Lady Gertrude Talbot,' wrote his brother Christopher to their sister Mary in April, 1856. 'I know he has admired her for several years, so I fully expect he will propose to her.'[23] However suitable she may have been – she was said to spend 'all her days in the schools' and to be 'devoted to the country'[24] – the match did not succeed because she did not like her suitor. Her refusal to marry him certainly ruffled Tatton's feathers and it was ten years before he dipped his toes in the water again, with disastrous consequences.

Sometime in 1866, he was introduced to Lady Alice Hill, the only daughter of the fourth Marquess of Downshire. From the moment he met her Tatton became obsessed that he was going to marry her, an idea which was the very last thing on her mind. 'I have had three letters from your brother,' wrote her father to Tatton's unmarried sister, Mary. 'I know you are aware of his extraordinary infatuation about my daughter, and probably you are also aware that he has not spoken to her three times in his life, and that from our first acquaintance I tried to impress upon him the utter hopelessness of his suit.'[25] Tatton was not to be put off, however, and bombarded Alice and her family with protestations of his love. When, in the summer of 1867, she announced her engagement to Thomas, Lord Kenlis, he was inconsolable to the point of madness.

He first of all turned against Mary, who kept house for him at Sledmere, blaming her for having prevented the marriage taking place. Adding insult to injury, he further wrongly accused her of falsifying her household expenses. 'I am sorry now to have to speak very plainly to you,' he wrote to her in August, 'but if you have any regard whatever for me, my interests, my wishes, you will at once see the necessity of your leaving Sledmere . . .'[26] Poor Mary was obliged to pack her bags and move in with her brother Christopher, who since his father's death had been living at Brantingham Thorpe, a large country house close to Hull, which he shared with his maternal uncle, Sir William Foulis. Her sisters, Kate, Sophia and Emma, all now married with children, also rallied round, as did Lady Alice's father, Lord Downshire. 'I am truly sorry for all the annoyance your brother's sad state causes you,' he told her. 'Nothing can be a stronger proof of his Monomania (for I can call it by no other name) than his fancying that you prevented his marriage with my daughter. I can conscientiously say that Alice never for one moment entertained the least idea of such a thing, and nothing would ever have induced her to marry a man so totally unsuited to her in every way.'[27]

Having banished Mary, Tatton then fled to America, accompanied by his valet Wrigglesworth. His mental state appears to have been deteriorating fast, and on the journey across the Atlantic his behaviour was so odd that he alerted the attention of the whole crew. Soon after landing in New York he wrote a pathetic letter to Christopher, telling him 'I am broken hearted. I shall never be the same man again. My mind is going. I shall be an altered person.'[28] The journey across America was a nightmare for Wrigglesworth as he watched his master's condition go from bad to worse. He was up with him every night. 'I am very unhappy,' he wrote on 8 October, from St Paul, to the

Sledmere housekeeper, Mrs Baines. 'I have had no sleep, in fact I have not been in bed for 4 nights. If Sir T does not alter I don't know what I shall do . . . his mind is very weake.'[29] When they reached Chicago, three days later, he reported that Tatton moaned and talked to himself for hours. 'He has got so thin,' he wrote, 'and looks so retched . . .'[30]

When they returned to New York, Wrigglesworth managed to persuade Tatton to see a psychiatrist, who told him that he should return home as soon as possible. When they finally got back to Sledmere he summoned over Christopher, who found his brother in a dreadful state. 'I have come over here,' he wrote to Mary, 'and I am sorry to say I find Tatton worse than I expected; *talking of nothing* but Lady Alice and the efforts she made to catch him (which was quite imaginary). He looks *very* thin and very old; with all his hair cut short and a great bald spot on his head. Poor Wrigglesworth took me into the Housekeepers Room in tears, and said he had had a most *awful time of it . . .*'[31]

Tatton's doctor in Malton told the family that he considered his case a very serious one and recommended his referral to a top man in London 'who has paid special attention to nervous and mental diseases'. They should at all costs, he said, prevent their brother from any attempt he might make to carry out his obsessive desire to get married. To Mary he wrote 'A Gentleman who declares he is "breaking up both in mind and body" and yet that "he will be married" is clearly not in a fit condition to take such a step. Suppose he were to make a proposal and it were accepted . . . would it not be the duty of the family to make known to the young lady and her friends all that has taken place during the last six months? Hitherto you do not deserve the reproach which Sir Tatton throws at you – in future you might do everything in your power to merit it.'[32] In this she singularly failed.

CHAPTER VII

Jessie

The 'wedding of the season', as it was dubbed by the press, took place on 3 August, 1874. From the moment the service began, the church bells rang out in Sledmere and the neighbouring villages and continued ringing for a whole hour. The proceedings were widely reported. 'On Monday,' wrote 'Rasper' in *Vanity Fair*, 'I hear there was a quiet little marriage between Sir Tatton Sykes and Miss Bentinck, assisted by 1,000 or so other people, at a suburban retreat called Westminster Abbey.'[1] Britannia, determined to ensure that the anxious bridegroom was at the church on time, collected him in her brougham and drove him directly to the Abbey, where, puffed up with pride and self-importance, and 'richly dressed in pink silk trimmed with jet and Spanish lace',[2] she was escorted in on his arm. By the time Jessie herself arrived, half an hour later, and wearing 'a dress of white satin, looped up on one side with a wreath of orange blossoms, and a long flowing veil of white tulle',[3] Tatton was a bundle of nerves. The full choral service was officiated by the Archbishop of York, assisted by the Dean of Westminster. It was, wrote one columnist, 'impossible for a masculine pen to do justice to such a scene of dazzling brilliancy'.[4] There were those who considered it the height of vulgarity. 'The Prince of Wales,' wrote Christopher from the Royal Yacht, *Castle*, to which he had conveniently escaped in order to avoid the celebrations, 'is so disgusted with the account of the wedding in the Morning Post. He says if it had been *his* there could not have been more fuss.'[5]

When the service was over, 200 favoured guests were invited back to Grafton Street for a sumptuous wedding breakfast. There were tables groaning with elaborate French food, of the kind that had been made so fashionable by the greedy Prince Albert – dishes such as

Galantines de Volailles Truffés au Four, *Filets de Cailles à la Strasbourg*, *Consommé d'Eté à la Duchesse*, *Pains de Foie-Gras à la Condé* and *Cotelletes d'Agneau à la Granville*, to name but a few, followed by an array of desserts like *Nougats à la Chantilly*, *Babas* and *Poudings Venetienne*. In another room the wedding presents were laid out for all to admire. They reflected the grandeur of the occasion, particularly the groom's gift of 'a suite of diamonds, consisting of a magnificent tiara, necklace of large brilliants, pendant, earrings, bracelet, and set of brooches forming head ornament, collaret etc., all of the finest water, and a pearl necklace of four rows with fine diamond clasp'.[6] Other gifts included forty-two more items of jewellery, decorative timepieces, bottles, candlesticks, inkstands, card cases, fans, boxes and a riding whip, while from the servants at Sledmere, there were a gilt timepiece and an aneroid barometer.

Jessie was disappointed in any hopes she may have had that her new husband, so celebrated as a traveller, would be whisking her away to distant and exotic lands. Instead, the honeymoon was spent first as the guest of the Duke and Duchess of Cleveland at Osterley Park, just outside London, and then with an elderly bachelor friend of Tatton's, George Tomline, at Orwell Park, near Ipswich, a vast and gloomy pile by William Burn. She was even denied the excitement of the rousing welcome the people of Sledmere had planned for her when she finally arrived there, for Tatton had written from Osterley to his agent, Mr Salton, to say 'I should prefer to come to Sledmere just as usual . . . Please let them know at the house that we shall be at Sledmere all being well on Saturday next.'[7]

The Cavendish-Bentincks were thrilled by the wedding, particularly Jessie's mother. 'You looked such a darling and behaved so beautifully,' she wrote to her. 'I can dream and think of nothing else.' She attempted to allay any fears her daughter might have had by heaping praise upon her new husband, who she described as a man of worth and excellence of whom she had heard praises on all sides. 'He has won a great prize,' she told Jessie, continuing, 'I believe firmly he knows its worth and you will be prized and valued as you will deserve. All your great qualities will now have a free scope.'[8]

Her younger sister, Venetia, bombarded Jessie with questions about Sledmere. 'Is the Park large?' she asked. 'Have you a farm? What is the garden like, is there any produce? Have you any neighbours? What sort of Church have you. Where is it and is the Clergyman high or low? What sort of bedrooms?'[9] In fact the Sledmere to which Jessie arrived on 15 August, 1874, was badly in need of a facelift. Virtually nothing had been done to the house since it was built, and as four of Tatton's sisters had left home to be married, the last in 1863, he had lived there with only his spinster sister Mary to look after the place, until she was so unceremoniously thrown out. She had little opportunity to decorate and imbue the house with a woman's touch, since Tatton was extremely careful with his money and he was, anyway, abroad for six months of the year. But it wasn't just that the house was shabby; it stank. In March, 1858, a civil engineer, Mr C. S. Newman, had been called in to inspect the existing water supply and sewerage, and had delivered to the agent a damning report expressed in the very strongest terms.

'I feel it to be a duty to myself as well as to those who have consulted me,' he wrote, 'to express how much I was surprised to discover a nuisance of such magnitude in the very heart of a family of rank.' The main problem was that the house had no drains, only a central 'soil shaft', running down the middle of the house, and directly communicating with 'cabinets' on each floor. Every time one of these 'cabinets' was opened, strong currents of air poured out into the staircases and corridors, 'currents charged with offensive effluvia and noxious emanations from the decomposing mass accumulated at the bottom and even adhering to the sides of the shaft'. Sledmere was unusual in having such an old-fashioned and dilapidated system of sanitation for by the mid-nineteenth century water-closets, the most efficient being that patented by Joseph Bramah in 1778, were becoming more and more common in large country houses. It did in fact have one, attached to Lady Sykes's bedroom, and it was the engineer's recommendation that this 'modern improvement' should be extended to every part of the house. As for the soil shaft, the only solution was its 'entire abolition at any cost'. He finished his report by stating that 'rarely even in the poorer districts of populous Towns are the conveniences so offensive as those I have here described'.[10]

Nothing was done. Old Sir Tatton would have considered it unnecessary modern nonsense, while his son was too mean to pay for it, so the soil shaft continued to fester. There appear to have been no bathrooms either. The family would still have relied on hand-filled hip baths for this purpose. On arriving at Sledmere, Jessie made up her mind to change all this but her determination to renovate the house met a major stumbling block in that trying to get money out of Tatton to carry out her schemes was like trying to get blood out of a stone. 'It has been practically impossible,' she was on one occasion to write in a letter to her lawyer, 'to persuade Sir Tatton to pay any comparatively small sums of money, nor to induce him to contribute to the keeping of our ... establishment in town and country.'[11] Though the improvements to the plumbing were eventually implemented, it was not for another fifteen years, so like everyone else she just had to get used to the smells.

Had the eighteen-year-old Jessie not been brought up in a similar establishment, she might have found the experience of suddenly having to run a large household such as Sledmere, with its sixteen live-in servants organised according to a strict hierarchy, a daunting one. She was, however, used to such a set-up, her parents employing seventeen indoor servants at their London house. At the head of the line-up assembled to meet her was the housekeeper, Mary Baines, an elderly spinster aged sixty-six, who had begun her life in service under Tatton's father. She ruled over two housemaids, three laundry maids and two stillroom maids, and was responsible for the cleaning of the house, overseeing the linen, laying and lighting the fires, and the contents of the stillroom. The other senior female servant was Ann Beckley, the cook, who was on equal terms with the housekeeper, and who had under her a scullery maid and a dairymaid. The butler, Arthur Hewland, was in charge of the male servants, consisting of a pantry boy and two footmen. Tatton's personal valet was Richard Wrigglesworth. The servants were housed in the domestic wing, enlarged and improved by Sir Christopher in 1784, and they welcomed the young mistress to Sledmere. After years of living with the introverted Sir Tatton, her extravagant and outgoing nature came to most of the household as a breath of fresh air.

The exceptions were two of the senior members of staff. The long-serving Baines found it hard to accustom herself to her new mistress. She was used to doing things her way and did not hide her disapproval of Jessie's immediate plans to cheer up the house. 'She [Lady S.] wants measurement of Music Room, Dining Room, Billiard also Drawing Room for *Carpets*,' she wrote disdainfully to her former employer, Mary Sykes. Beckley, the cook, evidently agreed with her, for both of them soon found themselves out of a job. 'I have had a letter from Lady S. this morning,' Baines told Mary, 'to say that there is a housekeeper, also a cook coming down the 1st Jan and that Beckley and me have to give up all to them and leave . . . I feel much put out at such treatment.'[12] She received great sympathy from amongst the family. 'I am so very sorry about poor Baines,' wrote Christopher, who had after all grown up with her.[13]

One of the first tasks that Jessie set herself was to breathe new life into some of the rooms. In *Algernon Casterton*, one of three semi-autobiographical novels she was to write later in her life, Jessie described her approach to decoration through the eyes of Lady Florence Hazleton, recently wed and attempting to instil some life into her new home, Hazleton Hall. 'She had made it a very charming place – it was in every sense of the word an English home. She found beautiful old furniture in the garrets and basements, to which it had been relegated in those early Victorian days when eighteenth-century taste was considered hideous and archaic. She hung the Indian draperies she had collected over screens and couches; she spread her Persian rugs over the old oak boards. The old pictures were cleaned and renovated, and among the Chippendale and Sheraton tables and chairs many a luxurious modern couch and arm-chair made the rooms as comfortable as they were picturesque.'[14] This could well have been a description of the Library at Sledmere, which was the first room on which Jessie made her mark. She plundered the house for furniture and artefacts of every kind, and soon the vast empty space in which her father-in-law had taken his daily exercise was filled to overflowing with chairs, tables, day-beds, china, pictures, screens, oriental rugs, bric-a-brac from Tatton's travels and masses of potted palms, which were all that were now grown in the hothouses.

For the first two years of her marriage, Jessie threw herself into the role of being the mistress of a great house. She organised the servants and the running of the houses, she attended church and took up her deceased mother-in-law's interest in good works and education, she read, wrote and hunted. She also tried hard to be a good wife, accompanying Tatton on his travels abroad, and to the many race meetings he attended when he was back home. But it was an uphill struggle. She could never have guessed when she took the fatal decision to bow to her mother's wishes the life that was in store for her with Tatton. Their characters were simply poles apart: while she had a longing for gaiety and company, he wished wherever possible to avoid the society of others. Like his father, he seldom varied his routine. Each day he rose at six, and after taking a long walk in the park, he would eat a large breakfast, before attending church. He spent the mornings attending to business in the estate office, before returning to the house at noon for a plain lunch, which always featured a milk pudding. After lunch he would snooze, then return to the office for further business. He took a light supper and was in bed by eight. He did not smoke and the only alcohol that passed his lips was a wine glass of whisky diluted with a pint of Apollinaris water, which he drank every day after lunch.

This was hardly a life that was going to keep a young wife happy for long, and her frustration and boredom was reflected in a pencil sketch she secretly made on the fly leaf of one of Henrietta Sykes's manuscript books. It depicts an old man lying stretched out asleep in a chair, snores coming out of his nose. Above him are written the poignant words 'My evenings October 1876 – Quel rêve pour une jeune femme.[15] J.S.' Jessie was later to confide to her daughter-in-law that it had taken six months for Tatton to consummate their marriage, and then only when she had got him drunk, and with the utmost clumsiness. In the light of this knowledge, it is scarcely surprising to learn that sometime in 1876 Jessie struck up some kind of romantic

friendship with a German admirer, Magens Frijs, whom she met on her travels with Tatton. Though it was almost certainly a platonic relationship – his letters to her are quite formal and she is addressed in all of them as 'Chère Lady Sykes' – there is no doubt that she was in love with him.

Though Tatton kept no account of any of his travels abroad, there are one or two journals which were written up by Jessie and which throw light not only on their journeys, but on the state of their relationship. The earliest of these describes a journey across America which took place between August, 1877 and March, 1878.[16] They left Sledmere on 10 August, accompanied by Tatton's valet, Dillon, and Jessie's maid, Gotherd, taking the early train from Malton to York. The Sledmere land agent, Walter Salton, had, wrote Jessie, 'with exertions squeezed twenty-five pound note out of T and gave me another of his own'. From York they travelled to Liverpool, arriving in the late afternoon. No sooner were they settled in their hotel than Jessie rushed off to the post office. 'Found a letter from Magens,' she wrote in her journal, 'it was very cold and I was dreadfully cut up.' The letter sympathised with her worries at going away for a long journey, not knowing how things might be between them on her return. 'Je vous prie de croire,' he wrote, 'que vous avez laissé en moi un ami sur lequel vous pouvez compter en tout occasion et pour lequel votre souvenir restera toujours comme un point lumineux.'[17].

The Sykeses boarded ship the following morning at 11.00 a.m. Jessie thought 'the accommodation very miserable', though there was one consolation. 'Luckily Tatton and I have a cabin a piece.' In New York, which they reached on 21 August, they were met on the pier by Jessie's brother George, to whom she was devoted and who was to spend some of the holiday with them. 'New York is the dirtiest, fumiest, untidiest place I ever saw,' she wrote. 'The streets are dreadfully rough and ill paved.' They spent two nights at the Brunswick Hotel, before heading off to Newport, Rhode Island. Since its 'discovery' after the Civil War, Newport was where all the fashionable New Yorkers assembled for the summer season. It had a balmy climate, so perfect after the oppressive heat of the city, and a beautiful natural harbour to attract those with yachts and one by one sumptuous summer 'cottages' were springing up along the ocean. The first person to build there on a large scale had been the China trade merchant, William Shepherd Wetmore, who in 1852 had set the standard with an Italianate-style villa at which he held elaborate entertainments, such his 'Fête Champêtre' in 1857, a grand country picnic for over 2,000 guests. In the 1870s his son, George Peabody Wetmore, remodelled the house in the second empire French style and called it 'Château-sur-Mer'. After that wealthy families like the Vanderbilts, the Oelriches, and the Berwinds were tripping over one another to build grander and grander houses.

Following hot on the heels of William Wetmore came America's Royalty, the Astors, John Jacob III and Charlotte, who built Beaulieu, a splendid house in the French style, where they gave extravagant balls and dinners. The memory of the Civil War was still very strong, and the rich reacted to it in much the same way as the flapper generation in London did in the aftermath of the First World War; money was no object; conspicuous consumption was the order of the day. Writing to his brother, William Waldorf, on 31 March, 1865, John Jacob spoke of 'days of magnificence, when money was poured out like water. Nothing but the best was good enough and so the best had to be procured regardless of cost.'[18] Beaulieu was one of the first homes visited by Tatton and Jessie, on the very night of their arrival. 'After dinner went to Mrs John Jacob Astor's reception,' she recorded. 'The House was handsome and decorated with splendid flowers. The Astors are the richest people in America. To our great surprise, Tatton went too . . . Supper was good, but the American system of picnicking all over the room instead of sitting up to the table is trying to say the least . . . After supper they danced a little but on a carpet.'

The next day, Jessie discovered that picnicking was all the rage. 'We went to a picnic got up by a man called McAlister. He is a Virginian, the most talkative creature I ever met and a thorough gossip, but better to have as your friend than enemy. McAlister took me to dinner which was served at two long tables on the grass . . . [his] plan is for every lady to bring a dish of some kind of food and every man a champagne, he providing the ice-cream, waiters, music etc, but his friends are wicked enough to insinuate that he finds his picnics rather profitable. He was very civil to me and I laid the butter on so made a conquest of him for all the time.' She had cast her spell on the right man, for Ward MacAlister was the leading arbiter of New York society, organiser of the Ball Committee, which virtually ruled over who was a member of society and who was not. With him and the Astors as their friends all doors would be open to her and Tatton.

Though the Sykeses had planned to spend a month at Newport, basing themselves at the Ocean House Hotel, which she described as being 'the great hotel of the place', Tatton only lasted a week, before he took himself off on a solitary sightseeing trip to the White Mountains of New Hampshire. Jessie, left with George as her escort, threw herself into an endless round of parties. There were breakfasts, luncheons, teas and dinners, polo matches, yachting parties, horse races, picnics and numerous balls. On Sunday, which was the day of rest, everybody promenaded along the cliffs. She enjoyed it all hugely and her outgoing, lively and flirtatious nature attracted her many admirers, such as Percy Belmont, son of the banker, August Belmont, 'to whom', she wrote, 'I took a fancy. He is small, dark, clever, and like all the men here fancies he knows a lot about horses.' She spent a lot of time with Mrs Astor, who she described as being 'killing with her long words'.

In early September, her brother Freddy and a group of friends joined the party. On 7 September, the day after his arrival, Mrs Astor gave an afternoon dance. 'We all went,' wrote Jessie. 'It was pretty good fun.' As it happened, Freddy had arrived just in time for the ball of the season, a 'much talked about' fancy dress party being given by Mr and Mrs Kernochan, a couple who failed to impress Jessie. 'Mrs Kernochan is one of the nouveaux riches and her father was in the Muff trade,' she wrote, adding caustically, 'she is truly vulgar and very common besides. To my mind she has a husband rather more plebeian than her. The general effect of the Ball was poor, the house pretty. I worked hard all the morning preparing dresses for all the boys. They were as scholars and looked very well – in little blue blouses and slates and toys hung round their wrists.' A Mrs Dundas, who came as Marguerite de Valois, she described as looking 'gorgeous but absurd'. Once again she was not short of suitors. 'Danced the Cotillion with Brookes. This sadly wearied me but Hutton and Michleman consoled me. Hutton is the sort of man like the colonel in an old fashioned novel. He called on me this afternoon.'

This was the last big social occasion attended by Jessie before she had to return to New York to meet Tatton, something she did, after making all her farewells, with a somewhat heavy heart. She knew what was in store for her; a three month trip to California without the company of George, who was to stay behind. She arrived in New York, on Friday, 14 September, and on Sunday attended morning service with Tatton at Trinity Church. His mood did nothing to lift her spirits. 'He was very cross,' she wrote. 'I was so hot I went out before the sermon which made him crosser still.' The following morning they started out for Niagara via the Hudson River. 'George left at the wharf,' she noted, 'to my great regret.'

Jessie arrived in Niagara, late in the evening of 18 September, 'feeling cross and disgusted', but things took a turn for the better when she discovered that Freddy and his friends were there too. She accompanied them to see the Horseshoe Falls. 'I was really pleased with the Falls,' she recorded. 'We dressed up in waterproof skins and went underneath it. Got very wet.' They also went to look at the rapids, which she thought 'very beautiful', but just at the moment when her spirits were temporarily lifted, a dreadful scene took place. The party were gathered together in the large sitting room of the hotel when she and Tatton 'had a great row about Dillon who was insolent. Tatton made a beast of himself. Freddy was much shocked.' When Freddy left the following morning, Jessie felt very downhearted. Toronto, where they arrived on Monday, 24 September, and where she found 'nothing much to do except drive about and go to very bad theatre', did little to improve her state of mind, and she continued to feel very low and homesick. 'Oh! How I hate America,' she wrote on 27 September. Her spirits hit a new low three days later when she failed to receive an expected letter from Magens Frijs, who she had not heard from since she left England. 'He does not love me,' she confided, 'I feel so miserable.'

From Toronto, they travelled to Kingston, then Montreal, which Jessie found 'decidedly more picturesque than the United States', and Quebec, which, though the town was 'clean and pretty', she thought 'decidedly dull'. On 13 October, after a tedious railway journey, they arrived in Ottawa, where the Governor-General, Lord Dufferin, had his residence. A dashing figure, who Queen Victoria had hesitated about appointing as a Lord-in-Waiting because he was so 'good looking and captivating',[19] he was much loved by the Canadians, and was renowned for his hospitality. He kept a close eye on who was passing through, especially those, like the Sykeses, who might bring him news from the home country. Tatton, however, whose mood swings appear to have been erratic in the extreme, preferred to be left alone. 'An invitation came to dine tonight with the Governor,' wrote Jessie, 'Tatton raved and cursed and said he would not go.' His temper was not improved by a visit in the afternoon to the nearby town of Chelsea, which Jessie described as being 'a wretched settlement consisting only of a few log huts', during which he 'was asleep most of the time and the rest swearing and abusive'. By the time evening came, Tatton had changed his mind again and decided that he would after all go to Government House, where he contributed little to the party. 'We had a very good dinner,' wrote Jessie, though 'Tatton was very silent and cross. I tried my best to please.' She found Lord Dufferin himself 'a man of charming manners', and concluded, 'How glad I was to see again a few educated and agreeable people after this wretched travelling.'

On the following day, the Sykeses returned to Government House for lunch, at which Lord Dufferin and his young, 'exceedingly pretty'[20] wife, Harriet, pressed them to stay with them. 'But of course,' wrote Jessie, 'such luck was out of the question.' Jessie had made a profound impression on the Governor-General, and he on her. 'Lord Dufferin . . . is simply quite the most charming man I ever met,' she noted. 'He is to my mind the most perfect realisation of the Grand Seigneur I ever saw. His manners are quite delightful and he has that extraordinary gift of appearing interested with everyone.' After lunch Lady Dufferin took Jessie for a drive during which she pumped her for news from home. 'I, as I always do,' she recalled, 'felt awkward, self-conscious and uncomfortable', adding revealingly, 'these are the results of constant snubbing in early years'. That night at dinner, she found Dufferin 'more agreeable than ever' and returned home feeling very happy and cheerful. Her spirits were immediately dashed, however, by Tatton's announcement that they were to leave in two days for Chicago. The next night, at her last dinner with the Governor-General, Jessie 'made a discovery,' she wrote, 'which pained me', adding, somewhat cryptically, 'It is always sad to find weakness.' Subsequent events suggest that His Excellency may well have paid her more attention than he should have done. 'But I have certainly enjoyed these few days,' she concluded her entry for 17 October, 'they have been so delightful. Now for three weeks' true misery, ugh!'

The nineteenth of October found the Sykeses back in Toronto, where Jessie took Gotherd to see a 'sensational American Melodrama called *Escape From Sing Sing*', which had 'about ten murders and sixty pistol shots in it!' They caught the early morning train to Detroit, which she found 'a thriving place', though with 'very nasty food'. When they reached Chicago on 22 October, she found a 'very civil and kind' letter awaiting her from Lord Dufferin. Jessie did not like Chicago, which she described as 'an enormous dreary town rather like the new parts of the City in London'. Tatton's idea of sightseeing was to take her 'out to the places where they killed hogs – saw about twenty scalded and cut up, a filthy sight'. From Chicago they travelled to Omaha on a train which had the novel addition of a dining car. 'It seemed strange,' she remarked, 'to dine at a little table while whirling along at thirty-five miles an hour.' Omaha itself, however, was not a success. 'Omaha is I think the most desolate God forgotten place it ever has been my luck or rather ill luck to visit . . . cows and pigs are feeding in the streets.'

On 31 October, en route to Salt Lake City, they crossed the Rocky Mountains. 'They are fine,' wrote Jessie, 'but I think they appear so more from the contrast with the dull dead level of the thousand miles of Prairie that precede them than for any merit of their own.' She loved Salt Lake City, which she considered 'a really pretty town', noting that it reminded her of Assisi. She persuaded Tatton to stay in a hotel run by a Mormon, 'thinking it would be more amusing', and attended one of their meetings, which she found 'curious but dull'. In the evening they went to see a conjuror and Jessie 'was much amused by the rough audience'. On the train to San Francisco the next day, the valet, Dillon, was once again 'excessively insolent'. Tatton paid no attention and Jessie was 'reduced to sitting in the smoking car'.

Jessie neglected her diary during the time she was in San Francisco, recording only that in 'the first week we amused ourselves by walking about, driving in buggies etc.'. She did remark, on 26 November, that she was 'disappointed not hearing from Ld. D.',[21] This may have been because she failed to tell him she was going to be there; in a letter to her dated 3 December, he wrote 'I wish I had known you were to have been in San Francisco . . . I would have told some pleasant people to call upon you, through whom you might have had a glimpse of the queer world which disports itself on the Pacific Slope.'[22]

Leaving San Francisco at the end of November, they went first to Sacramento and then back to Salt Lake City. The fifth of December found them in Ogden, a low point of the trip. 'The Hotel is awful, quite a hot-house,' reported Jessie. 'Our bedrooms were so horrible, the food so bad, and Tatton having a corpse for a next door neighbour, a poor girl who died this morning of fever, all included have induced him to allow us to proceed today for which I am truly thankful.' They moved on to Denver, which she thought 'not a bit picturesque. There are the Rocky Mountains in the distance it is true but nothing but the hideous Prairie everywhere else.' It is quite clear that Jessie was by now pretty much at the end of her tether. 'Oh! How sick I am of this journey and with what longing I think of New York,' she wrote on 8 December. 'Please God another fortnight will see this trip out.' The only consolation on that day was the 'very good-looking young' German coachman who took them for a drive on the plains and amused them with his anecdotes, and of whom she made a little sketch.

The entry for Saturday, 9 December, is perhaps the saddest in the whole journal and speaks volumes about the miserable state of Jessie and Tatton's marriage after only three years. They were out walking when 'the sole came off my boot, a pair I had bought at San Francisco and which, costing twelve dollars, nearly broke poor Tatton's heart. He scolded, gibed and insulted me the rest of the time – I had a weary walk home with him, particularly as my foot naturally hurt me a good deal. No one could imagine how truly terrible are the daily and constant nagging insults and one continual worry and tease. God only knows how much and how deeply T. has made me suffer – I really do try to please him and am so meek I quite despise myself, as after all those dreadful scolds I always kiss and try to make it up. But of course I have not the slightest spark of love or respect for him. How could I and the only thing I can look forward to is his death. This is really shocking – and I do as I grow older feel such a longing for all I might have had: children, a kind affectionate *gentleman* for a husband, a home, oh! . . .' Here she breaks off with a bitter reprimand to herself, 'A truce to these sentimental whinings.'

Happily for Jessie their return to New York, for which she was pining, was in sight and she managed the final part of the trip without again falling into such depths of despair. In Chicago, which they reached on 14 December, she found two letters awaiting her from Lord Dufferin, which cheered her, and a week later she was able to write in her diary 'Reached New York at 10.00 p.m. Joy!' While Tatton remained firmly ensconced in the Brunswick Hotel, Jessie, escorted by her brother Freddy, immersed herself wholeheartedly in the usual round of luncheons, teas and balls. Her success with Lord Dufferin had done little to curb her flirtatiousness and she soon appears to have been somewhat taken with a man called Freddy Bell, who she met with the Livingstons; 'Bell seems a clever amusing man,' she wrote on 29 December, 'enjoyed myself very much indeed'; and on New Year's Day, at Mrs Astor's Ball, annually the most important social event of the season, 'the party that broke more hearts than any other event before or since',[23] she 'talked to Bell who I found rather pleasant – he was Consuelo Mandeville's beau I believe'.[24]

On 15 January, to Jessie's great joy, Tatton set off on a journey to the South leaving her and Freddy in the Brunswick with an allowance of £50 a week, quite enough to take care of their everyday needs, considering that they would be living most of the time at other people's expense. 'I think the following four weeks,' she noted in her diary, 'were the happiest almost I ever spent in my life – we had no worries, we never quarrelled and entirely had a "good time".' There were several good balls: 'I had two or three devoted admirers and Freddy fell in love with Miss Astor.' Towards the end of January, Lord Dufferin turned up. He stayed at their hotel and, wrote Jessie, 'paid me the most devoted court which really quite touched me'. When he left, after extracting a promise from her that she would make a return visit to Ottawa, he wrote to her telling her how fond he had become of her and that she was a 'glorious and beautiful creature'. He finished his letter by expressing his hope that 'you will trust me absolutely and allow me to be to you all that I desire'. After all, he said, 'you cannot live all your life in your present barren joyless fashion . . .'[25]

It is easy to understand why Jessie was flattered by a man like

Dufferin, even though the age difference between them was the same as between her and Tatton. They shared a love of literature and art, not to mention their Irish blood. 'He had all the best qualities of an Irishman,' wrote a contemporary, Lady St Helier, 'and as a companion there was no one like him. He had read enormously, and his knowledge of books, pictures and music was unbounded.' He also had one other quality, which would have appealed to her in her unhappy state. 'No one was too insignificant, or too humble for him to be kind to.'[26] What he loved about Jessie was her originality and her independence of thought, and the hours of conversation he had with her about home and art. After one such session he told her 'I have not had such a treat for many a long year, as nobody in this country either knows or cares about such things.' In the middle of February, accompanied by Freddy, she turned up at Government House for a three week stay. 'On the whole it was very dull,' she wrote afterwards, 'except that I made a lasting conquest of the Excellency. He is as foolishly in love as a boy of twenty.' His devotion had evidently not gone unnoticed by his wife, however, for she added 'I was not well treated by the Dufferin females.'

When Jessie returned to New York to find Tatton still away, she and Dufferin exchanged letters almost every day, his becoming progressively more ardent and often including rather lurid sketches by him of classical subjects featuring Rubenesque naked women. 'How am I to thank you sufficiently, darling, for your dear letter which arrived this morning,' he wrote on 6 March. 'It made a great lump come in my throat.' He pressed her to tell him 'what sweet things a woman can say to a man who feels for her as I do for you'. But he also expressed his fears about indiscretion and begged her to be careful about not letting his letters out of her sight. 'I have written to you every day, but this d—d post can never be depended on. Moreover I have never dared to write freely, I am so fearful lest some disaster should overtake my missive; and yet I have a thousand things I should like to say if I dared. Are you quite, quite certain that no accident can happen, and do you destroy every letter directly you have read it? So much mischief can come of foolish letters, but I would give anything to write *au coeur ouvert*.'[27] Tatton's return in the middle of March did little to slow down either the flow of correspondence, or Jessie's endless partying. 'Lady Sykes suddenly made her appearance this evening in the hotel dining room,' wrote Lord Ronald Gower in his diary on 28 March, 'a blaze of diamonds; she was on her way to some friends who were giving a ball in honour of the Mi-Carême. Sir Tatton was dining in solitary splendour.'[28]

Jessie and Tatton returned to England in April 1878, and though Dufferin's ardour remained as strong as ever, hers appears to have cooled somewhat and her letters to him became fewer and fewer. 'It is so difficult to carry on the conversation,' he wrote exasperatedly to her in May, 'when one of the interlocutors persists in remaining silent.'[29] There is no doubt that Jessie was greatly flattered by and enjoyed the attention of the Governor-General. She certainly encouraged it, but she was never in love with him as he was with her. She referred to him in one of the entries in her diary as 'a sad fellow'. Though he continued to write to her, her mind was elsewhere. At some point she had decided that she desperately wanted a child.

CHAPTER VIII

Sykey

Tatton had as great a desire to have a child, in particular a son, as Jessie. The last thing he wanted to see was the Sledmere estate, with its 34,000 acres, go to the current next-of-kin, namely his younger brother Christopher. Christopher was a socialite, a leading member of the Prince of Wales's Marlborough House set, a dandy and a hopeless spendthrift. Like his older brother, he had been a great disappointment to his father who had hoped upon hope that, following on his education, first at Rugby and then at Trinity College, Cambridge, he would take up the squire's mantle which had been cast off and disdained by his elder brother. But however hard he had tried to interest Christopher in country pursuits – such as encouraging his maternal uncle, Sir William Foulis, a be-whiskered hunting, shooting, fishing countryman of the old order who styled himself 'Sir Gallop Away', to take him under his wing and steer him in the right direction – it had been to no avail. He was cut out for different pursuits. 'I thought of my Father,' he once wrote, doubtless envisioning the old man mud-splattered astride a horse, 'as I went up stairs to bed in green slippers with medieval cipher embroidered in gold on the toe; blue dressing trousers with red stripe; blue cashmere jacket lined with crimson silk; my cambric pocket handkerchief, gold watch, and a novel in my hand.'[1] In the end the old squire was forced to admit that Christopher was good for only one thing, and that was 'handing ladies into their carriages'.[2]

He learned his trade in his mother's drawing room in 21 St James's Place, a meeting place for many of the 'heavy swells' of the period, where he had his first taste of the glamorous world of London society. He was soon chasing about with the best of them, chalking up as many social 'kills' as he could muster. 'Went to Lady Salisbury's,' he wrote in his diary on Saturday, 19 June, 1852. 'Flew about the room endeavouring to get to the Duchess of Beaufort's on Monday, but without success. Took Lady Westminster to her carriage, and had to wait an hour in the hall, and then to walk all down Piccadilly in the rain to look for it. Hope such devotion may be rewarded.' Lady Westminster's husband, Richard Grosvenor, was described as 'the richest nobleman in England', and Christopher's prize should have been an invitation to Grosvenor House, his palatial London home. 'Nothing can be handsomer than this . . . house, and the gardens behind, it is really a palace,' wrote an American, Ellen Twisleton, in July, 1852, going on to describe 'the great works of ancient Art, set off by the living presence of everything that taste and money combined can give, the greatest splendour consistently carried through every point of the arrangements'.[3] But the following week at a dinner given by Lady Bradford, Lady Westminster gave Christopher 'half one finger' to shake. 'Ingratitude,' he grumbled, 'after going all down Piccadilly for her carriage.'

Christopher's diaries, kept between 1852 and 1859, in which he meticulously recorded his failures as well as his successes, give a fascinating account of the machinations of contemporary society at that time. They also provide an insight into the character of an intelligent and over-sensitive man who understood only too well the pitfalls of being a social butterfly. He moved with a set of young men, all richer and better connected than him, whom he had befriended at Cambridge. 'I am so thankful that as yet I have not lost sight of my college friends,' he wrote on 24 June, 1852, 'for I am sure I shall never make any I like so well.' Of this Cambridge group his boon companions were the Hon. Gilbert Heathcote, Sir John Ramsden and in particular Lord Annesley, whom he lionised. 'How foolish to let anyone have such an influence over one as I let him,' he wrote of him. 'He makes my days gloomy or sunshiny as he likes. From my heart I look up to him as the cleverest, most amusing, most refined in taste.' He appears to have acted as Court Jester to this coterie, though they did little for his self-esteem as they were constantly teasing him and reminding him of the disadvantages of his birth.

Owing to the system of primogeniture, which operates amongst families of the English nobility, Christopher was aware that as a younger son he had to work twice as hard to make his way in society, relying mainly on his charm, which he appears to have had in spades. Lady Lucan, wife of the third Earl, who gave the order for the famous cavalry charge at Balaclava, described him as being 'a concentrated lump of amiability', and hostesses were only too happy to help oil the wheels of his progress. 'Went home in high spirits,' he wrote after an evening at Lady Southampton's, 'Lady Lucan having got me a card for Lady Glamis's Ball, and Lady H. Cory promised me one for Lady Aylesbury's.' When it came to the question of his suitability as a prospective suitor for their daughters, however, the spectre of being the younger brother rose up to haunt him. At a ball given by Lady Aylesbury, on 8 July, a man, only identified as D, 'gave me a most insolent nod leaning over Lady Lucan's chair'. Christopher wrote anxiously, 'I hope he didn't tell her I was only the younger son.' Two days later, at Lady Gage's, 'Lady Lucan asked me to take a walk with her in the garden . . . she said, "Pray, Mr Sykes, have you many brothers?", "Oh, no!" I exclaimed, "only one." She then said, "Oh, somebody said you had several. But your brother is older, is he not?" "Yes," I said.'

He also imagined himself constantly snubbed because of his lack of rank. On 15 June, 1852, after attending Lady Sondes's Ball, he wrote 'Not received as I expected. Muncaster who came with me most graciously received. "Pray have you left Cambridge Lord Muncaster?", and those horrid distinctions of rank.' He was thoroughly put out. 'I shall be a Chartist,' he fumed, though when things began to look up, his social ambition soon banished such high-minded thoughts from his mind. 'Sat by Lady Charlotte Egerton in the evening, who was very gracious,' he noted on 25 June. 'She is a good indication to one's position in London. Her civility is a sign that I am getting on in the world . . . Went to Lady Glamis's Ball in the evening. Danced with Miss Leslie who told me I wanted elevating and not snubbing.'

In July, at a ball given by Sir Thomas Cochrane, Christopher heard the news that Annesley had been elected as MP for Grimsby. Secretly harbouring his own political ambitions, he was consumed with envy.

'I believe if he only *wished* to be Archbishop of Canterbury,' he confided to his diary, 'he would be immediately made so. He is so lucky . . . I wish I was out of London before these MPs come up. They will be in such overpowering spirits.' He didn't quite make it. While sauntering through Hyde Park on 13 July, the last day of the season, dressed in his best and most fashionable clothes and 'contemplating the "swells" as they rode by', he ran into Annesley, who began at once his customary banter. ' "Lord! How melancholy and *delabré*[4] you look in that seedy old great coat," was his Lordship's exclamation. I was dressed in a clean white waistcoat, patent leather boots, new trousers and a light-blue great coat. This was being *delabré*! He proceeded to tell me he had secured stalls at the Opera . . . "Do come," said he, "it is the last night I shall see you," and, seeing me hesitate, added as an attraction "and you can tell me your beastly plans." Strong contemptuous emphasis used.'

Ever a glutton for punishment, Christopher accepted the invitation, agreeing, 'foolishly', as he put it, to be collected from home by the Annesley coach.

After a hurried dinner, and before I could get my much-loved cup of tea, his Lordship's brougham was announced and in I bolted, and then waited to pick him up at the Coventry.

'Oh,' said he, 'my dear fellow, can you manage to get home alone, for Charlie Webster has promised to take me at eleven to see the new Ballet.'

With my usual pride I begged he would not think of me.

'What a coat! Is it a coat?', poking my new and fashionable opera cloak . . .

When we arrived at the Opera our stalls were immediately under the boxes of Lady Howard de Walden and Lady Carrington. His Lordship was frantic and restless until he left the stalls and rushed into the boxes where he sat in Lady Carrington's with Augustus Lumley, leaving me feeling very wretched and lonely, with a sort of horrid feeling that he and the Carringtons were looking at me . . . At length I met him rushing about the lobby looking for Charlie Webster.

'Goodbye. I'm looking for Webster, where is he? Take care of yourself. Is he gone? Write to me.'

This was his adieu for a year or so.

Christopher wrote this story down to remind himself, he said, not to become the following year too dependent for society 'on a person so capricious and thoughtless . . . who would not put himself out of the way for me.' Sadly his weakness for such people was to prove his downfall.

With the season over, he retired to Sledmere, confiding to his diary his disappointments. 'I have seen nobody I admire, and I have made few new acquaintances. I have been about as unhappy and as discontented as usual all the time . . . Shall I marry next year or not?' All such worries were soon forgotten, lost in the simple joys of country life. 'The weather lovely,' he wrote on 20 July, 'and Sledmere looking beautiful, the air so fresh and sweet.' Christopher adored Sledmere, where he felt able to be himself. 'When I come back here,' he recorded in March, 1854, after returning from a long trip abroad, 'all the time I have been away seems like a dream. Everything is exactly the same here; the same conversation, the same jokes, the books in the same place on the same tables. My rooms just as I left them. One cannot believe that five months of incident and excitement have passed away. Home seems very calm and comfortable; a refuge quite inaccessible to any of the vexations and troubles of the world.'

Christopher's routine at Sledmere, of reading and exercise, never varied. 'I am enjoying myself here exceedingly,' he wrote on 3 April, 1854; 'the days are not long enough. From half-past eight until a-quarter-to eleven I translate Lamartine's *History of the Girondists*, and write a French verb. Then I take half an hour's quick walk; read letters and answer them. From half-past eleven till twelve write French. From twelve until one read Girot's *Life of Cromwell*. Ride until five. Read *Life of Charles I* until six. Dine. In the evening read the newspapers.' Away from the temptations of London, he seriously contemplated a career as a diplomat, and had made several applications to be taken on by the Foreign Office. On 24 May, 1854, they offered him a trial job as a supernumerary clerk. The requirements for the post were daunting:

> You must be well grounded in Grammar, Orthography, Calligraphy, and Geography, and familiar with the use of Globes. You must speak fluently and write correctly French, German, Italian, Spanish, Portuguese, Dutch, Flemish, Modern Greek, Turkish, Arabic, Chinese, Persian, Hindustani and Sanskrit. In consequence of the suspension of our Diplomatic relations with Russia, the language of that Country will not now be indispensable to your admission into this Office . . . You will however be expected to make yourself Master of the Dialects spoken on the shores of the Baltic.

Perhaps if this letter had arrived while he was at Sledmere, Christopher might have considered the offer seriously, but on 24 May he was back in London, dining with Mrs Ramsden, and his thoughts were elsewhere. 'Miss Fitzwilliam the new Heiress was there, a nice plain girl who I thought I could marry with great satisfaction.' He ended his entry for that day with characteristic honesty. 'What a different person one is in London to anywhere else. You have no time to think.'

The London season of 1854 was overshadowed by one subject which affected everyone: the war with Russia, which had broken out in March. 'The papers ring with war,' wrote Christopher on 5 April. 'The Danube has been crossed, the Queen has received the Address of the Houses. The Duke of Parma has been stabbed. Well I remember him three years ago, one of the handsomest young men I ever saw, walking in St Marks Place at Venice.' Christopher began to question the nature of his life more closely than ever, particularly when compared to that of his friend Annesley, who was now immersed in politics. After walking back home with him late one night from a party and listening to his account of a great debate in the House on the subject of the war he was in self-critical mood. 'Talking about it made me feel the emptiness and folly of an evening spent like mine; sheer folly; dancing with ugly girls I have known these five years. I came home quite resolved not to make such a business of society.'

By the end of the summer the fighting, which had begun in Wallachia and Moldavia – present-day Romania – had spread into the Crimea. In September, in the first major confrontation with the Russians at the Battle of Alma, a river to the north of the Black Sea port of Sebastapol, 3,000 French and British and 9,000 Russians lost their lives and as the war escalated news of the deaths of friends began to filter back to London, penetrating, as Christopher put it, 'into regions where ordinary misfortunes are carefully excluded by wealth and power'. On 30 October, he wrote, 'At Burton Constable I heard of the death of my poor friend Frederick Leveson Gower, on board the Bellerophon in the Black Sea. It is but yesterday since he came up to Cambridge, surrounded by all the prestige of youth, innocence, the highest rank; refined, joyous like a child, all life before him . . . To die so soon, after lying ill, uncared for, on board a wretched transport in those Crimean Regions. Adeane and he are gone, both with all to make life valuable and dear . . .'

Annesley's brother was seriously wounded, which sent Christopher racing to comfort his old friend, and during the following week came the accounts of the Charge of the Light Brigade. 'Bad news from the Crimea,' he noted, '600 cavalry and 200 Infantry cut in pieces . . .' The twenty-second of November was a black day, on which the first full list arrived containing the names of all the killed and wounded. It was an event that 'filled London . . . with horror'. On his way to Arthurs, his club in St James's, Christopher passed lines of carriages on their way to the War Office, 'filled with anxious mothers'. When he reached the club, he assembled in a group with his friends, while one of them read out the list from the *Gazette*. 'Poor Frederick Ramsden killed, poor Henry Neville and many others,' he wrote. 'Alas! It is sad indeed . . . Never to the end of my life shall I forget the appearance of London this morning.'

There was one question which occupied Christopher much during this period of his life, and that was the question of whether or not he should marry. In spite of his being a second son, he appears to have had no lack of potential suitors. He was, in fact, something of a flirt. In June, 1854, he professed himself to be the 'slave' of Lady Lavinia

Bingham, second daughter of the third Earl of Lucan. 'I wonder if she perceives,' he questioned, 'that I . . . tremble all over before her.' In November he had a new fancy, Miss Katherine Cocks. 'At two I went to K's, and really made love so furiously that I was quite alarmed.' She liked him because he was 'fresh and new' and 'in fashion', and she wanted 'things to advance'. She moved too fast for Christopher, however. 'Things took such a material form,' he recorded, 'that I fairly fled and dined at Arthurs in a fury with myself for having done so.' When he returned to her Chapel Street house, he was disappointed to find 'rage and fury on her face'. The following March, while on a trip to Paris with his friends the Baillies, 'they talked a great deal about who I was to marry, and assured me I should marry a "Lady Somebody", a very probable event I think'.

Both these ladies slipped out of his hands, each into the arms of an eldest son. Opening the *Morning Post*, on 31 August, 1855, he read of Miss Cocks's marriage to the seventh Earl of Stamford. 'A Countess! £150,000 a year; the double coronets of Stamford and Warrington; the owner of historical Bradgate of Durham,' he fumed. 'I can hardly credit it when I think of this time last year, and of a certain small packet of letters in my writing box. Madame La Comtesse!' He had come much closer to marrying Lavinia Bingham, with whose name he had been joined during the summer of 1854 and with whom he admitted to having been 'greatly in love and much smiled upon by the beauty'. Their names, he wrote, 'had been in every old woman's mouth'. Yet in April, 1856, he read of her wedding to Arthur Hardinge, the future Viscount, commenting rather bitterly, 'that scene is closed for ever'.

When Christopher needed to lick his wounds, there was always his beloved Sledmere and its never-changing routine to retreat to. That spring, feeling tired and run down, he tried out a new health regime – 'out in the open air all day; meat at breakfast; a glass of ale at luncheon, port wine at dinner' – while a visit by his sister, Kate Cholmondeley, and her four small children gave him the opportunity to indulge in a bit of family life. He was amused how the Crimean War, which had ended in March, had rubbed off on the two eldest, Hugh and Beatrice. He wrote on 23 April,

Dear little B and Hughie sing a song,

> All round Sebastapol
> All round the ocean
> Every time a gun goes off
> Down goes a Russian

Touching to hear their little voices uttering such bloodthirsty words. B is a good girl; Hughie a charming little blue eyed white haired boy with a droll little manner; Essex is a fat round ball with large soft eyes, exactly like her Mother, the same sweet tempered expression; Henry a miserable little baby.

Letters from his cronies, Ramsden and Heathcote, soon heralded the approach of another London season. 'I half dread, half long for it,' he admitted, adding 'God! That wish to make oneself charming! What a bore it is!' When another letter arrived from Ramsden bringing the news that he was soon to be married, Christopher saw it as the end of an era. 'The drama of the last five years ends,' he wrote, 'five years spent in utter frivolity and laborious seeking after what I have by no means found.' It was time to turn over a new leaf, to banish the idleness that had been the curse of his life. 'Well – begin a new life,' he vowed, 'be energetic and independent – health this autumn, and in the winter make a vigorous effort for Parliament.'

The knowledge that his three best friends all had Parliamentary careers and were doing something more than just leading frivolous lives, had inspired Christopher seriously to consider entering the House himself, all the more so since the outbreak of the Crimean War. His problem was that he tended to think about the possibility more than actually do anything about it and being an intelligent man this often made him depressed, especially when those around him were going from strength to strength. 'I am most ungrateful for my numberless comforts and blessings,' he moaned on 24 February, 1857, 'but I cannot but feel somewhat low-spirited when each paper that I open contains some fresh success, political or social, of Ramsden's; while I live a listless, objectless luxurious life; everything that mere money can obtain; like a great spoilt child, kept at home and allowed everything but independence.' A year later, however, in April 1858, he was still only thinking about asking his father to let him stand for the City of York.

Over the next year the subject of Parliament, though ever present, was pushed to the back of Christopher's mind. He considered it 'much too great a fortune to come to pass'. Instead he decided upon a new project. 'I am going to try and write an account of my family,' he recorded on 26 May. This would seem to have been the perfect pastime for him. He was completely under the spell of Sledmere. Each time he returned there, after an absence in London or abroad, he would be overcome with delight. He had his own suite of rooms which were 'an unfailing source of pleasure' to him, 'all bright with fires and wax candles; the silver dressing case apparatus laid out on the dressing table; the gilded picture frames on the walls and the numerous pieces of quaint china and majolica reflecting the light of the fire. Luxuriously carpeted and curtained; the Tables strewn with books and all the Reviews and Pamphlets . . . letters littering my desk and blotting book.'

He began with enthusiasm, writing in his journal on 29 May, 'I searched the dusty piles of letters in the old Bookcase in the Study, for papers relating to the earlier branches of our family, settled at Sledmere; old Mark Kirkby, Richard Sykes and the money-lending Doctor of Divinity and first baronet, and having found some I laid 'em aside to be made use of in that sketch of the Family History which I meditate writing.' He got no further, his mind distracted by society, by travel, by what he described as 'idle groundless uneasiness' and by a liver overburdened with the fruits of too much good living. 'I think now I have fairly traced my enemy that for many a long month has tortured me, and given a bitter taste to every pleasure and distraction,' he wrote on 30 January, 1859. 'My Liver is out of order and I have begun a regime of starving which has already had most successful results. I begin again to look forward . . .'

On 2 February 1859, Christopher received the news for which he had waited so long. 'My reading interrupted,' he recorded, 'by meeting my Mother in the Hall who told me Robert Bower had sent a message by Reid to say there were to be three Members for the East Riding and I was to be the Third. My father had received the news without positively expressed displeasure.' He admitted to having at first been startled by this announcement and then doubtful that it was true. His spirits were raised, however, when he thought of the triumph it would give him over all those people he conceived to have slighted him over the years. Once he got used to the idea it excited him. 'How I should like to be in Parliament,' he wrote, 'and enter at once upon a new career.' But once again, disappointment loomed. 'I cannot write as usual,' he noted on 18 February. 'My whole train of thought has been upset. My father said quietly at dinner "James Walker or Willie Worsley are talked of as third members for the East Riding and I think Walker would be very suitable." I was chiefly grieved because my poor Mother seemed so vexed, and Mary too; the only two people who really care for me. I am very foolish and know I am like a child that cries for the Moon.'

It is on such a despondent note as this that Christopher's journals end. The 1850s had seen him establish himself as a well-known man of fashion, but he had singularly failed to achieve anything else. In 1859, aged twenty-eight, he was unmarried, without employment and still living with his parents. Being far too clever to live this kind of aimless life, his dissatisfaction was beginning to lend an air of lugubriousness to his appearance, which was to remain with him for the rest of his life. He was just as charming, only a little more solemn.

In July 1865, two years after the death of his father, Christopher finally did make it into Parliament, elected, aged thirty-four, as Member for Beverley. Described by contemporaries as a man whose 'carriage and grace made those about him seem common',[5] his tall, austere figure was noted by the correspondent of *Punch* as he took the oath in front of the Speaker, before taking his seat for the first time. Much to the amusement of the former, Christopher, as he was about to leave, noticed Mr Speaker leaning towards him, and taking this gesture as some kind of official farewell, walked up to him and graciously touched the tips of his fingers before leaving the House. This was not the only time that his perfect manners were to be a source of hilarity.

In spite of the long years of yearning to become an MP, when he finally achieved his ambition, Christopher hardly distinguished himself. In the twenty-seven years he was to sit in the House, representing first Beverley and then the East Riding, he made only six speeches and asked only three questions. His redemption was that he did introduce a bill into Parliament which actually reached the statute book. It was a bill intended to curb the slaughter of sea birds for sport, a pastime which was widespread, particularly on the east coast sea cliffs at Flamborough and Bempton, as well as to limit their commercial exploitation for the Millinery trade. Passing into law in June, 1869, as the Sea Birds Preservation Act, it provided protection for thirty-five species by introducing an annual close season running from 1 April to 1 August. Unfortunately for Christopher, his association with this bill earned him a nickname, the Gull's Friend, which he was never able to cast off and which led to his becoming the butt of endless jokes on the subject.

Christopher's parliamentary career might have gone further had it not coincided with a new friendship that was to have a profound influence on his life and which was to take up increasing amounts of his time. Since the death of Prince Albert from typhoid in 1861, Queen Victoria had retreated behind a deep cloud of gloom and remained there way beyond the normal period of state mourning. This had a profoundly depressing effect on society in general, so when in March 1863 the twenty-two-year old Prince of Wales, Albert Edward, fondly known as Bertie, married Princess Alexandra, the eldest daughter of the future King of Denmark, there was great cause for rejoicing among the fleshpots of London. They saw him as the sun breaking through the clouds, bringing the Monarchy back into Society. He did not let them down.

Over the next few years, at Sandringham House in Norfolk and Marlborough House in London, at yachting parties in Cowes and shooting parties in every grand house in the country, at Ascot, Goodwood and Epsom races, in the clubs and dining rooms of the capital, this golden couple ruled over English social life. There was not a rich and pleasure-loving aristocrat in the country who did not wish to be part of their charmed circle, and those who were lucky enough to be invited to join it found no doors closed to them.

The Prince's particular friends were a raffish set, chosen for their wit, their wealth and their reputations as *bons vivants*. Amongst them were Charles, Viscount Royston, known as 'Champagne Charlie', a man who 'was not slow in dissipating the fortune that his father had been at such pains to build up for him';[6] Henry Chaplin, an Oxford crony and one of the leading men of the Turf, who 'warmed both hands at the numerous fires of life';[7] the Marquis of Hastings, who gambled away a fortune and died of consumption at the age of twenty-six; the Marquis of Waterford, a wild Irish peer, who had eloped with his best friend's wife; and Lord Hartington, known as 'Harty-Tarty', lover of both the courtesan, Skittles, and the notorious Duchess of Manchester.

With an insatiable desire for novelty, the Prince was perpetually casting his net for new blood, and at some point in the latter half of the 1860s he ensnared Christopher. He would certainly have heard about him, as a fashionable man about town who mixed in many of the circles that he did and who was an acquaintance of the Prince's uncle, the Duke of Cambridge. No doubt stories had also filtered through to him of Christopher's 'patient and enduring good nature'.[8] In his biography of the fifth Earl of Rosebery, Lord Crewe, discussing the custom of the day in various stately country houses of finding great amusement 'in the generally harmless but often rough pleasantries popular with subalterns of a sporting regiment', wrote that 'Christopher Sykes was often the subject of such jokes'. This was for no obvious reason, he went on to say, except that 'he joined in them with sufficient good humour'.[9]

The nature of the sort of pranks referred to by Lord Crewe was described by Herbert Vivian, a well-known country-house creeper, in an article called 'Country House Caravanserais'.

In one house you may find a jug poised upon your bedroom door and fire-irons nestling between your sheets; artificial ghosts, in the shape of bobbins, in your bath, disturb your slumbers; seidlitz powders are secreted in your sponge, onions in your shaving water, or pepper in your face-towel; and you may be thankful if your fellow guests do not shake sugar-castors over your hair nor pull away your chair when you are about to sit down. A wet day suggests an obstacle race along the corridors, pillow fights in the hall, or water fights with the fire hose on the landing. Your evenings are dedicated to high gambling, in which you may easily lose more than you can afford, or win large sums which you will never be paid.[10]

It is clear, from a letter written to Christopher on his return home from a house party at Raby Castle, seat of the Duke of Cleveland, that as early as September 1867, his leg was being regularly pulled. Raby was famous for its visitors' book, in which every guest, without exception, had to express some sentiment and state the object of their visit. It was, wrote Lord Warwick, 'the dread of all, save the quick-witted'.[11] Lord Rosebery, for example, had no difficulty in coming up with a suitable quip, stating the reason for his visit as being,

> To see their Graces
> And shoot their Grouses.

A Miss Vernon, on the other hand, wrote in desperation,

> Who'll burn this book?
> I, said Di Vernon,
> If the Duchess won't look;
> I'll burn this book.

As soon as Christopher left the house, the pens of the wits were evidently out in force. 'Your absence has brought a sense of repose,' ran one letter. 'Much as we regret it, we must inform you that the age of buffoonery and wit has ceased with your dear presence ... Many paragraphs have been written about yourself in the Visitors' Book, of which no doubt you will soon hear. The spelling of the word "butt" by you has convulsed the whole house with laughter. As we find that writing to you is as tiresome as conversing to you we will now conclude with fervent hopes for your health and happiness.'[12] It was signed THE VISITORS AT RABY.

While there is no account of their first meeting, Christopher did record that his 'second invitation to a Royal dinner was given by the Prince of Wales by word of mouth, riding in Rotten Row in the summer of 1867. "Come on Sunday and dine to celebrate the Birthday of your great friend the Duke of Cambridge." On Sunday I went . . . We dined in the small Library, sitting between Lord Clanwilliam and A. Ellis . . . After dinner the Prince motioned to me to sit close by him.'[13] Within a very short time, the two were inseparable. Christopher was the perfect courtier. Ten years older than his new friend, he combined wisdom with the ability of knowing exactly how to conduct himself in the Royal presence. At the same time, both Bertie and the Princess were captivated by his wit and charm and were amused by the way he could hold his own. He was, recalled Lord Crewe, 'a man of no little shrewdness and observation, who, when it came to repartee, could give his not too brilliant banterers more than they bargained for'.[14] He suddenly found himself the envy of the fashionable world. Even those who had formerly looked down upon him for being a second son were eager to be seen with him. The invitations flowed in, the old disillusionment began to fade away, and he was set on a path to disaster.

In 1869 Christopher seemed well placed to be the best friend of the Prince of Wales. The death of his father had left him rich enough to be the owner of a country house in Yorkshire, Brantingham Thorpe, an imposing Elizabethan pile near Hull, and to rent a grand house in Mayfair, 1 Seamore Place. This was all the party-loving Prince needed, and he decided to test Christopher's powers as a host by inviting himself to stay at Brantingham Thorpe in September for the races at Doncaster. Christopher was determined that this, of all parties, should be a success. When the Royal train arrived, it was met by a string of carriages to transport the guests to the house, where a huge staff was assembled to greet them. The Prince loved comfort and no expense had been spared in the preceding months to upgrade the rooms to the standard of luxury expected. As for the food, Christopher, himself a connoisseur, referred to by his friend Lord Claud Hamilton as 'The Prince of Sykes Wines',[15] had employed a top chef from London who he knew would cater for his guest's famously extravagant taste. From mutual friends of HRH Christopher also had a good idea of his preferences when it came to after dinner entertainment. At Sandringham, they played bowls, took part in crazy gymkhanas and tricycle races in the ballroom, and sometimes even turned the stairs into a toboggan run, using silver trays as luges. The diversions provided at Brantingham were more likely to be cards and dancing, though later on in the evening, when the ladies had retired to bed and the gentlemen were in their cups, there was a fair amount of horseplay along the lines of soda-water fights and apple-pie beds.

Christopher found himself the victim of Bertie's teasing almost straight away. In the course of that first house party, he had employed a photographer to come and immortalise the visit and the result, a print of which still hangs in one of the backstairs lavatories at Sledmere, shows a small group assembled by a tree in the grounds, a corner of the house showing in the background. The figures represented in the foreground are the Prince and Princess of Wales, the Queen of Denmark, the Duke of St Albans and, looming rather gloomily over them all, the bearded, frock-coated figure of Christopher himself. Behind them can be seen the photographer's cart and his two assistants. A copy was sent to the Prince at Windsor Castle, and a day or so later Christopher was somewhat surprised to receive the following letter from the Prince's Private Secretary, Francis Knollys.

Dear Sykes,

The Prince of Wales desires me to 'sit down and write to Christopher at once' and ask him what he means? What is this indecent practical joke – sending or causing to be sent to HRH a photograph of your place in Yorkshire – in the foreground of which are inserted figures who are presumed to be caricatures of the P and Pss of Wales, the latter standing by an individual with a face like a malefactor who the unkindest enemy of his would not call Christopher Sykes!! What does this all mean? HRH is at a loss to understand what can have induced you to allow such an abomination to be sent as a recollection of so pleasant a visit as the sojourn with you undoubtedly was.[16]

A harmless tease indeed, no more than the affectionate joshing of a friend, but once the word got out that the Prince too had seen the point of pulling the leg of 'Sykey', as Claud Hamilton affectionately called him, there was no holding his friends back. If it amused HRH to see him the victim of jokes, then jokes would surely be played. It was the perfect way of sucking up, even if it was at the expense of an old friend. The situation appears to have got so bad by the autumn of 1870 that Christopher decided he should stop accepting invitations to house parties given for the Prince. A letter from Knollys made it quite clear that his master was not happy with this decision. 'His Royal Highness regrets to hear,' he wrote to Christopher on 31 October 1870, 'that you do not deem it to be consistent with the duty you owe to the "important constituency which you represent nor to the Party which you support", to meet His Royal Highness, for the future, at Country Houses in Yorkshire, in case jokes should be played upon you at them. He has however been told by several men lately, that during the ten days or fortnight you were "out" with your Yeomanry this year, you were the victims of jokes played upon you daily & nightly, and that you took them all with your usual good nature and temper.'[17]

These jokes, which to begin with consisted of little more than schoolboy pranks, had taken a nasty turn in July 1870, when somebody, no doubt motivated by jealousy, had sent out elaborate invitations to the cream of society, supposedly from Christopher, inviting them to a great dinner at Seamore Place, in honour of HRH. Word was then leaked out that this was a joke and that the host had no intention of turning up. Christopher was, so to speak, turning the tables on his tormentors. People were outraged and word soon reached him that 'society . . . was up in arms'[18] against him. Even the Prince, wrote Francis Knollys, 'began to think, if you played tricks of this description, whether he would be able to keep up his acquaintance with you'.[19] Luckily Christopher recognised the handwriting of George, Viscount Dupplin, on one of the invitations and the dinner was revealed to be a hoax perpetrated by him and the Duke of St Albans. 'These noodles can never distinguish between a fair practical joke in private and a vulgar hoax in public,' wrote his friend Claud Hamilton, adding wisely, 'You must really set your face against any such nonsense for the future and we will all support you in putting an end to it. As long however as you let the Prince set the example, you may be sure his admirers will be only too anxious to emulate him.'[20]

If only Sykey had heeded his friend's advice things might have been different. He was in too deep, however, and his lack of self-respect led him to believe that his role as court jester was all that kept him in the position he valued so much within the inner echelons of the Royal circle. The result was that one terrible night he allowed the Prince to set an example which was pounced upon by his tormentors, and which became the yardstick for a new and much crueller form of teasing. The incident took place in the Marlborough Club, a gentleman's club which Bertie had founded after he had been reprimanded by a member of the staff of Whites for smoking outside the confines of the Smoking Room. It was a popular haunt for MPs after a late-night sitting of the House, when, to quote *Punch*, 'the uxurious went home to supper, and the luxurious to gin slings and cigars at the Clubs'.[21] On the night in question, Christopher had arrived from the House to join Bertie for a supper party, in the course of which, inspired by who knows what flight of fancy, the latter tipped an entire glass of brandy over his friend's head. Completely taken aback by this event and temporarily at a loss for words, Christopher sat there while the golden liquid trickled down his face and into his beard and the room descended into a stunned silence. When he did finally speak, after what seemed a lifetime, it was to say graciously to the Prince, his head slightly bowed and with not a trace of irony, 'As Your Royal Highness pleases.'

Led by Bertie, whose initial childish giggle soon turned into bellows of helpless laughter, the room fell apart, and as the assembled company whooped, wept, fell off their chairs and gasped for breath, Christopher sat there, the brandy dripping on to his plate, his face a picture of solemnity. From that tragic moment on, there were no holds barred. Wherever he went, whether on his own or in the company of the Prince, Christopher was mercilessly baited. The brandy glass became a decanter, sometimes poured for a diversion down his neck. He was pushed under billiard tables where he would be imprisoned on all fours, his escape prevented by his tormentors spearing him with cues. He could not even find escape to the solitude of his bedroom, for the gang would almost certainly have already been there to souse his sheets with water or to leave something in his bed, on one occasion a live, trussed-up rabbit and on another a dead seagull, a particularly cruel jest under the circumstances.

One story is told of how the Prince persuaded Christopher to attend an important fancy dress ball, in the costume of a medieval Knight in full armour. He had arranged on purpose, without telling his victim, that their party was to be let into the house by the back door. Unfortunately for Christopher, when it was his turn to be admitted the door was slammed in his face. No amount of beating on the door with his fist or bellowing through his visor resulted in his rescue so, encased in armour, he had to clank his way round to the front of the house at a snail's pace, getting hotter and hotter by the second, and all the time gathering followers. When he finally reached the front entrance, by now accompanied by a large crowd of gawkers, and revealed himself to the guests assembled there as 'Sykey', there was a near riot.

At one house party in the North of England, Lord Charles Beresford took advantage of Christopher's slavish adoration of the Prince of Wales, a fellow guest, to play another unkind trick. He rushed into his room in the middle of the night in a highly excited state yelling, 'I say, Sykes, get up at once, Tum Tum wants to see you directly . . . hustle old cock, perhaps the Crown's in danger.' Christopher jumped out of bed, donned his dressing gown and raced to the door, but as he left the room, his feet encountered a rope stretched across the frame and he tripped up, falling head-over-heels into a tin bathtub filled with cold water. This was too much even for his patient self and, mortified, he left the house without even taking leave of his host.[22]

All the time that Christopher was proving himself to be such an endless source of amusement to the Prince, he was also providing him with considerable material comforts. Bertie used 1 Seamore Place not unlike a hotel and expected his friend to be on call to entertain him at all times. There was no host, he used to say, like 'dear old Xtopher', and he used him shamelessly, commanding dinners whenever the whim took him and providing the guest lists, which were liable to be changed at a moment's notice. These evenings were sumptuous affairs, exemplified by a dinner given on 19 February 1870.

MENU: DINNER 1 SEAMORE PLACE. 19 FEVRIER. 1870.

Premier Service.

Potages: Tortue Claire. À la Bonne Femme.

Poissons: Turbot, sauces Homard et Hollandaise.
Darnes de Saumon, sauces Tartare et Genoise.

Entrées: Kromeskys de Huîtres.
Crème de Volaille à la Conti.
Côtelettes de Mouton aux Pois.

Relevées: Poulardes aux Truffes à la Perigord.
Hanche de Venaison.

Second Service.

Rôts: Canetons,
Mauviettes.

Entrements: Asperges, sauce Hollandaise.
Pâté de Strasbourg.
Gelée au Madère.
Abricots à la Condé.

Beignets à l'Allemande.

His friends, no doubt aping the example of the Prince, were equally ready to take advantage of him. They started 'The Sykes Club', which met weekly in Seamore Place, with Lord Rosebery as Chairman. Its minutes for 14 April, 1874, for example, stated:

1. That cooling and various cups be always provided between the hours of 12 and 4 at 1 Seamore Place.
2. That when Ale is called for by a member it be drawn from a permanent and resident cache, and not fetched ostentatiously in a Pewter from a neighbouring Pothouse.
3. That fresh Caviare as supplied by Bannisters of Hull be kept on the sideboard during luncheon time. Hot and crisp toast to be provided **ad libitum.**
4. That fragrant and cunning Salads, or, in default of such, mayonnaises of lobster and chicken, be always kept in a place known to the committee but not to Uncle Foulis or casual strangers.
5. That plovers' eggs be provided from this time forth to the Derby day.[23]

When the London season was over, the parties moved to Brantingham Thorpe, for the racing at Doncaster, and for shooting and hunting. As they increased in size, swelled by legions of hangers-on, and the house began to run out of space, Christopher obligingly extended it to accommodate them. In 1882, he entertained 980 for dinner and 638 for luncheon, along with 5,289 'servants and strangers'. At Brantingham Thorpe alone, they consumed 10,650 lbs of meat.[24]

Had Christopher had the income of some of the nouveau-riche millionaires that Bertie like to surround himself with, he might have been able to continue meeting the enormous expense of this endless entertaining, but as a second son his pocket soon began to severely feel the strain. The orders kept coming and the Prince's 'obedient, loyal and most tried servant'[25] kept obeying them. 'Christopher was out today, he was very gracious and affectionate,' wrote Jessie to a friend in November, 1886; 'he says the Prince of Wales has ordered him to entertain with all the magnificence in his power the Comte and Comtesse de Paris and he is accordingly going to have a huge party for them in December. He invited me to go and do the honours.'[26] He remained stubbornly blind to his true position and raced headlong along the road to bankruptcy.

CHAPTER IX

Lady Satin Tights

Towards the end of February, 1879, Tatton received a letter from a Miss Mary Smith of 193 Sloane Street, London. 'I beg respectfully to inform you,' she wrote, 'that Lady Sykes came to my shop yesterday and ordered Baby Linen which she requires to be supplied in the course of a week, but after receiving your instructions not to supply her Ladyship without your written authority, I shall be greatly obliged if you will kindly give me your sanction to supply the goods . . . I should be exceedingly sorry to offend her ladyship and it is evident she will require the things very shortly.'[1] This letter, which bears out Jessie's constant assertion that she could never get Tatton to pay for everyday things, even clothes for her imminent child, was a bad omen for the future.

Jessie gave birth to a son on 16 March. He was christened with the names of his forefathers, Tatton and Mark, but in true style, she made her own addition to the litany of Sykes names by inserting in between them the name Benvenuto, a confirmation both of the joy of his arrival and of her great love of Italy. He was born in London, but was brought immediately to Sledmere for a full choral christening in the parish church, at which special books printed for the occasion were handed out to each member of the congregation. It was a longed-for cause for celebration and after the ceremony the doors of the big house were thrown open and a banquet was given in the baby's honour for 200 tenants and their families. The feast took place in the Library, which was fitted up as a dining room, with long tables spread from end to end. Jessie was presented with the gift of a pearl necklace and little Mark was cooed over and passed round by the village women. It was probably the happiest moment of her life.

'I am delighted to hear what has fallen out, and congratulate you on your freedom,' wrote her admirer, Lord Dufferin, from St Petersburg, where he was now Ambassador. 'I should have been very jealous,' he added, 'of anything that might have compromised the perfection of what is ideal.'[2] He told her the child would give her a new interest in life and would be a pillar of strength to her as he grew up. One person, however, was not so happy about the birth, ending, as it did, any future interest he might have had in Sledmere. 'CS,' wrote Sir George Wombwell, a Yorkshire neighbour, 'don't like it at all.'[3]

Jessie was sadly mistaken in her belief that giving birth to a child would be the end of her troubles. Her 'new interest' calmed her for a while, and even Tatton seemed easier, but as the novelty began to wear off and she became once again aware of the reality of her marriage, she felt the old restlessness stirring within her. She had done her duty and produced a son and heir for Tatton. Now she threw caution to the wind. Her American journal shows her to have been an outrageous flirt and men were only too ready to fall under her spell. Desperate for love, she indulged in a number of affairs, beginning in 1880 with the dashing Captain George 'Bay' Middleton, one of England's finest riders to hounds and pilot on the hunting field to Elisabeth, Empress of Austria, during the five seasons in which she hunted in England and Ireland. When this liaison ended, at the end of 1881, Jessie took up with a German Baron called Heugelmüller, a serial womaniser who eventually ran off with her cousin Blanche, Lady Waterford. 'Oh Blanche, how you have spoilt my life,' she wrote miserably in her diary in August, 1883. 'He is selfish, poor, ugly and a foreigner, and yet I like him better than anyone or anything.'[4]

According to a note sent to her by Bay Middleton, Jessie had also suffered a miscarriage in August, 1881. 'That walk on Saturday,' he scribbled, 'the consequence of so much quarrelling must have been too much for you, and am very sorry your second born should have come to such an untimely end. Altho' the little beggar was very highly tried . . . Goodbye and hoping this will find you strong, but don't play the fool too soon.'[5] One can only guess at the troubled state of Jessie's mind during this period of her life, nor does it appear that she was exactly discreet in her liaisons. 'She is in danger of becoming a cynical disbeliever in the existence of sincerity among men,' wrote the Catholic architect George Gilbert Scott Junior to Father Neville, secretary to Cardinal Newman at the Birmingham Oratory. Jessie's intelligence and her 'luxurious beauty' struck Scott, who had been recently introduced to the Sykeses while he was working on the restoration of Driffield Church. Shocked by how neglected she was by her husband and fearing that her 'vivacity and healthy sensuous temperament' might expose her to temptation and a possible 'disastrous *faux-pas*', he appealed to the Cardinal to offer prayers for the Sykeses' conversion. 'The securance to the Catholic Church in England of *a great name*, a great estate, a great fortune,' he wrote, 'is in itself worth an effort . . . But to save from a *miserable decadence* two such characters (as I am convinced nothing but the Catholic Faith can do) is a still higher motive.'[6]

In fact, conversion was already on Jessie's mind. 'You have not forgotten,' she wrote to her old friend and Yorkshire neighbour, Angela Lady Herries, 'that many years ago I told you that I was in heart a Catholic, only I had not the moral courage to change my religion.' After 'many struggles and many misgivings,' she told her, she was at last ready to embrace the faith, adding 'and I shall have the happiness of bringing my little child with me'.[7] She had tried her best to persuade Tatton to join her, but while he encouraged her to do so, he was reluctant to take the step himself for fear of offending the Protestant and Methodist villagers of Sledmere.

Angela Herries, sister-in-law to the Duke of Norfolk, England's leading Catholic, was delighted to hear the news of the conversion. It was through her family connections that Jessie had been given an introduction to the Cardinal Archbishop of Westminster, Henry Edward Manning, and she was pleased that he had not wasted the opportunity of adding another wayward soul to his flock. He had indeed taken a very personal interest in Jessie, who bared her soul to him in her letters. She wrote to him in November 1882,

Since I returned from London, I have thought much and sadly of all the wasted opportunities and the useless and worthless life I have led up to the present time, thinking of nothing but my own amusement, and living without any religion at all for so many years. I sometimes fear that the voice of conscience and power of repentance has died away from me and that I shall never be able to lead a good or Christian life. I feel too how terribly imperfect up till now my attempts at a Confession have been, and how many and grave sins I have from shame omitted to mention . . .[8]

With Lady Herries and Lord Norreys acting as her godparents and Lady Gwendolyn Talbot and the Duke of Norfolk as Mark's, Jessie and her son were received into the Catholic Church at the end of November. The conversion caused some upset in Sledmere, as Tatton had predicted it would, and in an attempt to soften the blow, Cardinal Manning wrote a 'long and eloquent' exposition on the subject for the vicar of Sledmere, the Revd Mr Pattenhorne. Nevertheless, Jessie was riddled with guilt at the unhappiness she had caused to him and his congregation. Her inner struggles continued, and she was devastatingly self-critical in her letters to Manning. 'I . . . fear steady, everyday, useful, commonplace goodness is beyond my reach,' she told him. 'Honestly I am sorry for this – I have, alas, no deep enthusiasm, no burning longings for perfection, no terrible fears of Hell – I am wanting in *all* the moral qualities and sensations which I have been led to believe were the first tokens and messages of God the Holy Spirit working in the Human heart.'[9]

She decided to dedicate herself to a noble cause. If she could not persuade Tatton to join her in the Catholic faith, then she would persuade him to finance a project which would be the climax of his career as a builder of churches: the design and construction of a new Catholic cathedral in London. She chose the right time to approach him. He had not built a church since 1877, when Street completed St Andrews in East Heslerton, and had been toying for some time with the idea of rebuilding St Mary's Sledmere. According to Scott, writing in February, 1881, 'He is now about to build a big church on which many say he will not grudge £200,000.'[10] On a trip to Vienna in 1882, he had been greatly impressed by the Votifkirche, the great cathedral erected by Kaiser Franz Josef I as a thanksgiving for having escaped an assassination attempt in 1853. 'For nearly eight years,' wrote Jessie, 'he has had the desire to find a model which should in every respect satisfy his ideas and imagination as a perfect specimen of Gothic – he thinks he has found it in the Votivkirche – and he will build after that design or none.'[11]

The architect of the Votifkirche was Baron Heinrich Ferstel and Tatton was so taken with it that he approached Ferstel and persuaded him to design a version for him to be built at Sledmere. However, a letter from Jessie, dated 24 September, 1882, shows the Sledmere site to have been abandoned almost immediately because it would not have 'the dignity that the Votivkirche demanded'.[12] Jessie knew that one of the projects close to Cardinal Manning's heart was that London should have its own 'Metropolitan Catholic Cathedral', a scheme he had inherited from his predecessor, Cardinal Wiseman, and which had never got under way owing to a lack of resources. Using all her wiles, she began to sow the seed in Tatton's mind that London was the place where Ferstel's new church should be built, and there could be no better cause than that it should be the new Catholic cathedral. If he were to finance this great work he would go down as one of the most important ecclesiastical builders in history.

For a while, egged on by Jessie, Manning and other leading Catholics, it looked as though Tatton was prepared to see the project through. He sent his man, Creed, to Vienna to prepare a proper report on the Votifkirche, Baron Ferstel came to London to look at the proposed site, and on 27 December 1882, Jessie was able to write to the Cardinal, 'I have never seen [Tatton] so tranquil or so resolved to commence the Church, as soon as he finds he has the actual means, as he is today. He said to me this morning that when I next wrote to you I was to say he hoped that Mark might build a chapter house and Cloisters when the edifice was completed.' Two days later she told him, 'one thing you may be perfectly sure of. The Cathedral in the future is a certainty, with the permission of the Almighty.'[13]

In the excitement of the moment, however, Jessie had forgotten a simple truth: the extreme fickleness of Tatton's mind. He may have been persuaded by what she referred to as the 'hostile influences' around him. A correspondent in the magazine, *Truth*, for example, wrote 'it seems to me that the only individuals to whom the perversion of the weak-minded Sir Tatton Sykes is a matter of the smallest moment are his relatives, who must be horrified at the manner in which he is apparently to be plundered, the building of a new Roman Catholic Cathedral at Westminster being the earliest undertaking to which his accumulations are to be devoted'. [14]What is more likely is that he looked at the books and the figures didn't add up.

Tatton had worked out that the financing of the Metropolitan Catholic Cathedral would cost him an outlay of £25,000 a year for fifteen years. In the boom years of the mid-nineteenth century, when the annual income from the Sledmere estate had been as much as £52,542, with expenditure no more than £16,000, this might have been acceptable, but the last quarter of the nineteenth century saw a serious agricultural depression hit the East Riding, as it did many corn-growing districts. The depression was the result of a combination of wet seasons – those of 1878–1882 being particularly bad – subsequent poor harvests, and tumbling prices aggravated by imports of cheap corn from abroad. Wheat prices fell by a half and those of barley and oats by about a third. Landlords were reduced to giving large rent rebates, and were forced to invest money in providing new buildings for their tenants and paying for such costs as the conversion of plough-land to grass. The Sledmere estate suffered along with the rest. Between 1881 and 1889 its annual income had sunk to £39,226, while expenditure had gone up to £23,580 in 1885. In the light of these figures, it is hardly surprising that Tatton got cold feet.

Jessie chose to ignore his increasingly nervous attitude towards the whole project and continued to assure Manning that things were on target. 'Tatton has a dread the Cathedral may eventually cost a million,' she wrote to him on 23 January, 1883, 'and wishes to work at it for two or three years before touching the capital, which is a little under £300,000. I will take care before he leaves England that a will is prepared and signed leaving this sum to the purpose he destined it while it was accumulating . . . I know you will derive most pleasure from the fact that your Cathedral is as sure and as certain a thing as anything on this earth can be.'[15] She could not have been more wrong. Tatton kept dithering and eventually the death of Ferstel in July, 1883, gave him the perfect excuse to abandon a project which, had it been successful, would almost certainly have led to the financial ruin of the Sledmere estate. It was not the end of his church-building, however – he was to build a grand new church in Sledmere a decade later – nor did Jessie give up her attempts to persuade him that he was wrong. 'Tatton got a new mania to build a church at Driffield instead of Westminster,' she wrote in her diary in August, 1883; '– have been trying to show him the folly of it.'[16]

At least the Westminster Cathedral scheme had, for a while, given Tatton and Jessie something in common. With its collapse, they increasingly led separate lives. While Tatton remained at Sledmere immersing himself in his horses and churches, Jessie spent more and more time in London in the pursuit of a happiness that continued to elude her. She broke up with her German lover in December, noting in her diary that she had 'shed the last tears I intend ever to waste on a heartless and unprincipled roué', and wasted no time in finding a replacement: 'Monday, 10 December, lunched at George's and met a man called Watson who I hear is a well known man about town, a great gambler and a friend of the P of W . . . I found him clever and unlike most people.'[17] He kept her amused throughout most of the following year.

The great love affair of Jessie's life began early in 1885 when she was twenty-nine. The man in question, who was the same age as her, was Lucien de Hirsch, the only son of Baron Maurice de Hirsch, a Bavarian Jew who had amassed a colossal fortune by snatching from under the nose of the Turkish Government the concession to build the first railway through the Balkans to Constantinople. The Baron was consequently nicknamed 'Turkish Hirsch'. He was a consummate social climber with a craving for crowns and coronets that verged on the comical. Lucien was his only son and his ambition was to secure the boy an English wife. One of the women with whom he broached the subject was Margot Tennant, the lively daughter of Sir

Charles Tennant, a rich businessman. In her memoirs she related how the Baron invited her to dinner in a private room in the Café Anglais in Paris, where he told her that he wished her to marry his son, whom he described as being very respectable, a collector of books and manuscripts, and highly educated. In fact, Margot knew him. 'Your son is the man with the beard who wears glasses and collects coins, isn't he?' she asked. 'I don't suppose he would even care much for me,' she continued, 'I hate coins.' 'Has he ever been in love?' she wondered. 'No,' replied the blissfully ignorant Baron, 'he has never been in love; but a lot of women make up to him and I don't want him to be married for his money by some designing girl.'[18]

Lucien and Jessie met sometime in 1884, and it seems that the discovery that cemented their friendship was their mutual love of the ancient Greeks. In his first letter to her, dated 13 October, 1884, and addressed 'Dear Lady Sykes', he wrote, 'I am very agreeably surprised to find that your taste in art matters is quite congenial with my own; the proof that I am a sincere admirer is that I have myself a small collection of Greek things: vases, terracottas and bronzes, a few of which are really very fine: but I never confess it except to people who have some understanding of these things as one only gets laughed at.'[19] In the course of their subsequent love affair, they wrote hundreds of letters to one another, often as many as two or three a day, and those written by Jessie, luckily returned to her after his death, give a fascinating if chilling account of what life with Tatton was like.

They gave him a nickname, sometimes 'the Alte' – the old gentleman – and at other times 'the Alte Herr' – the father – and Jessie did not spare the details of the tribulations she had to suffer. 'I got three letters from you, my own dearest love, this morning,' she wrote in the early summer of 1885, '*quelle embarras de richesse* – I assure you they come most *à propos*, for that vile old Alte being now stronger and better (from the milder weather I suppose) has been simply too devilish – last night when I got back from hunting – very tired and very cold – he saluted me with the news that he had spent the afternoon going to the Bank and playing me some tricks, and after dinner, when I remonstrated with him and told him this kind of thing could not continue, he pulled my hair and kicked me, and told me if I had not such an ugly face, I might get someone to pay my bills instead of himself . . . I was afraid to hit him back because I am so much stronger I might hurt him.' She went on to describe how, in spite of the brutality, Tatton was at the same time completely dependent on her for everything, like a child, and had come to her room only half an hour after this incident, to ask her to write a business letter for him to the Duke of Westminster. 'I am writing this letter under difficulties,' she concluded, 'in the refreshment room of York Station while he is pacing up and down covered with coats. It has turned cold today so perhaps that excellent Person who I always believe has a sneaking affection for me will affect the old brute with a bad cold again.'[20]

Embarking on a new love affair brought out all Jessie's insecurities, but this time it seemed as if she had at last found someone who really did love her for herself. 'It is very silly of you to imagine, as you seem to do, that I only want to have fun with you or whatever you may call it,' he wrote to her on 24 July. 'To be quite honest I must say that I do love you sensually as well, but what I feel chiefly for you is a peculiar sympathy in heart and mind and *the sincerest affection*. Such as one does not meet with very often in one's life.'[21] Happy though this may have been for her, their meetings were infrequent since Lucien was very much at the beck and call of his father, whose calls upon his time were numerous. As a result, her life was a series of highs and lows, the latter dominating. Writing to him from Sledmere on 4 October, 1885, with a reunion about to take place, she perfectly described her emotional turmoil. 'For a long time when I first knew I really cared for you, I was wild and excited, almost mad – then we parted – I was very unhappy – I tried to drown my cares and longings in excitement and change of scene – as I should have done had it been the winter in violent exercise – Now I feel you are coming back all my old longing and desire to see you and be with you again has returned with tenfold vigour.'[22]

She longed for him to be with her at Sledmere. 'This place is just at its best,' she wrote on 21 October; 'the lovely trees which are its principal beauty are gorgeous in their autumn tints, the weather for

England is excellent – and I should have had *you* for two or three days all to myself.' She added, 'it is a really beautiful house, and so comfortable'. In her daydreams she had planned how they would spend their time. 'We would have got up early, driven three miles to the meet, hunted on these beautiful open Wolds till two, ridden home, had a bath, dressed, come into this delightful Library, where I am now sitting, had tea and then sat about three hours by the fire till it was time to dress for dinner. We should both have felt that delightful sense of fatigue (which is not weariness) that one has after a pleasant day's sport . . .'[23]

The times Jessie dreaded most were the trips abroad with Tatton, taken during the winter months, long journeys of three months or more which separated her from her son as well as her lover. 'Je suis excessivement malheureuse,' she wrote to Lucien from Paris on 4 November, en route to India, 'de quitter mon enfant – qui est vraiment le seul être au monde excepte toi que je desire ardemment revoir.'[24] But it was not the parting alone which was the cause of so much anxiety, it was equally the difficulties of travelling with Tatton, as her descriptions of the trip in her almost daily letters to Lucien bring to life. Things could be so bad as to be almost comical. They got off to a bad start, for example, when the group, consisting of Tatton, his valet, Bellingham, Jessie and her maid, Gotherd, arrived at the railway station in Paris.

'Just before it was time to start,' she described, 'the Alte had a panic – that he had no tea with him, so we had a regular comic Pantomime enacted at the Buffet. The Alte in his peculiar French saying "S'il vous plait Madame, je veux acheter une livre de thé." Then explanations that they did not deal in the article, then a band of waiters flocking up, a tremendous argument, and finally the Alte retired the proud possessor of an ounce of tea in a screw of paper . . . We then mounted on board our Wagon Lits and passed a singularly unpleasant night. He had a cabin all to himself, and my maid and I shared the next one. I took as I always do the top bed and was just going to sleep when the Alte roused us and everyone on the car with the news his bed was hard and uncomfortable. We made him alright, as we thought, and all went to sleep. In about two hours, tremendous knocking and cries of Help! Help! proceeded from Sir T's cabin. It then appeared he had turned the bolt in his lock and could not get out. Such a performance – shrieks and cries – it was nearly an hour before we got his door open and then he was in a pitiable state.'[25]

By the time they reached the Indian Ocean, two weeks later, on board the SS *Paroumatta*, things had deteriorated further. Tatton was in 'a terrible state of health' and Jessie was being driven mad by the constant playing and singing by amateur musicians at the piano in the Saloon. The worst offender, she told Lucien, was a fellow Austrian called Ellinger. 'He is a terrible little creature whose passion is singing and he never stops. He is now hard at it singing "My Queen, My Queen" in stentorian tones. I sometimes think music is a perfect curse. One has to suffer so much from the shrieks and groans of amateurs.'

At night there was no peace either. Tatton would announce at eleven that he was going to bed and would retire to his cabin. Scarcely would Jessie and her faithful maid, Gotherd, be settled in their adjoining cabin, than they would be awoken by Tatton complaining that he couldn't sleep. There then followed a great deal of toing and froing as various members of the crew helped to move all his bedding to either the Saloon or the deck depending on his particular whim that night. He would then remain there for about half an hour before having everything taken back to his cabin. '. . . this kind of panto-mime,' she explained to Lucien, 'continues till five o'clock in the morning,' adding, 'He is really dreadfully ill and looks terrible. It will be an awful thing for me if he should die in India . . .'[26]

They arrived in Bombay at the end of November, from where they set out eastwards on an expedition to Calcutta. In spite of the constant frustrations, Jessie was occasionally able to see the funny side of their group. 'I wish you could have seen us leave the hotel at Poona,' she wrote on 15 December. 'We had thirty-five packages, including nine cases of wine, a bath and bassinoire, three native servants, an ayah, a cook, and a man servant, all one more helpless than another – the majestic Gotherd and the idiotic Bellingham topped up by Tatton, eyes closed, hands clasped and feet raised, the whole tableau too comic. I assure you I feel sometimes obliged to sit down and laugh, when I

think that I am in charge of the whole of this motley crew.' When they reached the railway station, they discovered that there was a half-hour delay to their departure and the special carriage they had ordered was sitting out in the blazing sun. 'I shall die, I shall die, I shall die if I get in that hot carriage,'[27] moaned Tatton. They calmed him down by making up a bed in the ticket office out of three chairs, and stretching him across them. Jessie did a little drawing of the scene to amuse Lucien.

Tatton's extraordinary habits drove Jessie to distraction. He had, for example, a mania about food. He would not eat at regular hours, forcing her to eat alone, while his own mealtimes were often erratic. Every two hours or so he would devour large quantities of half-raw mutton chops, accompanied by cold rice pudding, all prepared by his own personal cook and eaten in the privacy of his bedchamber. 'He has also adopted an unpleasing habit,' wrote Jessie, 'of chewing the half-raw mutton, but *not* swallowing it, a process the witnessing of which is more curious than pleasant.'[28] He took no exercise, and when not driving about in his carriage, lay on his bed 'in a sort of coma'.[29] At night he would often call Jessie to his room as much as eight times, leaving her frazzled from lack of sleep.

Of all his obsessive whims, however, the most worrying was his fixation that he was going to die. 'The Alte is a sad trial,' she wrote to Lucien on 20 December, from Spence's Hotel in Calcutta. 'About two this morning Gotherd and I were woken by loud shrieks and the words 'I am dying, dying, dying (crescendo). We both jumped up thinking at least he had broken a blood vessel – We found absolutely nothing was the matter . . . We were nearly two hours trying to pacify him. He clutched us . . . and went on soliloquising to this effect, 'Oh dear! I am dying, I shall never see Sledmere again, oh you wicked woman. Why don't you cry? Some wives would be in hysterics – to see your poor husband dropping to pieces before your eyes – oh God have pity. Oh Jessie my bowels are gone, Oh Gotherd my stomach is quite decayed, my knees have given way, Oh Jessie, Jessie – Oh Lord have mercy.' 'This is not a bit exaggerated,' she added, 'quite the contrary', concluding 'My darling, I think of you every day, I dream of you every night . . .'[30]

As the full horror of life with Tatton emerges, one can only sympathise with Jessie's search for happiness elsewhere. She thought she had found it with Lucien, who was her own age and shared her love of art and literature. 'There is I am sure a true happiness in caring for another person,' she wrote to him in February, 1886, from Cathay on the Red Sea, 'and perhaps it is the greatest the world contains.'[31] When she at last returned to England, they discussed his renting a house in London, one with 'no opposite neighbours', where they could spend more time together. 'I will help you any way I can about servants etc,' she told him, 'and if we are discreet in public, I do not think we shall have anything to fear.'[32] Her love for him deepened after a visit to the British Museum when she discovered that his love of art was just as strong as hers. 'All my old love of drawing seems to have come back,' she told him, 'and I really think I must seriously take it up again.' She had given it all up, she said, when she married Tatton and felt 'so miserable and lonely and disgusted'.[33]

Though Jessie snatched every moment she could with Lucien their times together were still painfully few. 'Our intercourse,' she wrote to him, 'is like that of two persons travelling in separate express trains and only meeting at the stations . . . What a cruel shame. I do not think I should love you any the less if I saw you every day, on the contrary the more I see of you the more I love you.'[34] Sadly for her, the house she had so hoped Lucien would rent never materialised, and by the time she managed to persuade Tatton that he should buy a house in London they were off again abroad. 'The Alte . . . is suddenly seized with a desire to revisit the capital of your ancient race,' she wrote on 8 January, 1887. 'He has made his horrible plans which are to leave here in a fortnight, spend two days (only two days!) in Paris, take the "rapide" to Rome, remain there a week, a week at Naples, and a fortnight in Sicily, from thence to Corfu and see Olympia, Athens and Corinth, all à la tourist which I *hate*, no time to enjoy anything, then to Beyrout – ride down the coast, five days in tents!! to Jerusalem.'[35]

Jessie had a bad omen about the forthcoming journey, and wrote to Lucien on 25 January, 'I am haunted with a dreadful fear that all is not quite right.'[36] She was worried about him, because he had been ill with a stomach complaint, but they managed to snatch a meeting in Paris where he reassured her that all would be well. She carried with her the memory of their farewell on the corner of the Rue de l'Elysée. 'You are the dearest and best creature in the world,'[37] she wrote to him from Bologna. They arrived in Jerusalem on 24 February and Jessie painted for Lucien a depressing picture of her circumstances. 'My darling, here we are and here we seem likely to remain – The Alte has exactly got what he likes best – an ailment, a bed in the sitting room, a stove which makes the apartment unbearably hot, and that general dirt and discomfort and untidiness which are his ideas of the pleasures of travelling . . . You can imagine how miserable I am – it is almost impossible to settle to any occupation, either reading, writing or drawing in a room like this – full of slop pails, dirty linen, relics of horrible meals and old clothes.'[38]

All that kept Jessie going on this trip was the thought of seeing Lucien again. Memories of their time together filled her every waking moment and each time a post was due she could barely contain her excitement. The disappointments were crushing. 'My darling, I have just had a most cruel deception,' she wrote from Jericho, en route to Beirut, on 5 March. 'As you know we have now been in this gay Jordan Valley since 2 March – a Post was to arrive in Jerusalem this morning, so I gave a Bedouin a Napoleon to ride to Jerusalem and fetch the letters. He has just returned and *there is not one from you*!!! . . . I do feel desolate.' She had not heard from him since 13 February, in spite of the fact that she had been writing to him almost every day, and frustration was beginning to get the better of her. 'I *hate* the East,' she cursed; 'the days are boiling, the wind is howling, the tent is flapping – I feel a beast!'[39]

The truth is she was frantic with worry, reading into Lucien's three weeks of silence every possible calamity that might have overtaken him. Her anxiety was relieved when, a few days later, she reached the small town of Tiberias on the shores of the Sea of Galilee and found a telegram from him assuring her that he was well. 'It was a great comfort to me,' she replied from Beirut, on 23 March, 'to feel that at any rate you were alive.'[40] Her fears for his well-being were now overtaken by worries that by the time they were reunited he would no longer care for her. 'You know I always think "Loin des yeux, loin du coeur",' she wrote the following week, 'though I am sure it is not the case with me as the longer I am separated from you the more I miss you – How I wish we were in a "bonne petite chambre" together.'[41]

When Jessie wrote this, late at night, she was alone in her tent, halfway from Beirut to Damascus, with no chance of sending or receiving any further letters for several days. Consequently she was champing at the bit by the time she and Tatton reached their destination. She described her excitement in a letter written to Lucien from Damascus on 6 April. 'On the morning of the fourth,' she told him, 'I got up at 5.00, started at 5.30 and galloped all the way to Damascus, seventeen miles in two-hours-and-a-quarter, reaching this hotel at 7.45 – I was so anxious to get my letters. I had to go to the English Consul for them. I felt in such high spirits, this odious journey being within a reasonable distance of ending.'[42]

One can just see her, dusty from the journey, breathless with exhaustion and anticipation, striding into the consulate to collect the letters which she so hoped would be awaiting her from Lucien. Instead there was a telegram from his friend Paul Goldschmidt in Paris. It read 'Lucien gravement malade depuis huit jours.'[43] She was distraught. 'We have a proverb,' she wrote, ' "He who laughs in the morning, will cry before night." And truly it was my case.'[44] She returned to her hotel in a state of abject misery, not daring to imagine the worst and with no one except her maid to pour out her heart to. She could not sleep. She spent the time composing a love letter. 'I hardly dare write not knowing how you are,' she told him. 'Mon cheri je t'embrasse mille fois. Je souhaite et je prie de tout mon coeur que tu puisse aller mieux . . . Je sens que je ne pouvoir vivre sans toi. Je t'adore – Jessie.'[45]

It was to be the last letter she was ever to write to him, and she never sent it. On 10 April, a further telegram arrived from Paul Goldschmidt.

> J'AI REÇU VOS DÉPÊCHES. PAUVRE LUCIEN EST MORT D'UNE PNEUMONIE COMPLIQUÉE DE FIÈVRE TYPHOIDE. LE TOUT N'A PAS DURÉ QUINZE JOURS. IL N'A PAS SOUFFERT . . . IL A PARLÉ DE VOUS ET M'A DEMANDÉ SI VOUS AVIEZ ÉCRIT UN TÉLÉGRAPHE. VOUS ÊTES PEUT-ÊTRE LA SEULE PERSONNE QUI SACHEZ QUELLE PERTE JE FAIS ET MOI DE MON CÔTÉ JE SAIS COMBIEN IL VOUS AIMAIT ET CE QUE VOUS PERDEZ EN LUI. SOYEZ SANS CRAINTE VOTRE SECRET EST ENTRE DES BONNES MAINS . . . [46]

Jessie's heart was broken. In the short time she spent with Lucien, she had had a glimpse of what life could have been like for her had she married a man of her own age and with her own interests. Both the knowledge of this and the loss of him proved too much to bear and she began to lose control. As part of a deal she had struck with Tatton before setting out on their last trip to the Middle East that she would stay with him in Palestine as long as he wished, he had agreed to take a lease on a London house for her, 46 Grosvenor Street. This is where she retreated when she returned home and where she was to spend more and more time in the years to come. Away from 'the Alte' and with a healthy disrespect for the conventions of society, she attempted to drown her sorrows in a hedonistic lifestyle. Soon the grand ground-floor rooms of this impressive Mayfair house were filled with the scent of cigarette smoke – smoking was a habit forbidden at Sledmere – and the sounds of merry-making, dominated by the rattle of the dice and the clink of the bottle.

Forty-six Grosvenor Street drew an eclectic crowd, all of whom were attracted by their hostess's keen mind and razor-sharp wit. Regular visitors amongst the old guard were the Duchess of Montrose, 'a woman of majestic manner, much humour, and extraordinary command of pungent Johnsonian language'; 'evergreen Maria', Marchioness of Ailesbury, known as 'Lady A.', who used to say, 'Nerves, my dear! What are nerves?', and the old Duchess of Cleveland, who once said in reference to some people she was criticising, 'they are not nice people; they are not gentle people, had they been poor they would have committed crimes'.[47] There were politicians like Randolph Churchill, who delighted Jessie with his 'eternal charm and his delightful conversation' and who privately sympathised with her dislike of the middle-classes. 'I much prefer real democracy,' she once told him, 'to the tyranny of the petite bourgeoisie.'[48]

Her cousin, the dashing Lord Charles Beresford, a naval commander who was something of a hero after his participation in the bombardment of Alexandria and the Nile expedition in the early 1880s, was another regular, along with assorted intellectuals, ambassadors and diplomats befriended by Jessie on her travels and raffish types she met on the racecourse. Then of course there was her brother-in-law, Christopher, of whom she was very fond, and who gave parties the occasional *frisson* by bringing along the Prince of Wales. A reporter from *The World* wrote of one of these evenings:

> Lady Sykes's ball on Thursday night was a distinct social success, although HRH and his sons did not arrive till nearly one. The dancing was in the back drawing-room, lit up with electric light. Mr Liddell furnished the music; 'ce bon Christopher' did the honours (*vice* Sir Tatton); and Prince Henry of Orleans was amongst the guests. Supper was served in a tent hung with Tapestry, and the hostess wore white with pink roses and a broad pale green sash . . . Mr Albert Stopford led the cotillion admirably; the Prince of Wales never danced with greater vigour; the cotillion did not end till after four, and the sun was shining brightly when Lady Sykes's friends departed.[49]

There were more lovers too, mostly bounders in the mould of Bay Middleton, who took advantage of her generosity and did nothing to improve her state of mind. As her drinking increased, so did her indiscretions, until the vicious gossips and jealous spinsters of London drawing rooms were whispering in each other's ears with undisguised pleasure the new name coined for her by one of the wittier amongst them. To them she was no longer Lady Tatton Sykes, but Lady Satin Tights.

'Nevertheless,' she had written to Cardinal Manning in 1882, 'I have . . . a real reverence for goodness and wisdom . . . and a desire . . . to try and utterly abandon my sinful and useless life.'[50] She did not give up the struggle. Society may have laughed at her behind her back, but amongst the poor and needy she was revered and blessed with a kinder nickname – 'Lady Bountiful'. When she was at Sledmere, much of her time was spent in daily visits to dispense food, clothing or money to families in need, while in Hull, where slum housing and conditions for the poor were particularly bad, she was something of a heroine. She was known particularly for her work on behalf of poor children, and Lady Sykes's Christmas Treat, for the Catholic children of Prynne Street, had become an important annual event. 'I gave a Tea in Hull for the children of the Catholic School,' she had written to Lucien on 31 December, 1886, 'which lasted from midday till 6.30 . . . There were 520 children, and I was carving meat for three hours. I think they enjoyed themselves poor things. Certainly they were very poor and 21 boys and 1 girl amongst them had *no* shoes or stockings, and in this bitter weather too. We made a huge sandwich for each child and gave them besides various mince pies and cakes. It was a great pleasure to me.'[51]

Her charity was not confined to Sledmere. She lived at a time when philanthropy was almost a social imperative and in London there was no shortage of directions in which she might turn her attention. Her particular interest was the Catholic poor in the East End, mostly Irish immigrants who were flooding in to look for jobs which were better paid than back home, or at least thought to be so. In they swarmed into the cheapest and already most overcrowded districts, creating appalling slum ghettoes from which it was difficult for them to escape. 'Whilst we have been building our churches,' thundered the author of a pamphlet entitled *The Bitter Cry of Outcast London*, 'and solacing ourselves with our religion and dreaming that the millennium was coming, the poor have been growing poorer, the wretched more miserable, and the immoral more corrupt.'[52] It was typical of Jessie to combine her social life and her charity work in a flamboyant style and she would often astonish people by leaving a party in full swing and going straight to the East End to dispense soup. Still dressed in her ball gown and sparkling jewels, she appeared to the homeless like a fairytale princess.

Though she now led a life which was increasingly independent from her husband Jessie was still Lady Sykes and she continued to play that role as she was needed, acting, for example, as Tatton's travelling companion. She accompanied him to Russia in 1887, India in 1888 and Egypt in 1889. Her powers of flirtation remained undiminished and each trip netted her new admirers. In Russia a General Churchyard fell under her spell. In India, where her old paramour, Lord Dufferin, was now Viceroy, two young men, Richard Braithwaite and David Wallace, were rivals for her love, but it was in Egypt that she came closest to finding again the happiness she had felt with Lucien. John Eldon Gorst was a young diplomat, a rising star in the Foreign Office and assigned to the British Consulate-General in Cairo under Sir Evelyn Baring. Five years younger than Jessie, he was immediately struck by her frank, direct manner. 'It was in January of this year,' he later wrote in some autobiographical notes for 1889, 'that I first made the acquaintance of J.S., a woman who exercised a great influence over my life for the next two years and who undoubtedly contributed very largely to the formation of my character and general views of life during that period. Some years older than myself, she possessed great intelligence coupled with an extraordinary variety of knowledge and a force of character unusual in one of her sex. All these qualities made her in those days a most delightful and instructive companion.'[53]

That Jessie fell in love with the young Gorst, who she always referred to as Jack, is without doubt. 'I never imagined I could have such feelings again for anyone,'[54] she once told him. Once more, however, she had chosen to form an attachment to a man she would see only briefly. Their short times together were intensely happy and passionate, their separations were filled with misery. 'My own darling,' he wrote to her on 26 October, 1889, 'it is just twelve hours since I last saw you and I feel more miserable every moment at the thought that I shall not see you for so long. I am quite lost without you and have no other interest in life.'[55]

The happiest period of their time together was in 1890, when Tatton decided to spend the winter in Cairo, throwing Jack and Jessie together in a whirl of social activities which Jack recorded in his diaries. When Tatton finally departed on a trip up the Nile, for once leaving Jessie behind, they engaged in numerous assignations, many of which culminated in their making love. These sessions were recorded by Jack with an *x*, while those on which there was no sexual contact were marked with an *o*. The former far outnumbered the latter, with 132 *x*s and a mere 18 *o*s being noted for that year.[56] Their meeting place in Cairo appears to have been the Villa Rolo in Garden City, an imposing villa built by the Austrian architect, Eduard Matasek, which belonged to the Rolos, a family of rich merchants and financiers. 'This morning I went over the things broken and missing in the Maison Rolo,' he wrote to her on 15 April, 1890 when she was on her way back to England. 'It gave me quite a pang to see the loathsome Madame Rolo in the rooms where we have spent so many happy hours together.'[57]

Over the next two years, Jessie and Jack spent as much time as they could together, both in Egypt and in England, when he was home on leave. He came to London in June 1890, having previously instructed Jessie to look out for some rooms where they could meet safely, 'but please do not run any risks in doing so,' he had told her, adding, 'I would rather live in the most loathsome lodging than that anyone should have any suspicions.'[58] In late July, she took him to Goodwood races, where he won £200, and in mid-August he recorded in his diary, 'My present for Lady S – a bracelet – arrived. Very pretty diamonds and sapphires.'[59] It was a blissfully happy time for them both.

The idyll ended in September when Jack was suddenly recalled by Sir Evelyn Baring to accompany him on an urgent diplomatic mission to Italy. The news came, he noted in his diary, as 'a dreadful blow'.[60] When he finally returned to Cairo, he was missing her terribly. 'My own darling Jessie,' he wrote on 16 October, 'here I am once more writing to you in the "Nid" and feeling very, very melancholy at the thought of all the happy moments we have spent here together . . . the whole place is so full of memories of you . . . On the steamer I was really too depressed to write and passed the time away in thinking of you.'[61]

A long separation followed and they did not meet again until March of the following year when the Sykeses paid another visit to Egypt. Though they had the better part of a month together, they failed to recapture the happiness of the past and there were quarrels and recriminations. When Jessie left on 7 April, Jack wrote to her 'You always say that my letters are so much more satisfactory than myself . . . With me it is otherwise and your very nicest letters seem to me a poor substitute for your own charming but rather independent self.' He had dreaded her leaving, perhaps because he sensed it was the beginning of the end. 'It has only been during the last two or three days that we really got to know one another again,' he told her, 'and we are now in for a longer separation than any we have had to go through hitherto. It would indeed be a pity if we drifted apart.'[62]

That is precisely what happened. Jessie began to allude in her letters to the fact that neither she nor Jack would be capable of remaining faithful if separated for too long. This was self-destructive in the extreme, since it made Jack feel very insecure and he became convinced that Jessie was losing interest in him. Their letters started to become quarrelsome. 'I quite agree with what you say in your last letter,' he wrote on 3 July, 'that you are an unsatisfactory woman – almost more unsatisfactory to yourself I should imagine, than even to me.'[63] Hurt by his criticism, she did not answer, and this he attributed to indifference. 'I think it best that our liaison should come to an end,' he wrote to her on 24 July. 'We have been very happy together for two years and I can never be sufficiently grateful to you for that . . . Our ways lie far apart and you have to drift along yours and I along mine. Goodbye then my Darling for the last time.'[64]

Jessie's reaction to this was a fit of bravado. She wrote to Jack telling him that she had been seeing a great deal of a man who was very attractive to her. Jack was naturally jealous, especially since she refused to name names. 'I am quite in the dark as to which of your numerous admirers has come to the front,' he replied. 'On the whole I am inclined to think it must be Braithwaite and that you are continuing the idyll begun in India. For the credit of my *amour-propre*, I trust it is not Wallace.'[65] Two weeks later he was declaring 'I am very much attached to you, I know you alone can make me really happy, and there is nothing I desire more than that we may be once again be upon our former footing.' He finished the letter with the addenda, 'I can honestly assure you that I do not love any other woman . . .'[66]

They were both telling the truth. Jessie's misery at being parted from Jack for such a long period and her deep-rooted need to be loved had undoubtedly led to her having been unfaithful to him. Guilt made her feign indifference. For his part, he obviously still loved her and was only waiting for reassurance that she felt the same. The affair was doomed. As soon as Jack realised this, his attentions began to stray in the direction of a half-American, half-Armenian woman called Mattie Rees, with whom he formed 'a strong attachment'. When Jessie eventually returned to Cairo in March, 1892, Jack told her to her face that this time the break was final. She took the news calmly and with generosity.

'Only a really great nature could afford to be magnanimous on such an occasion,' he wrote to her the following morning, his tears staining the pages of the letter. 'It makes me inexpressibly sad to feel all that I have lost. I shall never meet a woman to suit me like you or for whom I can care as I have cared for you. If I had known that you really loved me, things might have turned out differently, but alas! I did not make the discovery till too late . . . it quite breaks my heart to leave you . . . Please don't hate me Jessie. I feel so utterly broken down and miserable.'[67] On the boat home, Jessie scribbled on a scrap of paper, 'the Physiology of love is extraordinary . . . here I have been living for eighteen months with another man and going through agonies of self reproach and misery at the thought I was throwing Jack over, and now I know he has another mistress *I* am broken-hearted'.[68]

There was no consoling Jessie now. Aged thirty-six, her life was beginning to cave in on her. Her drinking became heavier, her promiscuity more flagrant, and she began to haunt bookmaker's shops and the premises of money-lenders. Those who cared for her looked on in horror, powerless to help, foremost amongst them her thirteen-year-old son.

CHAPTER X

Mark

In taking Mark with her into the Catholic Church, Jessie well and truly staked her claim on him, and there is no doubt that she was the overwhelming influence upon him as he grew up. She did not believe in pampering children. She saw them as small adults who should quickly learn how to stand on their own two feet. As soon as he had started to master the most basic principles of language, she began to share with him her great love of literature and the theatre. As well as the popular children's books of the day – the fairy tales of Grimm, Hans Andersen and George MacDonald, the stories of Charles Kingsley and Lewis Carroll, the tales of adventure of Sir Walter Scott, James Fenimore Cooper and Robert Louis Stevenson – she read him her own favourites, Swift, Dickens and Shakespeare, much of which she could quote from memory. She encouraged him to dress up and act out plays, and she was delighted when he began to develop a talent for mimicry and caricature.

By regaling him with tales of her travels across the world, and of all the people she had met and the strange sights she had seen, Jessie also gave Mark a sense of place and of history. She described to him the architectural wonders of medieval Christendom, and told him of the important ideas and ideals which grew out of the Renaissance. Fascinated by politics since childhood, she brought to life for him all the great statesmen and prominent figures of the past, heaping scorn on modern politicians, bureaucrats and businessmen, none of whom had any romance. She also passed on to him her hatred of humbug. The result of all this was that by the age of seven he was advanced beyond his years.

'He is a charming child and most intelligent and precocious,' Jessie's mother wrote to her in December 1886, 'which under the circumstances makes one tremble, for there is no doubt that he is now quite beyond the control of women.' She referred to the fact that his father was a relatively distant figure, who was away for half the year, and in the often frequent absences of his mother Mark was left in a household dominated by women. There were eleven female servants in the house, under the housekeeper, Mrs Tracey, and three males, under Broadway, the butler. Mark apparently ran rings round them. 'If he remains for much longer surrounded by a pack of admiring servants,' continued his grandmother, 'and with no refined well-educated person to look after him . . . and check him if he is not civil in his manners, he will become completely unbearable . . . When he goes to Sledmere he is made the Toy and idol of the place and each servant indulges him as they please.'[1]

If anyone was a father to Mark, it was old Tom Grayson, the groom, who had been at Sledmere since the days of his grandfather. A tall, white-haired old man in his eighties, with a strong weather-beaten face and a kindly smile, he was an inseparable companion to his young master, a friendship that brought great happiness to his declining years. He taught him to ride – 'this is t'thod generation Ah've taught ti'ride,' he loved to boast – and helped him look after his pride and joy, an ever-growing pack of fox terriers. He also contributed greatly to his education, sharing with him his great knowledge of nature and the countryside. In keeping him endlessly entertained with tales of local folklore and legend, he gave Mark a strong sense of locality and of his origins.

Tom Grayson was a wonderful storyteller, and Mark never forgot the bloodcurdling tale of the death of 'Old Coatee', an elderly woman, who lived in a cabin in the Derwent Valley, and was so called because she always had a leather coat wrapped tightly around her. One day she disappeared and her battered and mutilated body was discovered at the bottom of a well. A man who had been spotted coming out of her home was arrested and confessed to the murder. He suffered a dreadful fate. A cage was erected by the roadside, into which he was locked without food or drink. To add to his tortures, each day a loaf of bread, fresh from the oven, was placed outside the cage just beyond his reach. It took ten days for him to starve to death, and Grayson loved to tell Mark how he had witnessed the scene and had been haunted by the man's shrieks ever since.

Grayson was like a rock to his charge. As a highly intelligent and sensitive child Mark could hardly have failed to be affected by what was going on as a result of the worsening relations between his parents, and when things got bad he always knew he could escape to the kennels or the stables. January, 1887, was a typically bad time. Jessica was beside herself with fury after the latest of Tatton's outrages. She loved to sit in the Library, which she had filled with palms and various potted plants. 'I am very fond of them,' she wrote to Lucien, 'and when quite or so much alone there is a certain companionship in seeing them.' The room being so large, however, and having eleven windows, it was only made habitable by having two fires lit in it. Having gone away for a few days, she had instructed the servants to keep a small fire burning in one of the grates until she returned.

'After my departure,' she told Lucien, 'the Alte in one of his economical fits ordered no fires to be made till my return. The frost was terribly severe – the gardener knew nothing of the retrenchment of fuel and when he came three days later to look round the plants he found them all dead or dying from the cold.'[2] Morale throughout the household appears to have been at a very low ebb. 'The confusion here is dreadful,' wrote Jessie, 'everyone is so cross, all the servants quite demoralised. Broadway leaves Monday – I am very sorry for him – The coachman cries all day – I can do nothing! Gotherd is in a fiendish temper – and the Alte is in his most worrying state.'[3]

With his parents about to head off again on a long trip to Jerusalem, Mark's grandmother felt very strongly that he should have a tutor. For a start it would give him a male companion, who was younger than Grayson, to ease the loneliness of his life at Sledmere. Jessica herself admitted this in a letter to Lucien, on the eve of her departure for the Holy Land. 'The house is to be quite shut up, all the servants that are left to be on board-wages, the horse turned out, and poor little Mark left by himself . . . and not a soul in whom I have any confidence in the neighbourhood to look after him.'[4] She left having even forgotten to buy him a birthday present, writing to Lucien in February, from Jerusalem, '16 March is Mark's birthday – it would be very kind of you if you would send him a little toy from Paris for it – as I fear the poor child will get no presents, and he would be so delighted.'[5]

So far as Mark's education was concerned, the elementary part of this had taken place at the village school. Here he had learned to write and spell under the worthy schoolmaster, Mr Thelwell, but had shown little aptitude for anything else. 'He was not a diligent scholar,' commented Thelwell; 'book-work was drudgery; but having great powers of observation and a splendid memory, he stored a mass of information.'[6] Almost everything else he had learned was at his mother's knee, but in 1887, Jessie gave in to her mother and hired a young tutor, Richard Dowling, who Mark nicknamed 'Doolis' and with whom he was soon sharing the joys of the only 'schoolroom' he ever loved. 'I enjoyed an advantage over most of my age,' he later wrote in a memoir, 'in having access to the very large library at Sledmere, and, before I was twelve, I was quite familiar with the volumes of *Punch* and the *Illustrated London News* for many years back.'[7] He learned as much of modern history and the English language from reading these, as he would have done from any school text book. There were other rarer and more forbidden books too, such as Richard Burton's translation of the *Arabian Nights*, mastery of the notes of which contributed to his sexual education.

He was particularly fascinated by military history, no doubt inspired by the large collection of old uniforms and muskets which lay about the house, a reminder of the days when Sir Christopher had raised a troop of yeomanry to defend the Wolds against the French. Amongst his favourites were Marshal Saxe's *Art of War*, and Vauban's seventeenth-century treatise *New Methods of Fortification*. A childhood friend of Mark's, Tom Ellis, later Lord Howard de Walden, once recalled his attempts to put Vauban's theories into practice. 'Nothing would satisfy Mark but a model siege upon the lawn, so shortly there rose a fortress about ten foot square, laid out strictly according to Vauban,

Lawrence's portrait of Sir Mark and Lady Masterman Sykes, and Tatton Sykes.

Watercolour of Sir Mark Masterman Sykes out hunting.

Grant's equestrian portrait of Sir Tatton Sykes, 4th Baronet.

An early photograph
of Tatton in boots and
high-collared frock coat.

Jessie and Venetia
Cavendish-Bentick.

The engagement photograph of
Sir Tatton Sykes, 5th Baronet,
and Jessie.

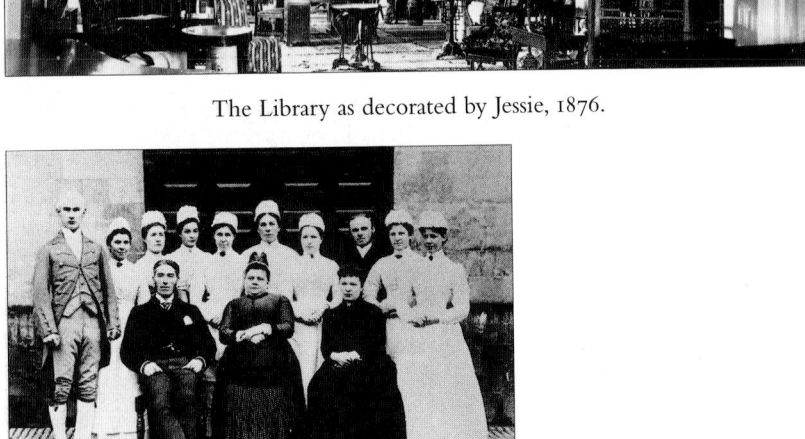

The Library as decorated by Jessie, 1876.

The Sledmere servants, 1876.

A shooting party at
Blenheim Palace, 1873,
with Sykey (4th from left)
and the Prince of Wales
(wearing hat, 2nd from right)

Mark Sykes and Grayson with Mark's beloved fox terriers.

'Master Mark' in soldier's uniform.

Mark Sykes with his faithful travelling companion, Isa Kubrusli.

Sledmere ablaze, with Sir Tatton, wearing several overcoats, seen anxiously pacing up and down as the villagers fight to save the house's contents.

Workmen in front of the house under reconstruction, 1913.

Edith (in hat) with (left to right) Freya, Chistopher, Petsy and Richard.

The Turkish Room, conceived and built by Mark.

Mark and Edith's
children in 1915.
(left to right) Freya,
Richard, Chistopher,
Petsy and Angela.

Mark's effigy engraved in brass on the Eleanor cross.

The Sykes family on the occasion of Richard's coming of age, August 1926. (Left to right) Freya, Richard, Daniel, Edith, Christopher, Petsy and Angela.

bastions, lunettes, redans and all else. Guns were represented by door bolts, and I was told to invest the fortress scientifically ... By the third day of the siege the lawn was a nightmare. I had closed upon the doomed fortress, and, joy of joys, I looked like beating Mark at one of his own games. About this moment Sir Tatton glanced at what had once been a fair lawn and was now a mole's Walpurgis night. I faded into the horizon, but Mark came out of the situation manfully. Sir Tatton was then ploughing up the park "to sweeten the ground". And Mark maintained that our performance was doing the same for the lawn!'[8]

These military games became more and more elaborate, with Mark calling on children from the village to play the part of troops which he, being the young master, could command without opposition. He devised complicated battles in the park and paddocks, in which he devoted great attention to the working out of tactics and the designing of fortifications. Poor old Grayson often found himself drawn into these. 'Witness the battle of Sledmere Church,' remembered Tom Ellis, 'which nearly brought about the death of Grayson ... Mark ordained that the church was to stand the onslaught of the heretics, represented by old Grayson and the twins of Jones, the jockey. After a prolonged siege the heretics attempted to take the outer palisades of the church by escalade, and were repulsed with one casualty. Old Grayson, being eighty, was not of an age to stand a fall from a fifteen-foot ladder.'[9]

A bout of illness at about this time heralded the beginning of the next part of Mark's education. He was bedridden for a while with what was diagnosed as 'a congestion of the lungs'[10] and when he recovered it was decided that the damp climate of Yorkshire winters was the worst thing possible for him. From then on he was to spend the winter months abroad travelling, at first with both his parents and later, when Jessie ceased to accompany Tatton on these journeys, with his father alone. In the autumn of 1888, he went to Egypt where he acquired a fascination for and some knowledge of antiquities from the cicerone of the ruling Sirdar, Lord Grenfell, to whom Tatton had been given an introduction. This elderly guide later recalled him as having been 'the most intelligent boy I had ever met. Mark took the greatest possible interest in my growing museum; he very soon mastered the rudiments of the study; he could read the cartouches containing the names of various kings and, with me, studied . . . hieroglyphics.'[11]

In Cairo, Mark made a new friend in George Bowles, the son of Jessie's old admirer, Thomas Bowles, who was staying with his family at Shepheards Hotel. They accompanied the Sykeses on a trip up the Nile, and the two boys became inseparable. Soon they were exploring on their own and Mark passed on to George his new passion for ancient artefacts. At Thebes the two boys bought themselves a genuine mummified head. 'That it will one day find its way into the soup,' wrote Thomas in his diary, 'unless it soon gets thrown overboard I feel little doubt.' They were nicknamed 'the two English baby-boys by the Arabs' and 'distinguished themselves by winning two donkey races at the local Gymkhana, Mark having carried off the race with saddles, and George the bare-backed race; but two days ago they fell out, and proceeded to settle their differences by having a fight according to the rules of the British prize ring, in the ruins of Karnak – a battle which much astonished the donkey-boys. Having shaken hands, however, at the end of their little mill, they are now faster friends than ever, and are at present, I understand, organising a deep-laid plot to get hold of an entire mummy and take it to England for the benefit of their friends and the greater glory of what they call their museum.'[12]

This was the first of many trips that Mark was to make over the next ten years, which were to contribute more to his general development and education than anything he ever learned at school. 'Before I was fifteen,' he later wrote, 'I visited Assouan, which was then almost the Dervish frontier . . . Then I went to India when Lord Lansdowne was Viceroy. I did some exploration in the Arabian desert, enjoying myself bare-footed amongst the Arabs, and I paid a trip to Mexico, reaching there just when Porfirio Diaz was attaining the zenith of his power.'[13]

In the spring of 1890, Mark returned from a trip with his father to the Lebanon, to find that he had been enrolled by his mother as a student at the junior school of Beaumont College, Windsor, a Roman Catholic school often called 'the Catholic Eton'. She chose Beaumont, against the wishes of Tatton, who would have preferred Harrow, not so much on religious grounds, but because it was more likely to nurture an unorthodox character such as Mark's. The Rector of Beaumont, Father William Heathcote, was a known libertarian who believed that qualities such as humour and loyalty should be encouraged. She also approved of the emphasis placed by the school on theatre.

Having been exposed to far more than most boys of his age, and with his precocious and rather rebellious nature, Mark was an object of curiosity from the very moment he arrived at his new school. 'He was quite unlike any other boy,' wrote a contemporary, Wilfred Bowring, 'and most of the boys certainly thought him eccentric. He took no part in the games, but soon gathered round him and under him all the loiterers and loafers in playroom and playground.'[14] Instead of games, he devised elaborate war games of the kind he played at Sledmere and could often be seen with his motley gang charging across the playground, perhaps in the guise of an Arab warrior or a Red Indian Chief. He kept a stock of stag beetles, with which he amused people by getting them intoxicated on the school beer, and was also the subject of much hilarity on account of his haphazard manner of dressing and his scruffy appearance, a trait shared by his close friend Cedric Dickens. 'I can see the two of them,' recalled Cedric's brother Henry, 'wandering into a certain catechism class . . . on Saturday afternoons, always dishevelled and invariably steeped in ink to the very bone. It must have taken years to get that ink out.'[15]

It is a tribute to the monks of Beaumont that they made no attempt to force Mark into a mould which he would never fit. Accepting that he would never have to earn a living, they seemed instead content with teaching him his religion. They made little attempt to ensure he did his school work and his exercise books, rather than being crammed with Latin Vocabulary and translations, were filled with entertaining histories based on Virgil and Cicero, illustrated with witty caricatures, a talent he had inherited from Jessie. When his eccentric mother, as she did from time to time, swooped down on the school to remove him to far-off places, the authorities simply turned a blind eye. 'On several occasions,' remembered Wilfred Bowring, 'Lady Sykes, generally half-way through term, announced that she proposed to take Mark on a journey of indefinite length. Mark vanished from our ken for about six months, when he reappeared laden with curios from the countries he had visited. These curios nearly always took the shape of lethal weapons, most welcome gifts for his school cronies. He returned from these trips with a smattering of strange tongues.'[16] Most boys, one might expect, would have been spoiled by this kind of upbringing. 'Not so Mark,' wrote one of his teachers, Father Cuthbert Elwes. 'Though he was undoubtedly a remarkably intelligent and intensely amusing boy, his chief charm was his great simplicity and openness of character and entire freedom from human respect.'[17]

On his return from these journeys, he was encouraged to develop his gifts for storytelling and acting. In the playroom he invariably attracted a large crowd around him to listen to the extraordinary stories he had to tell. Sitting cross-legged and often puffing on a hubble-bubble, he regaled them with tales of the weird Druses of Lebanon, whom few schoolboys could name, let alone place; of sleeping in tents on the edge of the Sea of Galilee; and of the dreadful scenes he witnessed in the lunatic asylum in Damascus where wretched madmen imprisoned in tiny kennels, each six feet by five, 'clamoured and howled the lifelong day; over their ankles in their own ordure, naked save for their chains, these wretched beings shrieked and jibbered! Happy were those who, completely insane, laughed and sang in this inferno.'[18]

Mark's talents, for acting and storytelling, found their truest expression when he went up to the senior school in 1892, and gained him the only award he was ever to win at school, the elocution prize for a play he wrote and directed himself, *A Hyde Park Demonstration*, in which he took the leading role of the orator. He also published his first piece of writing, an article for the inaugural issue of the *Beaumont Review*, entitled 'Night in a Mexican Station', which was an account of an incident that had taken place during a trip to Mexico he had made with his father in the winter of 1891–2. They had taken an overnight train to the north of the country, and Mark demonstrated his powers of observation in his amusing descriptions of some of the passengers in the different carriages. Those in the 'Palace on Wheels', for example, included 'the Yankeeised Mexican – viz, a Mexican in frock coat and top hat; the Rurales officer, a gorgeous combination of leather, silver and revolvers, etc; the American drummer, a commercial traveller . . . and lastly, the conductor – a lantern-jawed U.S. franchised Citizen, a voice several degrees sharper than a steam saw'.[19]

One can only wonder how much Mark knew what was going on in his mother's life at this time, but his powers of observation being what they were, it is unlikely that much passed him by. His friend Tom Ellis, who used to go and stay with him at Sledmere during the holidays, wrote of 'nightmare scenes amongst the grown-ups that faded as strangely as they began . . . Through these Mark walked quite steadily, with myself trailing dutifully in pursuit.'[20] The fact is that Jessie's behaviour was steadily deteriorating. Her beloved father had died in April, 1891, a loss that was compounded by the end of her affair with Jack Gorst. She was not only drinking heavily to drown her sorrows, but she was severely in debt and had begun to resort to dubious methods of getting her hands on more money, without regard to the consequences. As early as 1890, for example, she had owed as much as £10,000 and, when pressed for the money by the Union Bank, had given them a letter purporting to be a guarantee for that amount signed by Tatton. When the bank had asked him to confirm this, he had denied that the signature was his. Jessie told him he was mad to suggest such a thing and to avoid a scandal, Tatton had paid up.

In later years, when she found herself in the most serious of trouble, Jessie would always claim that she was driven to running up huge debts because of Tatton's refusal to pay for the upkeep of their establishments. It is certainly true that there were some huge expenses at this time. A ledger exists at Sledmere, from the London firm of Maples of Tottenham Court Road, which shows that between April, 1892 and June, 1893, the considerable sum of £7,656. 3s. 5d. was spent on refurbishments. As well as carrying out the usual tasks of reupholstering much of the furniture, painting walls and putting up new wallpaper, beating carpets, and making new curtains and blinds for most of the rooms in the house, those of the servants included, the major part of the work was the long-needed installation of a new drainage system. This enormous task involved the building of a new cesspit, the laying of numerous drains and the installation of enough modern water-closets and bathrooms to cater for a large household. One can only imagine what a relief it must have been for both the family and the servants to now live in a house which no longer stank of sewage.

Whatever the money was required for, the incident of the forged signature had shaken Tatton, and, encouraged by his new agent, his nephew, Henry Cholmondeley, he decided to take a tougher stand. From now on he ignored Jessie's pleas for more money. In desperation she had taken to gambling and was losing sums as high as £530 a week at the tables and in the bookmaker's shops. Her behaviour began to lose her friends, including Blanche Howard de Walden, the mother of Mark's friend, Tom Ellis. A nervous and delicate woman, she became afraid of Jessie, and put an end to the friendship between their sons. 'I must admit,' Tom later wrote, 'that Jessica, partially caged and embittered, was terrifying. At last Mark and I saw that our friendship could not continue. Mark had been more than a friend. He had been a sort of miraculous Philistine striding through the difficult age of adolescence and bowling over the conventions that I could only blindly resent.'[21] For the first time in his life, Mark began to dread visits from his mother, fearing that she would be begging him to intervene on her behalf with his father, or worse still, that she would be drunk. 'I can still see Lady Sykes,' recalled Henry Dickens, 'descending on Beaumont like a thunderbolt, entering into tremendous fights with Father Heathcote, the then and equally pugnacious rector.'[22]

It may have been one of these spats that led Jessie to suddenly remove Mark from Beaumont at the end of 1894 and send him back to Sledmere. He immersed himself in the care of his terriers, becoming so devoted to the dogs that he could not bear to be parted from them. This may be the reason that, for once, he did not accompany his father on a long journey to warmer climes. Equally he could have been forbidden to go by Jessie, whose relations with her husband were at a new low. Whatever the reason, he spent the winter alone. Sensing his isolation, in the early part of 1895, Jessie hired him a new tutor, a young Catholic called Egerton Beck, who was extremely widely read and was already the author of a number of papers on Monastic history. A man of impeccable dress and manners, with a fascination for the past, he hit it off at once with his new charge, of whom he was to become a lifelong friend. Mark could not wait to take Beck into the Library. Together they spent hours studying the papers of the Sykes ancestors, poring over the wonderful folios of engravings by Piranesi, and devouring the military histories that Mark loved so much.

In the spring of 1895, at the age of sixteen, Mark's education took a further turn, when he was sent to an Italian Jesuit school in Monaco, an unusual choice inspired by his mother's friendship with the then Princess of Monaco, the former Alice, Duchess of Richelieu, whom Jessie had met in Paris, at one of her celebrated salons in the Faubourg St Honoré. Jessie, Beck and three of his terriers accompanied him there, and they moved into a rented house, the terriers living out on the flat roof. 'The atmosphere at Monte Carlo,' Mark later wrote, 'was a peculiar one for a boy of my years. It is quite natural to think of people going there for pleasure, but for study seems rather curious. I knew everything about the inner workings of the tables and knew most of the croupiers.' Not as well as Jessie, however, who haunted the tables while her son was at school. One day word got out that she had disgraced herself by flinging her hat down on the table in fury after sustaining a particularly large loss.

As for the school itself, which Mark attended as a day-boy, he found the discipline stifling after the relaxed atmosphere of Beaumont. 'The Italian school system is extraordinarily rigid and hard,' he wrote. 'It was no child's play at Monaco.'[23] According to Beck he was more interested in his terriers than his school work, and by the time they returned to England in July, one of them had littered and their number had grown to eight. Sadly in the autumn he had to leave them behind when he left for Brussels to undergo the final part of his education before going up to University. The Institut de Saint Louis, a slightly less rigid school than the one in Monaco, but where the boys were still 'very much overworked', forbade pets and Mark had to bid farewell to his little family. He was heartbroken.

They were briefly reunited at Christmas. Amongst the guests staying in the house that December was Thomas Bowles, known as 'Tap', with his daughters, Sydney and Dorothy, who was nicknamed 'Weenie'. Sydney wrote an account of the stay in her diary. They arrived on Christmas Eve. It was snowing heavily and the Sykeses were giving a Christmas party in the house for the tenants. 'Two whole cows [were] cut up, and the mince pies were without number. There were ... fifty or sixty people come for the beef and we were struck by their good-looking, well-fed appearance.' At dinner, Jessie gave presents to the two girls, a 'lovely little box' to Sydney and 'a handsome writing desk' to Weenie. 'Lady Sykes is *very nice* and *extremely kind-hearted*,' she noted.

On Christmas Day, which was 'all snow and glitter', a 'great number of Carol singers came round all day, beginning as soon as we got down to breakfast', but there was no church since Tatton had demolished the existing one in order to build a much grander Gothic church. Instead 'Father Theodore and Mark and I and Grayson *and* the dogs (an ugly little crew of ten fox terriers) went for a long walk through the wood.' She later noted, 'Mark keeps ten together in order to observe their habits when living in lots. One of their habits is that when their *leader* gets old, they kill and eat him!' At lunch they had the nicest crackers she had ever seen. 'There was one I should think quite a yard and a half long, which Mark and I pulled. It went off with such a bang that Tap was quite frightened.'

Sydney found Tatton very kind, but also thought him rather silly. 'It is impossible to help laughing at him,' she wrote. 'For instance, Mark is still very fat, too fat really, though not so bad as he used to be. But Sir Tatton, seeing him a trifle thinner than when he last saw him, said "Ah Yes! Yes! Wasting away, wasting away." I roared. I simply couldn't help it.' There were more crackers at dinner, after which they played charades 'which were very funny,' noted Sydney.

'One word was "Preposterous", another "Drunk-ard", another "Dyna-mite", etc, etc. Mark seems to have a great talent for acting among his other accomplishments!'[24]

This was to be the last happy Christmas that Mark was to spend at Sledmere for many years to come, for it was at this point that the relationship between his parents reached its lowest ebb. Jessie's drinking had reached a stage where her faithful maid, Gotherd, had on several occasions to hide her scent to prevent her drinking that too. She also occasionally resorted, when her mistress was in a particularly bad state, to hiding her stays so that she could not go out and disgrace herself on the street. At 46 Grosvenor Street, the bills were piling up. To pay them, she was borrowing money from unscrupulous moneylenders – a Mr Sam Lewis was one, a Signor Sanguinetti another – at the most exorbitant interest rates, and she was speculating on the stock-market. She often found herself borrowing merely to pay back some-one else she had borrowed from. She even sank to asking Mark to lend her money from his allowance. Supported by the Bank and backed up by Henry Cholmondeley, Tatton did not waver in his determination not to help her.

At some point, his patience snapped and, driven into a terrible rage, he made a vicious attempt to lash out at Jessie through an act of unbelievable cruelty to his son. When Mark returned from Brussels for the Easter holidays, instead of his terriers racing out of the house to greet him, barking wildly, tails wagging and tongues eager to lick his face, there was no sign of them. There was silence. The servants would not look him in the eye. Then, under instruction from his father, one of the grooms took him down Sylvia's Grove, a long carriage drive named after his great grandfather's favourite dog. There, beneath a tall beech tree by an iron gate, he met with a dreadful sight; the bodies of his beloved dogs, suspended from a branch, hanged to death on the orders of his father.

Such a vicious, cruel act shows the depths of Tatton's hatred for Jessie. Driven into a terrible rage by her behaviour, he had lost all control over himself and exacted a bitter revenge by his cruelty to the son she loved so much. It was knowledge of incidents such as this which prompted Mark's first tutor and lifelong friend, Doolis, to write to him on the occasion of his first communion, 'unless you strive and fight against circumstances, you will grow up a worthless, cruel, hardhearted, frivolous man'.[25] They were words he took to heart.

In the winter of 1896, Tatton's advisers, in particular a ruthless lawyer called Thomas Gardiner, Deputy Sheriff to the City of London, persuaded him to take a drastic step. A recent amendment to the Married Women's Property Act of 1882 stipulated that a husband would be declared free from all debts subsequently incurred by his wife if he advertised to this effect in a daily newspaper. In spite of his abject horror of the impending publicity, and the fact that this was hardly a gentlemanly thing to do, Tatton went ahead and became the first man ever to publish such a notice. It appeared on the morning of 7 December in *The Times*, *The Morning Post*, *The Standard*, *The Daily Telegraph* and *The Daily News*.

> I, SIR TATTON SYKES, Baronet, of Sledmere,
> in the County of York, and No. 46 Grosvenor
> Street, in the County of London, hereby give
> notice that I will NOT be RESPONSIBLE for
> any DEBTS or ENGAGEMENTS which my
> wife, LADY JESSICA CHRISTINA SYKES,
> may contract, whether purporting to be on my
> behalf or by my authority or otherwise.

It was a shameful act which would have had his father spinning in his grave.

What saved Mark from being completely dragged down by the hideous events being played out around him was going up to Cambridge University, in the Easter term of 1897. He was accompanied by Beck and an Irish valet, MacEwen, an old servant of his mother's. Jessie had chosen Jesus College, for reasons thoroughly typical of her. She had originally intended him to go to Trinity, but on arriving late for her appointment with the Master had given as her excuse, 'I'm sorry to be late, but I've been at the Cesarewitch.' When he replied

'Oh, and where may that be?' she interpreted his ignorance of turf affairs as stupidity, turned tail and headed to the neighbouring college, which happened to be Jesus, to put her son's name down there. 'I was going to make sure,' she said later, 'that my son was not put in the charge of a lunatic!'[26]

Mark was hardly the run-of-the-mill Cambridge student. 'I must say I was not impressed by him when he first came,' wrote one of the dons, Dr Foakes Jackson. 'He struck me as a rather undeveloped youth whose education had been neglected. I considered that he would soon vanish from the scene and be no more heard of. By slow degrees I realised that Sykes was a man of exceptional powers.'[27] His tutor, the Revd E. G. Swain of King's, whose job it was to coach him through the preliminary 'Little Go' exam, soon realised that his new charge had little, if any, interest in the task ahead of him, but was, on the other hand, head and shoulders above most of his fellow students when it came to knowledge of the world and of the important things in life, and was also excellent company. 'He never failed to be unobtrusively amusing,' he recalled, 'and, since none of us had had experiences like his, he was always interesting.' He was impressed too by how unspoiled he was. 'It would be hard to find,' he wrote, 'another instance of a wealthy young man, completely his own master, who lived so simply or held so firmly to high principles.'[28]

The most important friendship that Mark struck up in his first term at Cambridge was with the distinguished scholar, Dr Montague Rhodes James, then Dean of Kings, and later to gain fame as the celebrated writer of ghost stories M. R. James. It was his habit to hold open house each evening, and he would leave his door ajar for any student who wished to visit. He later wrote in his autobiography of 'the delirious evenings in which it was perfectly useless to think you could get anything done the moment you saw Mark put a round enquiring face (into which he would throw the expression of a stage yokel) round the edge of the door'. From nine until midnight he would hold the company spellbound with tales of his travels, impersonating the various characters he had met, or perhaps with a re-enactment of some melodrama he had seen, in which he would take all the parts himself.

James was greatly impressed by what he described as his 'amazing skill' as an actor. 'Whatever it was,' he wrote, 'there was genius in it.'[29]

Acting was a way of escaping from the troubles that overshadowed his life. His mother was now in deeper trouble than ever. The effect of his father's advertisement had been to bring all her creditors out into the open, each one clamouring for payment. Since no one would now lend her any money, she could no longer resort to the expedient of borrowing from one to pay off another. In a last ditch attempt to settle the matter once and for all, Tatton's lawyers drew up an agreement under which, in return for her promise 'not to speculate any more on the Stock Exchange or to bet for credit on the Turf', she would receive a lump sum of £12,000 to discharge her existing liabilities, and a guarantee of a future allowance of £5,000 per year plus 'pin money' out of which she would pay all the household and stable accounts in London. The signing of this might have solved the problem had it not been for the fact that there were still massive debts which Jessie had kept secret, and by the spring of 1897, the creditors were once again banging at the door. They were led by one Mr Daniel Jay, of 90 Jermyn Street, a money lender with the Telegraphic address, 'BLUSHINGLY, LONDON', who Mark was later to refer to as 'the biggest shark in London'.[30]

On several occasions, throughout 1896, Jessie had borrowed money from Jay, at the exorbitant interest rate of 60 per cent. The first such sum was £3,000 on 11 January, but by 22 October the amount owed had risen to £13,400. At an interview with Jay, Jessie had persuaded him to postpone repayment for three months while she accompanied her husband to the West Indies, after which all liabilities would be dealt with. On his return from this journey, Tatton apparently agreed once again to make a final settlement of her debts and to give her an increased allowance of £6,000 a year for the house in Grosvenor Street, so that Mark would have somewhere to entertain his friends when he began to go out into society. Mark himself was present at this meeting, one of three witnesses who heard Tatton's parting words, 'I am now going to Beckett's to get the money to settle your enormous liabilities.'[31]

The truth was he had no intention of doing any such thing. On the advice of his attorney, Gardiner, he conveniently disappeared. 'He immediately "bolted" to the Continent,' wrote Jessie to the family solicitor, James Mills, 'leaving no address, and his cruel and unmanly desertion of myself has disgraced him in the eyes of all decent people – a desertion coupled with every indignity the wit of Mr Gardiner could contrive or invent. Boards of sale were put up on the house, insolent clerks served notices on my servants in the front hall, letters to Sir Tatton were unanswered, no provision was made for my maintenance, and a number of offensive and ridiculous charges were brought against me . . .'[32]

Jessie tried one last manoeuvre. She decided to sue for divorce, her thinking being that, if she was successful, any settlement in her favour would take in the immense wealth of her husband and therefore be large enough to cover the payment of all her debts. In suing in the High Court for restitution of conjugal rights and petitioning for adequate alimony, her Counsel suggested that Tatton had a net income in excess of £70,000 a year, made up of £40,000 or more from the rents and profits of the Sledmere estate, £18,000 on various investments, and at least £14,000 from the annual yearling sales. Tatton's lawyers categorically denied this, and produced an affidavit, signed by Tatton, stating that it was no more than £17,000. In spite of Jessie challenging this and applying for an order compelling him to appear before the court for cross-examination on the subject, the Judge accepted his evidence and dismissed the case. When Jessie was offered alimony of no more than £3,000 a year, she decided to drop proceedings.

The hard-headed Gardiner now made it his business to collect any information he could which might be eventually used against Jessie. He sent his men to Yorkshire, for example, to collect statements from people willing to testify as to her drinking. One such affidavit, from the second coachman at Sledmere, James Tovell, told how he had collected her one morning in July 1894. 'I could not understand her orders,' he said, 'and she kept me driving her about from about ten until three o'clock and was unable to tell me where she wished to go.' He went on to state that 'her conduct was so notorious that onlookers frequently chaffed me on her condition'. Robert Young, the assistant station master at Malton, said 'her conduct was the subject of conversation amongst the men'.[33] It was unbearable for Mark to see his mother so humiliated, and the adverse effect this had on his schooling is reflected in his failure to pass the 'Little Go'. But there was worse to come.

Daniel Jay, impatient for his money and meeting a brick wall in the form of Tatton and Gardiner, decided to go to court to force payment of his debt. After an initial delay of one month, owing to Tatton having fallen victim to a bout of bronchial pneumonia, the case finally opened in the Queen's Bench on 12 January, 1898. Heard before the Lord Chief Justice, Lord Russell of Killowen, it was loudly trumpeted and closely followed by an eager pack of journalists from all the daily papers. Jay's claim was straightforward; that he had consistently lent money to Lady Sykes and, as evidence of this, the court would see five promissory notes all signed in 1896 by both Sir Tatton and Lady Sykes, for sums ranging from £1,200 up to £5,000. He had made repeated requests for their repayment, but to no avail. There was also an important letter, apparently signed at Grosvenor Street, on 2 January, 1897, asking Jay to accept security for payment until the return of Sir Tatton from the West Indies in March. The problem was that Tatton denied that the signatures on the notes and the letter were his.

It is easy to imagine how the ears of the press must have pricked up when they heard the opening address of Mr J. Lawson Walton QC, acting for Jay, for he did not understate 'the eccentricities of character which marked the defendant in the knowledge and estimation of his friends'.[34] He described a man of great wealth who had few outside pursuits other than church-building and horse-breeding and who, though he never betted himself, had sowed the seeds of such an interest in his young wife by expecting her to accompany him to racecourses all over England. As a result of this, he told the court, she 'engaged to a considerable extent in that form of excitement'. Sir Tatton was also parsimonious to a degree that he was prepared to allow an overdraft of £20,000 to permanently exist at his bank, in spite of the heavy interest, because he could not bear to call up the cash to pay it off. In addition to this, the jury were told that he was a recluse who never went out into society – and that since they were married, she had never once been out to a party or out to dine with him – and who shirked responsibility for the payment of almost all expenses necessary for the upkeep of two houses.

After giving a brief account of the charges, he called Jessie to the stand, and in his cross-examination of her enlarged the picture of the extraordinary Sykes marriage. Nominally, she told the jury, she was to have £1,000 a year, but it was always a fight to get it. She had found herself living in a house 'as large as Devonshire House'[35] to which very little had been done since 1801 and which then had no drains. Sir Tatton paid for nothing and whenever she applied to him for money he was very tiresome. At one point, before the birth of her son, she had even been obliged to sue him for her pin money. As a result of this attitude, she had, with his knowledge, begun to borrow money, and had been doing so for eighteen years. Her debts had consequently increased like a snowball 'and time did not improve them'. She knew, she claimed, it was 'an idiotic thing' to do, and would never have done it had she been able to get the money elsewhere.

Cross-examined by Tatton's junior QC, Mr Bucknill, she elicited laughter from the court when, in answer to his question as to whether she considered her husband was a sound businessman, she replied that in her opinion he was 'as capable of managing his own affairs as most women'.[36] As an example, she cited the fact that instead of reading his letters, many of which contained share dividends, he often just threw them in the wastepaper basket. She had once found, she recalled, a warrant for a very large sum from Spiers and Paul in the bin, and had asked him to give it to her as a reward. She also intimated to the court that Tatton knew about her betting and was very proud when she won. He would tell everybody he saw about it, and always wanted a hundred pounds out of her winnings. When asked if she was angry after he had placed the advertisement in the newpapers, she replied,

'You are not angry with people who are like children . . . He is like a child in many ways . . . Yes, like a naughty child.'[37]

Most of the notes in question, she told Mr Bucknill, were signed in Grosvenor Street, and she had explained to Tatton that she wanted him to sign them in order for her to get money. It was unlikely, she had assured him, that he would ever have to pay up. When questioned closely about the times and dates of the various notes, she became vague, saying Tatton 'did not mind what he signed' and repeating, 'He would not give me any money, so I had to borrow.' As Bucknill piled on the pressure she was reduced to repeating the defence that 'Sir Tatton knew all about it, but he had a bad memory.'

'I did not want a scandal,' said Jessie on the following morning, causing ripples of disbelieving laughter to flow round the courtroom. Her statement was in answer to a query by the Lord Chief Justice as to why, back in 1890, when she had applied to the Union Bank for a loan of £10,000, she had not simply sued her husband for the money to keep up his establishments. After then running through diverse earlier business dealings, Mr Bucknill astonished the court by claiming that altogether the colossal sum of £126,000 had gone through Jessie's hands. 'That extends over a period of twenty years,' she protested, '. . . to amounts borrowed in 1878 and 1879. I was borrowing and paying back . . . The money was necessary to keep up the sort of establishment which people in our position of life maintained.'[38]

Re-examined by Mr Walton, Jessie reiterated that all the signatures purporting to be Sir Tatton's were made by him in her presence. These included those on two cheques for £1,000 signed in 1895 in Monte Carlo, and cashed at Smith and Co.'s Bank, which Tatton subsequently claimed to be forgeries. 'Sometimes he used to say he had signed guarantees, sometimes that he had not,' Jessie rambled on, her testimony having become rather disconnected. 'It never made any difference to our way of living. He never treated me as having been guilty of a great crime. I do not think he realised what forgery meant. I have never had a cross word with him about it. I went over to Paris last October and lunched with him, and he said 'Oh, it's all the lawyers. It's not my fault.'[39] Once again, laughter filled the courtroom.

Two of Mark's tutors were now called. Robert Beresford, who succeeded Doolis, told Mr Walton that, in his opinion, the signatures, were those of Sir Tatton, though in cross-examination by Sir Edward Clarke he admitted that the last document he had seen him sign had been as far back as 1892, and that the more recent signatures 'were blurred and unlike his normal signature'. When asked by Lord Russell if he considered Sir Tatton an intelligent man, he caused a stir by answering that he had always thought him to be suffering from incipient insanity. 'He would go about in ten coats,' he told a surprised court. 'You don't mean that literally?' asked Lord Russell, adding, 'You mean two or three.' 'No I don't,' he replied. 'I mean seven or eight overcoats one over the other . . . I can swear to that distinctly, because there were five covert coats, and one or two silk coats.' When Egerton Beck was called to the stand and told the court that, in spite of Sir Tatton being 'habitually a sober man', one signature did not look as if it were written by a very sober person, Sir Edward asked, 'That observation as to sobriety does not apply to Lady Sykes?'[40] Luckily for Jessie, Lord Russell forbade that line of questioning.

The third day of the trial began with Lord Russell asking Tatton to make two copies of the letter of 2 January, with two different pens. While he was doing this, Sir Edward Clarke opened the case for the defence. The question before the jury, he said, was a simple, if serious, one. Did Sir Tatton sign the notes, or were they forgeries by Lady Sykes? 'A case more painful to an English gentleman,' he continued, 'could not be imagined.' Called to the stand, Tatton 'gave his evidence in a low voice with a slow, nervous, hesitating manner, and kept repeating his answers over and over again, repeatedly fingering the Bible which lay on the desk before him, and occasionally raising it and striking the woodwork sharply to emphasise what he said'. He had never seen the notes and he had never signed them, and he had certainly not written the letter of 2 January. He had never had any need to borrow money, he said, preferring to keep an overdraft at the bank, which could run to any amount, since the bank had securities. After the advertisement had appeared, he had agreed to make a final payment of his wife's liabilities 'to avoid scandal! To avoid scandal! To avoid scandal!'[41]

Cross-examined by Mr Walton, Tatton caused much amusement by asking if his lawyers could 'refresh his memory' about the details of the alleged Monte Carlo forgeries. So great in fact was the laughter when Mr Walton said 'No!' that Lord Russell had to threaten to empty the courtroom. Walton then did his best to try to show that Tatton really had very little memory of what he had signed and what he had not, but he could not sway him from the basic fact that when it came to the Jay notes, he was adamant that he had nothing to do with them. The copies he had made earlier of the 2 January letter were then shown to the jury, Tatton complaining that the pens he had had to write with were too thin. When Mr Walton said that that was because the original was written with a quill pen, Tatton stated, 'Well, I have not used a quill pen for forty years',[42] leaving his interrogator floundering.

In the end, the letter of 2 January turned out to be the evidence on which the outcome of the trial would hinge. It was alleged to have been written in London by Tatton and signed by both him and Jessie. Sir Edward Clarke first called three handwriting experts, each of whom voiced their opinion that the letter was not written by Sir Tatton. He also called Mr Pearson, manager of Beckett's Bank, where Tatton kept his account, a man who knew his signature better than anyone. He testified that he did not consider any of the signatures to be that of his client. Sir Edward then attempted to show that the letter could anyhow not have been written in London, because, according to the testimony of two Sledmere villagers, Sir Tatton was at Sledmere on that day, with his valet Simpson, who had returned for the annual new year village ball. Simpson, who told the court that he had never been away from Sir Tatton for a single night, confirmed this.

Mr Walton, who saw his case collapsing, now revealed that Mark was in court and, though he realised that 'it was a painful thing to ask him to give evidence on the one side or the other',[43] he invited Lord Russell to call him on to the stand so that he might be questioned as to the veracity of these dates. This the Lord Chief Justice refused to do, though he told him that he could do so himself if he so wished. Though at first Walton decided against this course of action, on the morning of the following day, destined to be the last of the trial, he changed his mind.

It was a devastating experience for Mark to be forced into the witness box to testify that one of his parents was a liar and, as Sir Edward Clarke told the jury in his summing up, his evidence was so vague and therefore so inconclusive that he might have been spared the ordeal. It was given in a barely audible whisper. In his final address, Sir Edward gave no quarter to Jessie, whom he described as a woman of 'discreditable character', for whom there could be 'no sympathy and perhaps no credence'. When it came to the turn of the counsel for the plaintiff, Mr Walton accused Tatton of being a man without honour. 'The disaster of victory,' he told the jury, 'would be infinitely greater than the disaster of defeat. To himself, if he won the case, there would be the degradation of the wife of twenty-five years, to Mr Mark Sykes the dishonour of his mother, and to Lady Sykes, it might be, other proceedings in a criminal court. At present Sir Tatton might wish to win this case, but in the evening of his days would he wish his name to be clouded with the dishonour of his wife?'[44]

In the end the jury took only forty-five minutes to decide that 'the letter of 2 January, 1897, was not in the hand of Sir Tatton Sykes'. As the newspapers were quick to point out, this verdict left Jessie in an unenviable position. 'The person upon whom the verdict of the jury fell with such crushing force last week,' commented The World, 'stands arraigned by that verdict, on a double charge of forgery and perjury; and any shrinking from the natural sequel of such arraignment will certainly be interpreted as a sign of partiality in the administration of justice.'[45]

Though a number of actions did follow the first trial, in particular an unsuccessful attempt by Tatton in February to recover various items of family jewellery pawned by Jessie, and litigation brought against Tatton by the Alliance Insurance Company – a case similar to that brought by Daniel Jay and one which he chose to settle rather than face another trial – there was never any criminal prosecution brought against Jessie, because of the problems arising from the fact that the main witness against her would have been her husband. Little good would have come of it anyway. The horrendous publicity was punishment enough, and the fact that public sympathy lay with Tatton. 'Sir Tatton Sykes may not have been the most judicious of men in the management of his household,' commented *The Times*' Leader of 19 January, 'but if his evidence is to be believed, as the jury believed it, he has shown great forbearance for a long time.'[46] On 25 April, Tatton made an application in the High Court to 'restrain Lady Sykes from going to her husband's houses in London and at Sledmere in Yorkshire'.[47] Jessie's humiliation was complete.

CHAPTER XI

The Traveller

It takes little imagination to understand the effect that the trial and the attendant cheap publicity had on Mark. 'The verdict in the Sykes case was for Sir Tatton,' wrote Sydney Bowles in her diary, 'which has hit Lady Sykes and Mark very hard. The latter told George he is not ever going to speak to or see his Father again, and he will never go to Sledmere again so long as Sir Tatton lives.'[1] The memories of his parents being held up to public ridicule and of his own experience in the witness box haunted him for ever, and he spent his life trying to escape from them. Love Sledmere though he undoubtedly did, he was to spend relatively little time there in his lifetime, preferring to devote his energies to the study and exploration of the Middle East, a part of the world that held happy childhood memories for him.

He had decided that as soon as the trial was over he would get out of the country as soon as possible and, with the permission of his Cambridge tutor, had planned a trip to Palestine and Syria. Much to his annoyance, when he informed his mother of his plans, she immediately told him that it was fine for him to go so long as he took her and her maid with him. Exasperated by her reaction, which he considered 'ridiculous', he wrote bitterly to his cousin, Henry Cholmondeley, the Sledmere land agent, ranting that the only possible reason he could see as to why Jessie had encouraged him to go to Cambridge in the first place was so she could 'come down and extort a few shillings or pounds as the case may be, to read all the letters she may find in the rooms and return to London'.[2]

Jessie's behaviour towards Mark at this time was somewhat insensitive, but born out of desperation. She really felt that she had no one else to turn to. Her friends had all dropped her. Tatton's brother,

Christopher, who had always been her friend, was now bankrupt and suffering from ill health. She could not approach her brothers, who were respectably married with families. As for her younger sister, Venetia, married to the American millionaire, Arthur James, and one of Society's top hostesses, she would have nothing to do with Jessie, whom she considered to have disgraced herself beyond all measure.

Venetia was a crashing snob who favoured the company of royalty, politicians and ambassadors, as many as possible of whom she would attempt to gather together for weekends at Coton, her self-styled country 'mansion' near Rugby. She never bothered to soft-pedal her snobbery, and she was once heard to exclaim, after studying the guests seated round her dining table, 'What? Only one Baronet and one Viscount! What a mangy weekend!' If there was one certainty in Venetia's life, it was that she would not allow a single grain of dirt from her sister's life to rub off on her.

She also spectacularly lacked Jessie's generosity, and throughout her life practised a philosophy of economy that became laughable. It utterly superseded her snobbery. The Italian Ambassador was once staying at Coton for the weekend and when, on Monday morning, he had to take a train back to London, Venetia insisted that, in order to save on the cost of petrol, he should take a lift to the station in the butcher's meat van. He was only saved from this ignominy by a fellow guest, Lady Max Muller, who told Venetia 'the Ambassador travels in the meat van over my dead body'. She became a legend in the family for countless such incidents.

When the first underground railway was opened in London, Venetia was overjoyed at the thought of how much she could save on cab fares and took to using it as much as possible. A friend of hers was once passing through Dover Street Station, when he came across a large crowd of people assembled round a ticket machine. He heard raised voices from within the *mêlée*, one of which he recognised as Venetia's. Pushing his way into the middle, he found her shaking with rage and shrieking at a harassed-looking policeman, 'Officer, I refuse to leave until this machine has been taken to pieces. I put my coin in and no ticket came out.' The ticket was only worth a penny. She was the same with the telephone. In order never to have to 'waste money' ringing people who had called her back, she keep them hanging on the line for hours until she had completed whatever she was doing and was ready to speak to them.

There were no areas in her life in which she had not become an expert at making savings. Her niece, Audrey Coates, was once walking past Venetia's London house, 3 Grafton Street, 'my second mansion' she used to call it, when her Aunt unexpectedly appeared at the front door and asked her if she would like to come in 'for a little light refreshment'. Surprised by such an unusually generous offer, Audrey eagerly accepted the invitation. As she ascended the stairs to the Drawing Room, however, she was horrified to hear Venetia calling to her housekeeper, 'Emily, Emily, if the cat has left any of its milk, bring it up for my niece.' She could not bear waste, and, where she could, would persuade the butcher to let her buy meat on sale or return. On Monday afternoons she could often be seen walking down Bond Street, carrying a dreadful greasy parcel. It would be bacon she was returning after a weekend.

New guests at Coton were warned by the regulars to expect a parsimonious regime. During the winter months, fires in the bedrooms were strictly controlled. Married couples and single ladies were allowed one; bachelors none. The food too was organised with maximum economy in mind. Thus on Fridays she would try and include as many Catholics at her dinner table, knowing that their religion required them only eat fish on that particular day, which, being cheaper than meat, would help keep down the bills. 'Fish for the Papists!' she would hiss, as the food was served. If meat was to be served to everyone, then the servants were under strict instructions to keep portions to a minimum. On one notorious occasion, when a single chicken had been eked out to feed a whole dinner party, Venetia was seen to pass a note to her butler, Went, which mysteriously read 'DCSC'. It turned out to be a code for 'DON'T CUT SECOND CHICKEN'.

Isolated as she thus was, Jessie could not let her son go and relentlessly pursued him wherever he went, a circumstance that was eventually to alienate him from her. When, in February, 1898 Mark, accompanied by his manservant, MacEwen, set out for Constantinople he arrived at the Pera Palace Hotel only to find three telegrams from Jessie already awaiting him. They read:

RETURN AT ONCE IMPORTANT.

MUST RETURN AT ONCE FATHER WILL NOT SETTLE.

ABSOLUTELY NECESSARY YOUR RETURN WILL EXPLAIN ON
ARRIVAL.

'Having read these,' he wrote to Henry Cholmondeley, 'I replied that I could not return and proceeded to the Custom House.' He at once boarded a Russian steamer bound for Jaffa,[3] where he found the Russian skipper blind drunk and cavorting with 'two lady friends from the shore'. He did not, he told Henry, expect it to be 'a pleasant voyage as I am the only other passenger'.[4]

On arrival at Jaffa, Mark took the daily train to Jerusalem, where he was greeted by the same guide who had looked after him and his father on one of their previous trips to the Holy Land. Isa Kubrusli was a Cypriot Christian, a striking looking man with piercing eyes, a prominent hooked nose and a long white beard, who had served in the past as dragoman, or interpreter, to a number of important Englishmen, notably Frederick Thesiger in the Abyssinian Campaign of 1867–8, Sir Charles Wilson on his expedition to Mount Sinai, and more recently to the unfortunate Professor Edward Palmer, murdered by Arab terrorists while on a secret mission for the British Government in 1882. 'Thirty years ago,' Mark wrote in an account of one of his journeys, 'a dragoman was a person of importance; a man similar in character to the confidential courier who in the last century accompanied young noblemen on the Grand Tour. But he has degenerated and for the most part is now simply a bear leader, to hordes of English and Americans who invade Syria during the touring season.'[5]

By the time the Sykeses first met him, this was exactly the fate that had befallen Isa, who was working for the Jerusalem office of Thomas Cook, on hire to English tourists. Isa had a very poor opinion of most of his clients. Unlike the rich and cultured gentlemen he had encountered in the old days, who wore beards, could ride and shoot beautifully, and were liberal with 'baksheesh', 'many very fat and wear rubbish clothes,' he used to say; 'many very old men; many very meselable; some ride like monkeys; and some I see afraid from the horses. Den noder kind of Henglish he not believe notin; he laugh for everything and everybody; he call us poor meselable black; he say everything is nonsense and was no God and notin . . .'[6]

Mark's plan was to ride east of the Jordan, as far as it was possible, and then take a route north to Damascus through the remote, mountainous country of the Haurân, which borders the Syrian desert and was home to the Druses. After various delays, which gave him the opportunity to fill a note book for Monty James with copies of various Greek inscriptions he had found, the party finally set off. 'On Thursday, 10 March, 1898, I left Jericho,' wrote Mark in an account he later wrote up for the Palestine Exploration Fund, 'accompanied by my English servant, five muleteers, a dragoman, a native servant, a cook, an Armenian photographer . . . and by Sheikh Fellah, of the Adwân tribe.' They spent their first night at the Sheikh's camp at El Hammam, where the poor photographer was set upon. Mark related how 'The Arabs, every man of whom carried a weapon of some sort, struck terror into the heart of the Armenian. They dug him in the ribs with a pistol, upset his camera, whereat he wept, and remembered he had pressing business at Jericho. He wanted to return at once, but I persuaded him to take four photographs . . .'[7]

To begin with Mark religiously followed the route mapped out in *Murray's Handbook*, by far the best travel guide of the day, which would take him east towards the Jebel Ed-Druse and then north to Damascus. It was an exciting trip, full of incident and adventure, which served its purpose of taking his mind off recent events and strengthened his fascination with the Arab world. Wherever he went he befriended the Sheikhs of different tribes, who told him of the local sights, kept him fed and watered, and more importantly gave him their protection. At Jerash, for example, he was prevented from being arrested for not being in possession of the right papers by Sheikh Hamid Bey, who remembered having met him some years previously when he was travelling with his father. He invited him to dinner. 'Of course the meal was much richer than the simple Bedawîn fare,' Mark recalled. 'It consisted of rice, mutton, olives, several native condiments in saucers, sour milk, and a large flap of brown bread for each person, which was also used as a plate. As I was present, each person was provided with a spoon! When we had finished dinner and drunk the sour milk, it provided a meal for at least twenty men waiting outside.'[8]

En route from Jerash to Edhra'a, Mark was lucky enough to witness the extraordinary spectacle of a Hajj pilgrimage on its way to Mecca. They came upon it suddenly one evening, a mass of tents of every shape and form that seemed to go on for miles, and a gathering of people of an infinite variety. He reckoned there were at least 10,000 civilians in the column that set off at five the following morning, under an escort of 500 mounted infantry, and a mountain battery. 'The enormous procession, at least four miles long,' he wrote, 'glittering with red, green, and gold saddles and ornaments, was an impressive sight that I shall never forget; for every animal had at least four bells on its saddle or neck. I could hear it like the sound of the sea, quite half an hour after the last of the procession had started.'[9]

The highlight of Mark's journey occurred at Radeimeh, to the east of the Jebel, where the Sheikh was particularly hospitable, giving dinner not only to Mark, but to his muleteers and servants. 'The sight of MacEwen,' recalled Mark, 'sitting between two Druse Sheikhs and being solemnly crammed by them with rice and bread dipped in oil and pieces of mutton was, to say the least, quaint.'[10] When dinner was over, the Sheikh took Isa aside and told him about a place in the desert named Heberieh, 'where there were many arms, legs and fingers sticking in the stones'. No European had yet visited this strange site, which he said was a long ride away and would need an escort of at least fifteen men. Such a tale was every explorer's dream. *Murray's Handbook* made no mention of it, and Mark was determined to go there in the hope of making a discovery.

At four the following morning, the party set off and after two hours riding found themselves in country which Mark described as being some of the most extraordinary he had ever seen in the course of his extensive travels. He wrote of it as

> a fireless hell; nothing else could look so horrible as that place. Enormous blocks of black shining stones were lying in every direction; in places we passed great ridges some twenty feet high and split down the centre. One of these stretched over a mile and looked like a gigantic railway cutting. There was neither a living thing in sight, nor the least scrub to relieve the eye from the monotony of the slippery black rocks. My dragoman said to me 'I tink one devil he live here.' After four hours' hard riding through this inferno, the party reached an open space in the centre of which was a hill. The Druses announced that they had reached their destination.
>
> At first I thought the hill was only a mass of lava and sand, but on closer examination I found that it was a huge mass of bones and lava caked with bones. It was infested with snakes; I myself saw four gliding through the bones.[11]

The site covered three acres and must, he reckoned, have contained the remains of many millions of animals. After gathering a few specimens of the bones and taking a number of photographs, the party rode back to their camp, and thereafter continued on their way to Damascus, where the trip ended.

In the autumn of 1898, there took place what was to prove to be the most important event in Mark's life. It is somewhat ironical that his great love affair should have been with the sister of one of Jessie's lovers. Jack Gorst's father, Sir John Eldon Gorst, was MP for Cambridge, and Mark was often invited over for tea on Sunday afternoons to the family home, Howes Close, where he was welcomed into the fold. This was considerable, Jack having five younger sisters and a younger brother. The middle sister, Edith, a tall handsome girl aged twenty-six with masses of thick chestnut hair, was of immediate interest to Mark, since she was a convert to Roman Catholicism and, with this in common, the two struck up a firm friendship. She shared his love of the outdoors and was an accomplished horsewoman, and the two of them spent many a happy hour riding and walking. After the bitter intrigues of his own family life, Mark found the natural affection and good humour which existed between the Gorst children refreshing, and he began to spend more and more time with them. Edith had a down-to-earth approach to life, which attracted him to her, and the two became inseparable companions. 'I like you,' he was to write to her, 'because you are honest and unselfish, because you are the only truly straightforward person I have ever met.'[12]

His new friendship with Edith and his excitement about his travels gave Mark a new strength to deal with the omnipresent spectre of his mother, who, in spite of having been making a desperate attempt since the trial to turn over a new leaf, stopping gambling and cutting down on her drinking, was very low. She had moved out of her house in Grosvenor Street into 2 Chesterfield Street, a legacy, left to her in the will of her brother-in-law, Christopher, for whom she had done a great deal in the latter years of his life, when he was plagued by illness, and his financial troubles mirrored her own.

It was typical of Jessie that at a time when she was in dire straits, she should have simultaneously reached out to help others in similar circumstances. Blinded by his royal connections and quite unable to bow to the wishes of his bankers and curb his lavish spending, Christopher had simply run out of money. First had gone his beloved Brantingham Thorpe, then his house in Seamore Place had been sold to Alfred Rothschild, and then bankruptcy loomed. No help was forthcoming from his brother. As for the inhabitant of Marlborough House, upon whom this fortune had been lavished, he could do no more than whisper 'what a thoroughly bad business!' it all was. Jessie, outraged by his behaviour, took it upon herself to force Prince Albert to help out his old friend. 'He feels ill, old, lonely and miserable and impecunious,' she had written to him in the autumn of 1896. 'This is pitiable enough, if I may venture to say it. I do hope Your Royal Highness will not be hard on him. He is, as you know, so easily led, and is not morally to blame for much which in another one would with difficulty forgive.'[13] She demanded and got an interview. What took place during that meeting can only be a subject for speculation, though it was hinted that she threatened to reveal certain facts about HRH. which would have been severely embarrassing to him. Suffice it to say that soon after it took place, Christopher's debts were paid.

He was a broken man, however, who spent the remainder of his days as a displaced person, an endless guest on a prolonged tour of country houses. It was not a role which suited him, and his decline can be seen in the photographs which graced the visitors' books of the period, in which he appears no longer as the tall imposing figure of earlier years, but as a faded and tired-looking old man surrounded by a younger and more glamorous set. Ill health, brought on by constant anxiety about his finances, resulted in a number of minor strokes, the most serious of which took place in the summer of 1898. While recuperating in the fashionable Spa of Homburg, he received a summons from his old friend Prince Albert to visit him on the Royal Yacht, where he was languishing, bored, with a broken ankle. In spite of being too ill to travel, Christopher forced himself to make the journey, a decision that was to prove to be the death of him.

When the Prince saw his old friend, he bitterly regretted having summoned him and on his return to England he wrote to Tatton begging him to help his brother. 'If you could *without delay*,' he asked, 'make some permanent arrangement so that his remaining years could be peaceful and free from care, you would be doing what would be perceived by all his friends and relatives as an act of much needed and timely generosity. "Blood is thicker than water" and I feel sure that you must view with great concern the unhappy condition in which your poor Brother is.'[14] Such sentiments came too late, however, for Christopher's strength had failed him for the last time, and a month later he died. He was buried at Brantingham Thorpe on 20 December. Jessie was the chief mourner, neither Tatton nor the Prince of Wales choosing to attend, though the latter did attend a simultaneous memorial service at the Curzon Chapel in Mayfair. Perhaps it was lucky he was not present at the graveside, since he might not have been able to suppress a fit of laughter at the most solemn part of the ceremony. As the coffin was lowered into the ground it got stuck, being too big for the hole that had been dug, and had to be raised again. It was an unfortunate final moment for a man who, for so much of his life, had been the butt of practical jokes.

Before returning to the Haurân, which the Cambridge authorities had given him permission to do during the Lent term of 1899, Mark was determined to arrange a meeting with his father and the lawyers in order to persuade them to reach a final settlement with his mother. 'This is the last chance . . . and worth trying,' he wrote to Henry Cholmondeley in December; 'my mother is really broken and would accept any reasonable terms. I hope I can trust you to arrange this meeting as after that I should feel quite unresponsible for any further disgraces and that I had done all possible to stop it . . .'[15]

Confident that he had set the wheels in motion to try to help his mother, he prepared to set out for Syria. On the eve of his departure he went to Mass in Cambridge to take one last look at Edith, an event which reinforced his feelings for her. 'When I saw you leave the church and I went away without a word,' he wrote to her on his return, 'if you knew how I felt that day, how I shook as if with an ague, with my mouth and trembling steps, how I watched you go away further and further, and by quickening my steps I could have caught you up and didn't for fear that you might have some small inkling what was in my mind before I chose you should, because I thought to myself, perhaps I am only in love . . .'[16]

Though Mark's intention on his second Eastern trip was to spend three or four months in the Syrian desert, things did not quite work out that way, as when he reached Damascus in the early days of 1899, he found himself unable to get the necessary travel permit. Instead he decided to cover new ground, travelling to Aleppo, and east along the Euphrates to Baghdad, then north to Mosul, Van and the Russian border, coming home by way of Mount Ararat, Erivan and Batoum. It was a long and challenging journey. As well as Isa, who once again acted as his guide, he took with him 'a cook, a waiter, four muleteers and a groom; seven Syrian mules . . . two good country horses for myself and one each for the cook and the waiter; a Persian for the dragoman; and last, though not least, a Kurdish sheepdog that answered to the name of Barud, *i.e.* Gunpowder, and not only attended the pitching and striking of the camp but after nightfall undertook the entire responsibility of guarding it'.[17]

The party left Damascus on 17 January, and the weather was so atrocious, with constant heavy rain and hail storms turning to snow, that Mark was driven to telegraphing for a carriage to take him to Aleppo. An 'antique monstrosity', drawn by four horses abreast, eventually arrived. 'It had the appearance of a decayed bandbox on a brewer's dray,' he wrote in his account of the journey, 'and, as I found to my cost, was extraordinarily uncomfortable.'[18] Their first stop was at the village of Hasieh, 'the most desolate and filthy little village that it has ever been my luck to visit'. The guest house consisted 'of a large heap of offal with four rooms leading off it: the first and best was occupied by the cow; the second, which was not quite so clean, was given to me; in the other two most of the villagers were gathered together to watch my cook preparing what he called "roast whale and potted hyaena", that is roast veal and potted ham'.[19]

It was a miracle that they ever reached Aleppo, considering that the troublesome coachman made an attempt to sabotage the journey by deliberately overturning the coach. The ensuing scene was described by Mark as reminding him 'of those admirable pictures drawn in Christmas numbers of illustrated papers of Gretna Green elopements coming to grief in a ditch'.[20] When they did finally reach their destination, he found it 'not altogether a pleasant town'. The natives had a penchant for throwing stones at the hats of foreigners, and often had faces disfigured by 'Delhi Boils', which gave them 'a most sinister expression'. Almost everyone he met, he wrote, who was not a native, 'seemed to be trying to get away from the place, without success'.[21]

Six days in Aleppo was quite enough. The party then struck out for Baghdad. Not a day went by without Mark being either amused or frustrated by the Oriental character. 'Their ideas of time and space are *nil*,' he noted. 'If you ask how far away a certain village is, you may be told "one hour", be the real distance anything from five minutes to twelve hours; or, when you are beginning to feel tired, everyone you ask during the space of a couple of hours may tell you that you are only "seven hours" from your destination. This is really . . .

most annoying.' At Meskeneh he got his first view of the Euphrates, which did not greatly impress him. 'Its water is so muddy,' he noted, 'that it is impossible to see through a wine-glass filled with it.'[22]

Meskeneh was the first of a series of military outposts, manned by police or mounted infantry, which lined the high road from Aleppo to Baghdad. They were intended to help keep order in the valley, and to prevent the Anezeh Arabs from crossing the Euphrates, and it was at one of these that Mark now spent each night. When he finally reached the first bridge across the river at Fallūjah, the final stop before Baghdad, he was amused by what he found there. 'There is a telegraph wire which crosses the river but there is no telegraph office; the only official in the place is the collector of tolls who dozes most of the day on the bridge; there are no troops; and there is no police station within twenty miles of the bridge. There is therefore nothing to prevent any number of people crossing it . . . Truly the ways of the Unspeakable are inscrutable.'[23]

After days of trekking through the desert, the approaching minarets of Baghdad were a wondrous sight. 'The golden mosque appeared in the distance in the midst of a cluster of palm trees, and . . . the effect was very beautiful and inspiring.' Once within the city walls, however, although he was impressed by its cleanliness, Mark found little to inspire him, and after spending an enjoyable week staying with the English Resident, he was keen to be on his way to Mosul. Apart from a fairly close shave at Kirkūk, when they came under fire from some robbers, the journey passed without incident and as they approached the city, Mark was able to give further rein to his love of underlining the comic and exaggerating the grotesque. 'The first thing that struck me,' he recalled, '. . . was a splendid bridge. It is a fine piece of work-manship and has only one fault; it does not cross the river. The engineer commenced building it about 170 yards from the bank; he built twenty-four piers, and at the twenty-fourth came to the water. Then after due consideration he thought that he would build the bridge with boats, and these he chained to the end of the masonry. Though this structure is useless as a bridge, it makes an excellent rendezvous for beggars, lepers and sweetmeat vendors.'[24]

The hardships of the journey increased after Mosul. They were constantly on the look out for robbers, often mule-rustlers, and as they began to climb up into the mountains, the terrain became more treacherous, with rushing rivers and streams, non-existent roads and tracks that were impassable to anything but mules. It was bitterly cold, but the scenery was magnificent. 'Overhead was a blue sky, below, the vegetation, such as it was, was green as an emerald,' wrote Mark. 'We were among high mountains, whose ruggedness was relieved here and there by clumps of stunted trees. There was snow on the peaks, and down the sides of the mountains streams rushed frantically . . . In one place we had to pass a very rickety patched-up bridge . . . Isa when crossing missed his footing and only by the greatest good luck I caught him by the band of his Ulster. Even now it makes me shudder to think of what might have happened to him; for there was a drop of forty feet into a river running like a mill race towards the mass of rocks over which it fell.'[25]

As Mark and his party drew closer to Bitlis, a strategic Armenian town that was to see 15,000 of its inhabitants massacred by the Turks in July, 1916, they began to see more and more snow, which soon became so deep that they had to drag their mounts through it. His plan had been to head straight from here to the Black Sea port of Trebizond, and then home, but when this proved impossible he was forced to go to Van instead. This meant abandoning the muleteers in favour of fifteen man-sledges, each of which could carry a hundred pounds weight of baggage. One of them even had the added weight of Isa, who fearful of getting cold, had drunk a whole bottle of mastic, the local aniseed-flavoured spirit, and had become so drunk that he had to be tied face-down on to his sledge. Mark was astonished at the strength of the men who pulled these sledges. 'They kept up a pace of about three and a half miles an hour,' he noted. 'They mounted steepish hills with only raw hide lashed under the soles of their feet, and they only rested for five minutes or so every three quarters of an hour. The heavy breathing of the sledge-draggers, the gentle zipping of the sledges as they passed over the snow, the occasional moaning of the drunken man, and the stamping of the cold feet had such an effect on me that a couple of hours after leaving Bitlis I was fast asleep.'[26]

The sun rose on the waters of Lake Van, which the party now had to cross by means of a fifty-ton fishing boat, the *Jámi*, hired from and captained by its Armenian owner. Though at first all went well, after two hours the wind dropped, and there followed a fearful nocturnal storm during which the sail split, water began to seep in, and the boat began to list alarmingly. The crew, including the skipper, panicked and proved useless, and when Mark tried to get Isa to help him get the ballast straight, he became 'quite childish, and . . . screamed "Why you bring me to this debil country? I say bad word for the day I came with you; rubbish boat, rubbish captain, rubbish sea; I say bad word for the religion of this lake!"'[27] In the end he was reduced to watching over the ballast and bailing by himself. It was, he confessed, 'one of the most dismal vigils I have ever kept'.[28]

The storm had abated by sunrise, and the shore was in sight. Their plight had been noted from the shore by a Kurdish horseman, who galloped along the cliffs and, with the aid of a stout whip, persuaded a group of Armenians to tow the *Jámi* to safety. In Van Mark spent a week with the British consul, Captain Maunsell, before setting out on the slow and arduous trek to the Russian border. The last part of this journey, over a high mountain pass, was almost too much for Isa, the rarefied air giving him heart palpitations. He 'threw himself on the ground gasping,' wrote Mark, 'unable to walk any farther. I tried to carry him on my back but the result was that we both rolled head over heels in the snow; so I got out the medicine chest and gave him a mixture of ginger, brandy and opium which I find is a very good pick-me-up for Orientals.'[29] Eight days after finally reaching the Russian border, Mark reached Akstapha, where he boarded the Trans-Caucasian railway bound for Tiflis and Batoum, port of call for the steamer to Constantinople.

By the time Mark returned to England, it was six months since he had seen Edith, and as soon as he got to Cambridge, he invited her to dinner. In a letter he wrote to her the following year, he touched on his feelings that night. 'After an interval in which I neither wrote nor spoke of you to any man, you may remember how I dined with you the night after my return to Cambridge, and how little I spoke at dinner, and then only did I know that I had a real *affection* for you.' He added, 'I tell you, if . . . you had a hump in the middle of your back, a beard like a Jew, eyes that squinted both ways, were bald as a highroad, and had only three black teeth in a mouth like a cauldron, still my affection for you would be the same.'[30]

Not only was he in love, he was now, after his two great solo journeys, a *bona fide* adventurer, with the manuscript of a book, to be called *Through Five Turkish Provinces*, in the pipeline. He was also making a name for himself in college journalism, making regular contributions to his old friend George Bowles's *Granta*, in which, as well as writing leaders, skits and drama criticism, he exercised his burgeoning talent as a caricaturist. With a new friend, Edmund Sandars, he also co-edited a journal of their own, *The Snarl*, 'An Occasional Journal for Splenetics', which anticipated the snappish writings of modern-day journalists like Auberon Waugh and Michael Bywater. For the first time in his life, he seemed to be finding his way, only to find the road blocked by war.

Since 1897, Mark had had a commission in a volunteer militia battalion, the Princess of Wales's Yorkshire Regiment, and in November, 1899 he learned that his regiment had been called up to go to South Africa to fight in the Boer War. This news came only shortly after he had received a letter from his cousin Willie Pakenham informing him that Jessie, accompanied by her maid, and carrying with her two suitcases containing Bovril, jelly, tobacco and a number of Catholic prayer books, had herself set off for the war, her destination being a hospital for the treatment of enteric, situated in a former convent in Natal. 'Having had more experiences of travel in foreign and even barbarous countries, than most of my country-women,' she had explained, 'I thought I would go out to the Cape, spend six or seven weeks there, and try if I could not be some little use or service.'[31] Unfortunately her maid had panicked and abandoned her in Madeira, since when there had been no word of her. It was Willie's suggestion that Mark should waste no time in going out to look for her. All the old worries came flooding back. 'I never seem to get a month's peace,' he wrote exasperatedly to Henry Cholmondeley. 'No sooner does mother get fairly settled than she starts off on a wild goose chase like this and now I am forced to follow her, what I shall do when I get there, how I shall find where she is, or what she is doing I do not know, what I shall do when I find her I cannot conceive . . . If this is to be the kind of thing I am to be the victim of for the next thirty years I cannot say I look forward with pleasurable anticipation to the future.'[32]

As things turned out Mark never did have to go searching for his mother for she was home within three months, but his eventual departure for South Africa was greatly delayed by his desperate attempts to try to settle her affairs before he left. His solicitors had informed him that his mother's debts amounted to £120,000, being made up of £18,000 plus 5 per cent interest owed to the Alliance Assurance Co., £80,000 in gross liabilities, £10,000 plus £4,000 interest to the money lender, Sanguinetti, and £8,000 in private loans. Since his father claimed to have an annual income of no more than £17,000, and the total Sledmere assets were put at £350,000, Mark had an all-too-real fear that the whole lot might 'go to the thieves shelter'. The knowledge that his father would more than probably remain immovable put him under enormous pressure to step in himself, in spite of the dangers of such a move. 'If I make myself liable for all these immense sums,' he wrote to Edith, 'and no arrangement can be made with my father, with the Estate duty added to all, I shall stand in a somewhat precarious position, and that's annoying as I have never seen the money.' What he found most humiliating, however, was 'to be constantly arguing on a hypothesis of my father's death which is to me the most humiliating and loathsome feature of my repulsive affairs'.[33]

Round and round in circles Mark and his father went, with the Dickensian lawyer Gardiner always immovable, and his mother over-emotional and unstable. This war at home, and the war in South Africa, overshadowed all other events. Mark's coming of age, for example, on 16 March, 1900, which should have been the cause for great celebrations at Sledmere, passed virtually unnoticed, other than

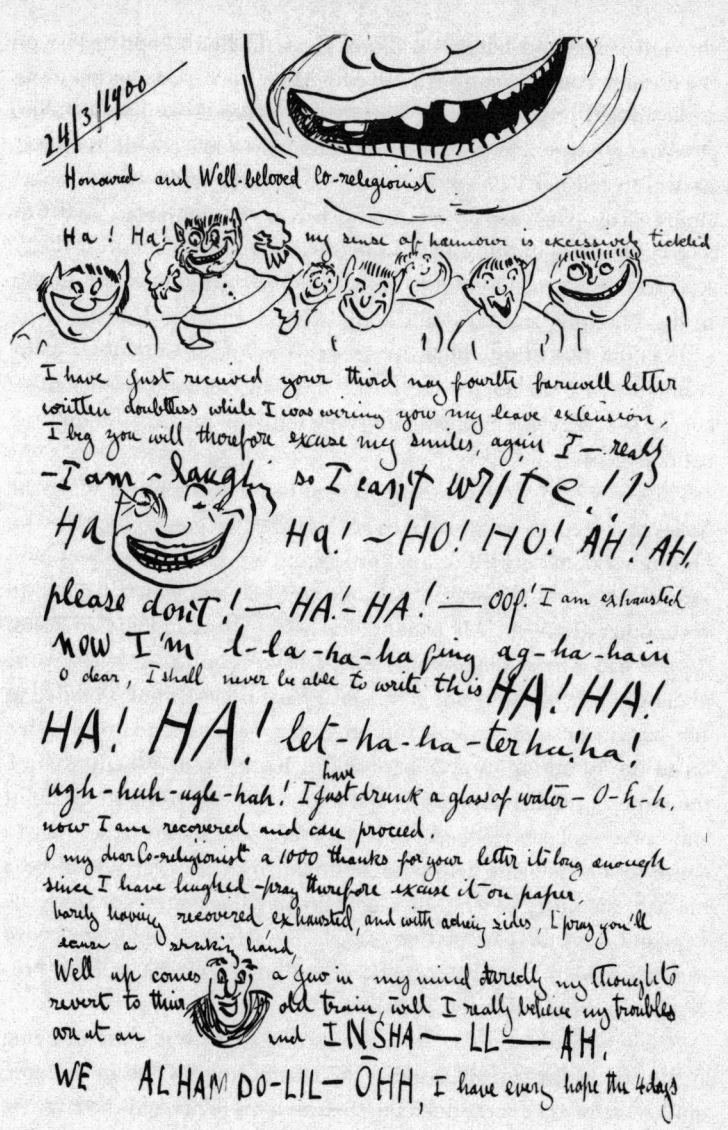

24/3/1900

Honoured and Well-beloved Co-religionist

Ha! Ha! my sense of harmour is excessively tickled

I have just received your third nay fourth farewell letter written doubtless while I was wiring you my leave extension, I beg you will therefore excuse my smiles. again I — really — I am — laugh, so I can't WRITE. !! HA Ha! ~ HO! HO! AH! AH! please don't! — HA! HA! — oof! I am exhausted NOW I'm l - la - ha - ha-fing ag - ha - hain o dear, I shall never be able to write this HA! HA! HA! HA! let - ha - ha - ter ha! ha! ugh - huh - ugle - hah! I have just drunk a glass of water — O - k - k. now I am recovered and can proceed.

o my dear Co-religionist a 1000 thanks for your letter it is long enough since I have laughed — pray therefore excuse it on paper, barely having recovered exhausted, and with achieg sides, I pray you'll excuse a shaky hand,

Well up comes a few in my mind directly my thoughts revert to this old train, will I really believe my troubles are at an end INSHA — LL — AH. WE ALHAM DO-LIL- OHH, I have every hope the 4 days

through letters and telegrams. Through it all, Edith kept the lid on
the pressure cooker, acting as a valve for Mark's occasional outpourings
of steam and probably saving him from a nervous breakdown. 'You
gave me courage and good humour enough to last out till the end,'
he was to tell her. 'Thank God you exist.'[34] He wrote to her on an
almost daily basis, always addressing her as 'Honourable and Well-
beloved Co-religionist,' and signing off TT, or Terrible Turk. 'Today
is a bad one for me,' he wrote on 2 April, 'my father now saying that
he'll do nothing at all. I don't know what is going to happen, there
is no doubt that other influences are at work and how they are to be
counteracted I do not know. I feel very dejected and suspicious of
everyone and everything, you are really the only person I can put my
confidence in . . .'[35]

For every step forward, there seemed to be a step back. When he
finally managed, two days later, to get his father to agree to a settlement,
his mother then decided to hold out against a portion of the proposed
agreement, which she was in no position to do and which resulted in
yet another deadlock. 'My patience has been exhausted,' he told Edith.
'I have had a most unpleasant scene, I have been called every name
under the sun but I do not care, and I have done I think as much as
any human creature would, the proverbial last straw has been piled
on to the labouring camel's back and it has broken. Whether you'll
think me an unfilial hound I do not know, but everyone has his limit,
and mine has been reached.'[36] He was then told by his father that to
come to a settlement before he returned from the war would be a
mistake, 'because, says he, "I might be killed and then of course he
wouldn't have to pay anything at all."'[37] All this achieved was to
strengthen Mark's resolve to settle everything before he went to prevent his mother being left penniless.

A letter written on 17 April, shows that Mark was close to being
at the end of his tether. Alone at the Marlborough Club in London,
on the eve of yet another meeting between his father and the lawyers,
he saw no end in sight to his worries. 'A surly misanthropy begins to
pervade my nature,' he confessed to Edith. 'I hate my kind, I hate, I
detest human beings, their deformities, their cheating, their cunning,

all fill me with savage rage, their filthiness, their very stench appals me ... The stupidity of the wise, the wickedness of the ignorant, but you must forgive, remember that I have never had a childhood, remember that I have always had the worst side of everything under my very nose.'[38]

Three days later, on the evening of 20 April, a solution was finally thrashed out at a meeting in the Metropole Hotel in London. 'After arguing, fighting, changing, erasing, quarrelling, cursing, to-ing and fro-ing,' he recounted to Edith, 'from 9.45 pm to 1.00 am', it was agreed that a mortgage of £100,000 should be raised from the Alliance to pay off the debts. From then on Jessie would receive an annual allowance of £5,000, from which a third would be deducted to help pay off the interest on the loan, while Mark would receive £2,000 per annum, out of which he would give his mother £500 annually. 'At last it is done,' he wrote, 'and I start for SA tomorrow, thank God! Alhamdollilah!'

The first nine months in South Africa were a pretty miserable experience for Mark, mainly because he was bored to tears. One of his first postings was at a place called Barkley Bridge, twenty-five miles inland from Port Elizabeth. 'My business is to guard a bridge with fifty men, sleep ten hours, read three hours, and eat, drink and smoke the rest of the twenty-four,' he wrote to Doolis.[39] He described himself as feeling like 'a squeezed lemon'.[40] Frustrated by the lack of any enemy activity, he kept the men employed building a rifle range, constructing a mud fort and carrying out endless alarm practices. The rest of the time he passed either reading them Shakespeare aloud, or dreaming up another Eastern adventure which he intended to pursue as soon as the opportunity arose. 'O for the East, the East and real feelings,' he wailed. 'Allah Ho Akbar, Din we el Mohamad! There fighting is real fighting, blind healthy rage and fury! Here it is stealth and dodging, nothing else!'[41]

In August a letter arrived which did little to raise Mark's spirits, containing as it did news that, once again, his mother's debts had been far greater than she had acknowledged. 'I am absolutely determined to do no more,' he told Edith. 'I have been cozened and humbugged long enough and I will not be responsible for a series of follies and extravagances which will continue for ever. Four years ago I said that there would be no peace or rest until my mother had no control of any money. I am more convinced of this than I was then.' He admitted to her that in his present frame of mind, it was no more than a sense of duty which compelled him to help. 'I have lost all affection,' he confessed sadly.[42] Self-pity, never far away, began to get the upper hand again. 'It is always the greatest puzzle to me how it can be that you should care about me . . . with my ridiculous appearance, which you will admit I never take trouble to conceal, my awkward manner, my eccentric ways, my sour, savage, unconditional nature which all go to combine TT in one foul excrescence . . . if you only knew the difference you made to me, it is you and you only who save me from being one of the most inhuman monsters that burden the earth.'[43]

In December, things began to look up when the regiment was transferred, on Christmas Eve, to Rhenoster Bridge. This was to prove a turning point in Mark's experience of the Boer War and for the first time he felt he was doing something that was worthy of his abilities. He also had his baptism of fire. 'At last we have had a fight,' he wrote to Henry Cholmondeley on 30 December, 'it was not a very grand affair, but at any rate we have been under fire, and so can wear the medal without shame . . . We stole about 800 sheep and looted ten chickens. The whole manoeuvre was on a par with that masterpiece of strategy of the late Duke of York who 'marched up a hill with 20,000 men/And when he got to the top/He marched them down again.'[44]

Feeling that he was now part of the war, even if he did despise it as a 'filthy business' with 'neither honour or glory in it', he threw himself into the business of soldiering, concentrating his attentions on a subject that had interested him since childhood, and that, in an era of trench warfare, was of the greatest importance: that of field fortifications. 'When I was a little boy,' he later wrote, 'I made myself familiar with the field work manuals of the eighteenth century, and when the Boers had lost all their artillery, eighteenth-century field works were the very thing – out of date against a modern army with artillery but perfectly sound against ordinary rifle fire. I adopted in the Boer War most of the hints I had picked up from Marshal Saxe's *Art of War*, (1740).'[45]

He devised a trench system, constructed at certain points along the railway, its purpose being to secure the line and save lives. Using his own initiative, and quite against army regulations, he had used black South African workmen, of whom he had a high opinion, to carry out the work. 'They are really rather nice people,' he wrote to Doolis, '(I like them better than Englishmen) but Hush-sh-sh-sh-sh-sh! what dreadful Blasphemy have I whispered. They cheer me every morning, and volunteer to work for me, I give them a good pinch of snuff every other evening . . . They are different to Arabs as they continually roar with laughter . . .'[46] Mark waged a running battle with the authorities over their inability to see the merits of using native labour to build fortifications rather than waste soldiers. He was shocked by the total disregard they had for either the lives or the abilities of the blacks, as demonstrated in the diet they were fed. 'How like our nicompoops,' he fumed to Edith, 'to feed them on salt beef, one pound per day, and biscuit, one pound per day, men who never touch meat, and whose fare from their infancy has been mealie pap and sugar. However I have put that piece of folly straight.'[47] Much to the annoyance of his superiors, he issued all his black workmen with army staff hats, of which they were inordinately proud and which encouraged them to work all the harder.

He had soon refined the defences of Rhenoster Bridge to a point where he felt that 100 men could hold out there against 600 of the enemy, and was told by the Chief Engineer that the bridge was the best on the line. But, in spite of being congratulated on his fortifications by the GOC in person and having them taken as a model for several other places, there was no promotion forthcoming and he received little credit for his innovations. Mark put this down to his reluctance to socialise with his senior officers at Bloemfontein or Port Elizabeth.

Somebody had noticed the young officer's ingenuity, however, for in the autumn, much to his dismay, Mark was taken away from his regiment and attached to the Royal Corps of Engineers at Honigspruit, where he was put in charge of a garrison called Amerika Siding. His instructions here were to transform a fortress intended for 300 men into one that could be defended by fifty. Though the work was hard and tiring, and he was supervising a labour force of eighty black workmen, 'some of whom are so old they cannot walk, others so ill they cannot stand', in three weeks he had completed five miles. 'I wish you could see me at work with the blacks,' he wrote to Edith. 'There is always a tremendous din and dust and howling and laughing and roaring and swearing, which combined with the heat makes an exhausting atmosphere.' Once again his attempts to promote black labour proved fruitless. 'I only got jeers and jokes for my pains,' he complained. The work at Amerika Siding did however earn him promotion.

Captain Sykes returned to England in May 1902 sporting a moustache and suffering from partial deafness, the result of poor treatment following an ear infection. Sledmere awaited his arrival there with anticipation, eager to push out the boat for the belated twenty-first birthday celebrations of the heir. 'The 3rd Batt. Yorks Regt. Is Dis-embowelled,' he wrote to Edith from Richmond, on 15 May. 'The men went away yesterday, I have to go to Sledmere tomorrow to be received in state.'[48] Since the railway was blocked between Malton and Fimber by a derailed train, Mark made the journey to Fimber by car, where he was greeted by a banner bearing the words WELCOME WELCOME, under which were assembled members of the 2nd East Yorkshire Battalion and a hundred leading members of the estate, all mounted. Much to his discomfort, after listening to a brief welcoming speech, Mark then had to ride the three miles to Sledmere in an open carriage flanked by postilions and led by a marching band, the procession following behind.

Unfortunately it was a typical East Yorkshire day. The rain pelted down and the village street was lined with people sheltering under umbrellas. A huge arch trimmed with horseshoes and bearing the words GOOD LUCK spanned the road, while a second proclaimed HONOUR THE BRAVE. From every building hung bunting, flowers and evergreen boughs, while children waving Union Jacks crowded the pavements. At the entrance to the village, a group of labourers and employees of the estate proceeded to take the horses out of the carriage, and draw it through the street to the main lodge gates where there stood a raised platform. Here, beneath another arch welcoming Mark home, the oldest tenant on the estate presented Sledmere's now rather damp hero with an illuminated address congratulating him on his service to his country. By this time it was raining so hard and the sky was so dark that proceedings were brought to a speedy conclusion. There was no sign of Tatton. He was travelling. That night, his first back at home for so many months, Mark dined with only his cousin, Henry Cholmondeley, for company.

Three weeks later, his coming-of-age celebrations, which had been previously postponed owing to his departure for South Africa, finally took place when several hundred local dignitaries, tenants and villagers were invited to a grand supper-ball. Two huge marquees had been erected in the park and no expense had been spared on their decoration. A multitude of pennons and flags decked the roof of the supper-tent, in which the guests first assembled, the walls of which were hung with crimson drapery, while every pole was adorned with a combination of laburnum, lilac, laurel and spruce. Each table was covered with flowers and behind the high table there hung a blue banner with 'MS 1879–1900' embroidered upon it in gold. When supper was over the speeches and toasts, to Mark's relief, were kept mercifully short. The company then moved into the equally splendid dancing-tent, whose green and white striped walls were hung with hundreds of ornamental oil lamps, their glittering lights reflected in a profusion of mirrored panels. Huge Japanese umbrellas, twenty foot in diameter, and baskets of flowers were suspended from the ceiling, while four enormous gilded Tritons stood in the middle of the floor. Mark declined any offers to dance, a pastime he had little time for. 'The more I think of dancing,' he had written to Edith earlier in the year, 'the more wildly unreasonable does it seem. It is not even a game.'[49] Instead he returned to the supper-tent, where he could smoke and talk to old friends.

Being back at Sledmere was no blessing for Mark. His experience in South Africa had taught him the benefits of freedom, and now he found himself once again assailed by pressures on all sides. To begin with there were the expectations which people had of him as the young heir. Scarcely had he set foot back in England, for example, than the local constituency of Buckrose were approaching him to ask if he would stand as their Conservative candidate in the next election. For the time being he was having none of it. 'I have told them,' he wrote to Edith, 'that I am neither A BUFFOON, AN OFFICE SEEKER, OR A HYPOCRITE, that I cannot talk sonorous twaddle for endless hours, that I have neither a large stomach nor a white waistcoat, and am in fact no way fitted for a local magnate, that I have no sympathy with the opposition, but I consider the present government the most hopelessly incompetent jelly that has ever quivered in a British cabinet, with which I left them and bade adieu to the Conservatives of East Yorkshire!'[50]

Then there had been his mother to face. He had gone down to London to visit her at her house at 2 Chesterfield Street, only to find her drunk and in a terrible state. 'I must admit that things are worse in every way than they were two years ago,' he told Edith, 'and I can see nothing before me but wretchedness.' Pouring his heart out to her, he reminded her of a conversation they had had a few days previously in which he had attempted to tell her what it was like 'being without a home'. He asked her if she realised 'what it is to be in my position', adding 'you are so sympathetic and large-hearted that I expect you do, but if ever I seem to you undemonstrative, pray remember my past and present life, and remembering that forgive my shortcomings'. He told her that he felt 'a beast' for writing such a letter, 'but it is a relief', he concluded, 'which I sadly need'.[51]

Mark's exasperation with his mother's behaviour increased over the next few weeks to such an extent that on 19 June, he wrote to Edith that 'the hopeless misery of it all for me is that I have no natural affection for my mother, alas that it is I who say it, it is a hideous confession to make'.[52] Her wise advice was that he should be patient, assuring him that Jessie's condition was sure to improve. She was, after all, carving out a new career for herself in the literary world. On her return from South Africa in 1900, she had written and had published a small book entitled *Side Lights on the War in South Africa*, and since then had contributed regularly to *Review of the Week*, and Frank Harris's illustrated magazine, *The Candid Friend*, writing articles on politics, profiles of personalities, the occasional travel piece, and book and theatre reviews. She had also founded her very own weekly, *The Sunrise*, a mish-mash of gossip and politics, which was much disapproved of by Mark. 'It is the sort of journalism,' he told Edith, 'that makes me foam with rage.'[53]

Nevertheless, it kept Jessie busy, and when in the summer of 1902 she amalgamated *Sunrise* with a revival of Samuel Johnson's magazine, *The Rambler*, she persuaded Mark to help her. Though this was a short-lived enterprise, it gave Jessie an opportunity to encourage Mark in his literary ambitions. *Through Five Turkish Provinces*, the book he had been working on just before he went to South Africa, had been published in the autumn of 1900. An account of his journey to the Haurân, it had received favourable reviews, though Mark considered them 'one series of ignorant, meaningless praise'. He was convinced that the book had only attracted attention because of who he was, and wrote to Doolis, 'I can perfectly imagine how it is done; Editor: O look here, here's a book by that young fellow Sykes! – cut it up – O no, he's a son of Tatton Sykes, you remember those trials, he'll be deuced rich! Result: 'Mr Sykes's brilliant little production on his trip to Siberia shows energy, valour, and literary talent of no small order.'[54]

His modesty was quite unfounded, for he had real talent as a writer, which he now put to use on a new project, undertaken with his old Cambridge friend, Edmund Sandars. Together they had spent some time at Sledmere reading all the latest books on Military Science, such as the *Infantry Drill Book* of 1896, which had been given to all soldiers heading out to fight the Boers, and *A Handbook on Field Artillery* by a Lt.-Col. Pratt. They then wrote a parody of these very serious works under the pseudonym of Major-General George D'Ordel, using the binding and format of the *Infantry Drill Book* as a blueprint. They called their great work *Tactics and Military Training*, and they dedicated it to General Sir John Barbecue KCB, an old warhorse who had learned 'modern warfare' in the Crimea, had ignored the Boer War on the grounds of its 'irregular conduct', and strongly disapproved of 'the new craze for learning and innovation'. *Tactics* was published post-humously as D'Ordel himself had died in his chair at the United Military and Naval Club after reading the new drill book by Lord Roberts, a serious army reformer. The book was open at the preface, and a deep nail mark underscored the following passage: 'Nor are the men allowed to degenerate into mere machines. The efficiency of the individual as a fighting man is the test of a good battalion.'[55]

Though strictly fictional, the characters of Barbecue and D'Ordel were rooted in reality, Mark having come across many such figures in South Africa. Moreover, he had only recently been exasperated by the short-sightedness of the military authorities over an experiment he had conducted for them. While passing the time at Sledmere on his return from the war, he had carried out various tests as to the best method of camouflaging a field gun, and after many trials had come up with the idea that the most effective way was to daub the gun in streaks of the three primary colours. He considered the results so successful that he managed to persuade some of the top brass to come and see them for themselves at the training camp at Aldershot. 'The gun is a great success as far as I can see,' he reported to Edith. 'One of the scornful today came up and said, "Haw-whe-ahs this blessed invisible jim-jam of yours, eh?" I said, "Within 400 yards of you in the open, look for it!" (My temper was getting rather short.) The fool then said, "It's an awfully clever trick, don't you know, but of course it's quite impractical. How could they march past if no one could see the guns? Haw, haw, haw!"'[56]

With the manuscript completed and lodged with the publisher, Mark set out one more time for the Middle East in order to gather material for a second, more substantial, travel book, thus fulfilling a promise he had made to himself in the trenches at Barkley Bridge. It was a trip he needed to get out of his system before addressing the other important question in his life, which was marriage to Edith. 'It was and is my intention, provided you agree, to marry you,' he had written to her from South Africa, 'but for anyone to marry before he is prepared to achieve some-thing, is to my mind absurd . . . when I have made my "Grand Tour" and worked at my books, I shall be in that position.'[57]

CHAPTER XII

A Restless Spirit

When Mark returned to England, in August, 1903, he brought with him material that would form the basis of his most ambitious travel book to date, *Dar-ul-Islam: A Record of a Journey through Ten of the Asiatic Provinces of Turkey*. The trip had not been an easy one, however, mostly owing to his misguided decision to take along a Cambridge friend, John Hugh Smith, the son of a rich banker. The motive for this, typical of Mark, seems to have been as a kind of tease for he regarded Smith, who was nicknamed 'Little John', as being far too soft and in need of a good dose of rough travel to toughen him up. No sooner had they boarded the steamer at Naples for the twelve-day journey to Beirut, than he was planning to 'frighten him with tales of disease and pestilence'. He wrote to Edith that 'one glimpse at the deck passengers will settle his decadent stomach I expect . . .'[1] By the time they reached their destination, on 13 November, he was able to report that Little John had improved beyond compare, had stopped talking endlessly about Molière and Wagner, and was 'bewildered beyond words'. When they reached Damascus, however, he had approached Mark 'with a face of horror saying "Do you know that three people sleep in the kitchen!" as if it were surprising'. 'He has much to learn yet,'[2] added Mark, rather scornfully.

Though he had at first enjoyed playing the role of cicerone to his innocent charge, he had soon begun to get annoyed by him. 'I don't know what's the matter with John Hugh Smith,' he wrote to Edith from Beirut, 'he sleeps the whole day . . . till there is a meal, sleeps in the carriage out driving, slumbers in the train and yawns on horse-back, he won't get up till ten o'clock, and complains that the food touches up his liver . . . The Mosquitoes also puncture him fiercely and he has broken out in spots. I had his decadent hair cut yesterday which apparently grieved him as he has done nothing but look at himself in the glass ever since.'[3] His colonial attitudes, eating with his mouth open, even though he knew it horrified the Arabs, and constantly spouting his ideas for reforming the East, also increasingly irritated him. Writing to E. G. Browne, his Professor of Arabic at Cambridge, Mark gleefully told him, 'He wants to try Hasheesh and says it will be a new emotion. I think I shall let him, particularly as the soda water is not of the excellent and hot-copper-cooling brand at Cambridge, it will cure him of any other dangerous investigations he may wish to perpetrate. O ye hammering anvils! O ye clanging Smithies!! O ye piercing broad-awls!!! O ye throbbing tom-toms! What a headache he will get!'[4]

The journey, led by hired a new dragoman, called Yussuf Haddad, and a Roman Catholic servant called Jacob-el-Arab, Isa Kubrusli having died while Mark was in South Africa, took them first from Beirut to Aleppo, where they split up, each taking a different route to Urfa – Mark the most rugged over the Taurus Mountains, and Smith the easier one down the valley of the Euphrates. When they met up again, Mark wrote to Edith that he found Little John greatly changed. He had, worryingly, become 'very bold, unconscious and manly' and was 'beating natives in the most unphilosophic manner'.[5] They did not stay long together, parting again at Diarbekr, where Smith embarked on a raft down the Tigris to collect stores at Baghdad. Finally reunited at Kirkūk, where Mark noted that the natives now felt nothing but hatred for Little John, who made no attempt to understand their customs, they set off for the Russian border on a leg of the trip that was plagued with disaster, and fuelled Mark's irritation with his companion. He blamed Smith's delicate stomach for the illness with which they were both struck down at Sulymaniyah. His temper flared outside Keui Sanjak, when Little John struck the dragoman, who threatened to stab him in revenge. The final straw came in the Kurdish mountains when the party were twice misdirected by some unco-operative Kurds, and Mark's fine Arab stallion collapsed and died from the strain. Though this was no fault of Smith's, his stubborn refusal to try out a new route on the final part of the journey made Mark vow never to travel with him again.

Edith who, through Mark's letters, was familiar with the minutest details of their journey, went out to meet the returning travellers in Constantinople, and they returned to England together in the latter half of August. Mark's first task on arriving home was to tell his father of his intention to marry, an announcement that was received with great enthusiasm by the old man, who immediately raised his son's allowance from £2,000 per annum to £4,000, a sure sign of his approval. His only stipulation was that the wedding should be in York, since a London wedding, with all the attendant razzamatazz, would only serve to remind him of his own disastrous marriage, and that it should be held at eight o'clock in the morning; 'I say eight o'clock you idle creature,' Mark wrote to Edith.[6]

The wedding took place on 28 October at St Wilfrid's Church, York. True to form, in the weeks leading up to the ceremony, Tatton changed his mind on a daily basis as to whether or not he would attend, but when the day came he was in his pew, sharp at eight. It was a quiet affair with no more than fifty guests and the Bishop of Middlesbrough performed the ceremony. Henry Cholmondeley acted as best man, and Jessie, accompanied by her brother Freddie, came up on the train from London the previous evening and stayed at the Station Hotel. For once, she behaved impeccably. After the wedding breakfast, which took place at the Station Hotel, the bride and groom departed for London, and the following day set out on their honeymoon, which took them first to Paris and Rome, and then to Constantinople and Jerusalem. Both parties were rapturous in their happiness. 'Neither was luckier than the other,' Mark's biographer, Shane Leslie, was later to write. 'It proved one of those few marriages made in Heaven.'[7]

Looking at the marriage from the point of view of Sir John and Lady Gorst, Edith's parents, Mark was quite a catch. Clever, good looking and charming, he was not only heir to a great fortune, but, with a growing reputation as a soldier, a traveller and a man of letters, there was the likelihood of a glittering career ahead of him. He had returned from his recent journey to find that D'Ordel's *Tactics* had been a best seller, going through six editions in its first few weeks. It had been widely and excellently reviewed in all the daily newspapers and weeklies, including *The Army and Navy Illustrated*, whose reviewer had recommended it to 'every soldier interested in the Service'.[8] The *Spectator* called it 'exceptionally amusing and perhaps exceptionally instructive', adding 'it is laughter compelling on every page'.[9] Now he was ready to start work on his next travel book, and had ideas for further D'Ordel publications.

The success of *Tactics* brought Mark's name to the attention of many distinguished people as being one of the brightest young talents around. One of these was the dashing Conservative and Chief Secretary of Ireland, George Wyndham, who offered him the chance to become his Private Secretary. Though Mark had a healthy disregard for politicians, he admired Wyndham, whose Irish Land Act had improved the lot of peasant farmers by helping them to buy land. Edith, who was ambitious for him, was certain that he had a talent for politics and thought that a career in them would give substance to a life that to date had been very restless. In spite of his own uncertainty, she persuaded him to accept the post and he left for Dublin on his return from their honeymoon, without his bride, the summons having come at too short notice.

He got off to a bad start, irked that, since Wyndham, or 'The Chief' as he was generally referred to, was not expected for another few days, he could have spent some more time at Sledmere with Edith. He sensed an atmosphere of slackness and disorganisation in the Chief Secretary's Lodge, and was annoyed that there was no one to show him the ropes. 'I have to pick up what they have been doing for four years,' he complained to Edith, 'with the end of a stick out of a dustbin.' One of the first jobs he was given was to précis an eighty-four page report for 'The Chief', only to find that a précis already existed at the back of the report. He had at first so little to do in fact that he paid two visits to the zoo to pass the time, where he was much amused by the fact that 'the keeper at the monkey house is so like a monkey, that one cannot help turning aside to smile'. So bored was he that he was almost ready to quit before he had started. 'Politics fill me with disgust,' he fumed, 'but I will go through with this infernal job as long as you can stand it . . . I don't know if I can possibly hold out in the office work. I want air and real work. Give me a native regiment to organise, a rebellion to raise, a map to make, a block-house line to construct, a Vilayet to govern and I will do it; give me an independent command, anything you choose but this, this life of a cat . . .'[10]

Things did not improve, even when 'The Chief' finally showed up, for Wyndham gave him little to do, tending to rely on his other long-standing private secretaries for most of the work. Mark wasted no time, however, taking the opportunity to start on his new book, and to correspond with Edith on the subject of where they were going to live during the months when Wyndham was based at Westminster. Having spent much of his childhood being dragged round hotels, he knew exactly what he wanted. 'Now about rooms,' he instructed her, 'we want our *own Kitchen and Cook*, you know how I and you Hate, Loathe, Detest, Abhor, Condemn, Spit Upon, and Utterly Damn Restaurants where The Vegetables are green, the waiters are greasy, the service disgusting, the company bestial, the surroundings vulgar, the IDEA LOATHSOME. Therefore find a roomy spot with a kitchen and a low rent even at Mile End!'[11]

Edith found a suitable flat in south-west London, 7 Lennox Gardens, which was conveniently close to the Irish Office, and they settled there in January, 1904. Mark dealt with his frustration at the little required of him by Wyndham by immersing himself completing his new book, *Dar-ul-Islam: A Journey through Ten of the Asiatic Provinces of Turkey*. Illustrated throughout with seventy of his own photographs and twenty pages of hand-drawn maps, it was an account of his travels with John Hugh Smith. Its success lay in its blending of history and descriptions of place with amusing anecdotes and sharp flashes of humour. One of the themes running through the book was his hatred of the way the West was beginning to spoil the traditions of the East. He gave as an example of this an inedible 'Dinny Vranzay' (Dîner Francais) prepared for him by the Sheikh of a village outside Palmyra, – rank soup, lumps of camel fat, and six other dishes 'enough to shake the strongest stomach' – which he described as 'a typical instance of smearing the East with the Gosmobaleet slime of the West'.[12]

The word Gosmobaleet, Mark's own rendering of the Levantine English for 'cosmopolitan', he described in a footnote as being 'descriptive of that peculiar and horrible sickness which attacks a certain percentage of the inhabitants of interesting and delightful lands. The outward symptoms in the East are usually American springside boots (Jemimas) and ugly European clothes ... The final stage is that in which the victim, hating his teacher and ashamed of his parentage and nationality, is intensely miserable.'[13] When the book came out in the spring of 1904, it was well received and widely reviewed, not only by the dailies and weeklies, but by distinguished writers like Rudyard Kipling, who wrote to Mark, 'I sat down to read it and stayed there for the rest of the evening ... I don't know Turkey, but I can see the chit and the delay and the confusion at the wayside *serais* as I can smell the smell (much like ours in India, I take it) of the towns.'[14]

As if it were not enough to have written a 300 page travel book, Mark also embarked on a new D'Ordel project with Edmund Sandars, this time a satire on another of his *bêtes noires*, cheap journalism. *D'Ordel's Pantechnicon, An Universal Directory of the Mechanical Art of Manufacturing Illustrated Magazines*, was the work of Prometheus D'Ordel, Gent., brother of the late Major-General, and introduced the reader to a 'Model Magazine' entitled *Scragford's Farthing*. Based on popular publications like *The Strand Magazine*, it suggested that magazines had gone downhill since the great days of the *Spectator* in the eighteenth century, and the quality of journalism with them. Conan Doyle was parodied as 'Doothey Boyle', author of *In Grypula's Grip, Grypula's Adventures, Au Revoir Grypula, The Strange Episode of the Brazen Face* and *More Grypula's Adventures*, while his latest novel, *The Search for the Iron Toe*, provided the obligatory serial. Though it did not achieve the success of *Tactics, Pantechnicon* was warmly praised, one reviewer describing it as 'probably some of the most brilliant nonsense ever written'.[15]

While Mark had been making his name in the world of letters, his mother had also been busy with her own literary efforts. In 1903 she published two books with Mark's publishers, Bickers and Son. The first, *The New Reign of Terror in France*, was a vitriolic attack on the Third Republic and the Dreyfusards, while the second, *Algernon Casterton: Some Experiences during the First Twenty-five Years of His Life*, was a semi-autobiographical novel, dedicated to the memory of Tom Grayson. Grayson appears in the book thinly disguised as Jack Saddler whose 'latter years were greatly solaced . . . by the teaching, gratis, of the little great-grandson of "t'oad squire" to ride. In fact the companionship of this little fellow was the great happiness of the declining years of Jack Saddler's worthy life.'[16] Though these books had only very limited success, this did not prevent Jessie from pursuing a career as a writer.

In the summer of 1904, she completed a play, the script of which she sent to the famous actor-manager, Herbert Beerbohm Tree. Typically of Jessie, it was just a little too *risqué,* and any hopes she might have had of seeing it performed at His Majesty's, Tree's theatre in the West End, were soon dashed. 'I have read the play very carefully,' he wrote to her on 2 August. 'I think it powerful and intensely clever. But it is very terrible, notably the scene in which the jockey makes love to the lady – it may be true to life, but everything on the stage comes out in letters of fire and one wishes . . . that the scene could be toned down somewhat.' He singled out two characters for praise. The Yorkshireman, he told her, was 'splendid', and Wolfgang was also 'a tremendous character'; adding, 'no doubt the thing would cause a sensation'. He concluded the letter, however, by telling her, 'Frankly I should shrink from producing it at my theatre for reasons that are perhaps obvious – and I hope I am not lacking in boldness . . .'[17]

The contents of her novels, undistinguished *romans-à-clef* of which she wrote a further two, were less controversial. The first, *The Macdonnells*, based on the Leslie family and published by William Heinemann in 1905, told the story of a widow's attempts to instil her own values into her sons and daughters, and painted a vivid portrait of Jessie's Anglo-Irish background. Her mother appeared as Mrs Macdonnell, while Jessie saw herself in the character of the eldest daughter: 'Georgiana was handsome, dark-eyed and dark-haired, and possessed a tall, well-rounded figure.

She was by no means her mother's favourite; her comparative freedom of speech and manner shocked her austere parent, from whose custody she escaped when only twenty years of age . . .'[18]

Her final novel, *Mark Alston*, was published by Eveleigh Nash in 1908, and was an exposure of the Bentinck and Lowther families. It told the story of an artistic young woman called Portia Bulstrode who, while studying painting and literature in Venice, falls in love with a young scholar, Mark Alston, based on Ruskin. Her mother forbids their marriage, having already decided that Portia should marry a 'misogynistic peer', Lord Beechfield, a thinly disguised portrayal of Tatton. 'Lord Beechfield was forty-eight years of age – a silent, serious, solemn personage. Twelve years previously he had succeeded to one of the largest estates in the North of England . . . He had not been on friendly terms with his father and spent most of his youth abroad. When he came into his title and fortune, it was naturally expected he would go into society and speedily marry, but instead of this he shut himself up in his country place, where he interested himself in building and improving his property. The farmhouses which under his father's rule had fallen into disrepair, he rebuilt; whole villages were pulled down and reconstructed, and numerous churches restored . . . He was supposed to be a confirmed bachelor, and never to interest himself in a woman . . .'[19]

Though Jessie's books brought her no great acclaim, and certain disapprobation from the families concerned, who bought up and destroyed every copy they could get their hands on, they kept her busy and, for the most part, off the bottle. 'I am very well indeed,' she was able to write to Mark in April, 1906, 'and feel about twenty-five.'[20] She would have revelled in the kind of literary success that was within Mark's grasp. Yet for him it seemed to hold little meaning, and though he continued to produce books, his ambition remained unfulfilled by writing. His restless nature made it hard for him to decide exactly what it was he wanted to do next. A stint of training with his Yorkshire regiment in the summer of 1904 gave him the idea that he might prove useful in helping to reorganise the militia, while another side of him craved a post on the staff of Lord Curzon in India.

'I must have an employment which I am capable of working in,' he wrote to Edith in frustration, '– that is to say one requiring energy, thought, and originality.'[21]

At the end of August, Edith gave birth to their first child, a healthy, fat baby girl they named Freya, an event which temporarily took Mark's mind off his problems. In the final weeks of her pregnancy, Edith had been with her family at Castle Combe, while Mark remained at Sledmere working with Edmund Sandars on another D'Ordel book, a treatise on 'spin' to be called *An Introduction to the Culinary Art of Preparing and Using Statistics*. He eagerly awaited her arrival. 'I have been fearfully busy,' he told her; 'we worked from nine-thirty in the morning till midnight yesterday, but we are getting on well ... I suppose Freya is as fractious as ever – you are expected here on Wednesday.'[22]

After pestering 'The Chief', for a change of job, and prevailing on Edith to bend the ear of her brother, Jack, then an Under-Secretary in the Foreign Office, Mark was offered a post as an honorary attaché at the British Embassy in Constantinople, a city in which he would be able to put to good use his extensive knowledge of the Middle East. His wife and daughter were to accompany him there but, before taking up the posting in the spring of 1905, he decided to take Edith on a holiday to Palestine, to be followed by a short solo journey in Syria. It was while they were in Jerusalem that another intrepid and outspoken traveller came into town, complete with an ego as inflated as Mark's, a situation that was sure to lead to trouble.

Gertrude Bell was the daughter of a wealthy Durham ironmaster, Sir Thomas Bell. Educated at Oxford, where she was the first woman to gain a first class honours degree in Modern History, she had proved herself an intrepid explorer and talented archaeologist, and was hot on the heels of Mark in his chosen career as an Orientalist. When she arrived in Jerusalem, she found an invitation to dine with Mark and Edith at their hotel. 'Dined with the Sykeses,' she wrote in her diary of 30 January. 'He is going up over much the same route that I intend to take. He has an immense camp, and what he must spend over it I tremble to think ... Both he and his wife are darlings; he is most amusing, but she is the more intelligent of the two I should think.'[23]

During the dinner, Mark was most put out by Gertrude's insinuations that he had been grossly overcharged for his horses and mules. He bore a grudge against her for this, which spilled out a month later when he discovered that she was taking the same route through Syria as he was, after telling him she was going elsewhere. 'An infernal liar,' he called her. '10,000 of my worst bad words on the head of that damned fool, Miss Bell,' he fumed to Edith, 'confound the silly chattering windbag of a conceited gushing flat-chested man-woman globetrotting rump-wagging blethering ass! . . . She leaves every place she visits in an uproar . . . if you see the loon before I do, give her neither encouragement nor entertainment as she is just a damned mischief-making woman, let loose out of a London Drawing room into the Syrian desert . . . Poor Richards the Consul has aged ten years in two – poor wretch, I needn't tell you Miss Bell has not lessened his worries, he could kill her.'[24] He let off steam a second time, six weeks later, when he found himself once again in close proximity to her. 'I hear that *Bitch* Miss Bell is coming up here, I am flying before her – so is everybody else. She is now known as the "Terror of the Desert".'[25]

Before taking up his new attachment in Constantinople, Mark returned to England to collect Freya and Edith, who was now pregnant with their second child. He also went to Sledmere to visit his father. Tatton's life had changed little since his separation from Jessie. He still spent the winter abroad, and the remainder of the year building churches and racing. Apart from the restoration of five local churches, his main ecclesiastical project had been the demolition and complete rebuilding in the Gothic style of St Mary's, Sledmere, the simple Georgian style of which had ceased to please him. It was an undertaking that caused some controversy since the villagers were left for five years without a place of worship. So far as the stud was concerned, he had achieved huge success, having established Sledmere as a top class nursery, whose progeny since 1893 had fetched the colossal sum of £133,093 at the annual Doncaster sales. His colt, John O'Gaunt, which he bred himself, had come second in both the 1904 2,000 Guineas

and the Derby, and his latest star, Spearmint, whose mother he had
bought in foal from Sir James Duke, would go on to win both the
1906 Derby and the Grand Prix de Paris.

One change which had taken place in Tatton's life, was the acquisition of a companion, Louise de Lichtervelde, a French widow with
a young daughter, who had originally come to Sledmere as his French
tutor. Her standing in the household, however, had immeasurably
changed after Jessie had left, at the time of the proposed divorce.
Referred to by the staff as 'Madame', she now ran the house and
accompanied Tatton on all his travels. Though he never grew to like
her, Mark accepted 'Madame', since he knew his father could not
bear to be alone. He also needed looking after because of his continuing
poor health, and had recently suffered from a minor stroke. Mark was
happy, however, to find him in good spirits. 'I have seen my father,'
he wrote to Edith. 'He is incredibly better, drives and walks round
the mares etc, etc, eats well but sleeps badly – the only result of the
illness is a slight clouding of his brain. It cannot be said that he suffers
from hallucinations but something very like them.' He gave as an
example of this the fact that Tatton had asked the Clerk at the Bank,
a Mr Pearson, if he could lend him £5,000. He was also 'stricken
with terror before and after every undertaking of the day'. Mark told
Edith that he accepted what he had been told by his father's physician,
Dr Tinsley, which was that 'as long as he lives you will always have
trouble with him'.[26]

Needless to say, Jessie could not stand 'Madame' and always referred
to her as 'that woman'. When news had reached her of Tatton's illness,
for example, she wrote to Mark to tell him that she was disgusted that
the opportunity had not been taken 'to get rid of that woman'.[27]
Though it was almost certainly platonic, Jessie was always suspicious
of the nature of the relationship. These suspicions came to a head in
1908, when she discovered that on a trip back from Australia on board
the steamship *Mongolian*, Madame was referred to in the Ship's Book
as Lady Sykes. Through his solicitors, Tatton made it clear that there
was nothing to read in this, admitting that he had heard of her being
dubbed 'Lady Sykes' at Colombo but, wrote his solicitor, 'he did not

bother about it'.[28] Jessie chose not to pursue this, but the incident only served to make her hate Madame even more.

Mark's usual boyish enthusiasm bubbled over when he started his new job in Constantinople. He was back in the Ottoman Empire, the part of the world he understood and loved most, and he had his heavily pregnant wife and child with him. Settled in Therapia, the summer residence of the Sultan's Court, awaiting the imminent birth, he wrote to Henry Cholmondeley, 'I am now very satisfied with my work, which is more "real" than the Irish Office.'[29] Four days later, on 24 August, Edith gave birth to a son and heir for Sledmere. 'I hope the boy will *not* be called Tatton,' wrote Jessie from a villa she had taken in Bavaria. 'Richard is certainly a better name and has a fine Anglo-Norman sound about it – also the founder of the Sykes family was really that Mr Richard Sykes whose letters you have read and who built the main body of the house.'[30] Richard he was named.

There was not a word from Tatton. The only communication from Sledmere was a letter from Aunt Kate, Henry Cholmondeley's mother, which included a hastily scribbled postscript from Henry. 'I see no reason why the birth of my son should be kept a deadly secret,' Mark wrote indignantly to his cousin. 'Personally I should have expected a telegram from Sledmere, from at least the people in the place, a thing not much in itself but still showing a little human feeling, and which if they had been told they would have done if I know them at all. As it is it is nine days since I telegraphed and I have not heard a single word . . . As you know I am far from sentimental but there is a degree of stoical frigidity which is beyond my philosophy.'[31]

As things turned out, Mark was to be as frustrated in Constantinople as he had been in Ireland. He had powerful convictions of the vital importance of Britain keeping up and consolidating the good relationship with Turkey, which had been forged in the nineteenth century when Russia was a common enemy to them both. It was paramount, he felt, that she should guard against British predominance in the region being undermined by the Germans, who were building railways and helping to train the Turkish army. Having travelled so extensively in the East, he considered himself a great expert and was certain that he would have the ear of the Ambassador, Sir Nicholas O'Connor. However, the copious reports he wrote on his journeys round the province, illustrated with maps and photographs, and which he used as a vehicle for his views, fell on deaf ears. He was after all no more than an honorary attaché and any ideas he might have had about influencing policy were soon squashed when he found himself engaged in boring tasks like reading newspapers and pasting press cuttings into albums.

It was during this period of his life that Mark, for the first time, began to seriously consider entering Parliament, as the only way he was ever likely to be in a position to influence government policy in the spheres in which he was interested. This decision was partly brought on by the incompetence and inefficiency he witnessed in the Levant Consular Service while on his last great journey before returning to England, a trip that took him on horseback all the way from Constantinople to the borders of Persia and back to Aleppo. 'When I see this country and think of our lost opportunities, it makes me mad,' he fumed to Edith from Diarbekr. 'Are we a declining nation? Are we falling into the hands of hidebound official cliques and setting everything by competitive exam? . . . Politics will be really great fun in a year's time, O don't you never fear I'm going into them. We will give battle to cant and incompetence.'[32]

Edith was to join Mark in June for the last leg of the journey. After two months alone, he was missing her dreadfully. 'All the muleteers are praying for your advent,' he wrote to her from the Kurdish town of Erbil, 'as they say I am getting so ferocious . . . six weeks we shall be together again never to part – it is terribly lonely – and reminds me of the dismal life I led before I was married.'[33] In the letters he received from her, Edith kept him informed of the progress of the children. She had endured dreadful anxiety over an illness suffered by Richard, who was now on the mend, though 'he must be kept on his back for six weeks'.[34] Little Freya was thriving. 'I show her your photograph every day and she says "bonjour Papa" to it. There is a picture of Our Lord that she insists on calling "Papa" or "Garçon". I tried to impress the name Jesus on her but she paid little attention to my religious instructions.'[35]

That she also missed Mark acutely is clear from the fact that she was prepared to leave her children for what was to be weeks, in order to be with him. 'Please dear little fellow *do* meet me at Constantinople,' she pleaded, 'then I shall not have to go so far to see you and have to wait such a long time . . . and I shall be so miserable at leaving the babies that I shall want you to console me directly. Nothing but you my dearest could make me leave them for such a dreadfully long time.' She declared herself unafraid of any dangers involved in the journey, except 'there is only one risk I don't want to run and that is being carried off to a Pasha's harem!'[36]

Husband and wife were reunited towards the end of June, not at Constantinople as she had hoped, but in the Black Sea port of Sinope. 'It will be like heaven when you come,' he had written to her, and he later wrote that he never forgot 'that glorious day' when he 'heard the whistle announcing' her arrival. Together they rode 1,000 miles, from Sinope east across to the Persian border, then west via Aleppo to the Mediterranean where they embarked for London. An account of this journey was included by Mark in his final major work, *The Caliphs' Last Heritage*, a study of Islam and the Ottoman Empire, work on which he had started while at the embassy in Constantinople, but which was not to be published till 1915, when the war in Europe had spread to Turkey and interest in the subject was suddenly revived.

The priority for Mark on his return home was to find a house for his wife and family. Since his father was firmly ensconced at Sledmere with 'Madame', and showed no more willingness than his ancestor 'Parson' had done to move out in favour of his son, he instructed Henry Cholmondeley to find them somewhere suitable. Henry came up with a 400-acre farm on the estate called Eddlethorpe, and persuaded Tatton to agree to pay for any alterations that might be needed to the house. Had the latter had an inkling of what these would entail, he might have thought again, for they turned out to be considerable.

Mark could never do anything by halves, and the conversion of Eddlethorpe was no exception. As it stood, he told Henry Cholmondeley, it was a 'masterpiece' of the 'hideous and revolting' school, 'a vulgar, heavy, clumsy, toneless, soulless image' of the builder's 'beastly mind'.[37] Using the estate architect, Mr Collett, a man whose experience up to date had been limited to the erection of cottages and farm buildings, he transformed the simple Victorian farmhouse into a flamboyant fantasy the like of which had never been seen on the Yorkshire Wolds. It was a hotchpotch of designs in a vaguely Arts and Crafts style, which might have been described as 'The Wolds meets the Orient.' He told his friend Edmund Sandars, 'I will excite your curiosity by saying there is a dash of Kastamuni in it.'[38] Two new wings were added, giving the house fifteen bedrooms. Attached to one of them was a three-storey tower, topped by a cupola, which was named 'Mark's Tower', and contained his study, library and dressing-room. There was also a chapel, a nursery, and a kitchen which was approached by four archways covered with Anatolian tiles, part of a consignment of 2,700 which Mark had brought back from his travels. Cufic inscriptions were inscribed over each arch.

The exterior was bold enough to draw astonished gasps from passersby. 'Half the effects in architecture of the domestic kind,' he had once expounded to Henry Cholmondeley, 'are gained by colour . . . just as much as by shape, only the colours must be laid on thick, and not too carefully.' The ground floor was entirely of red brick, the upper storeys were in grey stucco, the hipped roof tiles were red, the chimneys white, while the cupola, the balconies and the surrounding fence were all in black and white. A shield bearing the Sykes coat of arms was placed above the neo-Georgian entrance, topped by a large brass Triton. It was, to say the least, a highly eccentric building, but it suited Mark's extrovert nature. The children loved it. It reminded them of a house out of a fairytale.

While work on Eddlethorpe progressed, the family lived in another estate farmhouse, called Menethorpe, and it was here, on 17 November, 1907, that Edith gave birth to twins, a boy, Christopher, and a girl, Everilda, named after the patron saint of Kirkham Priory, a nearby ruined abbey. The name, which Monty James had originally suggested to Mark as a possibility when Freya was born, was soon found to be a bit of a mouthful, and she was nicknamed Petsy. When the new house was finally ready, at the beginning of 1908, it easily absorbed the fast-growing family and the large staff they had accumulated – a governess for Freya, nurses for Richard and the twins, a cook, butler, footman, chauffeur, coachman, groom, gardener and under-gardener.

Considering the unhappy nature of his own childhood, it is not surprising that Mark took to family life. He was able to do with his own children all the things he had missed out on himself, when he was growing up. 'He was a delightful father,' wrote Edith. 'In his leisure moments he invented wonderful games, and when we lived at Eddlethorpe, the whole lawn would be covered with a miniature railway system, each child being responsible for a point or signal.'[39] In the winter months, the railway, made by the firm of Bassett Lowke, was brought inside and laid out along the top floor corridor, the track winding in and out of the various bedrooms. The locomotives were clockwork and were wound up with a key. Mark took it very seriously, and had the children and their friends manning the points to guard against any accidents. 'We had to keep our heads to avoid collisions,' remembers Nino Hunter, a nephew of Edith's, 'watched closely by Uncle Mark who was terribly happy when all went well. But I do remember an occasion when poor Freya got it wrong, and there was a nasty mishap. That time Uncle Mark got quite cross with her.'[40]

He devised elaborate war games, played on the lawn, with coloured blocks and sticks representing cavalry, infantry, guns, wagons, trains and houses, while artillery and shrapnel rounds were signified by the throwing of different-sized bags. Since it was the children's job to move the sticks and blocks, while the adults had all the fun of throwing the bags, this was not their favourite game. They much preferred the Yorkshire stories he wrote for them, which he would recite in a broad East Riding accent, and the tales of his travels in far-off lands, often woven into *Arabian Nights* fantasies, with which he held them spellbound. There were also 'passionate family excursions led by him to York and Beverley and to little known churches in the East Riding, where there was a Norman arch or a Saxon font, or to some place where there was a ruin – it hardly mattered what – provided it dated from far beyond living memory'.[41]

His great skill as an illustrator was put to good use for 'the babies', as he used to refer to them, and they remembered his entertainments for the rest of their lives. On one occasion, recalled his son Christopher, 'he procured a copy of that most grotesque of English classics, *The Castle of Otranto*, by Horace Walpole, and every evening when he could he read us a chapter, accompanied by coloured illustrations of the more striking incidents made previously by himself. The pictures were of the kind that can make you laugh aloud, and I remember that he used to laugh aloud as he drew them.'[42]

When Mark and Edith were both away, the children were left in the care of the two nannies, Marie Duntz and Lizzie Nicholson. One day, Marie told them that she was taking them for a special treat. They were dressed up in their very best outdoor clothes and taken to the farm, which was across the road. There in the middle of the yard stood what Freya, a good little Catholic girl, took to be an altar. Beside it stood a man dressed in a long white coat, while on the ground were a number of large basins and bowls and various knives. Then two men dragged a large pink pig, shrieking its head off, into the yard. 'I suddenly realised what we were in for,' remembered Freya, 'and I became absolutely petrified. Richard immediately burst into tears and roared the place down. Lizzie tried to control the twins, who were only two! Before our eyes a sort of hammer and chisel were placed in the middle of the pig's forehead. It was in this way stunned and fell down, and at the same time its throat was cut from ear to ear. I have never seen so much blood in all my life. It was all collected in a basin. By that time I was pea-green in the face.' Luckily at that moment, Lizzie protested and the children were taken away. Later that afternoon they were taken down to have tea with their grand-mother, Lady Gorst. 'She was a very sweet old lady,' Freya recollected, 'and she asked, "And what did you do this morning, dears?" and I blurted out, "We saw the pigs killed!" There was the most awful rumpus.'[43]

On rare occasions, in the absence of their parents, the children were sent to Sledmere to spend a few days with their grandfather. It was an alarming experience. They would arrive with their nannies and take up residence on the top floor of the house, all other floors and passages being strictly out of bounds. Each morning they would be dressed up in their best clothes and led downstairs to the Boudoir, to say good morning to Sir Tatton. There he sat in state, with Madame by his side. The routine never varied. They would enter the room, shake his hand and say 'Good morning, Grandpapa.' Then they would leave, either to go out for a walk, or to return to the confines of the nursery. Until the house was burned down, this was their only experience of Sledmere.

Just as he had been by his mother, so Mark treated his own children as equals. His brother-in-law, Harold Gorst, once witnessed an episode which serves as a perfect example of this. While staying at Eddlethorpe one day, he was walking with Mark down a passage, when they were confronted with the sight and sound of Richard, aged two, in the throes of a major tantrum. He was lying on the floor on his back, kicking violently at anybody who dared to approach and screaming his head off that he would not go out for a walk. Marie, his nurse, and Edith were both at the end of their tether. 'Suddenly Mark,' recalled Harold, 'after surveying his son and heir with that queer little contraction of his eyebrows, swooped down, picked him up in his arms, bore him away kicking and struggling into a neighbouring bedroom, and locked the door behind him.' Harold and the two women then stood in the passage expecting any moment to hear the sounds of a hearty spanking being administered to the furious child. Instead, to their astonishment, the shrieks died away to silence. When Mark, three or four minutes later, emerged from the room leading a perfectly serene and normal Richard by the hand, they asked him how he had effected such a miracle. 'I sat him in a dry basin on the washstand,' replied Mark, 'and reasoned with him.'[44] This was his philosophy in a nutshell.

During the years from 1907 to 1911, Mark spent more time in England with his family than he ever had done and was ever to do again. The reason for this was his adoption as Conservative candidate for his late Uncle Christopher's constituency of Buckrose, which had been held by the Liberals since 1892. 'I am now home for good,' he wrote to his old tutor, Egerton Beck, 'and making a political plunge.

Tory Democracy is what I am going to try and push, for all it is worth.'[45] It was to be an uphill struggle, since the Conservatives were now out in the cold, the Liberals, under Campbell-Bannerman, having achieved a landslide victory in the 1906 general election.

In his acceptance speech, Mark cited his hero, Benjamin Disraeli, the great social reformer, who had advocated an alliance between the aristocracy and the working class, and under whom the Conservative Party had thrived. Since then, the party had lost its ideals; ideals such as unity 'between employer and employed, class and class, creed and creed, father and son, colony and mother-land, prince and subject, farm and village, village and city, city and kingdom, kingdom and colony, colony and Empire'. These were Mark's ideals too, and he was never to abandon them. The Liberals might be in power now, but in his opinion and in a remarkable flash of foresight, Radicals being better at demolishing than building, 'twenty years hence there will be only two parties – Socialists and Tories'.

Mark may have distrusted the Labour movement, which he considered too rooted in urban bureaucracy, but he never underestimated its power, stating openly 'If I were a working man, my house unsanitary, my wages low, my child sweated, my wife ailing, my employment hazardous, I should vote Labour.' He thus encouraged every member of the Tory Party to show himself at heart a true Labour member and to outdo the Trade Unionists in getting the working man 'a good house, a good wage, a good education', the cost of which could be met by higher taxation on wealth and imports.

Though Mark was undoubtedly extremely conscientious as a candidate, and worked assiduously hard on his campaign, his chances of election were hampered by the fact that he had chosen to stand at a time when local issues were very much overshadowed by more important national ones. In 1908, the Chancellor of the Exchequer, Lloyd George, had introduced the Old Age Pensions Act, which promised to pay between 1s. and 5s. a week to people over seventy. To pay for this, he introduced a People's Budget to raise revenue of £16 million, which included increases in taxation for the rich and a land tax. When the House of Lords chose to block this, their action precipitated a constitutional crisis and, in January 1910, the Prime Minister, Herbert Asquith, called an election. Mark's opponent, the standing MP, was Sir Luke White, a self-made man with a broad Yorkshire accent and, class feeling being aroused as it had been, the Liberals made capital out of the difference between their man and the aristocratic Sykes. 'Follow the Gospel and put Mark before Luke,' cried his supporters, but to no avail. The forces of Liberalism were mobilised, and Mark lost to White by 218 votes.

As it happened, there was a second election in 1910, in December, this time precipitated by Asquith's desire to force through a Parliament Act, designed to reduce the powers of the House of Lords. It was a punishment for their having attempted to block the People's Budget. Once again Mark was defeated but he had not helped himself by, in the heat of the moment at one meeting, referring to his opponent as 'an unpatriotic humbug'. Of this outburst, Sir Luke made suitable capital. He would appear at meetings bearing the meek expression of a martyr and, endeavouring to speak, would find himself overcome with emotion, only able to repeat, as the tears streamed down his cheeks, the words, 'E ca'd me a Oomboog!'[46] Mark was philosophical about his second defeat. 'If you choose to give me a political career,' he wrote, 'I will take it up, but if not, I have my books and can go back to my plough.'[47]

He did not in fact have to return to the plough, because exceptional circumstances gave him a third crack at the whip within only six months when the popular Conservative MP for Central Hull, Sir Henry Seymour King, had his election declared null and void after allegations that he had bribed voters by financing treats for children and giving away free coal to certain constituents. Being a local man whose reputation had already been established by his conduct in the two Buckrose campaigns, Mark seemed an obvious choice to the local Conservative Association for their new candidate. Add to this a little bit of history: namely the contribution made by his eighteenth-century ancestors to the growth and prosperity of Hull, and the charitable work of his mother on behalf of the poor Catholics of the city, and his adoption was assured.

Delayed by the coronation of George V, on 22 June, the by-election did not take place till 5 July, on which day Mark was returned as Conservative MP for Central Hull. It was the first good piece of news for him in a year that had been thoroughly blighted by the fire which had swept through Sledmere House on 23 May, leaving nothing of the beautiful creation of his proud ancestors but four blackened walls.

CHAPTER XIII

A New House

It would be no exaggeration to say that in the next eight years, Mark worked himself to death. Unable to do anything by halves and unwilling to delegate, he took on the avalanche of tasks which suddenly befell him without pausing for breath. He was not only preparing to throw himself headlong into a political career, he was faced with the difficult decision of what to do about Sledmere, which his father, on the day after the fire, had made it quite clear he intended to rebuild. 'Lieut-Colonel Mark Sykes had all the plans and copies of the decorative schemes,' Tatton had told the *Malton Messenger,* 'and these would be faithfully reproduced . . . He regretted the loss of the Library, which was the finest apartment in the house, and one of its chief beauties. He hoped, however, that it would be possible to replace it by a faithful replica, as well as the decorative designs of the other rooms.'[1]

This was no pipe dream. The house was well insured for £110,000, a sum that would more than cover the costs involved, and once a settlement had been reached with the two companies involved, the Sun and the Yorkshire Insurance, the decision was taken to go ahead. The chosen architect was W. H. Brierley of York, who was an expert on architectural restoration and a leading exponent of the neo-classical style. Since Tatton was too old and ill to assume practical responsibility for the rebuilding and spent much of the time travelling abroad, the task fell on Mark, who relished the challenge, feeling a sympathy with his amateur architect ancestor, Sir Christopher Sykes. To begin with it was agreed that the remains of the house would have to be totally demolished, and a new Sledmere built from scratch. Brierley was excited by this prospect, as it would give him the opportunity to build a really modern house. Unfortunately for him, Mark did not share his ideas. 'I detest modern houses,' he said. 'This is an inartistic and vulgar age. We will build a house that is as little typical of the second decade of the twentieth century as possible.'[2] The scene was set for a long drawn-out locking of horns.

With this on his mind, Mark took his seat in the Commons, where he found a warm welcome at the door. 'I found a nice old thing with a top hat,' he recounted to Edith, 'who looks after coats and who said, "I have seen two generations and you are the third; Mr George Cavendish Bentinck, Mr Christopher and yourself."' He was resolutely unimpressed by his fellow Conservatives. 'Our party are very bad and stupid,' he complained, 'and the speeches are enough to drive one mad with boredom – "while entirely agreeing – er – with the first remarks – er – of my rt. hon. – er – friend, I – er, hem – depreciate – er – deprecate – the further remarks – that is I am in agreement with a part – that is the first, the first part" and so on till I could scream . . . These men cannot deliver themselves of their ideas.' The greatest impression made on him was by Lloyd George, who he described as 'a very great genius', adding 'he is the brightest man in the House by lengths; he has charm, fascination, personality, sympathy, agility, and is much more than clever'.[3]

As it happened, during the first month he sat in Parliament, Mark witnessed some of the most dramatic debates of the century. In spite of his having recently won an election, Asquith had conspicuously failed to persuade the House of Lords to agree to his Parliament Act, without endless amendments. In the end he was obliged to go to the King to ask him to create 250 new Liberal Peers in order to force through the Bill in the form in which it had been drafted. On 24 July, Asquith went to the Commons to state his intentions. 'I have just come from the most disgusting performance I have ever witnessed,' Mark wrote to Edith. 'The House was packed from end to end . . . when Asquith came in our people began to howl like madmen and so continued, here are some of their cries: "Who killed the King?", "Have a drink", "Perrier Jouet", "Traitor", "Judas", "Not this man but Barabbas", "Scoundrel", "Dictator", "Tyrant". Asquith was angry, red, frightened, undignified – not a great man in any sense of the word – Balfour, frightened, ashamed, halting ... Lloyd George was intensely amused and laughed all thro' – GW bayed like a blood-hound – and our side without exception behaved like weak, hysterical girls, unstrung, leaderless and uncontrolled.' It was, he concluded, 'entirely a revolting spectacle I cannot find the heart to laugh at'.[4]

His opinion of the House of Lords, unsurprisingly considering his patrician background, was somewhat different. On 9 August he attended their own debate on the Bill and, sensing how close they might be to self-destruction if they refused to toe the line, wrote a vivid evocation of what he saw in the Chamber.

> The scene in the H of L was most wonderful – a scene perhaps never to be seen again. 400 English gentlemen – independent, honest, determined and at variance – no one knows how the division will go, every speech has its effect – the last deliberative assembly in Europe will have ceased to be as such in another five days or perhaps less. Even the hordes of Radicals at the bar among whom I stood were impressed. We shall never see such a scene again. The Lord Chancellor on the Wool Sack and around him Generals, Ambassadors, Lords Lieutenants, Governors, Diplomatists, Gentlemen, and Bishops – below the bar a knot of greedy adventurers, cranks and lawyers – what a contrast![5]

In the event, the Lords saw sense and voted through the Bill, an act which Mark saw as a betrayal of Toryism.

There was time to gather his thoughts and catch up with his family in the long summer recess which followed, the highlight of which was the arrival, on 6 September, of the Sykes's fifth child, a daughter they named Angela. This brightened up what had been a week of mixed blessings; on the good side, the fourteen yearlings sold at the Doncaster sales had fetched a record sum of £20,422. Unfortunately Jessie had made an unscheduled and disastrous appearance. 'Today's sale was quite spoiled for me,' Mark wrote to Edith, 'by the most inopportune arrival of my mother – *très très mal* – and in a vile temper – Henry and I have decided that next year some steps will have to be taken to prevent a repetition – It was not so bad as it might have been but I couldn't stand it and went away.'[6] Though he was not to know it, Jessie's health was in steep decline, owing to her drinking.

A considerable part of his time was spent arguing with Brierley about the exact form the new house should take. He did not like the initial designs, which reminded him of the Royal Automobile Club in Pall Mall, London. Their most glaring fault in his opinion was, that Sledmere's great library, its pride and joy, had been re-housed on the ground floor. 'Are you still absolutely fixed to [the] library on the ground floor in the new building?' he wrote to Brierley on 18 October, in a letter liberally sprinkled with amusing caricatures illustrating his worries. 'Consider it will cease to be a library – there will be gardeners carrying palms, friends looking in at the window, people climbing out of the window, people laying tea things, ladies and children arranging flowers, guns coming in at the door. It will not be a library, it will be a hall – a huge damnable hall. I want a library – it must be on the first floor.'[7]

Mark's strong views were not entirely motivated by practicalities. His sense of the aesthetic told him that a ground-floor setting would deprive the room of one of its most striking features, the beautiful

view out across the park. 'It should be in the air,' he told Brierley a few days later. 'The landscape effect from the house is a great part of the room – the windows at the church end do more than light the ceiling. Now if the library goes downstairs it loses six windows and gains four: but it gains shadows after twelve o'clock, so you may say it loses three windows – besides this it loses the light of the sky by having a high horizon.'[8] In the end these worries about the library contributed to Mark entirely rethinking the concept of building a new house and considering the possibility of recreating the eighteenth-century Sledmere.

When Parliament reconvened, it was time for Mark to put the problems of Sledmere to the back of his mind, and prepare to make his maiden speech. He did so on 27 November on a subject close to his heart: affairs in the Middle East, in particular Turkey, then in the throes of a war with Italy. To lend him moral support, Edith attended with her brother, Harold, and from the Strangers' Gallery, they witnessed the agonies of nerves he was going through as he sat waiting for the interminably long speech of the previous speaker, the leader of the Irish Party, John Dillon. 'I shall never forget the spectacle of the tortures he endured when waiting for his turn to speak,' Harold recalled. 'Every time that Dillon said something like: "and now, Mr Speaker, to go on to my seventh point," Mark cast an agonising look . . . and threw himself – quite regardless of appearances – into an attitude of hopeless despair. There was Dillon slogging away at his points without a sign of exhaustion. And there was Mark tossing about on his bench like a ship in a stormy sea. It was one of the most distressing spectacles I have ever witnessed.'[9]

When his moment came he shone, though he took time to get into his stride. 'At the commencement of a speech,' wrote a contemporary, '[he] at first gave the impression of extreme boyishness – a sort of silly, laughing nervousness or shyness, which made one wonder if one were about to listen to the speech of a man or a clownish boy. Doubts were accentuated by his peculiar habit of twisting round his fingers an untidy wisp of hair which invariably persisted in falling across the left side of his forehead. When first I heard him, he gave me a very peculiar quaking feeling for about three minutes, but suddenly the silly shyness or what-ever it was would drop like the discarded cloak of a clown, and thereafter he was the serious statesman. Not for a second longer did he lose the grip of his subject or the attention of his audience.'[10]

His speech was a passionate one, touching on the dangers of the government's lack of any real policy in the Middle East – in particular reminding them of the importance of a strong and united Turkish Empire to British commerce and strategy – and calling on them to give more support to the Turks. It was, wrote Aubrey Herbert, given 'in the rare complete silence that the House sometimes gives as recog-nition to a distinguished contribution to its debates'. Mark's good fortune was that the next speaker happened to be Mr Asquith, the Prime Minister. 'It is my most agreeable duty,' he said, ' – if the Hon. Gentleman will allow me to do so – to congratulate him very heartily on as promising and successful a maiden speech as almost any I have listened to in my long experience.'[11] Afterwards, Edith teased her Terrible Turk about his display of nervousness, reminding him that he had always said that most of the people sitting in the House were 'fools'. 'They are mostly fools,' replied Mark, 'but there are a few who count and of whom one naturally stands in awe.'[12]

Mark's reaction to the great success of his speech, given in a reply to a letter of congratulation the following day from the *Grande Dame* of the Tories, Lady Londonderry, was uncharacteristically modest. He attributed it to an extraordinary run of luck. '(A),' he wrote, 'Dillon had wearied the House till it was ready to cheer anyone or anything. (B) I knew the subject. (C) It was not controversial. (D) Asquith himself is a Yorkshireman. Take also into consideration that it was a pure fluke that the PM spoke directly after me . . .'[13] Still, it was a brilliant start to a parliamentary career into which he threw himself with gusto, thrilled at having at last found a calling that was worthy of his talents, and perfectly suited his restless and active temperament.

He had soon established for himself a punishing schedule which involved, not only putting in more than the requisite amount of time in the House, but also travelling all over the country to address political meetings and attend fund-raising social functions. Between his election in July, and the Christmas recess of 1911, he attended thirty-one meetings and twenty-seven social gatherings, spent fifty days in Parliament, taking part in eighty-eight divisions, asking sixteen questions, and made one speech. He was always in a frantic hurry. One day, for example, his brother-in-law, Harold, who was staying with him at Eddlethorpe, was just settling down to a delicious breakfast, his favourite meal of the day, when the dining-room door was flung open, and in rushed Mark, shouting at him to look sharp, as they had to be off at once. When Edith protested that her brother had not yet eaten his breakfast, Mark yelled at her, 'Breakfast! Here's his breakfast – I'll take it with me!'

'He rushed to the table,' Harold later wrote, 'and seizing several pieces of bacon on toast, thrust them into his overcoat pocket. A couple of grilled sausages and a slice of ham with plenty of fat on it followed suit. Into another pocket he stuffed the top of a loaf of bread. Then he seized me also, and rushed me out of the room into the hall. I was barely allowed to snatch up my greatcoat and hat before we were in the car and off.'[14] He usually had so many things on his mind that he could not be bothered with what he considered trifles. On another occasion, when he had to attend a very grand political dinner in Carlton House Terrace, and was changing to go out, he was so engaged in a political argument with Harold, that he failed to notice his footwear and left for the dinner dressed to the nines, except that he was wearing on his feet a large pair of muddy boots.

A political career meant big changes not only for Mark but for his family, who were moved to London, into 9 Buckingham Gate, an imposing four-storey town-house across from Buckingham Palace, and within easy walking distance of Westminster Cathedral. As well as a grand entrance hall and fine staircase, their new home boasted a series of large reception rooms, suitable for entertaining in, a mass of upstairs rooms for the five children and their nannies and governesses, as well as plenty of space to house the large number of servants then required by a family of their size and station. Edith immediately opened an account at Harrods, which supplied her with everything from sardines to shoelaces.

Though Mark adored his family, and spent as much time as possible with them, his new life meant that he was never able again to devote the time to them that he had done since his return to England in 1906. He was, more than ever, a workaholic and, with the exception of Sundays, when the family would attend Mass together in the morning, and pass the afternoon at a concert either at the Queen's Hall or the Albert Hall, they began to see less and less of him. On weekdays in London he rose every morning at dawn and either went riding in Rotten Row or walked to Mass at the Cathedral, where he would often act as one of the servers. If the children were lucky they might catch a glimpse of him at breakfast, though he would have little time to spare since, before heading off to the House at eleven, he had to read all the leading dailies, both from London and Yorkshire. Then he was off to his office in the Commons to go over his correspondence with his secretary, Walter Wilson, a fellow Yorkshireman.

In the evenings, if he were not out of town addressing a meeting, he would invariably be back in the House, or attending a dinner. Enjoying debate as he did, and being a man of such charm, he found no shortage of invitations to political dinners. He was invited to join an exclusive Conservative dining club known as the 'Tuesday Club'. This club, so called because it met on successive Tuesday evenings, had been founded by Sir Ian Malcom as a successor to the 'Hughlians', a name given to a group of friends, all supporters of Lord Hugh Cecil, who were bound together by their hatred of Asquith and his Parliament Bill. 'The members,' wrote Malcom, 'were linked by no engagement to act together politically, but only to observe with free Masonic fidelity the astonishing confidences that were exchanged at our weekly feasts in the Palace of Truth.' Mark shone at these gossipy dinners because of his great talent as a caricaturist and it became a rite that on each occasion he would draw a cartoon in the club book. 'Mark would grab at the book,' Malcom recalled, 'and, pushing his plate on one side with a sniff and a chuckle, draw forth his fountain pen and bend double over the page until his caricature was completed. We rarely knew what it was that had tickled his fancy so suddenly until the book was passed round, and we were convulsed with laughter at our artist's conception of the passing jest of the moment.'[15]

The caricatures were generally some in-joke connected to a recent exploit of a member of the club or some piece of political gossip. Sometimes they were rough scribbles but they could also be quite elaborate. In the latter category falls the series that he drew in 1917 when Chequers was presented to the nation as a permanent residence for the current Prime Minister. He illustrated a 'Code of Conduct' for the new incumbent, which included such rules as:

- Prime Ministers' eldest sons alone shall have the right to carve the names of their fiancées on the grand staircase.
- In the event of the Prime Minister being a woman, the Prime Minister's husband will be regarded by the domestic staff as mistress of the house.
- In event of a Prime Minister being engaged in conference with a member of his Cabinet who is of the opposite sex, members of the domestic staff will knock twice before entering the room.
- Gentlemen guests of the resident Minister will be required to wear evening dress at dinner. In order that the artistic unities may be preserved, they will be inspected by the President of the Royal Academy who, on behalf of the Trustees, will decide whether their appearance is in harmony with the traditions and surroundings of the Ministerial residence.
- An English country gentleman is to be kept on the premises for the entertainment of the resident Minister and to give tone to the establishment.

Scarcely were Mark and the family settled into Buckingham Gate than they found themselves in mourning. Jessie's drinking, a problem that would not go away, had led to a steady decline in her health as well as her behaviour, the latter having caused an almost complete rift between her and her son in the last few years. 'It is impossible,' Mark had written to Edith back in July, 1909, 'to remain on any particular or intimate terms with one who will neither listen or pay heed to

SOME OF THE RULES FOR "CHEQUERS."

anything.'[16] Now, aged only fifty-six, she was at death's door after a series of strokes. Though society may have turned its back on her, and the last years of her life were spent, as *The Times* put it, in the company of 'a small group of intimate friends', she had never ceased to win the love and respect of the less well off, and it was said at her funeral that as she lay in her room, insensible and dying, her servants crept in one by one and kissed her hand.

Her death, on 2 June, did not pass unnoticed by the press, much to the fury of both Mark and his father. In one paper she was referred to as 'the greatest plunger of her time',[17] while the *Daily Mail* called her 'a victim to all the excitements of the racecourse' and drew its reader's attention to the 'notorious litigation' of the 1890s.[18] Lord Northcliffe, the proprietor, received a stinging rebuke from Mark, who asked him 'to prevent the repetition of such vile outrages on the defenceless dead and the stricken living'.[19] When he subsequently apologised and threatened to sack the offending author, Mark begged Northcliffe to refrain from doing this, on the grounds that 'of all qualities in my mother, charity and mercy were the greatest'.[20]

On 7 June, a special train took Jessie's body up to Sledmere, from which station it was borne on a cart drawn by four farm horses to a temporary chapel erected close to the ruins of the house. There it was met by the Abbot of Ampleforth and a contingent of Benedictine monks, who sang a Requiem Mass, after which the coffin was carried by tenants of the estate to the churchyard. Two thousand people turned out to bid their farewells. The mourners did not include Tatton, who, unfit to travel, remained in London, but they did number among them her last and faithful lover, Major Braithwaite. In London, a Requiem High Mass took place simultaneously at the Church of the Immaculate Conception in Farm Street, the text of the funeral oration being, 'Charity covers a multitude of sins'. As Tatton left the church, he was heard to mutter 'A remarkable woman, Jessie, a remarkable woman, but I rue the day, I rue the day I met her.'

Tatton did not outlive Jessie for long. In the last few months he was to spend at Sledmere, in the summer of 1912 and living with Madame in a house in the village, he became obsessed with the idea that he was going to die at precisely 11.30 a.m. Each morning his groom would bring round his favourite mount, an old cob, for him to ride. On some mornings he would ride out, while on others he would dismiss them with the words, repeated over and over again, 'No, no, can't ride, can't ride, going to die, going to die.' As it happened, his premonition was not realised. Instead, on a trip to London early in 1913, he caught pneumonia and was laid up, seriously ill, at the Metropole Hotel. At some point, Mark appears to have completely lost patience with his father and all those who surrounded him, including Henry Cholmondeley, whom he despised for being so weak. As for Madame, whom he suspected of trying to take control, he saw this illness as an excuse to finally get rid of her.

The plot failed, because by the time he went to see Tatton, on 13 March, his eighty-seventh birthday, the status quo had changed. 'My father had made such progress by the time I came back,' he wrote to Edith, 'that nothing could be done as regards Madame – he is now recovering very rapidly but will not move . . . so all I have been able to do is arrange the food, and feeding shall be in the hands of the nurses, and that Madame is not to take her meals in the room with him – and that his letters are to go through Henry.' He bitterly regretted not having taken Edith with him, telling her that had she been there, he might have been able to achieve his objective. 'But alone it is impossible,' he complained. 'I feel very defeated and weary and depressed. Never had anyone such people to deal with as Henry, Gardiner, Madame, and my father.'[21]

Feeling that he was on the mend, Tatton told Mark that he was going to remain at the Metropole until he was strong enough to travel back to Sledmere, where it was his intention to 'start on more churches at once'. It was a wish that was never to be fulfilled. Soon after, his condition deteriorated. He remained at the Metropole, his health being the subject of weekly reports in the Court Circular of *The Times*. On 3 May, his state was described as 'grave', and he died in the early hours of 4 May. A death in a hotel is never good for business and the manager, thrown into a temporary panic, had the cheek to ask Mark if he minded his father being smuggled out of the premises in a hollow sofa, which had been specially constructed for such occasions. 'However my father leaves this hotel,' he remarked, outraged by the request, 'he shall leave it like a gentleman.' In the end he accepted a compromise, and the body was removed from the hotel in the middle of the night.

On 5 May, the early morning train from Malton to Sledmere carried with it Tatton's coffin, which was loaded on to a farm wagon and drawn by a pair of heavy horses the four miles to St Mary's Church. After a simple, brief service, attended mostly by estate servants and villagers and a few tenants, the coffin was placed on a bier in the chancel to lie in state for a few days. On the night before the funeral, Mark crept into the church and gave a Roman Catholic blessing over his father's body, in the belief that during his lifetime he had had the desire to convert, but had lacked the courage to do so. While this would certainly have caused Jessie to smile, one can only imagine that Tatton himself must have been scowling in the tomb.

As Tatton's coffin was being lowered into the ground, in the shadow of his most ambitious church, across the grounds a cat's cradle of scaffolding enfolded the walls of the burnt out house, and the occasional distant shouts of workmen and the sounds of their tools were blown in on the wind. Tatton's ambition that his beloved Sledmere should rise again was being realised, and in the way that he wanted it. He had told Brierley, in March, 1912, that 'you cannot do better than follow the old lines in every way'.[22] On this subject, Mark had been in complete agreement with his father. With the outer walls sound, apart from the west front, and the cellars all in good condition, he considered it a waste of time and money to pull them down and start anew, when the old house might be successfully recreated. He submitted to Brierley some sketches to prove his point. 'The offices and house I have roughly sketched are what we want carrying out,' he wrote in January, 1912. 'The old house was generally regarded by servants as most convenient because of its compactness, and both my wife and I consider that in the enclosed rough draft the old merits of warmth, closeness and convenience are retained.'[23]

Brierley was still determined to build a modern house and fought

Richard and fellow
'Bright Young Things' on
Bridlington Beach, 1926.

Wedding photograph of
the author's parents,
29 September, 1942.

Virginia Gilliat,
the author's mother.

Lily, Marchioness of Anglesey,
the author's maternal grandmother.

Henry Cyril Paget, the 'Dancing
Marquess' of Anglesey.

Familiar faces of Sledmere:
(clockwise from top)
Dorothy (housekeeper),
Michael (butler), and
Jack (chauffeur/valet).

The Sykes family in the Library, Christmas 1961.
(Left to right) Nicholas, Christopher, Henrietta, Mama,
Arabella, Papa, Tatton and Jeremy.

Papa playing the organ.

The author, in hippie mode, 1967.

1969 Christmas card: the last photograph of Mama with her family.

The Big House.

The Village School 1894, with Alice Carter standing on the right.

his corner hard. 'It would be infinitely better,' he told Mark, 'and only cost about the same, to entirely rebuild the house, and to place its principal and longitudinal frontage facing south.'[24] He told Henry Cholmondeley he considered Mark's scheme 'an impossible one'. He was up against the worst kind of client, however; an amateur who knows best – a particularly determined amateur at that – and the bottom line was that he had to either agree to his ideas, or back out of the contract. He chose the former course and, on 9 February, submitted plans based on Mark's scheme, telling him 'I think it has come out well and the arrangement is certainly more convenient and workable than I thought possible on such lines.'[25]

One modification upon which Mark insisted, curious in the light of the times, was the addition of an enormous servants' wing on the north elevation, almost as big as the principal block, containing the servants' hall, kitchen, laundry, brewery, gunroom, brushroom, etc, everything that would once have been needed to meet the require-ments of a grand Edwardian household. It was on these quarters that the rebuilding of Sledmere began early in 1913.

In the annals of difficult clients, there can have been few more exacting taskmasters than Mark. Nothing escaped his notice and his patience was stretched to its limits by what he considered to be Brierley's lack of interest in attention to detail, combined with a cava-lier attitude to his wishes. He was furious, for example, that his estate carpenter had not been consulted about the mantelpieces and grates for the fireplaces in the servants' wing, which was nearing completion in the summer of 1914. 'As this has not been done,' he commented, 'we have, as I expected, the usual monument of hideousness.'[26] The twelve '929 Glen Eden' fireplaces were what he most disliked – 'Ill-proportioned, Modern, Pretentious, Vulgar, Untruthful' – and he ordered them to be removed. In addition he was unhappy with the dado and skirting rails, the bedroom doors, the windows and the jambs of the shutters. 'So far,' he wrote exasperatedly, 'not one single detail has been correct.'[27]

With work about to begin on the central block, Mark was especially concerned that things should be done exactly the way he wanted them, and he insisted that Brierley was to go ahead with no work until it had been personally initialled by him. 'It is simply a question,' he told him, 'as to whether I am to have the old rooms in spirit or whether I am to have modern vulgarity.'[28] While he professed himself to be 'a lamb', when it came to construction, water, light and planning, 'on ornamental detail,' he said, 'I am and must remain a roaring lion . . . I have to live in the house – think how bad for you and me if I live to any age – that I should daily curse your name each time my eye was vexed by a detail my soul could not approve . . . it's not a question of leaving the design in your hands, but of not leaving it sticking in my eye. We are on the verge of the old house and we must come to an understanding.' A postscript added to this letter reveals the depths of Mark's irritation. 'I'll break your proud heart yet.'[29]

Contrary to what is often said about the present Sledmere, it is not an exact replica of the original, though it follows it closely. The west front, for example, which was completely rebuilt to an unexecuted eighteenth-century design, gained two new windows on each floor, and a central pediment supported on four pilasters. There were significant changes to the interior, in particular the creation of a grand hall, with a double-flight staircase sweeping up to an arched gallery along each side of it, with a secondary staircase hall behind it for the use of the servants. Mark also made his own additions, in particular a neo-Vanburgh smoking room, in which he was able to display the family's collection of banners and muskets from the Napoleonic era, and, most eccentrically, the Turkish Room, designed by an Armenian artist, David Ohanessian. Covered from floor to ceiling with copies of sixteenth-century Iznik tiles, made in Damascus under the supervision of Ohanessian, it was inspired by the beautiful decorations Mark had seen in the apartments of the Valide Sultan (Sultan's mother) in the Yeni (New) Mosque, which stands on the shores of the Golden Horn in Constantinople.

When it came to the principal rooms – the Drawing Room, the Music Room, the Dining Room and the Library – they were entirely remade, only the mahogany doors being repaired and reused, having been removed and carried out at the time of the fire. In the recreation of these, the original plans and drawings rescued from the Library proved invaluable, as did Sophia Sykes's nineteenth-century watercolours, and a set of photographs taken by *Country Life* in 1897. The plasterwork, by Martyns of Cheltenham, proved to be the single most costly item in the rebuilding. It was either copied from old drawings, or taken from moulds still in the possession of Jacksons of Hammersmith, who worked on the original house. When the restoration was finally complete, in the summer of 1917, the total costs amounted to £62,000, the equivalent of three times the sum expended on the original house.

At the same time as he was faced with the task of single-handedly supervising the rebuilding of Sledmere, Mark was making his name in Parliament, establishing a reputation as a spell-binding speaker and an MP of great adaptability, with a desire to see fair play at all times. His wide knowledge of the East was soon well known, but when he addressed the house in April, 1913 on the subject of foreign pilots under the Pilotage Bill, the correspondent for the *Sunday Chronicle* wrote, 'If he should subsequently turn out to be a ship's captain and a doctor of medicine, few will be staggered.'[30] The speech with which he really made his name, however, and gained the attention of the whole country was on the Irish question.

By the spring of 1914, the Home Rule crisis had brought Ireland to the brink of civil war, with the Unionists insisting that the four counties with a Unionist majority should be left out of any Home Rule scheme, and the Nationalists insisting that Home Rule must include the whole of Ireland. They had each formed their own brandnew military-style units, the Ulster Volunteer Force (UVF) and the Irish Volunteer Force (IVF), and were squared up against one another. In an article for the *Saturday Review*, published in March, Mark entreated MPs to put themselves above party on this issue. 'The Irish question must be settled,' he wrote; 'the Ulster question must be settled; the constitutional question must be settled; the Army must be saved from destruction . . . Parliament as a whole has a duty to the people, above all party pledges; no one was elected to help to bring

England to ruin; every member's duty now is to save her from revolution and disorder.'[31] In *The Times* he wrote, 'The essential to a settlement is that there should be no victory.'[32]

On 1 April, during a debate on the Irish question, Mark reiterated many of the points he had raised in his article, calling on Ulster to be temporarily excluded from Home Rule until a federal solution could be achieved. He appealed to both Nationalists and Unionists. 'I feel that the blame must lie upon us all,' he told the packed House. 'We have drifted on passions, and both sides have gone from one wild cry to another until we have divided class from class, creed from creed, in order to further our policies, until at the very end of it all one cannot deny that the military forces and the very Throne itself have been involved in our quarrels.' His words struck a chord with many ordinary people, and two days later the *Daily Sketch* carried four photographs of him, together with extracts from his speech and his prepared notes, on its front cover, under the headline,

THE GENESIS OF A GREAT SPEECH. THE NOTES FROM
WHICH SIR MARK SYKES, 'MP FOR ENGLAND', SAID
WHAT ALL SANE MEN ARE THINKING.

The most cursory glance at Mark's schedule at this time shows him, quite voluntarily, to have taken on an inordinate amount of work, giving him little time for either himself or his family. Extracurricular activities included a leading role in the recruitment campaign of the Territorial Army. The deteriorating situation in the Balkans had convinced him for some time that the British military should be better prepared in the event of a war. Since 1911 he had been a Lieutenant-Colonel in the Yorkshire Territorial Battalion, and he was determined to see that they were trained up to a standard high enough for them to be able to go straight from their usual work to the line of duty. He was proud to be commander of his 'Terriers', as he called them, and wearing the silk sash that had belonged to his ancestor, Mark Masterman, during the Napoleonic era, appealed to the romantic streak in him. So poor was their pay, however, that it was difficult to keep up their numbers, and up to 30,000 men were being lost each year. Mark feared that the truth about the Territorial Reserve was that it was 'a paper dragon'.[33]

One of his most original ideas during this period, inspired perhaps by reading about his great-grandfather's raising of a militia to fight Napoleon, came about after he had attended a wagon-driving competition, which was held annually on the Sledmere estate, when drivers put their horses and wagons through exacting routines, with prizes awarded for the best driving, the quickest harnessing, etc. It did not escape his attention that these men, with their profound knowledge and understanding of horses and their skill in the field, had great potential as field-battery drivers in time of war. His idea was to form a regiment of Wagon Drivers. When the War Office refused to back his plan, he went ahead and recruited 200 drivers from around Sledmere at a wage, paid out of his own pocket, of fifteen shillings per annum if they agreed to serve in the event of a war. He named them the 'Wagoner's Special Reserve', and gave them each a badge, designed by himself, consisting of an oval medallion with a horse's head in the middle. Finally the War Office took notice and decided to include the regiment in a new branch of the Territorials called the 'Technical Reservists', eventually providing them with the annual sum of £1,000. This enabled Mark to sign up 1,000 men in 1912. When war eventually came, the Wagoners proved extraordinarily useful and saw action almost immediately during the Allies' humiliating retreat from Mons.

As if these interests were not enough, he was also instrumental in the planning of the Royal Naval and Military Tournament, held annually at Olympia. This was boys' war games on an epic scale. Between 1912 and 1914 he produced pageants that became progressively elaborate. The first was a performance of the musketry drill according to the 1745 manual, still used in Napoleon's day. Armed with the flintlock 'Brown Besses' from Sledmere's armoury, the 5th Yorkshire Regiment marched into the arena to a slow drum beat, went through the twenty-one motion routine of preparation for the volley, and then let off a great thunder of fire before marching away. In 1913 he enlisted his old D'Ordel collaborator, Edmund Sandars, to help him produce *The Restoration of Charles II* in five scenes, filling Olympia with replicas of Ludgate Prison and Holbein's Gate at either end, and a huge bust of Cromwell, sculpted by Mark himself. The King, George V, who was in attendance, was so delighted with the performance that he called the two producers up to the Royal Box to personally congratulate them.

It was the last of these pageants, however, which was the most spectacular. *The Romans in Britain*, which opened on 14 May, 1914, would have done justice to Cecil B. de Mille. Six hundred men and 100 horses were involved, and the arena, which was surrounded by 25,000 yards of scenery, contained a simulated landscape of the Roman Frontier, and a model of Hadrian's Wall, weighing fifteen tons. The production opened with 'The Triumph of Claudius Caesar', in which the Emperor and Empress entered, to the strains of Tchaikovsky, in a chariot drawn by white horses and attended by Imperial Lictors, Consuls, Tribunes, Magistrates, Senators, Priests and Centurions, and followed by the captive Britons, Imogen and Cymbeline. Mark's second son, Christopher, was also in the chariot, playing the role of the young Nero. The climax of the evening was a fierce battle between the Centurion, Ausonius, and a Barbarian king, the latter's triumph ending Roman supremacy.

Six weeks later, Archduke Franz Ferdinand of Austria and his wife were assassinated in Sarajevo, and war looked increasingly as if it would no longer be confined to games in the arena at Olympia. This was grist to Mark's mill, as it would enable him to offer all his knowledge and experience of the East in helping to shape British policy out there. Within a month of hostilities being declared, and with a growing likelihood that Germany would involve Turkey in the war, he offered his services to Winston Churchill, then First Lord of the Admiralty, to serve in Syria and South Mesopotamia. 'I know you won't think me self-seeking,' he wrote on 24 August, 'if I say all the knowledge I have of local tendencies and possibilities are at your disposal – and you will forgive me for troubling you, if operations are to take place in those parts I might be of more use on the spot, than anywhere else.

My Battn. is practically willing for foreign service, i.e. eighty-five per cent, and with my personal knowledge of its possible antagonist in the regions I mention, I could make it serve a turn, raise native scallywag corps, win over notables or any other oddment.'[34]

Mark received little encouragement from Winston, and by November he was champing at the bit. 'It maddens me,' he wrote to Edith from the battalion's training camp in Newcastle, 'not to be where I could be most useful, i.e. in the Medn.'[35] Not a man to be sidelined, and a strong believer in the vital strategic importance to Britain of Constantinople and the Ottoman Asiatic Empire, he kept up the pressure on Churchill, writing to him in February, 1915, when the Dardanelles expedition was being planned, and encouraging him to 'take the Gallipoli peninsula . . . or to play the great stroke and take Constantinople by a combined attack by sea from North and South'.[36] Then he transferred his pestering to the War Office. In the end, this strategy paid off, but not quite in the way he had intended, for instead of being sent to the East with his battalion, as had been his request, he was separated from them. While they went off to fight in France, Mark was seconded to the War Office by Lord Kitchener, the Secretary of State for War, as an adviser on Eastern affairs.

In certain circles, both during and immediately following the end of the 1914–18 war, there were accusations that Mark was a coward for abandoning his battalion in this way. These were grossly unfair as he felt a very strong responsibility towards his men. 'A Battalion is like one's child,' he wrote to Edith in February, 1915, after he had been offered a post on General Maxwell's staff in Egypt. 'One must on choice choose the thing one is responsible for.'[37] In another letter, to Kitchener's private secretary, Oswald Fitzgerald, he declared 'I want to make it quite clear that I could only leave my battalion on a direct order & not as a volunteer. My personal duty is to my regiment . . .'[38] It was a direct order from Kitchener that brought him to the War Office.

Mark spent most of the war on special, often secret missions to the East, his first being a six-month trip to observe the military and political situations in the Near East and India. Leaving London in early June,

1915, he travelled to the Balkans, the Eastern Mediterranean, Egypt, Aden, India, the Persian Gulf and Mesopotamia. Missing Edith and the family dreadfully, he sent home a steady stream of letters. 'Isn't it wonderful,' he wrote in one from Salonika, '1901–1915 – and we love one another more than ever.' Edith and the children had moved from Eddlethorpe into the big house, work on which was coming on a pace, with the Drawing Room ceiling completed, and the one in the Library going up. Until the interior was finished, they were lodged in the servants' wing. For Freya, Richard, Christopher, Petsy and Angela it was heaven. This was now their home, with no grumpy old grandfather to tell them where or where not they could roam. They chased Petsy through the half-finished rooms playing hide and seek, while the Library, with its polished floor and numerous tall windows, was the perfect setting for endless games of 'rats and ferrets', played in the dark. Richard discovered Tatton's old wheelchair, and the long passages on the ground floor echoed to Petsy's screams of terror as she was raced up and down them blindfolded. 'The rubble in front of the house,' she wrote, 'was a wonderful place to toboggan down on trays, and when Papa was at home on his brief leaves, we had a wonderful time.'[39] Slowly but surely, new life was breathed into the house.

Mark saw little of it, for scarcely was he home than he was drawn into a new government intrigue, which required his presence almost permanently in London. As the man now considered indispensable by Kitchener for his knowledge of the East, he was appointed as his personal representative on a committee set up to consider the future of Asiatic Turkey. Under the chairmanship of a senior diplomat, Maurice de Bunsen, from whom it took its name, the committee faced a difficult challenge – the complicated dissolution, in the event of the defeat of Turkey, of the 400-year-old Ottoman Empire. Mark's appointment caused a few raised eyebrows since he was only a junior official, but the fact is that he was alone amongst the other members in having actually travelled to most parts of Ottoman Asia and was thus able to submit memoranda, supply detailed maps, many of which were used by the War Office throughout the war, and provide discourses on little-known subjects from the Kurds to the Caliphate.

In spite of his junior rank his work on the De Bunsen Committee impressed the British government enough to give him the task of presiding over secret negotiations with the French, who had their own claims to stake against the Turks. Though Mark and, to a certain extent, the French negotiator, François Georges Picot, scion of a French colonialist family and a senior diplomat, were both sincere idealists of the school of thinking which was eventually to lead to the formation of the League of Nations, they were up against extreme reactionary forces in Paris, led by two men, Etienne Flandin and Franklin Bouillon, who were determined to hijack this treaty to further their own imperialist ambitions. Since Picot was too weak to stand up against them, these two triumphed in their desire to see France dictate highly advantageous terms for themselves over the Arabs. Even though Mark's own goals had gone no further than creating a French buffer in the Middle East between Russian and British territory, his name was thus given and was for ever after associated with an agreement which went much further than this, and which, when it was revealed to the world, was, much to his resentment, derided as being 'iniquitous', 'unjust', 'nefarious', and an outstanding example of the methods of the 'old and evil diplomacy'.[40]

The Sykes–Picot Agreement essentially divided up Turkish-held Syria, Iraq, Lebanon, and Palestine into various French- and British-administered areas, giving at the same time the south Kurdish and north Armenian provinces to Russia. Between the French and British acquisitions, there was to be a confederation of Arab States or a single independent Arab State, divided into French and British spheres of influence. Palestine, because of its Holy places, was left under an international regime. Unfortunately, the treaty conflicted with pledges already made by the British in 1915 to Hussein ibn Ali, Sherif and Emir of Mecca and self-styled 'King' of the Hejaz Arabs.

The Hejaz, the long and narrow western section of the Arabian peninsula bordering the Red Sea, was of unique importance in the Arab world in that it contained Mecca and Medina, the Holy cities of Arabia, which gave great influence to its ruler. Though the latter was nominally the Ottoman Sultan, the great distance of the Hejaz from Constantinople gave it almost autonomous status, which meant that real power lay with the Sherif. Hussein had been promised that, in return for his bringing his people into revolt against the Turks, and thus ultimately preventing them from siding with Germany, he would be given dominion over all the land he liberated. This amounted to all the territory east of the Mediterranean, bounded on the north by the 37th parallel, on the east by Persia and the Persian Gulf, on the south by the Indian Ocean, and the west by the Red Sea and the Mediterranean.

For the time being the Arabs remained in ignorance for the very nature of the treaty, drawn up at a time when the Allies were in no position to implement it, meant that it had to be kept secret. The Russians however did have to be consulted, which is how Mark, in March, 1916, found himself in Petrograd enjoying an audience with the Tsar. 'General Callwell has come from England,' wrote Tsar Nicholas to Tsaritsa Alexandra, on 7 March, 'together with another very interesting man, Major Sykes, who has travelled all his life in Asia Minor and Mesopotamia, and knows the Turks and Arabs well. He has told me many strange and noteworthy things.'[41] The Tsar struck Mark as being like a well-informed schoolboy of fifteen, though one with a prodigious memory. He was impressed by his recalling the exact position of every unit in the Russian army, and by the fact that as he passed down the line of officers drawn up in the ante-room before dinner, he remembered exactly what each one had done.

But he also noted and, on his return to England, commented on the huge gulf that separated the Tsar from his people. It must have preyed on his mind, for on one occasion when he was entertaining his children with a rendition of Tchaikovsky's 'Marche Slav' on the pianola, he stopped in the middle of playing it to declare, 'With music like this, there has to be a Revolution!'[42] The Russian Revolution, when it came, effectively ended the secrecy of the Sykes–Picot agreement, for the Bolsheviks, in an attempt to discredit both the overthrown Tsarist Government and the capitalist governments of the Allies, published the details, along with those of other secret treaties in the archives of imperial Russia. When the Arabs discovered that the agreement clearly contradicted the promises that had been made to them, it stirred up powerful resentments, which formed the foundation of a long and bitter struggle in the Middle East.

Mark had great hopes at the beginning of 1917, when General Stanley Maude, at the head of a conquering army, marched from Basra to Baghdad, sweeping all opposition before them, albeit at considerable cost in men and equipment. Mark sincerely believed that the Arab troops, who had little love for the oppressive Ottoman Empire they were defending, would welcome this victory, and that it would be popular throughout the Arab world if handled well. With this in mind, he drafted a 'Baghdad Proclamation' which was delivered by Maude on March, 1917:

O people of Baghdad, our armies do not come into your cities and lands as conquerors or enemies, but as liberators. It is [Britain's] wish that you should prosper even as in the past, when your lands were fertile, when your ancestors gave to the world literature, science and art and when Baghdad City was one of the wonders of the world.

Though they welcomed the defeat of the Turks, many Arabs, however, were distrustful of the British, noting that, despite the rhetoric of freedom and representation, there was little concession to autonomy or self-determination. Their suspicions that the invaders were motivated by imperialist ambitions were strengthened within a few months with the revelation of the contents of the Sykes–Picot Agreement.

It would not be an exaggeration to say that Mark's subsequent and never-ending quest to find a solution to the Middle Eastern problem was eventually the death of him. He tried harder than anyone in the British Government to rationalise Arab aspirations with Allied interests. It was, he considered, his destiny and it was an all-consuming one, taking him away from everything else in his life that he loved, including his family, but, gifted and serious individual though he was, he was often used as a pawn, both by the more diplomatically seasoned and cynical Picot and the senior officials in Whitehall.

On one of his infrequent and ecstatic reunions with Edith, they conceived a third son, Daniel, born in October, 1916. Named after his Hull merchant ancestor, Mark was hardly to know him, so little time was he able to spend at Sledmere. This was a relief for Brierley, who was able to complete his work without constant interruption, though his employer still fired off the occasional broadside. When at home for a visit in September, 1916, for example, he crossed swords over the colour for the Hall, then about to be painted. 'I stick by pale blue,' he insisted, 'which was the old colour', adding, 'I have decided to marble the columns: that's final.'[43] A year later, when the work was finally complete, Mark paid Brierley the compliment of asking him for a crayon drawing of himself 'the same size as Rose's pastel, for me to hang in the Library'. He had finally given the ultimate seal of his approval.

It was Edith's habit to regularly invite her numerous nephews and nieces to stay, so that the new house was often full of children. On the rare occasions their visits coincided with Uncle Mark's leaves, they were aware of how he filled the house with his presence. 'All would be transformed,' Angela later wrote, 'and great excitement prevailed. Suddenly the house was filled with uniformed men, raised voices, impromptu games of football or archery, cavalcades of horses would be mounted and go galloping down the dales, while indoors my father would thunder out music on the American organ in the Music Room.'[44] His nephew, Nino Hunter, recalled 'the vividness of his personality, the ebullience and irrepressibility of his humour. He was the mainspring at the centre of all the fun we had, acting endless charades at his instigation.'[45] Mark loved to entertain them with his cartoons, a favourite of which was inspired by a painting, hanging in the Dining Room, by W. Hamilton, RA, of a group of people gathered round a tombstone in Stoke Poges Churchyard, the famous setting for Thomas Gray's *Elegy Written in a Country Churchyard*. An old man is regaling a child and two women with a story. They are leaning over him, as he rests on a walking stick. His caricature was called *What Would Happen if the Stick Broke*, and depicted the old man and child lying on the ground, beneath the winsome, respectable females who, with their legs up in the air, were displaying a wealth of frilly undergarments. It made the children howl with laughter.

There were adventurous games too, which could lead to episodes of a hair-raising nature. On one occasion, while at home on leave with an old friend, Lancelot Oliphant, he witnessed one of these scenes involving a chariot he had had made for the children by the estate works yard, always known in the family as 'the Raff Yard'. Inspired by his Roman scenario for the Royal Tournament, it was pulled by two Shetland ponies, Malvolio and Merry Andrew, running side by side. This time, Freya was at the reins, and her passengers were Lancelot Oliphant and Angela, aged four. As she raced across the lawn, standing upright like Queen Boadicea, Mark and the rest of the family who were observing the scene with mounting horror, began to flap their arms up and down in what they assumed would be interpreted as a sign for her to slow down. 'But I thought they were encouraging me to go faster,' Freya later recalled, 'so I did, and the ponies took the bit in their mouths and bolted. I screamed to Lancelot, who seized hold of the reins, but he couldn't stop them and they careered over the drive and were going absolutely full pace slap into the garden wall. He managed to hang on to one rein and he pulled them and they went under a tree. I remember he got a crack on the head from a branch. By this time Papa and Mama were tearing down the path towards us. The ponies had stopped and were heaving.' No sooner had they got Angela out and dismounted than the ponies took off again, knocking Mark, who had been holding them, to the ground. They careered across the main road, down a steep hill and smashed into a gate at the bottom, reducing the chariot to matchwood. 'But I thought you wanted me to go faster!' wailed Freya, who was in the doghouse for some time after.[46]

In the latter years of the war, Mark's letters home to Edith were full of yearnings for home and family. 'You cannot think what a happiness the thought of your dear self is to me,' he wrote to her from Cairo in April, 1917, 'we are never really apart, you are at my side every moment ... here we are darling, married twelve years, with our dear children and writing like young lovers'.[47] A week later, he was in India, his heart still beating for home. 'Oh my dearest dear, every day I pray for you and the children,' he told her. 'I suppose you are staying on at Sledmere where there will always be plenty for you to do – I see you in every place in the house – the house I know so well – or in the park or on the farm.'[48] Yet when the war ended, rather than return to his family, he volunteered to go out once again to the Middle East, believing that he was the only man who could sort out the problems there, in particular the friction between the French and the Arabs in Syria. He left for Jerusalem on 30 October, 1918.

While he was away a general election took place. 'I am absolutely in the dark as to what is going on or how the Election arose,' he wrote to Edith from Jerusalem. 'Anyway I cannot bother my head about it now as I have more important things to do. Is Europe in the throes of death or pangs of birth?'[49] Edith brilliantly managed his campaign, vigorously denying the accusations of his opponent, a Methodist Minister, that her husband had 'shirked' his duty. When the Prime Minister, Lloyd George, heard about this he sent her a letter of support. 'I see unfounded and cruel charges are being made against your husband,' he wrote. 'I have had frequent opportunities of seeing the results of Sir Mark's work, which has been of an exceptionally arduous and difficult character, both at home and on special missions to the Eastern fronts. I hope the electors of Hull will repudiate the false and unworthy insinuations made behind a man's back.'[50] Mark sent his election address from the Holy City. 'Complete ignorance of circumstances under which election has come about,' he stated unequivocally, 'oblige me to confine myself to principles ... Since the commencement of the war I have known no party. I stand for a League of Nations, disarmament and the abolishment of war. In peace terms I stand neither for aggrandisement nor revenge but for justice, reparation and security.'[51] On 14 December, Mark was returned as MP for Central Hull with a massive majority of 10,370 votes. 'I telegraphed the result to him,' wrote Edith, 'and the answer he sent me touched me deeply and will remain for ever imprinted on my heart – *Adjutrix mea et liberatrix mea es tu.*[52] And that is what I like to think I was and am.'

When he finally returned to England on 30 January, 1919, Edith

was shocked by his appearance. He had failed to tell her that he had
been struck down by a virus in Syria which had prevented him keeping
down any solid food, and that for three weeks he had been living on
nothing but three tins of condensed milk a day. He was emaciated
and worn out. Her attempts to persuade him to take a rest fell on
stony ground as he was insistent that he must travel at once to Paris
to report to the Peace Conference. He was depressed that things were
not going satisfactorily in the East.

After a brief two days in London, where at least he caught a glimpse
of four of his children, Freya, Everilda, Angela and baby Daniel,
Richard and Christopher both being away at school, Mark headed for
Paris, accompanied by a worried Edith. Unfortunately, no sooner had
they arrived and settled in at the Hotel Lotti, than Edith was struck
down by the epidemic that was sweeping Europe at the time, the
'Spanish' flu. This deadly strain of influenza, which had engendered
panic and chaos in communities across the globe and was eventually
responsible for between thirty and forty million deaths, struck with
amazing speed, often killing its victims within hours of the first signs
of infection. Edith had the strength to fight it; Mark was not so lucky.

On 10 February, he paid a visit to his old friend and D'Ordel
collaborator, Edmund Sandars, who was working for the War Office
in Paris. In his diary, Sandars noted how thin Mark looked and that
when he commented on it, Mark jokingly pulled in his belt and said
that he had been 'poisoned in Aleppo'. He asked Sandars for a chit
to get some condensed milk, and while this was being obtained, collapsed in a chair, telling his friend how fed up he was with the Peace
Conference. That night Sandars and his wife accompanied Mark and
a friend, Sir Arthur Hirtzel, to the opera to see Massenet's *Thaïs*. Mark
was in a merry frame of mind. 'As usual,' recalled Sandars, 'he facially
acted the music, and we laughed over the play (neither of us had heard
Thaïs before).' After the opera, he ate a good dinner at Henri's, before
being driven back to the Lotti, where the party bid their farewells.
Mark's bonhomie, however, masked a fearful truth.

'I've got it,' he told his faithful secretary, Walter Wilson, as he went
to bed, and Sandars finished his entry for that day with the melancholy

sentence, 'He never got out of bed again after that night.' The following morning, Edith rose from her own sickbed to nurse him, convinced
then that he had nothing worse than a chill. Supplies of Bovril, Oxo
and various patent medicines were sent up to her by the hotel, but
when the chill developed into full blown flu, she sent for their doctor
from England. He arrived too late. By then, Sunday, 16 February,
pneumonia had set in, together with a severe and agonising infection
of the ear, obliging Edith, by the end, to have to shout at her Terrible
Turk to be heard. He died at 6.30 p.m., a month to the day before
his fortieth birthday. Many years later, Petsy was to confide to a friend,
Coote Lygon, that her father appeared to her in London at the very
moment he passed away.

'So,' wrote Mark's childhood friend, Tommy Ellis, now Lord
Howard de Walden, 'the one man that I had met who seemed to me
to have in him the seeds of greatness was not to attain it after all.'[53]
Nor was he to attain his ambition to live to a ripe old age and, as he
had once told his brother-in-law, Harold, 'end his days at Sledmere
as a patriarch, after the Italian fashion, with all his married sons and
their families living in the house with him'.[54] Instead he left a yawning
gap in the lives of all those he left behind. John Hugh Smith wrote
to Edith:

> I shall always for the rest of my life live largely in the past because
> of Mark, and there is little in my mind which is not what it is because
> of him. His conversation was surely the best that one has ever heard;
> its interest, whether one agreed with his ideas or not, was mastering;
> its imagination never failed nor its unique humour. And what I feel
> myself will I know be felt by hundreds of men – not only his friends
> but his own people at Sledmere and his constituents at Hull and his
> soldiers: Bedawin, Druses, Kurds and Turks.[55]

Mark's friend, Ronald Storrs, who had been Oriental Secretary in
Cairo at the beginning of the war, said simply, 'I do not like to think
of England without him; it will never be the same place.'[56]

On the evening of Saturday, 22 February, Mark's coffin arrived at

Sledmere, where it was placed in the new family chapel and covered with a Union Jack. Three wreaths were placed upon it. One was from the villagers and read 'He who never rested, rests.' The others were from the children – 'To darling Daddy' – and Edith – '*Adjutor Meus Liberator Meus Fuistis.*'[57] The funeral service was held three days later in the presence of family and close friends, and afterwards an enormous crowd joined the procession to the graveyard. At its head were the Abbot and Monks of Ampleforth Abbey, bearing lighted tapers as they walked in front of the flag-draped coffin, which was borne on a gun carriage. Behind the coffin came Punch, Mark's favourite charger, carrying an empty saddle, with his field boots reversed in the stirrups. Edith, flanked by her two oldest boys, Richard and Christopher, followed closely behind, leading the rest of the mourners. As the cortège passed through the gates of the church, a band of the 5th Yorkshires struck up Chopin's 'Marche Funèbre'.

A reporter from the *Eastern Morning News* described the burial, which took place with full military honours.

The Father Abbot pronounces the committal service, and the body of Sir Mark is in its last resting place, close to that of his father and mother. The firing party fire three rounds into the northern sky, and following each the drums roll and the air seems to tremble with their sadness. Then bayonets are fixed and Buglers sound the Last Post. Each of the clergy sprinkle Holy Water on the coffin. The church has completed its offices. The widowed mother and fatherless boys fall on their knees, and the hearts of the multitude are filled with a great compassion, and their eyes brim over with tears as they watch their silent prayer.[58]

So Mark was laid to rest in the shadows of both the church built by his father and the great house rebuilt stone by stone by him. His image was also given a more permanent residence, where it could be looked upon for generations to come. During some of the darkest days of the war, when horrendous losses occurred at Passchendaele in 1917, and in the German offensives into France and Flanders in the spring of 1918, Mark had made a vow to commemorate some of the friends he had lost, both in his battalion and elsewhere. His father, in 1896, had erected, outside the gates of his new church at Sledmere, an Eleanor Cross, being a replica of one of the monuments built by Edward I to commemorate the resting places of the body of his wife, Eleanor of Castile, as it travelled from Nottinghamshire where she died to London. Into its niches, Mark had inserted memorial brasses depicting his departed heroes, each dressed in the garb of a crusading Knight, treading underfoot the barbaric Hun and chivalrously slaying the evil dragon of German imperialism with the sword of St George.

The first of eight panels had been in memory of his boyhood friend Edward Bagshawe, 'Captain of the 5th Yorkshire Regiment, killed in Flanders on 22 July, 1916, *Preux chevalie sans peur et sans reproche*.' Others were remembered by their trades and ranks. 'Ye who read this remember Walter Barker, a footman of Sledmere and a Private in the 5th Yorkshire Regiment', 'Harry Agar, an Agriculturist and a Private', 'Thomas Frankish, a Carpenter and a Sergeant', 'William Watson, a Saddler and a Lance Corporal', along with many others, officers and men of the same regiment, who died with them. By coincidence he had left one panel unfilled, and in this his own effigy was engraved in brass, bearing sword and shield, trampling underfoot the prostrate figure of a Saracen, for scroll the *Laetare Jerusalem*, and in the background the Holy City itself.

CHAPTER XIV

Richard

'Whenever he was at home,' wrote Christopher of his father, 'we all seemed to be involved in a world of romance and excitement and laughter.'[1] Now he was gone, and a deep sadness descended upon Sledmere. Edith was bereft, though she had her faith to help pull her through. Mark's constituency, devastated by their loss, tried their hardest to persuade his widow to take up his seat, but, believing that her duty now unquestionably lay with her children, she turned them down. Had she not done so, Edith would have become England's first woman MP.

Since her eldest son, Richard, was only fourteen, Edith was faced with the responsibility of running the house and estate, a task in which she was lucky enough to still have the invaluable help of Mark's cousin, Henry Cholmondeley. Invariably referred to by the family as 'Cousin Henry', he was always elegantly dressed in breeches and gaiters and spoke with an aristocratic, slightly nasal, drawl. His knowledge of bloodstock was unparalleled and his brilliant management of the stud had seen it go from strength to strength. Even during the war years, the progeny from Sledmere had brought in over £65,000. Edith too had a fine eye for a horse, and in the next ten years her input, combined with that of Henry, produced a golden era for the stud, the annual sales bringing in a total of £463,600. Four great foundation mares were bred during this period; Mumtaz Mahal, Lady Juror, Straitlace and Teresina, and their descendants, such as Oh So Sharp, descended from Mumtaz Mahal and winner of the 1985 Triple Crown, are still winning races.

The high prices began in 1919 when ten colts and six fillies, sent up by Edith to the annual Doncaster sales, fetched the astonishing sum of 61,300 guineas. The highest price was paid for a brown colt by

Swynford out of Blue Tit, which was bought by Lord Glanely for 11,500 guineas, and when the prices of four other yearlings, sold later, were included, the total sum for the year came to a record £66,260. Richard and Christopher accompanied their mother to the sales, and stood on the rostrum with Mr Tattersall as the Sledmere horses were knocked down. He prefaced the sale with an appreciation of their father, whom he described as having been 'not only extraordinarily clever, but most amusing and witty'.[2]

Edith was determined that the spirit of fun and laughter with which Mark had imbued Sledmere should live on, and so she made sure that in the school holidays the house was always full of children. Her nephew, Nino Hunter, the son of her sister Hylda, was a regular there. 'I spent some of the happiest moments of a happy childhood amongst my Sykes cousins,' he recalled. It was a children's paradise. They had freedom to roam wherever they wanted; through the enormous service wing, with its laundry, brewery and numerous outhouses; in and out of the kitchen and servants' hall; along miles of passages; up and down the staircases; round and round the reception rooms; sliding along the Library floor; and exploring the attics and the cellars.

There were many memorable characters inhabiting the house who were recalled by Nino. The governess was Mademoiselle de Loudovici, known always as 'Mouzelle', a lady of Luxembourg origins who had come to Sledmere in 1910 from the Earl of Scarborough at Lumley Castle, bringing with her not only her teaching skills but a wealth of ghost stories about the old castle with which, to their delight, she used to terrify the children and instil in them a love of the macabre. She had started by teaching Freya and Richard and now Angela and Daniel were her pupils. She was a very strict Catholic and part of her duties was the religious instruction of the children. 'Mouzelle struck me as prim and proper,' wrote Nino, 'and I was rather in awe of her displeasure should I inadvertently overstep the bounds of propriety in any way.' Being an Anglican, he was also always aware that Mouzelle disapproved of his family for being 'heretics'.

Catholic instruction came also from an Italian monk at Ampleforth College, Father Dunstan Pozzi, who came each Sunday to say Mass in the private chapel attached to the house. He was a humourless man, who spoke the English language in a learned way with very correct pronunciation, without any understanding of its meaning, and was thus regarded as something of a joke by the children. He had a penchant for giving long and incomprehensible sermons, and Christopher referred to him irreverently as 'Father Bumbore'. They were fond of him, however, and often used to include him in their games. In return, he would sometimes in the evenings read them ghost stories with his cowl over his head. 'It was very creepy,' said Nino, ' – so that on going to bed I used to have a good look underneath it, and behind the window curtains too.'

The butler was a burly Irishman called Cassidy, who had a voice which reminded Richard 'of someone moving squeaky furniture about'. 'He wore the dignity of the species,' recalled Nino, and had the ability to show profound disapproval to those whom he felt did not behave in the correct manner. A young American fighter pilot, training at Driffield with the RFC, once landed his plane in the park in an attempt to take a closer look at the 'lovely old house' he had spied from above. Invited to lunch by the enthusiastic bunch of young cousins who rushed out to greet him, he soon found himself seated in the middle of the long table in the Dining Room answering a barrage of questions. Before long he was approached by Cassidy and asked what he would like to drink. ' "Waal, I guess I'd like a port and lemon",' Nino remembered him as saying, adding, 'Trained servant as he was, Cassidy was unable to mask a disdainful surprise, for he well knew, which we then innocent children did not, that a port and lemon was the usual tipple chosen by whores in public bars.'

Mrs Wignall ruled over the kitchen. She was a first class Yorkshire cook and was renowned for her Christmas speciality, Goose Pie. Large country houses like Sledmere always had a special table for cold foods in the dining room, known as the Cold Table, and each year on Christmas Day this magnificent pie made up its centrepiece. Made with raised pastry, it had the appearance of a huge square pork pie. The ingredients for the pastry alone consisted of twenty-four pounds of flour, six pounds of butter and half a pound of suet, and the kitchen maid had to kneel on the kitchen table in order to roll it out. Then it was laid into a huge square tin that had been specially made for it by the local blacksmith, Mr Scott. Mrs Wignall was an expert butcher, whose skills were now put to good use, for the inside of the pie consisted of layer upon layer of boned game, each wrapped around the other. On the outside was a goose, then two ducks, two pheasants, a hare, partridges and, at the centre, six woodcock. The pastry lid was laid on and stock poured in through a hole in the top. It was then cooked for hours in the main oven of the black, coal-fired range that ran down one side the kitchen, and rested in the coolest part of the larder for eight days before being brought to the table. Once the two footmen who were taking the pie into the Dining Room on a huge tray dropped it, when one of the swing doors, which led from the kitchens to the front of the house, swung back and knocked the tray. Luckily, because it was so solid, it only broke in parts and they managed to get it back on to the tray and piece it together.

Being mechanically minded, Nino used to haunt the garage, where two cars were housed; a two-seater Humber and a large French Panhard. There he would often find the chauffeur, Flatters, lying beneath one of the cars and surrounded by pieces of engine. 'He caused us amusement because he had a passion for taking motor cars to pieces, not matched by an ability to reassemble them correctly.' He was inordinately proud of his cars, which were always kept clean and shiny, and even if he had been up late the previous night bringing the family back from a Hunt Ball, he would always wash the car before he went to bed so that it would be ready for use the next day. Flatters never quite got the hang of the Panhard, which had a very difficult straight-through, not a gate, gear change, making it hard to judge when the car was in the correct gear. 'I remember Flatters often making a nonsense of changing gear on a hill, stalling the engine and then having to dismount to wind up the engine to start it again by hand.' Nino was also fascinated by the small power station which provided the electricity for the house, and one or two houses in the village. 'Two DC dynamos,' he recalled, 'feeding a bank of lead-acid cells, were driven by hot-bulb heavy oil engines. The engines were started by heating the hot bulbs in the cylinder heads with a blow-lamp and were turned over by compressed air. It made a wonderful noise. I used to visit this little power station often, plaguing, I suspect, the electrician, Mr Horner.'[3]

As the electrician, Horner also spent a lot of time in the house, in particular in the cellars, where there were endless fuse boxes and miles of wiring. In these cellars, which like those in many country houses are large, dark and ghostly, Richard, who had become obsessed with the French Revolution, after reading A Tale of Two Cities, orchestrated the creation of a Grand Guignol. The walls were daubed with slogans, painted red in imitation of blood, proclaiming such things as VIVE LA REVOLUTION, with bloody arrows pointing to MADAME GUILLOTINE. He had even ordered a miniature guillotine to be made for him at the Raff Yard, which they duly constructed, perfect in every detail and complete with a real metal blade made from a ploughshare. Angela, who was fast becoming a talented sculptress, created corpses and gruesome decapitated heads. She almost became a victim of the guillotine, when one day she was seized by her two older brothers, and had her head placed beneath the blade. Luckily for her, the other children intervened. 'But it's only Angela,' protested Richard. When his mother found out what had happened, she was furious and had the guillotine taken away to have its blade replaced with a blunt wooden one. It reminded her of a previous incident when Angela was only five and Richard, dressed as an evil witch called Mrs Clixon, had been caught attempting to persuade his little sister to jump into a septic tank.

In spite of all the material advantages which life had laid at his feet, Richard, an artistic and sensitive boy, did not have an easy boyhood. 'From his earliest years,' recalled Angela, 'he had a pronounced and rebellious character. One can only guess what would have happened if he had had a wise and understanding father to guide him. As it was almost all the influences worked against his happiness.'[4] He was always being told by his mother what a wonderful man his father had been, and he found him a very hard act to follow. He made an early decision not to emulate him, a fact which was eventually to set him on a collision course with Edith. Harman Grisewood, a school friend, remembered him as having been 'somewhat critical and somewhat withdrawn' as a boy and rather spoiled. This is hardly surprising considering that he was only fourteen when his father died and that he became instantly heir to a large fortune. Since there was no one to discipline him at home, he became used to having his own way and began to assume a certain sense of self-importance. Grisewood noticed this when he and Richard found themselves at Ampleforth College, then a new school, which took in not only boys from public schools, but from other backgrounds. 'There were quite a lot of shopkeepers' sons and the like in the school,' he recalled; 'not the kind of people that Richard was used to living alongside, let alone sleeping along side and I remember him making it quite clear that socially these other people simply weren't acceptable as companions at all. They were barely tolerated.'[5]

As it happened, Richard's time at Ampleforth was short. He and Christopher were removed from the school in 1917 when it was discovered that they were being bullied, partly because their father was a baronet and a Conservative MP, but also because word had leaked out about the accusations against him of cowardice. They were sent to Downside instead, another leading Catholic school, which they both hated, claiming that it was 'a hotbed of homosexuality and sadism'. Fifty years later, Richard was to write to Christopher, 'The memory of that day of anguish is still vivid . . . the dreadful sight of the Quad, the entry by one of the hideous Gothic doors, the smell of coal gas lamps along the dingy passage, and finally being left in charge of the skirted Ramsey and Corney . . . Oh the horror of it all.'[6] He used to say that it was his experiences with the monks at Downside, writing once of 'the fearful scourgings the skirted rascals gave to their wretched charges',[7] that put him off the Catholic Church for ever. His unhappiness there eventually affected his work and when his mother discovered that there was a good chance he might fail his exams into Cambridge, she decided to send him to a crammer. She enrolled him as a boarder at an establishment in Camberley, run by a Mr Tinniswood, where his cousin Nino was already studying.

Richard got off to a bad start with Tinniswood. 'He said he *must* have a piano in his room,' recalled Nino. 'Tinniswood said "No!" Musical instruments were a distraction and were not allowed. Richard then ordered a piano to be delivered to his room and a window had to be removed to get it in. When Tinniswood discovered this he nearly had a stroke and ordered Richard to remove the piano or himself or, better still, both. In the end Tinniswood, being a snob, thought better of it, not wishing to have a real live baronet leave his establishment.' Nino told this story because, he said, 'it was then typical behaviour on the part of Richard, who invariably exhibited "impatience of control".

In spite of his problems with Tinniswood, Richard eventually passed the Cambridge entrance exam and found himself up at Trinity College, where he embraced the fast, rich set, led by Lord Charles Cavendish, the younger son of the 9th Duke of Devonshire, a set 'so exclusive' wrote Cecil Beaton in his diaries, '[they] don't know anyone out of it'. Though Beaton considered most of them 'rather brainless', he had a higher opinion of Richard. 'Sykes is different,' he wrote. 'He really is most witty and has sudden gleams of utter brilliance.'[8] So far as Cavendish and his friends were concerned, Richard was a welcome new addition to their group, especially since he was rapidly becoming a talented jazz pianist. Sing-songs in his rooms became a regular feature of their lives. 'We sat in Richard's rooms in candlelight,' recalled Cecil Beaton of one such occasion, '. . . Richard started playing the piano and he plays extraordinarily well, and we let ourselves go to the newest song tunes. We started to do a Charleston and Jack [Gold] became most vivacious. It was most awfully funny to see Jack leaping and kicking in the air like some cat doing a death dance.'[9]

Richard also loved practical jokes, a popular pastime of this set. In one of her memoirs, Daphne Vivian, later Marchioness of Bath, recalled his having got her into trouble with her uncle, Field Marshal Sir Douglas Haig, who had allowed her to give a dinner party in his London house. She had invited Charlie Cavendish but Richard, who was having his own party in Cambridge on the same night, wanted him there so he sent a telegram to Lady Haig which read 'So sorry cannot dine stop Have had a fit stop' and signed it 'Charles

Cavendish'.[10] It did not take Richard long to work out that, with the fortune due to him when he came of age, work was entirely unnecessary and he enthusiastically set about pursuing a good time. Champagne flowed, usually by the tumblerful, and his name soon became the subject of a jingle written by some college wit,

> Come on Boys,
> Let's make a Noise.
> I'm Richard Sykes,
> I does as I Likes.

For various reasons, not least amongst which was her disappointment that her eldest son was not showing the sense of duty, responsibility and obligation which she considered his position entailed, the relationship between Richard and his mother was somewhat strained. Stories of his wild and irresponsible behaviour, both at Cambridge and in London, drifted back to her and she did not like them. Looking at the unenviable position Edith was in – bereft of a husband and having to manage the running of a large house and estate, as well as cope with a wilful eldest son and five other children – one cannot help but compare her with the fictional character of Lady Marchmain in Evelyn Waugh's *Brideshead Revisited*.

Though there is no suggestion that the creation of Lady Marchmain owed anything to Edith, the character being a composite of many different people, the parallels between the fictional Brideshead and the real Sledmere are striking, and are an indication of just how close Waugh was to his subject. Sledmere was an example of the very Arcadia of which he was writing; a beautiful English house set in a perfect northern landscape and still inhabited by the talented and extraordinary family that built it, a family converted to Catholicism, beneath whose outward strengths lay an undercurrent of fragility. Daniel, the youngest, was to lead a life that closely paralleled that of Waugh's fictional hero, Sebastian Flyte. In fact Waugh never visited Sledmere, and is said to have based Brideshead on Madresfield Court, Worcestershire, home of the Lygon family. His contemporary, Cyril

Connolly, on the other hand, was a guest there and did fictionalise it. He spent the Christmas of 1928 with the family, as a friend of both Richard and Christopher. The former, he wrote, 'appealed to all the rake and the oppidan in me', the latter 'to the schoolmaster'.[11]

'I am fond of this family,' he wrote to his friend, Noel Blakiston, 'they are all interesting people. We act charades, make films and hope for hunting.'[12] Apart from Connolly, the party consisted solely of the family: Richard and Christopher, Freya, with her lawyer husband, Ricky Elwes, whom she had married in 1926, Petsy, newly wed to Adrian Scrope, a young land agent who had just taken over the running of the estate from Henry Cholmondeley, and the seventeen-year-old Angela. Sledmere wove its usual magic spell. 'Enjoyed riding . . . the countryside under snow,' wrote Connolly in romantic mode in his journal, 'the huge warm house, the tobogganing, the shoot, the smell of cartridges, the heavy winging and thud of falling birds on the smoky evening air. Standing in the wet woods listening to the beaters tapping and whistling, watching the farm cart full of birds bowling home over the park, drinking with Richard before and after dinner, making friends with Vermeer Freya over elaborate charades.' The atmosphere of the house, he said, transported him in his imagination back to 'the grim rich game-pie England of eighteenth-century squires, yellow waist-coats, brown woods, top boots and leather gaiters', and he had thrown himself without difficulty into the way of life. 'O the joy of lingering over port and brandy,' he wrote in his journal, 'with men in red coats telling dirty stories while it snows outside.'[13]

So completely did Connolly fall under the spell of Sledmere, that he wrote a story based on his visit there, in which the house appears as Nonsuch. It would not be hard to believe that his own arrival at Sledmere for the first time was similar to that of his fictional character, Miles, who has come up from London for a few days hunting with his friend, Stephen Nonsuch.

Stephen met him in the hall, where a butler, whose 'is this all Sir?' revealed that he had already made a dangerous enemy, was directing the disposal of his rusty suitcase.

'We're all pleased you managed to come,' he said. 'Have some tea.'

They went into a long hall, supported at each end by ancient columns; many doors opened off it, a marble staircase mounted at one end, in the middle the family were grouped around a log fire. Besides Stephen there were his two sisters, and his elder brother, Lord Nonsuch, who greeted him with casual and affectionate incuriosity. There was a strong likeness between all three which Stephen Nonsuch did not share, a quality of great fairness of hair and complexion, a languid elegance, something immature and not quite grown-up, coiled in their armchairs they seemed to look about with the sleepy good temper of a litter of expensive animals . . . The fire crackled, shiny illustrated weeklies went their rounds, he sipped his tea and listened to the amazing quiet of the country, feeling for the first time the two hundred miles that separated him from London over a waste of frost and snow.[14]

The making of films, to which Connolly refers in his letter, was a popular pastime with the Sykes family, Richard having returned from a trip to Hollywood with a passion for the medium. Using his brothers and sisters and their friends as his cast, he directed a number of short films for his own production company, Photo Richard. The first, a ghost story about a haunted cello, starring Angela and his maternal Aunt Hylda, was unmemorable, but the second was a far more ambitious affair. He both directed and starred in *Flames of Desire*, a story of brutal feudal oppression, playing with relish the leading role of Sir Otto Brightmire, who torments the pathetic and poverty-stricken Bugthorpes, a peasant family. After raping Florrie Bugthorpe, played by Angela, he is finally attacked and murdered in an act of revenge by her husband.

Photo Richard's masterpiece, however, was a brilliant comedy based on the life of Father Pozzi. *From Toe Dancing to Tonsure* told the story of how Dunstano Pozzi, a Neapolitan toe dancer, escaped the obscurity of the streets of Naples, when King Bomba fell in love with his beautiful sister. After a series of crazy adventures involving, among others, Garibaldi, Queen Mary and an American millionairess called

Mrs Cory, based on a real-life character called Laura Corrigan, he was finally driven to begging asylum from the Abbot of Ampleforth. Once again Richard commandeered the juiciest roles for himself, namely those of King Bomba and the Abbot, while Christopher took the lead as Pozzi. The completed film was received with howls of laughter, when shown to Pozzi's fellow monks, but they never dared show it to the man himself. Had he not been born the eldest son, with the predestination such a position entails, Richard might well have made a career in the movies.

With all the family living at home, and Richard and Christopher filling it with their friends, the second half of the 1920s saw Sledmere buzzing with life. It had begun with Richard's coming-of-age celebrations in August, 1926, which, as well as the usual party for the village and all the tenants, included a splendid ball, with a band brought up from London. Now that he was officially heir to all that he surveyed, Richard was determined to make the best of the situation and began a steady programme of spending. He entertained on a lavish scale, and travelled extensively, trips which provided an excuse to buy antiques and statues for the improvement of Sledmere. It is said that on one trip to Italy, he hired an entire freighter to ship back some gates he had bought. The recession of 1929 appears to have completely passed him by, and his mother was soon in despair. 'Richard's "improvements" are in full swing,' she wrote to Freya in February, 1929. 'I honestly believe he will have a financial crash. He has *no* idea of money. It seems so ridiculous when we are all economising that he should go on spending money like water.'[15]

'Mouzelle tells me you have bought another hunter,' Christopher wrote to him in 1930, 'making your total of horses five. It's a pity you don't hunt any more.' He also bought himself a Rolls-Royce. 'I hear also from all quarters,' continued Christopher, 'head-splitting tales of your great new car and how wonderful a spectacle it is when it heaves and billows over the graceful undulations of northern England. Your life is very hard.'[16] In her memoir, *Mercury Presides*, Daphne Vivian recalled an amusing incident involving Richard's beloved Rolls, when he was staying at Vaynol, on the Isle of Anglesey, the home of his friend Sir Michael Duff. There had been a picnic by the sea, and on the way home Richard had foolishly allowed Michael's cousin, a flighty young girl called Mary Erskine, to take the wheel. Daphne was in Michael's car, also a brand new Rolls, which was leading the way. 'As we were approaching the lodge,' remembered Daphne, 'Michael drew up, but Mary put her foot on the accelerator instead of the brake. The second Rolls shot into the first Rolls, which cannoned into the huge wrought-iron gates, which slowly toppled and crashed like the walls of Jericho. I felt there was a certain chic being in an accident which involved two Rolls-Royces.'[17]

Richard's extravagance was not the sole cause of a deterioration in his relationship with his mother. She lambasted him for his waning faith, and generally disapproved of what she considered to be his whole 'fast' way of life, epitomised, in her mind, by the fashion for cocktails which was sweeping through society, and which had been set in London by a trio of young Americans, Eugene Reynal, Ben Kitteridge and Bob Coe. The latter was a particular friend of Richard's who before long had imported the craze to Sledmere. Edith had a particular horror of gin, having watched her own mother-in-law drink herself to death on that tipple, and she was determined to see that none of her own children went the same way. Since any drinking had to be done in secret to avoid the wrath of his mother, Richard had set up a drinking parlour in the servants' wing. When his friends came to stay, they would retire here in the early evenings to partake of Bronxes, Sidecars and White Ladies – the house speciality – which were a potent combination of gin, Cointreau and lemon juice. One day a gaggle of 'Bright Young Things' were in the middle of a session, the room filled with the merry sounds of shaking ice, clinking glasses and chatter, chatter, chatter, when the door opened and in walked Edith. There was no time to hide as she froze the room with a look of utter scorn and announced coldly, 'I think you will find it is time to dress for dinner.' The ladies quickly and obediently left, leaving her to vent her fury on her wayward son. 'It was drunkenness as an act of defiance against the regime,' he later wrote to Christopher.[18]

Any restraining influence Edith might have had over her son

disappeared with her sudden early death, in July, 1930, after a bout of pneumonia. At the time she was living in a house in Rosedale, on the North York Moors, having moved out of Sledmere, so strongly did she object to what she considered to be his fast life and friends. This had led to constant rows, which made Edith increasingly unhappy. Richard's wild behaviour was always getting him into trouble and he was virtually on a blacklist in Yorkshire after an incident at the Middleton Hunt Ball, for which he had given a house party. To liven things up a little, two of the men in the group, Charlie Cavendish and Michael Rosse, had suggested that two of the girls, Zita Jungman and Jo Dunn, should attend the party dressed as men. 'With her long legs and short hair, Zita was the perfect person for this,' remembers her sister Baby, another guest in the house, 'but she did it so innocently.' The ultra-conservative County set were, however, anything but amused by this prank, which was revealed when Zita and Jo took to the floor with other men as their partners, instead of girls. 'The people at the Hunt Ball were perfectly livid,' recollected Baby, 'and I could never show my face there again. They were shocked to suddenly see two men dancing together.'[19] Lord Middleton threw out the whole Sledmere party, and Richard was told never to darken his doors again.

Sledmere was full to bursting point the weekend that Edith died. Among the guests was Lady Dorothy Lygon, known as 'Coote', who was one of the three daughters of the 7th Earl Beauchamp. It was her first visit, and the weekend had been filled with incident from the start, not least, because Tanis Guinness, daughter of the society hostess, Mrs Benjamin Guinness, was staying. Described by Cecil Beaton as 'a lovely, fat, painted tulip' with 'gigantic eyes with shiny long lids',[20] she was the current love of Richard's life, which spelt trouble since she encouraged his attentions whilst her own were usually elsewhere: when she was around and was not being nice to him, his temper was at its worst. On this occasion she was flirting madly with one of the other guests, Drogo Montagu, which did nothing for Richard's humour. The weekend got off to a bad start with a near-fatal accident when Drogo, who had flown up in his own plane, took Christopher up for a ride and promptly crashed close to the house. Miraculously they both escaped with minor bruising but it made everyone very edgy. Storms raged all the next day, and Richard was charging about in a fury. The guests went to bed on Sunday night, to be woken at dawn with the news of Edith's death. 'We'd all been leaving rather leisurely on Monday morning,' recalled Coote, 'and we were all suddenly shuffled off and taken to York station. Among those staying were Alice Wimborne and her daughter Cynthia. Alice had taken a sleeping pill and she didn't at all care for being woken up and got to the station for eight o'clock! It went down very badly. I remember her sitting there looking very po-faced. Then I remember looking out of my window and it was raining hard, and seeing Richard going off with a great collar turned up and all hunched against the rain.'[21]

By the time she died, Richard and his mother were barely on speaking terms and he referred to her for ever after, not in the affectionate way that children usually refer to their parents, but as 'Edith, Lady Sykes'. The other children all adored her, however, as did all her nephews and nieces, to whom she was especially generous, being the richest of their aunts. 'I remember her giving me, about 1912, a whole Golden Sovereign,' said Nino, 'which I squandered on buying a Musical Box.' Naturally, the child who was most devastated by her death was Daniel, who was only thirteen and who, being the youngest by five years, was very much the favourite. When Harman Grisewood first visited Sledmere, Daniel was still in the nursery, and was the proud owner of a magnificent toy car, which he occasionally used to drive about downstairs in the stone hall. 'Edith gave him very special attention,' he remembered, 'and he had a very dependent relationship with her. It was a terrible shock for him when she died, because there was really no one else for him.'[22]

Nino's visits to Sledmere and those of Edith's other nephews and nieces came to an abrupt halt with her death. 'I never saw Richard again,' wrote Nino in a memoir, 'but heard rumours of him enthusiastically sowing his wild oats in one of the fast sets of society.'[23] The 'fast set', so brilliantly and accurately caricatured by Evelyn Waugh as the Bright Young People in *Vile Bodies*, included some of Richard's Cambridge gang, such as Charlie Cavendish, Jack Gold and Cecil Beaton, along with many new friends made as he carved his way through the social whirl, aristocrats like Henry Weymouth and Harry Stavordale, rich Americans such as Bob Coe and Chips Channon, aesthetes Brian Howard and Cyril Connolly, city financiers like Eric Hatry, and scores of beautiful, fun-loving girls, including Daphne Vivian, Tanis Guinness, Baby and Zita Jungman, Sibell Lygon and Diana Bridgeman. 'We used to see each other every night at the same dances,' remembered Sibell Lygon. 'We were very gangish. Daphne was the great leader of this set. She was really very, very wild and got us in a lot of trouble. We used to go about late at night in taxis and shout outside people's houses. A favourite was Lady Powis's house. She was a very regal figure and we used to shout "LADY PO PO PO PO POWIS!;' until the butler came out to shoo us away. This was at two or three in the morning. At another time we all went about on bicycles made for two, cycling like mad up and down Piccadilly, in Hartnell dresses, on the way to some ball or other.'[24]

Richard continued to entertain extravagantly at Sledmere. 'It was marvellously relaxed and unsupervised,' recalled Coote Lygon. 'I went there a lot all through the 1930s. I used to go up for Christmas, and sometimes I'd take horses up for the hunting. At a big weekend there would be anything between twelve and twenty for dinner. All the rooms would be full.' In the absence of Edith, Mouzelle took on the task of allocating the bedrooms and ordering the food. The routine in the summer was invariably the same. After breakfast on Saturday, there would be a reverential viewing of the stud, with the yearlings all led out and paraded once, if not twice. Then there might be a race meeting somewhere. If there was no racing, motoring expeditions were popular in the afternoon, with a bit of 'sweeping' thrown in. This was the sport of viewing other people's houses unannounced. 'We used to go to Brantingham Thorpe,' remembered Coote, 'and he loved going up there just as it was getting dark and creeping up and peering in at the window.'

Winter days were spent hunting. In the evenings there were endless charades and dancing, either to Richard on the piano or to the gramophone. 'The great excitement,' said Coote, 'was always when he got all the latest Astaire records over from America. These were played endlessly. We danced to them in the Music Room.' Richard once even made his own recording of the Harry M. Woods/Mort Dixon song, 'Just Like a Butterfly (That's Caught in the Rain)', from the Broadway musical *Mum's the Word*, with a girlfriend, Mary Ashley Cooper, on vocals. So far as girls were concerned, Richard played the field, though his real love was still Tanis Guinness. 'There was also a figure called Jean Parrington,' Coote recalled, 'and he was rather ashamed of her. I think he used to have it off with her. As we all left for the station in the Rolls-Royce, after a weekend, chug-chug-chug up the drive would come Miss Parrington in her Austin 7. She was a Yorkshire girl. He thought she was of humble origin and was quite ruthless with her really.'[25]

One element that was invariably present during these weekends was a faint air of tension, caused by fear of Richard's occasional outbursts of furious temper, which often led to guests being sent home on the milk train. 'Richard . . . does like to be the centre of the party,'[26] Cecil Beaton had written in his diaries, and if he felt he was not being sufficiently appreciated, he would go into a sulk. This was when he was at his most dangerous, and those who risked crossing him at such a time suffered the consequences. Daphne Vivian, who could never resist seeing just how far she could go, once painted the mouth and genitals of the Apollo statue on the Hall staircase with lipstick. Her furious host was less than amused and she was on a blacklist for a long time.

Occasionally Richard bitterly regretted these demonstrations of anger, such as on the night of 7 June, 1931. During a card game at Sledmere, with Freya and a friend, Alice Lindley, because the cards were not in his favour, Richard began to rant and curse, uttering 'terrible blasphemies which rang through the halls'. 'We begged him not to speak so,' wrote Freya in a letter to Christopher, 'and I warned him that something awful would happen if he continued.' Sensing that he had gone too far, Richard was repentant, but that night, after they had gone to bed, something terrifying happened.

'Of a sudden I awoke,' wrote Freya. 'Oh! terror! The whole house was rocking, thumping and clanging. My bed bounced on the floor, the air was filled with a horrible noise as of thunder, and I thought the wrath of the Gods had descended on us ... A step upon the passage and in came my poor brother, quaking in his very shoes ... and described how he'd gone down and found the chandeliers swinging madly. Alice then came in and we all sat and shivered, thinking that the end of the world was nigh. It was very frightening.'[27] Though to Richard this may have seemed like the wrath of God visited upon him because of his wicked oaths, the truth is that they were experiencing the effects of an earthquake, the epicentre of which had been in the Dogger Bank area of the North Sea. Though the east coast of England felt the strongest effects, the after shocks of the North Sea Earthquake, which registered 6.1 on the Richter scale and was the largest earthquake ever recorded in the UK, were felt as far afield as London. 'I was woken up by terrible rocking,' wrote Angela to Freya from town, 'and clung in a state of nervous prostration to my heaving bed. The whole house rattled and my teeth were shaken in my head.'[28]

The rate at which Richard was living and spending did not go unnoticed outside his family. The Sledmere estate, which had lost some 10,000 acres to the tax man owing to the payment of double death duties within six years, now looked in danger, in a time of depression, of being further depleted by the profligacy of its young owner, whose overdraft at the bank had risen to the then considerable sum of £14,000. A crisis meeting of the trustees was called at which a number of drastic proposals were suggested in order to avoid the very real possibility that the bank could foreclose on the debt and, in doing so, thereby bankrupt Richard. These included reducing his allowance from £2,500 per annum to £500, selling the Romney portrait of Sir Christopher and Lady Sykes, and closing Sledmere, spending only so much on it 'as prevents waste'. A letter written in April 1932, by William Irons, a footman then in service at Sledmere, to his sister, confirms the gravity of the situation. 'The footman, kitchen maid and head housemaid have all had a month's notice,' he told her, 'and Sir Richard is closing the front part of the house down altogether. It is a pity to see a nice house like this going to rack and ruin, it breaks Sir Richard's heart.'[29]

There was one other stipulation made by the trustees, which was that he had to have every cheque he signed, however small, counter-signed by a chosen attorney, the unfortunate man in question being his agent and brother-in-law, Adrian 'Bunty' Scrope. Bunty, a boy-hood friend of the family and a man who lived and breathed horses, had spent some time working on the stud before taking over its management and that of the estate from Henry Cholmondeley in 1928, at the very young age of twenty-one. While riding round the domain on one of his thoroughbred hacks, he had attracted the attention of the twenty-year-old Petsy, who was soon regularly accompanying him on his long rides, elegantly mounted side-saddle. They were a perfect couple, she being a keen farmer and an expert judge of stock, as well as a talented naturalist. 'After dinner we used to go up to the Library to congregate,' recalled Harman Grisewood. 'Petsy used to open the windows and call to the owls, imitating them in the most marvellous way. And the owls would respond to her. It was extraordinary.' It was not long before Bunty and Petsy fell in love, and they were married a week after her twenty-first birthday She could now achieve her ambition, which, so she told Grisewood, was 'to have lots of children and turn them loose on the Wolds'.[30]

A friend and neighbour, 'Sim', 3rd Earl of Feversham, concerned for Sledmere, decided that the best way for Richard to extract himself from his dire financial situation would be for him to marry an heiress. He had just such a one in mind, none other than the richest girl in the world, Doris Duke, who at birth had been dubbed 'the million dollar baby'. Only nineteen years old, she was heiress to one of the greatest fortunes in America, that of the American Tobacco Company, and in 1932, she just happened to be touring Europe with her mother, Nanaline. When they paid a visit to Sim at his house near Malton, Nawton Tower, he arranged a trip over to Sledmere. Richard was impressed by Mrs Duke's apparent love of music. 'Whaat's thaat?' she asked, staring at the huge Panphonic radiogram which stood in one corner of the hall and out of which was floating the divine strains of Mozart. 'It's Figaro,' replied Richard, delighted at her appreciation of his musical taste. 'Hey, Doris,' said Mrs Duke to her daughter, 'we must order one as soon as we get home.' Doris smirked at her mother's *faux pas*, and Richard was smitten.

When Doris and her mother went over to France in the spring, he followed in their footsteps and caught up with them in Nice. He asked Mrs Duke, courteously, if he could take her daughter out to dinner. She told him that that would be fine on the condition that her own chauffeur drove them to wherever he was taking her. When Richard made no objection to this he was given her blessing and the plan was made. On the night arranged, the evening went without a hitch until the moment on the journey home when Richard was emboldened to press his suit. Hardly had his arm gone around her and the first steps towards a kiss been initiated than the chauffeur, acting on orders from Mrs Duke, stopped the car and ordered him out. When he indignantly refused to comply with this demand, another car drew up behind them out of which jumped two bodyguards who forcibly ejected the hapless young baronet from the back seat and roughly threw him into a ditch. The chauffeur then drove Doris straight back to her mother, leaving an embarrassed and furious Richard by the roadside.

The conclusion of this saga was Richard's involvement in what Randolph Churchill was to describe as 'a tremendous fracas', and the scandal of which was to dog him for the rest of his life. The following August, he found himself in Venice where the celebrated American hostess, Laura Mae Corrigan, a tireless social climber, was holding court at the Palazzo Brandolini. Her houseguests included Evelyn Waugh, the Duff Coopers and Chips Channon, but there were fashionable English everywhere, including Cecil Beaton, Emerald, Lady Cunard, Lord and Lady Castlerosse, endless Guinnesses, Oliver Messel and Randolph Churchill. Night after night this riotous crowd was summoned to Mrs Corrigan's for extravagant dinner parties, while in the daytime she ferried them to and from the Lido in her personal motor launches, where elaborate beach picnics were laid out and served by footmen in livery. This particular season was, wrote Randolph Churchill, 'one of the gayest the English and American visitors had ever known in Venice'.[31]

On 29 August, Chips Channon gave a party on the island of Murano to celebrate the fortieth birthday of Lady Diana Cooper, and every-body, including Richard, was invited. It began in elegant and pictur-esque mode, with glassblowers and gondoliers mingling and dancing with the guests. When dinner was served, Richard, whose tiff with Miss Duke had been the subject of gossip for weeks, found himself seated next to her. No sooner had he sat down and made an attempt to patch up their differences, than she got up and flounced off in a huff, leaving his vision of the rescue of Sledmere by the Duke millions in tatters. Drowning his sorrows in champagne, he wandered about tipsily until he was spotted by Randolph Churchill, who immediately dragged him off to kiss and make up with Doris. She was having none of it, and nor was Richard, who promptly removed the Lucky Strike cigarette she was smoking from her lips and stubbed it out on the back of her hand, telling her as he did so, '*This* is what I think of you and your Lucky Strike.' At which point Randolph took a swing at Richard and knocked him to the ground.

The fighting began to spread. Alfred Beit, who was standing close by, tried to intervene and got punched himself. Cecil Beaton started to throw bottles of champagne, while Bob Coe did his best to remove them from his hand each time he picked one up. Then Oliver Messel waded in and soon he and Cecil were 'fighting like bears'. All hell now broke loose as the entire party began to dissolve into a grotesque parody of a Western bar brawl. 'They were all terribly drunk,' Lady Diana Cooper later recalled; 'it was *too* frightening, fists were flying, bottles were broken, there was glass everywhere. People were pounding each other for no known reason. I hung on to Duff as he would have loved to join in.'[32] It was not long before he did.

'Mr Duff Cooper got roped into the mêlée,' wrote the Marquess of Donegall, gossip columnist for the London *Sunday Dispatch*, who reported the incident the following week, 'and eight men rolled onto the floor, dragging the crockery from the table on top of them. While all this was in progress, fifteen gondoliers were singing in the room and fifty more were watching. Unable to resist the fun, these sixty-five joined in, raising an Italian war whoop. The Baronet, practically unconscious, landed outside and was ministered to by eight Italians.

At which point the famous socialite Emerald Cunard arrived, fashionably late. "What a lovely party!" she said, from force of habit.'[33]

'When the British are carnivalling,' commented Diana Cooper, 'they behave disgracefully and become quite impossible.'[34] The Italian press were certainly outraged and the story filled countless column inches that weekend. According to Randolph Churchill, one of the fallouts of the affair was an immediate rush by the Italian aristocracy to purge themselves of the English nannies and governesses they had employed in the mistaken belief that the English aristocracy was so much better brought up than their own. So widespread, indeed, was the general outrage over the affair, that it was even said that Mussolini himself was most displeased. When he finally returned to England, Richard found it necessary to keep a low profile for quite a while. 'It was a tremendous *cause célèbre*,' remembered Coote Lygon. 'It was considered quite a shocking way to have behaved, even though Miss Duke was thought to be pretty silly.'[35] Evelyn Waugh, who was in the habit of inventing words, inspired by the characters of people he knew, coined a new one, 'to sykes', which meant to strike or demolish.[36]

The Doris Duke affair was the low point of Richard's life so far, and to a certain extent it brought him to his senses. When he returned home, he realised he would have to make an attempt to rein in, in spite of the humiliation of having, in effect, to go to Bunty for money. This did little for their relationship and led to endless recriminations and dreadful rows, one of which, having taken place in the Library, ended with Richard hurling a heavy book at his brother-in-law. Bunty could not help smiling at the title, which he noticed as it hit the ground beside him, open at a page about riding boots: *Sexual Aberration: the Phenomena of Fetishism* by Dr Stekel. In accepting his role as sole attorney, Bunty had had no choice for the alternative would have been ruination and over the years he brilliantly weathered the constant storms, never allowing his personal relations with his brother-in-law to deteriorate to a point where they would affect Petsy's friendship with her family. The result was that by the end of the 1930s, the situation was stabilised and Sledmere was once again on a sound footing, even if its size was reduced to 18,000 acres. With the outbreak of war, Bunty had to enlist, and Petsy took over as temporary agent.

When war broke out in September, 1939, Richard continued to live in Sledmere, commuting daily to Bridlington where his regiment, the 7th Battalion Green Howards, in which he was a full Lieutenant, was stationed. The men were all quartered in various large cafés which had been closed down, while the rest of the officers all lived in the Expanse Hotel, which had been turned by their Commander, Charles Richmond Brown, into the Officers' Mess. The only occasion on which it was not possible for Richard to drive back to Sledmere was when it was his turn to act as Battalion Orderly Officer, and these nights he was obliged to spend sleeping in the Orderly Room. A caricature drawn by Christopher, a fellow member of the Regiment, depicting one of these nights, shows the bleak surroundings of the room with black-out shutters on the windows, a naked electric light bulb hanging from the ceiling and the usual army trestle table, covered with a blanket. On the table, however, is a great spread of luxurious foods while footmen in gorgeous eighteenth-century liveries hand out other dishes to the diners. A manuscript account of Richard's short war, by Rupert Alec-Smith, a fellow officer in the Green Howards, shows it to have been like yet another episode from a Waugh novel. There were a number of local 'gents' based at Bridlington, and they used to congregate at the Britannia Hotel, always referred to by Richard and Christopher as the 'Britannique'. The Frenchification of names became a popular game with them. The adjutant, Captain Farmer, was always referred to as 'Fermier', Commander Richmond-Brown as 'Richmonde', Lieutenant Haycock as 'Meule de Foin', and so on. Bridlington School, on the playing fields of which the men were drilled, was given the name of 'Golgotha', by Richard, who for ever after referred to his time there as 'in Golgothian days'. The RSM, Sergeant-Major Westwood, who carried out these drills had a favourite catchphrase. 'Third Swine from the right!' he would yell at some unfortunate, which inspired Christopher to comment 'I feel like the Tsar at Ekaterinburg'.

Occasionally, one or two of the officers would be asked over to

Sledmere for dinner. 'It was not quite dark,' wrote Alec-Smith of his first visit there, 'when I drove through the main lodges, and saw the west front of Sledmere for the first time, very severe in its cold evening setting with a windy sky as grey as the house itself scudding against its silhouette . . . it seemed to please Richard that I found it so grave. However it was very heart-warming inside.' Most of the house was shut up, in preparation for its takeover by the army as a hospital, and the Dining Room had been turned into a sitting room. They ate in a small room in the servants' wing. On another occasion, just before the Battalion's departure for France in April, 1940, Richard gave a farewell dinner which was held in the Entrance Hall. After that he abandoned the house to the army, leaving only Mouzelle to keep an eye on it, and moved to the Villa, the house in the village that his grandfather had once inhabited with Madame.

'When we finally left Hull by train late one evening,' recalled Alec-Smith, 'to embark at Southampton for Le Havre, Richard and I shared a compartment, and before trying to get to sleep as best we could on ordinary seats, Richard produced a splendid hamper from Fortnums, filled with many delicacies and washed down with champagne, the whole served with grace by his batman.' It was their last taste of luxury for a while. They soon found themselves living in a tented camp on the Vimy Ridge, the Green Howards being engaged in pioneer work helping to build an airfield, and Richard was promoted to the rank of Captain. When the Germans invaded France, the Battalion were ordered to take up defensive positions along the Canal du Nord, in spite of the fact that their equipment for action was virtually non-existent. This was the first of many such positions they were to assume as they were gradually pushed back to the beaches at Dunkirk, finally returning to England in dribs and drabs. The action of the 6th Green Howards was of particular note. They held up the Germans for days at Gravelines, on the western flank of the Dunkirk perimeter, an action that greatly contributed to the success of the evacuation.

The early summer found the Green Howards concentrated once more, with its brigade headquarters in Parkstone, Dorset. Here Richard established a *modus vivendi* which suited him very nicely. He rented a sizeable Edwardian villa from a family called Farmiloe, manufacturers of Nine Elms paint, which had a sizeable garden overlooking Brownsea Island, and installed himself there, along with his butler, Cassidy, and cook, Mrs Wignall. The house had a tennis court and his fellow officers were often asked for a game before dinner. When the regiment moved to Castle Cary in November, Cassidy and Mrs Wignall went too, setting up house in Terndale Villa in Sparkford Road. 'The previous troops at Castle Cary before our arrival,' wrote Rupert, 'had been a unit of the Brigade of Guards, and their officers expressed surprise at the comfortable standard of living arranged by, and permitted to, Sir Richard Sykes in the Green Howards.'

The Battalion HQ at Castle Cary was in a large pseudo-Elizabethan villa called Florida House, and Rupert Alec-Smith found himself appointed adjutant, with Richard as his assistant. They sat side by side behind a pair of trestle tables in the orderly room, which was situated immediately above the Battalion detention room, fantasising about 'the wretched prisoners in the *oubliette*, groaning and clanking their chains in the room beneath us'. The CO, Major Guy Stansfield, also had a table in the orderly room. Once, when the telephone rang and Richard answered it, he suddenly waved it at Major Stansfield and said, 'Guy, will you take this call. I've *no* idea what they want.'

Their pleasure while posted at Castle Cary was their regular Sunday outings to engage in what Richard liked to call 'trespassing', which involved going out in his private car to view local houses of beauty and interest. 'We saw Dyrham,' remembered Rupert, 'and a near-derelict Doddington, the house used as a school. There was also talk of Baron de Tuyll at Chipping Sodbury, which was said to be an appropriately named residence. Other trespassings included Longleat, where late on a winter's afternoon we met the old Lord Bath, who, wearing an Inverness cape, loomed up out of the gloom on the drive . . . We drove up to Wardour and rang the bell, which was answered by a parlour maid. Richard gave his name and asked if we might see inside, but the message came back from Lady Arundell that she could not allow it. I think her son had been taken prisoner or was missing. He died on the way home and the peerage became extinct.'

What they had a horror of were the occasional 'exercises'. 'These dreaded events,' wrote Rupert, 'usually meant long journeys in some discomfort, and cold, sleepless nights. At one such, we spent the night in the village school at Shapwick, near Kingston Lacey. I sat up all night at my blanket covered table near the telephone. Other HQ officers lay on the floor and tried to get some sleep, but there was a constant stream of runners and dispatch riders, and our work was carried on in low tones. This night was ever after known by Richard as "the whispering campaign".'[37]

In April, 1941, Richard was taken ill with pleurisy and rushed off to Shaftesbury Hospital. It was the beginning of the end of his war. After two months, he returned to Sledmere, and moved into the Villa, the house having been taken over by the Royal Army Medical Corps. This was a blessing in disguise, since having the building full of doctors was infinitely preferable to it being subject to the vandalism that so often occurred in the many stately homes that were requisitioned as barracks. At a medical board in July 1941, Richard was declared 'permanently unfit for General Service'. It was the first of many he was to attend during the next few months, a period in which his spirits became very low. 'My own life has been very uneventful,' he wrote to Archie Scott, a friend on active service, 'and despite all your sufferings and privations, I envy you in many ways. Here life is quite intensely boring and depressing at times and often I yearn to be back with the horrors of battalion life.'[38]

Richard's military life ended for good in April, 1942, when he was finally and permanently invalided out of the army. By this time he had resigned himself to his fate, and was immersing himself in running the estate. Petsy, who had been doing the job for nothing since the outbreak of war, was unceremoniously squeezed out and given no credit for the work she had done, particularly with the stud, which was thriving. When Bunty realised just how unhappy this was making her, he wrote a furious letter to his brother-in-law telling him that his treatment of his sister was 'beyond contempt'.[39] To avoid further acrimony, he also offered his own resignation.

In resolving to leave, Bunty was making a wise decision, not simply because he was doing his best to avoid a permanent family feud, but because there was a new factor in the equation. Since early in 1942, Richard had been assiduously courting a pretty and lively young girl called Virginia Gilliat, the twenty-six-year old daughter of a dashing and successful banker, Jack Gilliat, and his extraordinary wife, Lily, the former Marchioness of Anglesey. Virginia, 'Ginny' or 'Gin-Gins' to her friends, had been a popular girl on the London scene for some years, and had caught the eye of some of the City's most glamorous men, including the young Joe Kennedy, whose father was American Ambassador, the dashing flying ace, Max Aitken, and the heroic soldier, Lord 'Shimi' Lovat. The courtship had not been an easy one, since Richard had to negotiate his way through a maze of admirers, but he had persevered, and in August was able to announce his engagement. 'In fairness to your wife,' Bunty had written, 'this matter should be cleared up before she arrives at Sledmere.'[40]

'My dear Pozzi,' wrote Christopher to Richard from Tehran, where he was stationed, addressing him by one of the numerous different nicknames he used in their correspondence, 'I got your . . . invitation, and, regretting my absolutely unpreventable absence from the feast of Hymen, presided over I trust by the immortal Dunstano, I offer you my most hot and ardent felicitations. I know Virginia and like her terrifically. I think she's colossally all right.'[41] The wedding took place in London on 29 September. It was followed by a party and a very short honeymoon, after which Richard brought his bride back to Sledmere, to carry her over the threshold; not of the big house – that would have to wait until the war was over – but of the Villa. Waiting for her she found a letter from her new brother-in-law, Christopher. 'I was really delighted and thrilled when I heard that Richard was going to marry you,' he wrote. 'The whole of what one now thinks of as "the past", that is the days before the war, seem so remote that it is difficult to remember how well, how intimately, one knew the given person! I remember that we met often, and I remember also, if I may borrow a phrase from Edwardian usage, my impression that you were a positive smasher.'[42] It was a charming welcome to her new family.

The new Lady Sykes was the result of an extraordinary union. Her mother, Lily, was the eldest of three daughters born to Lady Florence Chetwynd who, as a young girl, had achieved notoriety in Victorian England. Born Lady Florence Paget, she was the most outstanding beauty of her day, dubbed 'the Pocket Venus', and had become engaged, aged twenty-two, to Henry Chaplin, an intimate of the Prince of Wales. It was regarded throughout society as a perfect match. Shortly before the wedding, however, Lady Florence caused a sensation by eloping on 16 July, 1864, with the Marquess of Hastings, a notorious rake, after a rendezvous in the Oxford Street store, Marshall and Snelgrove. For ever after she was branded a worthless and despicable woman, and was never forgiven.

Considering that she had sacrificed everything for love, it is ironical that Florence should have chosen to force the first daughter of her second marriage, to Sir George Chetwynd, into an arranged marriage. The chosen husband for Lily, a radiant beauty with flaming red 'Titian' hair and white skin, was her first cousin, Henry Cyril Paget, Marquess of Anglesey, 'the Dancing Marquess', a delicate, effeminate young man, who had been brought up abroad, and whose interests were the theatre and jewellery, his love of which amounted to an obsession. It is said that, on their honeymoon in Paris, when Lily stopped to admire the window display of the famous jewellers, Van Cleef and Arpels, he bought the entire display for her, reducing her to tears by forcing her to wear them all to the races. At night he would make her undress and then cover her naked body with jewels until she was dripping in emeralds and diamonds. She was then made to sleep wearing the jewels. As a young and innocent girl from a very sheltered background, she found the whole experience humiliating, and eventually developed an obsessive hatred of jewellery.

Lily left her husband after only six weeks and began nullity proceedings against him almost immediately. Thereafter she never spoke to anyone about her marriage. It was as if it had never happened. She set about losing herself in the twilight Bohemian world that was emerging in the early 1900s. She moved into a house in London's Ovington Gardens, where she mixed with a set of artists and actresses. She spent

339

a lot of time in Paris, from where tales filtered back of wild behaviour, dancing on tables and lesbian romances. However much truth there may or may not have been in the rumours, they painted a picture of Lily as a woman of loose morals, and she was cold-shouldered by 'respectable' society. 'You shouldn't go near that woman,' Lilah Morrison Bell, a new friend of Lily's, was told soon after they had first met, 'you can't touch pitch without catching some smear.'[43]

When in 1909 Lily announced her intention to marry John Francis Grey Gilliat, who was seven years her junior, his family, who were eminently respectable bankers, were horrified. Socially ambitious, they had given their son the perfect upbringing for a country gentleman. He was good-looking and charming, a brilliant musician and all-round sportsman, and the last thing they had in mind for their beloved Jack was marriage to an older woman of questionable virtue. They pleaded with her to leave him alone, but she showed great strength in that the more they did so, the more determined she became to prove to them that they were wrong about her. As for Jack himself, he was infatuated, and they were married in December, 1909. Lily was now single-minded in trying to attain respectability in the eyes of society, but it proved an uphill struggle. After they had attended a party soon after their wedding given by Lady Evelyn Guinness, their hostess had received a letter from King George V and Queen Mary, who were the guests of honour, telling her 'We did not enjoy meeting Mrs Gilliat.'[44]

Realising that the gossip would never stop, Lily ceased to care and threw herself into a new life, with a younger set of friends who knew nothing of her history. She sold all her jewellery and with the proceeds bought a house called Woodstock, near Sittingbourne in Kent, where they brought up their three children, Simon, John and Virginia. Nannette Kenyon Slaney, a childhood friend of John's, remembered there being frequent large house parties there and Tallulah Bankhead being a constant visitor. Lily made herself into the perfect wife and mother and in so doing won over the Gilliat family, but in the late 1930s and early 1940s, her life was sadly marred by tragedy. As she worshipped Jack, she also worshipped her sons, but they were both killed. Simon, a pilot in the RAF, was burned to death in August, 1936, when his plane crashed on take off. John, who was a fellow passenger, was thrown clear and, though severely injured, made frantic efforts to save his brother to no avail. Eight years later he too died, when the Guards Chapel was bombed in 1944. A friend of Lily's who was with her when she received this news recalled her 'letting out a long, drawn-out groan of despair that I shall never forget.'[45] Her daughter was her sole surviving child. She was my mother.

CHAPTER XV

Sledmere Reborn

I was born on 23 July, 1948, the third of three sons, into a household that was still run on a scale that would not have disgraced the previous century. The bankruptcy worries of the 1930s had been long since forgotten, land sales and a thriving stud having put Sledmere back on a sound footing. When Uncle Christopher visited for the first time since Mama and Papa moved back in, it was, he wrote, 'like the return to Paris of Louis XVIII in 1815, such feasting and pleasuring and wild heathen laughter'. After the deprivations of war, his enjoyment knew no bounds. 'Rarely in the history of human conflict,' he told his new sister-in-law, 'have I enjoyed myself so much for so little for so long. It was most kind of you to throw open your maisonette to me, to make me slightly bottled so often, to feed me so unstintingly . . . and all the rest of it. I always love going to Sledmere very much and never have I seen it looking so perfectly lovely . . . I could embrace every gatepost.'[1]

They had used the excuse of the relatively slight damage left by the Army Medical Corps to redecorate and Christopher was liberal in his praise, calling it an unqualified success. 'The green of the Hall is a perfect bull's eye and it's wonderful how it harmonises with the blue tablets. I should jolly well put my foot down about the Boudoir if I was you, and decorate it in a thoroughly fussy humorous French fashion (this is incitement to mutiny formerly punishable with the lash) but I shouldn't have sham Van Dycks on the wall. Take Richard Cromwell (he's a unique and important picture) and Sir Julius Caesar and Mr Egerton and lots of miniatures – that sort of thing. Better a second rate original, than a copy of something good.'[2] This was a reference to his father's habit of exaggerating the importance of some of the picture collection by labelling obvious copies, such as the famous triptych of Charles I by Van Dyck, as being the original.

As a child, apart from being terrified by some sinister paintings hanging in dark passages, I paid little attention to the picture collection, being far too involved with the people who filled the house. The centre of the children's world was the top floor, where there was a day nursery, a night nursery and a schoolroom, and we rarely moved from here apart from being taken out for daily walks. Once a day, if they were at home, our parents would come up and visit us but they always seemed uncomfortable there for it was not their domain. At the nursery end, the nannies ruled; at the schoolroom end the governess, and an uneasy truce always existed between them. By the time I was old enough to remember, Nanny Talbot had been with the family for a number of years, assisted by various nursery maids from the village. The governess was Nellie Goodall, a Belgian, who was known to everyone as 'Zellie', short for 'Mademoiselle'. She and her family had suffered terribly under the German occupation during the war, and any mention of the Germans, in whatever context, would set her off muttering '*Sales Boches!*' between gritted teeth, sometimes quietly, but at other times, usually when we were in a public place, embarrassingly loudly. I remember her almost causing a riot in the local cinema in Bridlington during the torture scene in the Violet Szabo biopic, *Carve her Name With Pride*. We went to her for lessons from the age of four.

This was the magical age when we were, for the first time, occasionally allowed downstairs. Dressed in our best little shorts, shirts and socks, we would be taken down the back stairs and through to the hall where our parents were enjoying tea laid out in front of the fire. We would give them a kiss and shake hands with any guests who happened to be staying, before being whisked back upstairs again. Once I had tasted the fruits of life downstairs, however, and come to the realisation that there was another much more exciting world out there, the joys of life on the top floor began to pall. I listened eagerly to the tales of life on the first and ground floors told by my two older brothers, Tatton, aged eight, and now at prep school, and Jeremy, aged six, whose playmate I was about to become. Gradually I, too, began to get to know the people they talked about, the other huge family who inhabited the backstairs and amongst whom I spent far more time than I did with Mama and Papa, a not unusual situation in upper-class households of the day.

The most important of these was Mouzelle, who had been a constant presence at Sledmere since 1910, when she had taught Freya, Richard, Angela and Daniel in turn. She had taken on the position of Secretary when she was no longer required as a governess. After my grandmother's death, she had acted as hostess for Papa when he had house parties, and it was she who had single-handedly watched over the welfare of the house when it was in use as an army hospital during the war. Being well into her seventies, she had a unique position in the household and everyone adored and respected her.

Mouzelle lived in the Oak Room, formerly the School Room. So called because of the dark oak panelling on the walls, it was a large ground-floor room with three tall windows at the north-west corner of the house and was referred to by everyone as 'Mouzelle's room'. It was wonderfully untidy. Bookcases lined the walls, a large rolltop desk stood in one corner, overcrowded with books and papers, a long cloth-covered table filled the centre, also invariably piled high with papers, and there was an assortment of squashy sofas and chairs, curled up on each of which was one of Papa's lurchers, of which he rarely kept less than four. Since the room was also their indoor kennel, there were water bowls and plates of dog food littered about, which gave the room its special pungent smell. When the odours leaking out into the passage occasionally became too much, Papa would raid Mouzelle's room, in a fury, and hurl the dog scraps out of the window. Then dozens of joss sticks would be lit in an attempt to mask the stink – but it would soon be back again.

Much of our time was spent in this room, which was a children's paradise. She had a stereoscope on which we spent hours looking at 3D photographs of life in the trenches during the First World War, and which also had pictures of tanks and field guns. There was a hand-cranked projector which showed short flick-films of subjects

such as a girl eating porridge or a ride on a big dipper. In one corner
stood a large folding screen on which Mouzelle always hung her
outdoor clothes – an overcoat, her hat and walking stick – and we
used to love to tease her by putting them on ourselves, which always
drove the dogs into a furious frenzy of barking as they thought they
were about to be taken for a walk. But most of all we loved to listen
to her 'Mouzelle stories', anecdotes about our eccentric ancestors and
relations, about how wonderful our grandfather was, about Papa's
exploits as a boy, about Father Pozzi, all repeated over and over again
until they were imprinted on our brains. That she knew so much was
of little surprise to us, to whom she seemed a hundred. 'You are purple
with age,' we used to tell her.

When I was not haunting Mouzelle's room, I was in the Kitchen.
The present Duke of Devonshire told me that after the war, when
England was still gripped by the icy fingers of rationing, there were
only a few houses to which people longed to have invitations, and
Sledmere was one of them. Being a large country estate, it had the
advantage of being self-sufficient, and was known to be an oasis of
comfort, good company and, above all, for people who had suffered
the culinary deprivations of war, delicious food. The guests could
scarcely believe their luck to sit at a table on which there stood
unlimited amounts of thick yellow butter and cream, straight from the
farm, and they did not hold back. Mrs Wignall was the first cook I
remember. We called her 'Wiggie', and she was an absolute wizard
with pastry. She also introduced a house speciality for which Sledmere
became famous, a delicious home-made lemonade, a jug of which was
always on the dining-room table.

Unhappily, Wiggie's career came to an abrupt end when she pierced
one of her fingers with a pheasant bone. The wound turned septic,
and the finger eventually had to be amputated. It was a sad day for
the Sledmere kitchen. She was succeeded by Mrs Scott, another great
pastry cook, who I nicknamed 'Gretel'. I spent hours watching her
make her delicious pies, such as rabbit and pigeon pie, which had puff
pastry which melted in your mouth. She had a kitchen maid to help
her with the preparation of food, and two scullery maids to prepare

the vegetables and wash up all the pots and pans. The kitchen was a hive of activity all day, beginning first thing in the morning with the delivery of the fresh milk, cream and rich yellow Guernsey butter from the Dairy. Then one of the gardeners would arrive with baskets of vegetables and, in the summer, delicious fresh fruit, such as strawberries and raspberries, white peaches, nectarines and grapes. The butcher came mid-morning with meat and poultry from the farm, sometimes veal from a newly-slaughtered calf, the occasional suckling pig or, my own favourite, duck. In the winter the gamekeeper brought pheasant, partridge, woodcock and pigeon, as well as an abundant supply of rabbits and hares. By the time our family was complete, with a sister, Arabella, born in 1950, another brother, Nicholas, in 1953, and one more sister, Henrietta, in 1957, there were a lot of mouths to feed each day; six in the nursery, six in the Dining Room, and eleven in the servants' hall. If there was a house party, the numbers would be swelled by anything up to fourteen.

Cassidy (never Mr in those days), was still butler, and the whole household were expected to look up to him. His domain covered the pantry, the brush room and the wine cellar, and he ruled over a staff of four, consisting of a pantry maid, a footman, a hall-boy and, at the bottom of the tree, a pantry boy. While footmen and hall-boys came and went, Marion Marshall, the pantry maid, was a permanent feature and was mercilessly teased by us children. Since she was a keen gossip about everyone and everything, we nicknamed her 'Marion of the Daily Clarion' which annoyed her intensely. The hall-boys were a mixed bag. Coming as they often did, owing to Mama's charitable nature, from what were then known as 'approved' schools, they tended to be far more experienced in the ways of the world than us children and were thus objects of fascination. Our keenness to befriend them, however, often led to trouble and there were a number of unfortunate incidents that were hushed up. On one occasion I remember, when I was about eleven, I had a narrow escape when just as I was about to get into bed, one of these boys appeared at my bedroom door. 'Master Christopher,' he asked me, using the form of address that the children of the house were called by, 'I wondered if I could have a look at your mouse.' 'I haven't got a mouse,' I replied, wondering who on earth had told him I did. 'You know,' he continued, 'your bird.' 'I haven't got a bird either,' I told him, feeling increasingly perplexed. 'Yes you have,' he insisted, 'it lives in your pyjamas.' At this point I cottoned on to just what he had in mind. 'No you can't,' I told him. 'Go away.' I never told a soul.

Michael Kenneally, the pantry boy, arrived in 1952, aged eighteen, from Glenarm Castle, my Aunt Angela's home in County Antrim. His position was at the very bottom of the hierarchy and his jobs included cleaning the silver, sharpening the knives and doing lots and lots of washing up. He slept in a tiny bedroom in the attics, with a bathroom on the floor below, and even his room was not sacrosanct, because if a servant of higher rank came to stay, such as the valet of an earl, Michael had to move on to a truckle bed in the corridor. In spite of these early hardships, Sledmere became his life. He loved to tell how, soon after his arrival, he was told to get a notebook and familiarise himself with the house. While in the Library, he noticed *Miller's Sexual Systems* on one of the shelves. 'I thought,' he used to say, 'I'll read that when I get the chance. It was seven years before I got the opportunity, and when I opened it, it was the sex life of plants and flowers. After waiting for seven years!'

It was also seven years after he had arrived that Michael, having first graduated from pantry boy to footman, was appointed butler. He faced an early challenge. Not long after his appointment, Queen Elizabeth the Queen Mother came to stay. 'Sir Richard told me she was coming,' he used to relate, 'and asked if there was anything I needed to know. I said "I beg your pardon, Sir Richard, but there is something. Being Irish, I can't bow to anyone, especially the British Royal family." Afterwards he said to me, "Michael, you didn't bow beautifully!"' This was typical of Michael, who was never obsequious and used to love to repeat the mantra 'I'm not servant to any man, nor is any man my master.' There were times when the long hours and constant demands on his time got the better of him, and he would let off steam. 'Let the buggers wait!' he would shout as the bell in the Dining Room rang and rang, demanding his presence.

In the forty years in which he was to serve at Sledmere, Michael became the subject of numerous anecdotes, not least those involving his occasional over-indulgence in 'butler's perks', as half empty bottles of wine are often referred to in grand houses. One memorable evening, for example, he was bewildered while serving dinner by the fact that the guests were all refusing the delicious dish of lemon chicken he was handing round. 'I think, Michael,' said Papa after a while, 'that it might be an idea to lay the plates first.' On another occasion, inspired by a recent TV commercial in which a butler drove a Fiat car round the dining table, towards the end of dinner he rode into the Dining Room on a bicycle, a tall stack of dessert plates balanced on the rack behind the seat. Solemnly he managed to complete one circuit of the table with his load intact, but on the second lap, he lost control, ending up in a heap on the floor, his plates, miraculously intact, scattered around him.

The person we were all most in awe of in the house was Dorothy, the housekeeper. Short, with pebble-lens spectacles and one leg slightly shorter than the other, which meant that she walked with a curious rolling movement, she was a devout Catholic with a strong character and a short temper, which meant that she was absolutely not to be crossed. She knew every inch of the house like the back of her hand and woe betide anyone who moved anything without her permission. If you broke anything, you were dead. Dorothy's threats were promises. I once built a mansion out of Minibricks, a popular toy of the time, on the Library floor. It had columns, a portico and dozens of windows and I was incredibly proud of it, but I had failed to ask Dorothy's permission to use that particular location. Unimpressed by its beauty when she saw it, she told me to move it or she would do so herself. Foolishly I ignored her and when, the following day, I rushed to the Library to continue adding on to my prized palace I found nothing but a pile of small rubber bricks piled unceremoniously back into the box. In my anger at her, I remember letting out a torrent of swear words, none of which I knew the meaning of, and which I didn't even know I knew. A hundred Hail Marys wouldn't have atoned for my sin.

The first and second floor pantries, tall rooms with black and white tiled floors and huge china sinks, were the centre of Dorothy's world. These were the repositories for the brushes and dusters, the mops, buckets and cleansers with which her team of four or five ladies armed themselves for their daily battle against dirt and dust. They started at dawn and the first sign of life each morning was always the sound of shutters being opened and blinds drawn, followed soon after by the smell of wood smoke as, one by one, the fires were lit. Dorothy, in her second role as lady's maid, would then call my mother and take her breakfast in bed, which always included a glass jar of freshly made yoghurt, quite a rarity in the fifties. After laying out her clothes for the day and running her bath, she would then go upstairs to the linen cupboard, a long room lined from floor to ceiling with drawers and cupboards that were filled with beautiful white linen sheets and pillow cases, rough white cotton bath towels in every size, linen face towels, piles of soft wool blankets, and magnificent embroidered bedspreads. It was a treasure chest, the key to which was kept permanently in Dorothy's pocket.

Dorothy treated us as children all our lives, even when we were grown up. At the age of thirty when my first book, *The Visitors' Book*, was published in 1978, a bookshop in the local town of Driffield held a signing. I decided to ask a few friends to stay, including Ed Victor, my literary agent, and the theatrical impresario, Robert Fox. Since none of them had been to Sledmere before, I was keen to show them the Library, but when we went up there, it was to find the door firmly locked. I called to see if Dorothy was about and she soon appeared from one of the passages in her distinctive pale blue and white uniform. I asked her if she would kindly open the door so I could show my friends inside. She looked at me with complete astonishment and said, 'Master Christopher, I am *not* having you and your *mucky* friends sliding about on that library floor.' As I reasoned with her and persuaded her to hand over the key, I could hear stifled guffaws of laughter behind me, and from that day on Robert has always referred to me as 'Master Christopher'!

There was one other key character in the Sledmere household. Jack

Clark, always 'Mr Clark' or 'Jack', was my father's chauffeur and valet, and was so indispensable to him that we used to joke that he slept in a basket at the bottom of his bed. He certainly saw more of Papa than he did of his wife, Lilian, who ran the village post office. He had first come to Sledmere in the late 1930s, when he took over from the then chauffeur, Spencer. The car was a Rolls, and Jack was sent to the Rolls-Royce School to do a course. After the war, during which he had served as batman to Bunty Scrope, he returned to Sledmere at a time when Papa, who had recently returned from America, was developing a craze for Cadillacs, the first of which was delivered in 1948.

Cadillacs were almost unheard of in post-war Britain, and a sale was such a rarity that the head of the company which shipped it, Lendrum and Hartmann, delivered the car, a Fleetwood, personally. 'He came up for a weekend with his wife and child,' remembers Jack, 'but unfortunately there was something not quite right with the car, and Sir Richard complained that it wasn't giving him the results he expected. So the chap came down to our house with a bit of a long face and I took him for a drive down Monument Hill. I remember we went a hundred miles an hour!' The Cadillac had automatic gears, power steering, electric windows, cruise control and air conditioning, a combination of advanced features to be found in no other car on sale in Britain. It was also so futuristic looking that it gathered crowds around it wherever it went, especially when Jack was trying to park, a manoeuvre made all the more complicated by the fact that the car was left-hand drive. 'They couldn't believe that I could get such a large car into such a small space. The reason was that the tail fins were so long and so high up that I could see the lights through the back window and you could back the car within an inch of another car. That was helped by the power steering, which meant that I could turn the wheel with no effort.'[3]

How I hated those cars! They were upholstered in a type of material which set my teeth on edge, the ride was so springy that it made one feel permanently sick, but worst of all was the fact that it drew attention to one. I could not bear the sea of faces peering in wherever we drew up and wanted only to hide under the seat. The cars, which were regularly changed, got bigger and bigger, culminating in the 1959 model, celebrated for its rocket-ship tail fins. After that, though they may not have got any bigger, they certainly got no less vulgar, their interiors becoming plusher and plusher. 'The last one he had was a bit overdone inside,' recalls Jack, 'all red velvet and frills. We used to call it "the tart's bedroom"!'

Jack was the living incarnation of Jeeves. When on duty, he was always immaculately dressed in a dark blue suit, accessorised when driving by a chauffeur's peaked cap in the same colour. His routine never varied. He would come in just before eight to call Papa and bring him his breakfast, after which he would run his bath and put out his clothes. 'I chose his clothes,' he says, 'because I knew exactly what he would wear.' When he had finished this, he was off to the garage for the rest of the day, where one would find him in his overalls tinkering with an engine, his hands and face streaked with oil. There was nothing he did not know about the inner workings of a car and he would often astonish even professional mechanics with his expertise. Legend has it that when travelling one time through Italy with my parents, they came across a friend of theirs broken down on the autostrada, their car, a Rolls, surrounded by Italian mechanics scratching their heads. Jack pulled up alongside, and within half an hour had the car running again, earning the undying admiration of the Italians. At the end of the day, Jack returned to the house to lay out my father's dinner jacket, since he changed for dinner every night, even if there was no one staying. When Papa went down for cocktails, he would turn down the bed and lay out his pyjamas. Then, if there were guests staying, he would often help out in the Dining Room.

If my parents were going away, only Jack could do Papa's packing. No lady's maid could pack like Jack. Watching him was like watching an artist at work; shoes beautifully wrapped in tissue paper, everything ironed and neatly folded, layered between sheets of tissue. Then when they arrived at whatever house they were visiting, he would never allow the house servants near Papa's suitcase. Only he could unpack it, and when he had done that he would invariably be found helping to wait at table, or even, with his jacket off and sleeves rolled up, doing the washing up. Wherever my parents went, everyone loved Jack. The guests loved him because he was the perfect valet, the male servants loved him because he was so helpful, and the ladies because he was unfailingly courteous and dashingly handsome. After the first Bond film came out he was always referred to by Mama as James Bond, because he bore more than a passing resemblance to Sean Connery.

On the many travels he made with my parents, Jack made many friends and acquaintances, but none of them were as notorious as Harold Winstanley. Winstanley was a footman at Knowsley Hall on the outskirts of Liverpool, the home of the Earl and Countess of Derby. John and Isobel Derby were close friends of Mama and Papa, who were regular guests at their shooting parties, and during their many visits to Knowsley, Jack and Winstanley had become quite friendly. 'One day he said to me,' remembers Jack, "Here Jack, come with me, I've got something to show you", and he took me down the cellar and proudly showed me this collection he had of guns. They were mostly German, I seem to remember, but it was a real arsenal. I assumed they were just curiosities. It never occurred to me that he might have had bullets for them. I don't think anyone else in the house knew about them. He would confide in me where he wouldn't with the others.'

On 9 October, 1952, a year after Jack had seen the guns, Isobel Derby was alone at Knowsley in her sitting room when Winstanley entered the room in his shirtsleeves, smoking a cigarette. She had just told him off for not having let out the dog, which had consequently made a mess in the house. When she asked him what he was doing, he pulled a gun on her, a German Schmeisser 9mm calibre machine pistol, and shot her at point blank range. The bullet passed through her neck and she fell to the ground, wounded and bleeding profusely. On hearing the shot, Stallard, the butler, rushed in and was shot dead, his body falling across that of Lady Derby, who lay still, paralysed with fear. Then the under-butler, Stuart, arrived and in spite of pleading for his life was also mortally shot. Leaving behind what he assumed were three corpses, Winstanley then went on the rampage, wounding

Lord Derby's valet, Sullivan, and threatening the housekeeper, Mrs Turley, before fleeing the house. The alarm was eventually raised by Doxford, the lady's maid, and Winstanley was arrested later that night in Liverpool city centre after giving himself up. Lady Derby survived these horrific events but was severely traumatised and eventually moved out of Knowsley Hall to a new house in the park. Winstanley was judged insane and was sent to Broadmoor for life.

If Jack had a fault, it was that he spoiled Papa, constantly fussing over him like a nanny fusses over a baby. 'I don't know what it was about your father,' he once told me, 'but he was treated like royalty. People would bend over backwards for him and I couldn't understand why. Once when we were staying at Hambleden Manor, the hot water had broken down and Lady Hambleden and myself were running up and down the stairs with buckets of hot water from the kitchen so that Sir Richard could have a hot bath!' On one occasion, Papa went too far and nearly lost his beloved Jack. They had been on a long trip abroad, and on the day after their return to Sledmere, Jack was getting ready to take Lilian out for the day when Papa turned up at the door saying that he wanted to go to the races. 'Well I hadn't had a day off for ages,' Jack told me, 'and I saw red and told him "I could get a better bloody job than this anywhere", which was true because people were always saying that, if I ever left, please would I come and work for them. Then he turned his toes up and said he would give me anything. There was a lot of horse trading and running to and from the office. Lilian said to me "What's the mad panic going on?" I told her I'd just given in my notice. There was a right ding-dong for a while.' Luckily for all of us, the storm passed and Jack stayed on, acknowledging that 'working for Sir Richard was never easy'.

If we did spend rather more time backstairs than we did with our parents that did not mean we did not have fun with Mama and Papa. The latter, for example, even though he was a rather remote figure of whom we were slightly in awe and who knew how to wield a slipper if we got into too much mischief, was at the same time an expert provider of childish amusements and time spent with him was full of adventure and laughter. He had embraced Sledmere since moving in and his whole life was devoted to the running of the estate, which, with the help of his enthusiastic new agent, Norman Cardwell, was kept in apple-pie order. He carried a small notebook and a gold pencil with him wherever he went, into which he would write his observations as to which gate needed a lick of paint or where a fence needed repairing or some tiles replacing on a roof. Nothing escaped his notice, and we would often accompany him on these inspection expeditions, during which he would enthuse us to love the place as much as he did. I remember these trips as if they were yesterday.

In the summer he would drive us about in an old Austin 7 he had bought for Mama when they were first married. It had a soft top, so we could stand on the seats and stick our heads out to breathe in the delicious summer smells. With the lurchers running behind, we would go grass burning, a great favourite, to rejuvenate some area of straggly, dying meadow or stop near one of the stud paddocks to fill a basket with fresh field mushrooms, or 'fieldrooms' as he called them. Some-times he brought a .22 rifle with him and we used to take pots shots at crows sitting in the beech trees. On winter afternoons he took us out in the Land Rover to watch the lurchers course hares over endless ploughed fields. The lucky ones among us got the front seats, the rest being forced into the back with the dogs. This was bad enough before they started coursing but sharing it with them after a long run, when they were hot and sweaty and breathing steamy foul breath, was akin to being locked up in the Black Hole of Calcutta. The most memorable expeditions were when it snowed, and Papa would tie a huge four-seater sledge, made at the Raff Yard, to the back of the jeep and drag us at speed, squealing through the snow.

But of all the things that conjure up happy memories of my father, and still bring a smile to my lips, it is the organ that tops the list. As Cecil Beaton and many others testified, Papa was a brilliant musician who, as a young man, shone as a jazz pianist. As he got older, his musical interests changed and he began to play classical, no longer on the piano but on the organ. In true extravagant style he bought himself not a simple two-manual electric instrument but a full-size, three-manual Cathedral pipe organ, which had formerly graced the private chapel at Dunecht House in Aberdeenshire, the summer home of the Earls of Crawford. It was installed in Sledmere in 1947 by Binns, Fitton and Haley, organ manufacturers from Leeds, who set the console at the bottom of the main staircase and all the pipes in a loft on the top floor. Every evening without fail, when he had finished listening to the six o'clock news on the radio, Papa would emerge from his study, saunter over to the organ, roll back the lid with a noisy rattle, switch on the light beside the keyboard, which sometimes threw a sinister shadow of him on the wall so that he resembled a sort of country-house Dr Phibes, and begin to play.

LA DA DA . . . LA DA DA DA DA . . . DA . . . LA DA DA . . . DA DA DA DA . . . would trumpet out the opening bars of Bach's Toccata and Fugue in D Minor and the windows would rattle, the floors would vibrate, the bath water would tremble, and the whole house would sit bolt upright. It was an unforgettable experience; for those who lived in the house and heard it nightly; for those regular visitors who were primed and looked forward to it; but particularly for those who were unprepared and who must have jumped out of their skins the first time they heard it. It is still a great surprise to me that at no time was it ever the cause of a fatal heart attack. We loved it for the thrill it sent down our spines and from the pleasure we got watching Papa's face as he played. It took on a look of absolute concentration, personified by piggy eyes and pouting lips, and was referred to always as 'the organ face'. It was the cause of much childish giggling and amusement.

Life at Sledmere during those golden years was never, ever dull. For one thing, the house was rarely without visitors. Mama, who people used to say would light up a room when she walked into it, had an extraordinary talent for friendship and picked up new friends of all ages wherever she went. As a result, countless guests came to visit throughout the year, to indulge in an endless round of country pursuits. They came for the races at York and Doncaster, for the shooting and the hunting, the tennis and the croquet, for Christmas and Easter, high days and holidays, filling the house with their chatter and laughter, the distant hum of which would float up nightly to our bedrooms on the nursery floor. Then how we longed to join in; later we did so with gusto.

Christmas and Easter were family times when the uncles, aunts and cousins came to stay. Aunt Freya, nicknamed 'Frypots' by her brothers and sisters, and 'Moot' by her nephews and nieces, always came for Christmas, with her husband Ricky, a famous high court judge, and their five children, Ruth, Polly, Mark, Jessica and Hughie. The routine never varied, the festivities beginning on Christmas Eve with a party for all the children in the village. First a film, usually Laurel and Hardy, was shown in the Drawing Room on a noisy old projector operated by a Mr Dent from Hull, a small, rather fussy man with spectacles, whose professorial air earned him the nickname 'Doctor', as if he had an honour in the art of Projectioning. An immense tea in the Dining Room followed this, where the table, covered by a huge white cloth, was laden with sandwiches, cakes and jellies, and loads of crackers. Then we all trooped into the Hall and stood at the foot of the stairs, looking eagerly upwards to the great glass dome above. Suddenly balloons would begin to fall as if by magic from the sky, and we all knew this signalled the arrival of Father Christmas; in reality Uncle Ricky, who bounded down the stairs to distribute presents round the huge tree which stood in the Hall and had been decorated by Mouzelle. When he was finished, he ran back up the stairs, always pausing on the first flight to do a little dance, before waving goodbye and disappearing from view. It would all have been lovely had it not been for the fact that the mask that he wore, which had no eyes and hung off his face in a sinister way, was so frightening that it often reduced the younger members of the party to screams and tears.

Each year, when the party was over, a very feudal ceremony took place, when all the men from the village who worked on the estate would come up to the house for their Christmas presents. A long trestle table was erected in the back passage on which were placed dozens of ducks. Mama and Papa stood at one end of it with all of us children and the agent, Norman Cardwell. The men, who had been waiting outside in the yard, then came in, their caps in their hands, and were given either one or two ducks, according to the size of their families. We would all wish them 'Happy Christmas' and off they would go back into the night. Though we all quite enjoyed this ceremony when we were little, as we grew older we began to find it excruciatingly embarrassing, but it went on relentlessly throughout Papa's lifetime.

The grown-ups and the older children all went to midnight Mass on Christmas Eve. This took place in the family chapel and was taken by a priest who was lent to Sledmere for Christmas by the Abbot of Ampleforth, a continuation of a long tradition that had started during Papa's boyhood with Father Pozzi. We now had a charming Benedictine monk called Father Anthony. Papa never attended these services, his hatred of religion being just as strong as ever, which meant that he missed the annual sight of Uncle Ricky being reduced to hysterical giggles during the hymns by the caterwauling of one of the female parishioners. Instead he preferred to remain behind to prepare all the ingredients for the post-Mass supper, which he always called the *Réveillon*. Served in the Dining Room, this consisted of fresh veal consommé and York ham, washed down with champagne.

Christmas was never without its dramas, whether it was the invariable noisy argument that sprung up between the judge and the priest on the merits of capital punishment – perhaps not surprisingly it was Uncle Ricky who was the liberal and Father Anthony the reactionary – or some more sensational event such as the Christmas Day that was cancelled. Amongst the Elwes family there was a sharp divide when it came to how they liked to pass their time, most simply classified as the 'Outdoor Set' and the 'Indoor Set', the Queen of the latter being Moot, whose idea of heaven was to sit all day by the fire in the Music Room chain-smoking Gauloise cigarettes and poring over *The Times* and the *Telegraph* jumbo crosswords. The Christmas Day routine at Sledmere was to open presents round the tree at teatime, when the candles on the tree would also be lit.

One particular Christmas, at about four in the afternoon, when we were all beginning to gather around the tree for present-opening, it was noticed that there was a strong smell of smoke coming from the Music Room, the door of which, since the Indoor Set had an aversion to draughts, was firmly closed. When it was opened, an extraordinary sight was revealed. A fog of smoke filled the room and through the gloom could be made out the figure of Moot sitting on the sofa puffing away and studying the crossword, completely oblivious to the fact that the chimney was on fire. That it was serious was clear from the fact that more smoke was seeping out of a crack in the wall above the chimneypiece. Moot remained quite unfazed throughout the panic that followed. The fire brigade were called and Papa insisted that the rest of Christmas should be cancelled till the following day, to the great disappointment of the younger members of the party, most of whom were reduced to tears. The day ended on an amusing note. We were all sitting round the dining-room table at the end of dinner, having just pulled the crackers. Papa was sitting at the head of the table puffing on a huge cigar and wearing a pink paper hat and a large pair of plastic earrings, when Michael approached him with the news that the chief of the Bridlington Fire Brigade was waiting to see him in the Hall. Oblivious to his get-up, he went off to meet the officer, and when we all followed him out, we were thoroughly entertained by the sight of these two men talking to one another, quite unphased, the one in full fireman's uniform, the other sporting earrings.

At Easter we would sometimes be visited by our favourite uncle, Uncle Christopher, the most brilliant and genial of men who being number four in the line of Christophers in the family was consequently known as 'Fourth'. Of all Mark's children, he was the most like his father, sharing his love of travel and the Middle East, and having inherited his talent as a mimic and caricaturist, as well as his sense of adventure and a certain devil-may-care attitude. He once told his great friend Harman Grisewood about a game – his own word for it – that he used to play on the London Underground, which consisted of him following a departing train by running through the tunnel to reach the next station before the train behind him ran him down. He had played an even more terrifying version when he was a member of the Oxford University Railway Society and had lain flat out on the track between the rails to see if an oncoming train, in this case the Irish Mail would pass over him, leaving him unharmed. It had done so, three times. 'Why do you do such things?' Grisewood had asked him. 'To see what it felt like,' he had answered with an amused smile.[4]

Christopher had enjoyed an extraordinary life. After leaving Oxford without a degree, he had joined the Foreign Office, serving in Berlin and Tehran, before deciding that he wanted to become a writer. He travelled extensively in Persia and Afghanistan, where he was for some time a correspondent for *The Times*, in which guise he also acted as a spy for the British Government. He published his first book in 1936, *Wassmuss*, a biography of 'The German T. E. Lawrence'. Much of the war was spent in Cairo, working for SOE, though he almost got himself court-martialled for criticising the organisation in a novel he published in 1943, *High Minded Murder*. He returned to England and joined the SAS, and in 1944 was parachuted into France behind enemy lines where he fought with the Resistance. 'He showed great courage,' wrote his commanding officer, 'and . . . was ready to take anything that was coming to him, including my cigarettes.'[5] He was subsequently mentioned in dispatches and awarded the Croix de Guerre. When the war was over, his career as a writer really took off with the publication of the critically acclaimed *Four Studies in Loyalty*, a series of biographical sketches, including one of his great-uncle, Sykey.

Uncle Christopher was Papa's best friend and I never saw him happier than when he was in his company. They talked and laughed all the time, mostly about their childhood and kept us endlessly amused with tales of the past. They loved to take us on what they called 'Mystery Tours' when we would all pile into the Cadillac, the two brothers in the front, with Papa at the wheel, and drive for several hours round various places which held special memories for them. The stories they told soon became imprinted on our minds so that whenever we were close to any of these places we knew that they were about to say 'Look at the Scubby-Scubbies', 'Lady Mary Clough-Taylor lived there', 'there's the Slipper Hill', 'remember the Dog Stoop ghost?', 'it's so sad the Fimber Paffa has gone', and so on. A particular favourite was Burdale Tunnel, a deserted railway tunnel, about a mile long, on the abandoned line from Fimber to Malton, which they discussed endlessly. One day Uncle Christopher took us on a walk through it, leading us through its dank dripping interior with only a torch to light the way, and regaling us with ghost stories as we walked. It was a terrifying experience.

Sometimes they whispered about a man called Mitchell, a name that was meaningless to us, but because it was spoken so secretly we realised that it was something that we were meant to know nothing about. On occasions when this name was mentioned, someone would mutter under their breath '*Pas devant les enfants*', though since we'd all been taught French by Zellie, it must have been clear to the grown-ups that we would know what it meant. It did not take long to garner from our older cousins the information that Mitchell was our mysterious Uncle Daniel, about whom we knew very little since his name was never mentioned. He was nicknamed Mitchell after Miss Mitchell, a piano teacher whom Papa and Uncle Christopher remembered from childhood, and of whom it was said, 'The only person who plays the piano worse than Miss Mitchell is Daniel.' Though I was never allowed to meet him, over the years I have gathered together information about him from surviving friends, and his story was a sad one.

The youngest of the family by five years, Edith had indeed doted on Daniel. 'He came in all the time thinking wasn't he wonderful,' remembers Sibell Rowley, a frequent guest at Sledmere in the 1920s. 'His mother spoilt him thoroughly. He was very much the younger son and thought to be wonderful. Richard and Christopher were very fed up with him and all the attention he got.' When his mother died so young and so suddenly, he found himself adrift. 'He seemed awfully lost,' Sibell told me. 'He never fitted in, and he used to come round and see me and complain how his family didn't understand him.'[6]

Being very Catholic and quite conventional, one of the things they didn't understand about him was that he was quite openly gay. 'I think being homosexual was at the root of his troubles,' Moot told me, 'and a terrible lack of initiative, of being able to stick to any one thing.' A talented artist, he first tried architecture as a career, but dropped out of school after six months, and then drifted around in a succession of jobs.

When war broke out the following year, Daniel decided to go into the RAF, but his career was short-lived. He went absent without leave and fled to London, much to the disdain of his family. 'Does he realise,' wrote Uncle Christopher to Papa, 'that people who spend this war in that manner will never live it down under twenty years and he will *never* be able to show his great monstrous painted face at Sledmere again unless he wants to be pelted with rotten turnips.'[7] It was in London where the eighteen-year-old John Richardson first came across him. 'I was living with the Hope-Nicholsons in More House in Chelsea,' he told me. 'All the rooms had huge closets which were filled with fancy dress, because Mrs Hope-Nicholson used to rent out clothes to theatres and for parties. There was a closet off my room and there was obviously someone in there because I could hear rustling sounds. I went in to investigate. There was a window in the closet, so it was like a kind of room, with crinolines and dresses hanging everywhere, and there was a man sitting there, partly in RAF uniform, painting his toenails. It was Daniel.'[8] He had been hiding out for several weeks, though the RAF appeared to have made little effort to trace him. 'They were almost certainly relieved by someone like Daniel deserting,' commented John. They soon became lovers and Daniel introduced John to the extraordinary Bohemian world he inhabited in wartime Chelsea.

At that time, Daniel's life revolved round the home of Marno and Odile Hornak, referred to in family letters as 'the Hornakery', a large eighteenth-century house on the corner of the King's Road and Royal Avenue, the deep basement of which attracted a floating population of artistic like-minded people, many of them gay, who gathered there to shelter during air raids. 'Thirty or forty people used to come,' recalled Odile Hourani, the former Mrs Hornak, 'bringing picnics and bedding, and one day Daniel was among them. We took to him immediately, he was so witty and clever and a great raconteur and gossip. We – Marno, myself and our baby daughter, Julia – became his family. He used to come every day, and read stories to Julia and sometimes cook for me. He was very happy in those early days with John.' Marno, who ran an antique shop, gave Daniel a job scouting for him. 'He had a brilliant eye,' remembered Odile.[9] None of this impressed his family, who considered him a lost cause. Writing to Papa a few days before his wedding, Uncle Christopher commented 'I hope Mitchell doesn't turn up rouged, wearing a wig and drunk.'[10]

Daniel's flair and sense of style soon came to the attention of a clever, rather sexy refugee from Germany called Gaby Schreiber, who was a talented designer, and together they set up a decorating business called Sykes and Schreiber, employing John, who had been exempted from service in the army after a bout of rheumatic fever. One of the areas of design in which they became interested was the use of plastics, encouraged by Gaby's lover, a fellow German refugee called Bill Fischbein, who was a brilliant expert in the field and was the inventor of Bartrev, the precursor of chipboard. He had futuristic ideas for the design of a plastic car and soon Daniel was producing drawings for him and beginning to believe that his fortune was about to be made. 'Daniel began to see himself as a genius businessman,' remembers John, 'and suddenly bought himself a huge briefcase and double-breasted suits and started having meetings and business lunches all over town with Fischbein and other tycoons, and they were going to make all kinds of things out of plastic.'

At Sledmere, there were audible sighs of relief. 'I understand that Mitchell has returned to a life of decorum,' wrote Uncle Christopher to Papa in March 1943, 'that he has abandoned the joys of Sodom, and wears a black hat and carries blueprints in a bag. Long may that last. I cannot say that I always knew the boy would win through because I was always convinced that he wouldn't. But then I also thought the French would hold, the Greeks wouldn't, and the Russians would collapse. Possibly Mitchell is among these major miscalculations.'[11] As things turned out, however, he was not. The scheme came to nothing, and Daniel was soon back to decorating and looking for antiques.

When the war was over, Daniel went to Paris, where he fell in with a group of artists and intellectuals whose number included Jean Cocteau, who befriended him, and introduced him to opium, the joys of which he was only too happy to extol on his return to London a year later. 'We were all convinced that it was just an affectation,' Odile

THE BIG HOUSE

told me, 'but he went on and on about how wonderful it was.' In their London house, the Hornaks had an extravagantly beautiful eighteenth-century bedroom, decorated by Odile in the style of Marie Antoinette, and it was much admired by Daniel, who one day asked if he could hold a opium party there. 'I very foolishly agreed,' remembered Odile, 'and about nine or ten of his opium friends came here. They all became like purry pussycats, half crouching in corners, and it seemed to go on for ever, silent and deadly boring. Then out of sheer despair, I smoked some. I remember it smelt of damp leaves and chestnuts and I had a most annoying dream of pink and blue teddy bears walking down a steep hill. I never forgave him for it.'[12]

Unfortunately the opium proved to be more than just an eccentric phase in Daniel's life. He became hopelessly addicted to it, establishing a string of suppliers, most of whom worked in various Latin American embassies, and when the sources began to run dry and it became more and more expensive, he turned first to injecting cocaine, and then to heroin. He continued to work in Marno's antique shop, and spent much of the time at their home. 'He used to come in almost daily for lunch and for a fix,' said Odile. 'He was becoming more and more dependent.' In spite of the fact that he became a registered addict and could thus get his drugs on the state, something that was possible in the 1950s, the policy was to reduce the dose each time to try to wean the sufferer off the drug. While this undoubtedly worked for some people, others like Daniel continually craved more, so the expense of supporting his habit began to get him into severe financial difficulties. When the last pennies of his inheritance had gone to the dealers he turned to his sister Angela.

Angela, who had married Ran, 8th Earl of Antrim, in May 1934, lived at Glenarm Castle, a Gothic turreted pile in County Antrim in the north of Ireland. A devout Catholic and the closest of the family in age to Daniel, she had shown herself to be the most approachable of his siblings when it came to asking for help. In August 1953, he invited himself to stay with her for ten days. She very quickly found out the reason. 'The truth is out,' she wrote to Moot, 'and it is not funny. He is an advanced heroin addict, needing at least four and a half grains a day. Three would kill you or me . . . He is in a desperate state, blackmailed and squeezed by the dope racketeers. I don't know how much it costs to buy his needs, and suspect the price is generally what you have got plus threats . . . He takes injections four times a day and is in a really shaky state after missing only one, and might do some violence to himself or some rash deed if he was desperate.'[13] Angela sent him home with enough money to pay for his drugs and organised accommodation for him, which she persuaded Papa to pay for. His attitude was that he would pay up to help his brother so long as he did not have to see him. This was the sad pattern of the rest of Uncle Daniel's life, right up to his early death in 1968 at the age of fifty-two.

The Easter holidays were the quietest time of the year at Sledmere, most of the social life revolving round events that took place in the summer and winter. In November, December and January there were three big shooting parties when the house burst at the seams with visitors, many of the guests bringing their own valets and maids. To make room for everyone, the youngest children were farmed out with their nannies. Chauffeurs would be sent to the village pub, the Triton Inn. Mama was in her element during these house parties, priding herself on her ability to gather together not just the best shots, but the most glamorous and amusing. If there were bachelors among them, then she would have been sure to ask beautiful, single women in need of a husband.

Mama was like a great conductor with her orchestra: not a note was left out. The house always smelt delicious, a combination of sweetly scented plants from the hothouse and fragrant oils in burners. There was the constant clink of glasses and the rattle of ice in the cocktail shaker – she mixed a mean martini. When people were shown to their rooms, they would find their suitcases unpacked, a fire burning in the grate and their baths run. The vast black coal-fired boiler in the cellars ensured that there was never a shortage of hot water. The food was exquisite. She spent hours in the kitchen with Mrs Scott, telling her about dishes she had tasted on her travels in Italy and France, and getting her to try things out, using the wonderful local ingredients. Dinner was always four courses, the menu written out in pencil in French by Mouzelle on white china menu cards. Soup to start with, perhaps clear *Consommé de Veau*, accompanied by thin triangles of white toast; followed by a fish course such as *Goujons de Sole, Sauce Tartare*; then a simple meat course like *Côtelettes d'Agneau*, with a delicious home-made ice cream to finish, such as *Glace à la Vanille* made with the thick Guernsey cream from the farm.

When dinner was over, the party would retire to the Music Room and the Drawing Room for charades, cards and chatter, against a background of Mama's Ray Conniff records played on the radiogram. As the evening wore on and the champagne flowed, the laughing, gossiping voices got louder and louder, the noise often waking us up and luring us down from the top floor to peer through the railings of the first floor balcony to the Hall below. Sometimes we saw elegant dancers waltzing round the stone floor, other times a drunk being helped up the stairs, and very occasionally we might recognise the face of someone famous, such as David Niven, a former admirer of Mama's, or Noel Coward, a protégé of her father's. It was always fascinating and enchanting and filled one with a longing to be grown up.

In the summer, the house parties were all connected with the stud and racing, the highlight being the annual three day meeting at York during the third week of August. This seemed to attract a younger, more raffish set, with bloodstock agents like the More o'Ferralls, and trainers like Bernard van Cutsem, mixing with glamorous owners like the Duke of Devonshire. Hopefully, Mama would have hooked an American multi-millionaire, such as Paul Mellon or Jack Clayburg, into the party in the hope that they might buy one of the season's yearlings, which were paraded round the paddocks each morning. When Jack Clayburg, owner of the King Ranch in Texas, came to stay, he was sleeping in one of the bedrooms on the first floor, which have a balcony outside the door overlooking the Hall. After a hard night on the Bourbon, which Papa had specially provided for him, he retired to bed in the early hours. His neighbour, Shimi Lovat, was awoken at dawn by the sound of what he thought was a running tap outside his room, and got up to investigate. When he opened the door of his bedroom he witnessed the amazing sight of Clayburg standing half awake, peeing over the balcony into the Hall below. He had evidently woken up and, thinking he was back on the King Ranch, decided to take his early morning piss from the balcony on to the Texas earth. He did buy a yearling, but whether it was out of shame or not, no one ever knew.

As we got older, our sense of detachment from the curious world of the grown-ups began to get less, especially when, as we entered our teens and left prep school for public school, we were allowed to take the first steps towards joining in, the most important of which was being allowed down to dinner. Now we were able to observe at close quarters what formerly we had only been able to watch from afar, and we were able to listen, our ears picking up far more than they should have. We began, for example, to squirrel away various anecdotes about Papa's rather colourful past, in the days before he was married. Some of them, such as '*Une Espèce de Roi*', were funny stories about his attempts to impress. In the 1930s, for example, he used to travel each year in October to Paris to attend the Arc de Triomphe. He always went with the same group of friends, and one night they overheard him in a night club chatting up an attractive blonde with the words, spoken in faultless Franglais, '*Je vous avoir savoir que en Yorkshire où j'habite, je suis une espèce de roi!*'

Others, such as the Doris Duke incident, concerned his temper, another favourite being 'The Wentworth Woodhouse Affair'. Papa had accepted an invitation to shoot at Wentworth Woodhouse, the ancestral pile of the Earl of Fitzwilliam, which, with its 600-foot frontage, is thought by many to be the grandest house in England. During the weekend, however, he was the butt of various practical jokes, designed by the other guests to see how easily they could make him fly off the handle. The culmination of these, which he discovered when he retired to his bedroom, a small room on the Bachelor's Passage, was the snipping off of the arms and legs of his tweed suit, which were put in a bucket of water, and an apple-pie bed. Unlike his Great-Uncle Christopher, who had suffered so much teasing with such stoicism, Papa was not prepared to take this lying down, and he went berserk, grabbing a heavy stone match holder from the bedside table, and proceeding to smash every piece of furniture in the room into smithereens and throw them out of the window. He then dressed and left the house without ceremony, and drove himself home through the night. The following morning, Admiral Lord Beatty, who had been Commander of the British Navy during the First World War, and had been sleeping in the room directly below Richard, told his host that he had not heard such a noise since the Battle of Jutland.

Another story, which demonstrates the awe in which Papa was held by some of his friends, was 'The Affair of the Burnt Chair'. During one York Races house party at Sledmere, a group of guests were playing Racing Demon. They were seated round a card table on part of a very fine set of eighteenth-century French chairs. One of the participants, John Wyndham, the future Lord Egremont, who was having a hard time of the game, became very agitated and bounced up and down in his chair so hard that he broke one of its legs. The chair capsized, catapulting him to the floor. His fellow guests, being alarmed at the effect this breakage would have on their host, picked up the chair and placed it hard against the wall, balancing it on the broken leg. The next person to move the chair would get the blame. They returned to their game, and eventually, after much drinking and laughter, they all retired to bed, hopefully to sleep soundly.

Not so John Wyndham. Tormented by the spectre of being on the wrong side of Papa's notorious temper, he sat upon his bed, remaining wide awake until he knew that the last person had retired to their room. He then crept downstairs into the Drawing Room. Opening the writing desk he found a large pot of Grip Fix glue, which Mama kept for sticking photographs into her numerous albums. He took the offending chair apart again and applied liberal amounts of the glue to the chair leg, which he then carefully stuck back on to the base of the chair. He waited patiently for twenty minutes or so before slowly lowering himself back into it. Scarcely had his bottom touched the seat than once again the leg broke and the chair collapsed.

John was now convulsed with fear. What on earth was he to do? He thought long and hard before the solution hit him. After reinforcing his courage with a stiff Scotch from the drinks tray, he broke the chair into pieces and burned them on the drawing-room fire. The next day, he spent the few hours before he was due to leave in a state of absolute terror, imagining that any moment the wrath of his host would be upon him. But Papa never noticed, not on that day, nor the next, nor the next month, nor in the years afterwards. In fact he would die innocent of the facts. For a man who prided himself on having things perfect, he failed to notice that his priceless set of eight French chairs, was now a not so priceless set of seven.

These stories, whispered behind his back, were taboo in front of Papa, who would fly of the handle at the merest hint of them being mentioned. 'Your father,' Mama once told me, 'is haunted by his past.' Such outbursts, being extremely alarming on the relatively rare occasions when they occurred, earned him a nickname from us, 'the Mutant', after a creature we saw on the television programme, *Dr Who*. As we passed puberty and turned into real teenagers, the name became more relevant as Papa grew increasingly impatient with both our demeanour and our appearance. In his letters to Uncle Christopher, he began to refer to us all as 'the snake pit'. 'The snake pit season is on,' he wrote in August, 1965, 'and consequently I am frequently in a vexed state.'

The Mutant did not take kindly to the sixties. 'Oh why can't you have your hair like Peter Irwin?' he used to wail, referring to a particularly short-haired and smart neighbour of our age, as our hair began to inch over our collars. Each evening as he either played the organ in the Hall before dinner, or afterwards sat listening to concerts of classical music on his radiogram, he had to compete with 'non-stop Beatle music from the Library'.[14] Night after night I used to creep out of my room and listen to him arguing with Mama in the Hall below, complaining about the long hair and the dreadful clothes. He had reason to despair, certainly on my behalf, for I was well and truly caught up in the hippy craze of the time, wore an earring, and had so many bells hanging from my torso that you could hear me coming half a mile away. After a while, however, when he realised that we paid scant attention to his disapproval, the Mutant learned to live with our appearance, and even showed signs of being amused by it. 'York Races is just over,' he wrote to Uncle Christopher in August, 1967, 'and we had a great party of the snake pit and their colleagues all dressed in sensational costumes.' The outfits of their own contemporaries, he added, 'the Misses Dunns, Hope Vere, Maggie Guinness, Lygons, were fit for Vatican audiences in comparison'.[15]

Mama loved the new fashions, and embraced the young. I remember meeting her and Papa one day for lunch at Claridges Hotel, their London residence. I was wearing a floral-patterned Deborah and Clare shirt and a pair of gold crushed velvet trousers from Granny Takes a Trip, the hippest boutique in the King's Road, and as we walked together across the foyer, a friend of hers, Zara Cazalet, came up to her and said, 'Darling, how can you be seen in public with Christopher dressed like that?' Mama turned to her and said, 'I think he looks absolutely lovely!' and walked straight on. She had a completely open mind and wanted to try everything. One evening, during a York Races house party, the snake pit were all gathered in the Library after dinner, dancing to the Beatles and smoking large numbers of joints. The door suddenly opened and in walked Mama, attracted by the sounds of her favourite pop group, which had wafted down below. 'Darling, is that marijuana you're smoking?' she asked, peering into the gloom and wrinkling her nose. 'Do let me have a puff,' she begged, and took three heavy drags on the spliff she was offered. We waited for her verdict with baited breath. 'I just don't see what all the fuss is about,' she then said. 'It's had no effect at all.' The fact that her eyes had taken on the appearance of boiled sweets told another story.

When Mama was around it was impossible for the Mutant to be angry for long, even in one of his famous tempers. Over the years she had become an expert at pouring oil on troubled waters, her easy-going nature and *joie de vivre* helping her to pull him out of his black moods. She adored him, though he often appeared to take her for granted. She once wrote to him 'I think of you all the time, which I hope makes you feel ashamed, you self-sufficient creature'.[16] But the truth is that when she was away he was quite lost. In her fifties she had the energy and youthfulness of a woman in her thirties.

One day, early in April, 1970, I went into her room in the morning and she told me that she had had a stomach ache in the night, the doctor had been called and had told her he suspected appendicitis. An ambulance was coming to collect her to take her to the cottage hospital in Driffield, the Alfred Bean, where she was going to have her appendix removed. Later that morning we were told that the surgeon, Mr Patrick, had discovered, not appendicitis as suspected, but a stomach ulcer, and that this had been operated on successfully and that Mama was now in recovery. I happened to be at home at the time because I was recuperating from an attack of pneumonia, so I was able to go and visit her every day. Mama had never been in hospital before and was finding it difficult to regain her strength after the operation, though the hospital was not remotely concerned about her.

On 28 April, Papa went away for a couple of nights to fulfil a long-standing engagement to stay with his friends the Derbys at Knowsley, near Liverpool, having been assured by the hospital that there was nothing to worry about. When I went in to see Mama that day, this was confirmed when they told me she was being sent home the following day. She was over the moon at this news and as I left her room, promising as I did so that I would start reading her *To Kill a Mockingbird* when she got home, she squeezed my hand and said 'I love you all.' That night I had a strange dream that my best friend from art school had died, and I woke up crying into my pillow. Then I felt a hand on my shoulder shaking me, saying, 'Wake up, Christopher, wake up.' It was Tatton, my eldest brother, come to tell me that Mama had died during the night of heart failure. She was fifty-four.

Papa was devastated. 'She made my life for me,' he wrote to his old friend, Rupert Alec-Smith, 'and having been a somewhat moody character . . . she had a great knack of being able to pull one out of one's weaknesses. The blow has been terrible.'[17] We were all bereft, but at least we had him to worry about to take our minds off our own misery. He was haunted by guilt; that he should not have gone away, that he should have transferred her to a better hospital, that he did not do enough to prevent it, though the truth is that she almost certainly had some weakness of the heart which, because she had never been ill before, had escaped diagnosis. He went through all the stages of bereavement. He had black despairs, he drank too much, he took pills, he even once attempted suicide, but gradually he began to pull through. It would be a falsehood to say he ever really recovered from Mama's death. For ever after he was only half the person he had been, but encouraged by his children and helped by his friends, he really did make an effort.

Seeing us all rally round, made him think that perhaps we weren't such a snake pit after all, and he became more mellow and affectionate. The first Christmas without Mama was a hard time for him. 'We had Xmas here with all the ex-snake pit,' he wrote to Uncle Christopher. 'Wonderful snow which came on Xmas Eve, with the trees looking as though they had been bought from the Xmas Tree department at Fortnum's, and tobogganing such as we did 100 years ago and I used you as a guinea-pig to see how dangerous the slope was. It was a dreadfully nostalgic time for me – Virginia so much loved Xmas and all the silly things that go with it – but all those activities did much to divert my mind.'[18]

Sledmere really saved Papa's life. He immersed himself in its cocoon and allowed it to nurse him back to some kind of life. Though after two or three years, we tried to persuade him to consider remarrying, producing a number of possible candidates, some of them old friends and one of whom we actually persuaded to accept if he were to propose, in the end we abandoned this project, realising that Sledmere now stood in Mama's place. All he wanted was to be there, surrounded by his dogs and horses, his trees, and his family, or 'the beatniks'[19] as we were now known. In the mornings he went to the estate office to 'frown at papers', as we called it in the family. In the afternoons he drove out in his Land Rover, the back packed with lurchers, to go coursing over the Wolds. In the early evening he played the organ, and listened to music in the Hall after dinner. Slowly, he once again achieved some kind of contentment.

There were still the occasional outbreaks of eccentric behaviour.

After all, he was the Mutant. One of these was the Stalinesque habit he developed of erasing people with whom he had fallen out from the Visitors' Book. The first person to whom I consciously remember this happening was a boyfriend of Arabella's called Hamish McGregor-Petrie, who came to stay soon after Mama's death, and who accompanied the Mutant into his study one evening and told him that the best way for him to deal with his grief was to 'drop acid'. Though the Mutant's initial reaction to this was that Hamish was 'a remarkable young man', after a few days pondering the incident, he changed his mind and set about erasing his name from the Visitors' Book with Tipp-Ex. Perhaps Hamish's behaviour did border on the outrageous, and more often than not people were confined to oblivion for the most innocent of reasons.

A more typical incident was as follows. An old friend of mine, Candida Lycett-Green, the daughter of Sir John Betjeman, was staying on one occasion, when at lunch she got into what started as a friendly argument with the Mutant over the merits of Victorian architecture. He was teasing her about her enthusiasm for the beauty of the village school, a distinguished Victorian building by the architect, Street, saying that in his opinion, it and all similar architecture was hideous. Not realising that they were built by him and were his pride and joy, she retorted with 'Well at least it's a great deal better than those dreadful neo-Georgian council houses at the top of the village.' From long experience, we always knew when someone had made a *faux pas*, because the Mutant's eyes went piggy, and on this occasion they went especially so. Somehow we diverted attention away from Candida to avoid him shouting at the table, and as she was leaving after lunch, the crisis seemed to have been averted. After she had gone, however, he made his displeasure about her quite clear and we later noticed that wherever her name appeared in the Visitors' Book he had Tipp-Exed it out and written over it the crudely falsified signature of some other more favoured guest. Candida was one of many distinguished people whose memory was expunged in this way.

Shortly before Mama's death, and for a variety of reasons connected to tax relief, Papa had taken the decision to open the house to the public for one hundred days each year. This gave him a new interest, and also the excuse to refurbish some of the rooms, beginning with returning the Drawing Room to the way it was before the fire, by putting back the mirrors between the windows, which Brierley had replaced with bookcases. 'I was lost in admiration of the Drawing Room Revividum,' wrote Uncle Christopher after a visit in October 1976, 'and of it may truly be used the historic words "You have done great things!" . . . I think that in all its history, Sledmere has never looked so beautiful as now.'[20]

Had Mama been alive, she might well have persuaded Papa against carrying out the last eccentric act of his life, which was to change his name from Sykes to Tatton-Sykes. Like many landowners, Papa was convinced that Harold Wilson's government spelled the beginning of the end. 'The political situation is dreadful for places like here,' he had written to Uncle Christopher in February, 1975, 'and I see absolute ruination looming ahead.'[21] In the New Year's Honours List of 1977, to Papa's horror, James Callaghan, who had replaced Wilson after his resignation, awarded a knighthood to one of his supporters who happened to be called Richard Sykes. 'Every time there is a Labour banquet,' he wrote, '"Sir Richard Sykes" appears as being present. Now everyone thinks I must have joined the Labour Party and some-one wrote to me recently and said they were so pleased I am now a friend of Callaghan as he really is such a nice man! In effect I detest him . . .'[22] When, at the beginning of March, he received a letter sending him 'hearty congratulations' on being appointed as the next Ambassador to The Netherlands, a job just awarded to the new Sir Richard, Papa decided that he would put a stop to these errors once and for all by taking the now extinct name of Tatton, which had once belonged to the family of Elizabeth Sykes, wife of Sir Christopher. Though he tried hard to persuade the rest of the family to do the same, his efforts fell on stony ground.

In 1978, I was travelling round America with the Rolling Stones, publicising a book about them I had produced with the photographer, Annie Leibovitz, when on 20 July, in Los Angeles, I received a telegram from home saying that Papa was gravely ill and that if I wished to see him, I should return at once. I flew to New York and from there on Concorde to London, and on the evening of 22 July was at his bedside in the hospital in Hull. He looked dreadfully frail. The next day, my thirtieth birthday, I showed him the proofs of a book of old family photographs, which I was putting together. He smiled as he looked through it, his life passing before him. There he was in his pram in 1907, standing in a line with his brother and sisters in 1912, with his mother and father in 1917, with Pozzi in 1924, with a group of 'bright young things' in 1933, at the wheel of his Rolls-Royce in 1934, at the piano in the Music Room in 1936, and finally with Mama on his wedding day in 1942.

The following morning, there was a message from the hospital to say that he had had a relapse. Gathering up Jack, we set off for the hospital and were soon assembled round his bed. At one point he opened his eyes and I asked him if there was anything he would like. 'A Double Diamond,' he whispered weakly, naming his favourite pale ale. With the approval of his nurse, one of us went to the pub opposite the hospital and returned with a bottle, the contents of which were administered in a beaker. As he sipped at it a faint smile crossed his face, and he whispered the word 'Delicious!' He died that afternoon.

Sometime after, we were all sitting around in the Hall, when one of us suddenly said 'We are orphans now.' My youngest sister, Henrietta, burst into floods of tears, and I think that a great sense of emptiness assailed us all. This really was the end of childhood, the cracking of the great cocoon that Sledmere was.

It really struck home a few months later when I rather nonchalantly said to Tatton, 'Oh, by the way, I'm coming up for the weekend and I'm bringing a couple of friends.'

'Who said you could do that?' he asked me with some surprise.

'I don't have to ask,' I replied indignantly 'It's my home.'

'Not any more, it isn't,' he told me, firmly, 'it's *my* home now. You'll always be welcome here, all of you, but from now on you must ask if you want to come and stay, not just presume you can.'

I stalked off in a fury, but when I thought about it, I realised he was right. As the head of the family, it *was* now his home, and it was time for the rest of us to move on, to make our own nests. It has been a difficult task, for whoever I am with and wherever I go, I never feel so much at peace as when I return to the big house.

My Unexpected Uncle

In early June 1976, quite out of the blue, my Uncle Christopher received an extraordinary letter, which threw new light upon one of the more bizarre episodes in our family's history. It came from a complete stranger and read as follows:

Dear Mr Sykes,

I have something to tell you and a request to make. I am in some perplexity as to how to begin, so I will jump straight in with what I have to say.

My father, who is now very ill, is the son of your father and Alice Carter, and was born in 1895, when they were both pretty young. I understand that Mark Sykes and Alice Carter eloped from Sledmere and were eventually found by Lady Sykes in London. Sir Tatton had threatened to disinherit his son and Lady Sykes arranged things by sending Mark away to school and looking after Alice. Her child was born in April, 1895, and put into the care of a foster mother. Alice stayed on under Lady Sykes's protection in a house in Mount Street. She later became a teacher in, and later headmistress of, a school in London.

Lady Sykes made excellent financial provision for my father, paid for him to go to a good boarding school, and used to visit him from time to time. He was also kindly treated by Sir William Pakenham who helped him in 1919 to find a job.

You will be wondering why I am bringing up this old history now. My father had always been very reticent about any of it until a few years ago, when he had a serious illness. At that time he told me more and I realised that emotionally he had suffered deeply as an adolescent and that his memories still grieved him. Last year I bought him Adelson's book.[1]

It seemed to me that Adelson had found the events of 1894–5 difficult to explain, especially the vengeful killing of the dogs, and I wondered whether the family had chosen not to make more explanation available or had simply not known any more.

This brings me to my request. Now that he is so ill, and knowing how rejected he has felt, I would dearly like to be able to tell my father that his existence was at least known within the family. Had you ever heard anything of this history before? I am writing to you because you seem particularly to have followed up your father's works.

I expect this letter will have caused you some surprise, but I hope it does not distress you.

Yours sincerely,

Veronica Roberts.

Astonished by what he had just read, Uncle Christopher was for a while in some doubt as to what was the wisest course to follow. Since Mrs Roberts had given her address and telephone number, he began by writing to her to acknowledge her letter and then had a lengthy conversation with her on the telephone. In the meantime he sent a copy of the letter to his older sister, Freya, whom he telephoned on the following day. Together they came to the same opinion, which was that, for all its surprising character, the document rang true. They also both agreed that for the time being it would be best not to tell Papa on the assumption that he would immediately think that Mrs Roberts's family were cranks who were after money. 'I feel if I were to send it straight to him,' he told Freya, 'he would tear it up in a rage and write a poison pen and goodness knows what!'[2]

He decided first, with Freya's encouragement, to make a few discreet inquiries. In his telephone conversation with Mrs Roberts he had learned that at the time in question, around 1894, Alice Carter was a teacher at the village school in Sledmere. An initial difficulty in Christopher's investigation was that as far back as he or anyone else he questioned could remember, there had been no family in Sledmere called Carter. Parish records also appeared to support this fact.

He then turned to the Sykes archives and the correspondence of Mark's cousin, Sir William Pakenham, a close friend of Jessie's, to see if that would throw any light on the story. 'I turned first of all to the Pakenham–Sykes letters of 1894 and 1895,' he recalled, 'and then to those of ten or twelve years later when [the child] George would be beginning his schooling . . . I gave particular attention to the letters after 1894. To my surprise and disappointment I found no mention of Alice Carter, George, or my father, anywhere in the letters. I found fewer letters than usual for the years 1894 and 1895. I found, in short, an absence of evidence. I came to wonder whether the story was true . . .'[3]

Then suddenly there fell a ray of light. His youngest sister, Angela, remembered a sketch which used to hang in his bedroom at Sledmere, when he was a child. It represented among others, old Tatton out hunting with two friends. The figures were coloured, the rest was in black and white. At the bottom of the picture, the names of the figures were written in, the central one being Sir Tatton in his red coat, with behind him his companions in the chase, Lord Middleton and the Sledmere parson, dressed in ordinary riding clothes. In front of them, however, also clad in red, were the Huntsman and the First Whipper-In, and their names were Will Carter and Tom Carter. So far as she recalled, the sketch was dated around 1830, which would have made one of these men Alice's grandfather. An elderly lady in Sledmere village who had been a child in the 1890s supplied further evidence. She remembered that there had indeed been a family called Carter living there. Mr Carter was Sir Tatton's coachman, and had left the village suddenly. 'She said,' Christopher recalled, 'that she and her friends guessed the reasons for his unexpected departure, but she would not say more.'[4]

The whole story, as told to Uncle Christopher by Veronica Roberts, was as follows. When Alice was quite young, nineteen or twenty, and Mark was only fifteen, she was teaching in the village school in Sledmere. Her father, who had come to Sledmere from Castle Howard, worked as a groom. Alice was tall and good-looking, probably quite beautiful, and quite stylish in the clothes that she wore. She was intelligent and literate. 'There was nothing "village maiden" about her,' commented Veronica. She met Mark when she was at the stables with her father, who had taught Mark to ride, and, even though he was only fourteen at the time, was soon captivated by him. To a girl like her, who had seen little of the world, he was a romantic figure, fascinating her with tales of his travels through the Ottoman Empire, and impressing her with his fluency in Oriental languages. But he was also, she said, 'very lonely'. A strong attraction soon developed between them, which eventually led to an affair. 'I do remember,' Veronica recalled, 'that it was my father's belief that he was conceived on the Dairy floor.'[5] The romance lasted long enough for them to plan to elope to London, which is where they were discovered by Jessie. They were immediately separated.

Jessie then had the unenviable task of breaking the news of his son's behaviour to Tatton. He was angry enough on hearing of the elopement to threaten Mark with disinheritance, a threat which Jessie managed to dissuade him from carrying out. Instead he was taken out of Beaumont school and sent abroad, first to Monaco and then to Brussels. The Carter family had to leave Sledmere, and Jessie gave them a job working for her in London. When it was discovered that Alice was pregnant, Jessie decided to keep the news from Tatton for as long as possible, and secretly arranged for Alice's cousin, Mary Page, and her husband, Frederick Lott, to adopt the baby, a boy they named Frederick George, the names of Jessie's brothers. Known always as plain George, he was born two months prematurely, in April, 1895. Curiously enough, his birth was never registered. Though this may have been because he was not expected to survive, such a blatant flouting of the law seems more likely to have been the work of Jessie trying to cover tracks.

Because Jessie believed strongly that the Sykes family should pay for the upbringing of this child, she could not keep his birth a secret from Tatton for too long. It is a tribute to her strength of character that she succeeded in persuading him to take financial responsibility, in spite of his incandescent rage at the news, which was the true reason for his hanging of the dogs. George was brought up in Sheerness, where his adoptive father, Frederick, worked in the docks, and here Alice was allowed to visit him in the guise of his aunt. It was impressed upon her by Jessie that on no account was she to attempt to make any contact with Mark, whose interests and honour were not to be compromised. 'She totally accepted this,' said Veronica. 'I imagine that Jessica must have been very persuasive and very forceful too. Alice also probably had a great feeling of guilt. She no doubt felt that she had misled this boy and was now paying for it. She always held this strong belief that nothing whatsoever should damage Mark's reputation.' The result was that Mark was never to know that he was the father of a son by Alice.

From time to time, Jessie would turn up in Sheerness to visit her grandson, and this would cause quite a stir, as her carriage drew up outside the small terraced house and she climbed out – tottered on the occasions she was drunk – dressed to the nines. In spite of the fact that she brought him presents – he always had the best and newest kind of bicycle – George detested these visits because he had to stand there and be questioned by her to see how he was getting on. When 'Aunt Alice' used to come and see him, she and Mary would sit together by the fire chatting and occasionally looking at him, and he would hear the words 'Sledmere' and 'Sykes' mentioned, and he very soon began to realise that there was something different about him. Eventually, when he was about eleven, he asked what all this was about, and was told the whole story. When he said that he wanted to meet his father, he was met with blank refusals, something he bitterly resented for the rest of his life.

When he was old enough, George was sent as a boarder to Borden Grammar School, in Sittingbourne, Kent, and after that joined the Merchant Navy. At the beginning of the First World War he went to see Willie Pakenham who told him to present himself at the Admiralty where he had arranged for him to have a commission in the Navy. But by that time George had rushed off to the nearest recruiting office and had joined the Royal West Kents. Though this meant that he never did get his commission, it did lead to a close encounter with his father. Early in 1915, George's regiment were sailing to Gallipoli, and by a strange coincidence Mark was on the same ship.

'I said to him,' Veronica remembered, 'why didn't you send him a note?'

'You don't understand,' he replied, 'you don't go writing notes to officers if you are a ranker. I'd have been in dreadful hot water. It just wasn't possible. Anyway it wouldn't have been the best time, would it, going up to him in front of all the other officers and saying "I'm your long lost son!"'

In fact, George was struck down with an illness and was shipped back to Jerusalem, so luckily for him he never reached Gallipoli. It was the only time he ever saw his father in the flesh.

George married in 1919, and the following year his first child, Veronica, was born, to be followed in the next nine years by another five children. He kept his secret religiously, destroying all his mother's letters, and remaining absolutely determined that he was never going to tell *anybody* about his past. 'He didn't even want to tell my mother,' recalled Veronica, 'though she must have had hints of it, because she made various cryptic remarks to me. I remember once that I said to her "It's a funny thing. But Daddy can sing and he can speak several languages and he's marvellous with words and so forth, but his parents and his sister are not like that at all. It's odd that he's so different." "Well," said my mother, "haven't you ever heard of throwbacks, when people resemble an ancestor? Hasn't it occurred to you that your father might be in that class?" I didn't ask any more, but I was stunned by the idea that my father might resemble some antique ancestor who was perhaps something like a pirate! I thought, how wonderful, a pirate for a grandfather!'

It was not till after her mother's death that Veronica herself finally found out the truth. In 1969, her son, Dicky, a student at London University, was working on a project involving making a family tree, and asked his grandfather to help him. He was particularly interested in finding out about his mother's family, since she seemed to know so little about them. When Veronica went to visit her father, then living with his second wife, Marjorie, he told her that he didn't want his grandson, of whom he was very fond, to base his research on facts which were untrue, and piece by piece he then told her the story. Since it was obvious that it really grieved him that he had never known his brothers and sisters, Veronica asked him why he had not made more of an effort to approach the family?

'He answered,' she told me, '"If we hadn't been so desperately hard up with all you children, I would have contacted the family. But I was not going along, shabby as I was and hard up as I was. They would merely have thought that I was going to ask for money. Unless I could do it in the way I wanted to do it, I didn't want to see them." I understand his point. He really thought of himself as someone who ought to have known Sledmere. He was after all the eldest son.'

Given the nature of the story and the fact that it had remained a secret for so long, Veronica decided that it should stay under wraps, and thus the embargo stood until 1976 when, after a holiday in Spain, George fell desperately ill with Legionnaire's Disease. At one point the family were told he had only twenty-four hours to live.

'While he was at the height of his illness,' Veronica recollected, 'my stepmother rang me one day and said, "Do you know what he talks about in his delirium? You won't like it very much because he doesn't mention you or any of your brothers and sisters or even your mother. All he talks about is his father, his regrets that he didn't know him and his regrets that his brothers and sisters don't know of his existence. It's really sad to hear the way he goes on about it. He knows all their names." I thought to myself, "Why the hell shouldn't they know?" Suddenly the worm turned. Instead of accepting all this duty to Mark's memory, for God's sake, I said to myself, "Well why shouldn't he have that comfort?" I suddenly felt fiercely on the side of my father's rights.' She then sat down and wrote a letter to Uncle Christopher.

Knowing nothing about the family before she decided to write, Veronica had looked them up in *Debrett's* and noted that Christopher Sykes, the second son, was a respected writer of biographies. He was the one she sensibly chose to approach, suspecting that a letter to the head of the family might be misconstrued as an appeal for money, which was exactly the attitude taken by Papa on receiving the news of his new sibling.

'I feared a tempestuous reply,' wrote Christopher to Freya, in June 1976, after he had first broached the subject to his brother, 'as Richard's family pride passed all reason ... To my relief ... I had a good-humoured reply about unsuspected "family skeletons".' But, as he suspected, this was the calm before the storm.

'I had not to wait many days before the extreme family pride burst forth in an avalanche of misinformed fury. "This tale of the alleged bastard brother," fumed Richard, "is indeed strange, and I find it hard to accept on such flimsy evidence. Why the bombshell so late? Mark was born on 16 March, 1879, and the child born April, 1895. Therefore Mark was only fifteen when it was supposedly sired by him. I have always been led to believe that fertility is rare before the age of seventeen ... That Mark should elope with a local schoolteacher does not accord with his character at any period. At that time he had recently been converted to Catholicism by bigoted Jesuits and would have been much too frightened of the flames of Hell to break the sixth commandment so brazenly."'

In a letter written to Freya a couple of days later, Christopher added 'what you have written to Mrs Roberts seems to have eased him on his deathbed so things had better be left there, but I hope his six children (my 'nephews and nieces') don't come knocking at my door'.

Luckily, George did not die as soon as expected, and lived long enough to have one of his wishes granted, that he should have personal acknowledgement of his existence by one of his siblings. It was Aunt Freya who decided to go and visit him.

'Yesterday was a great day,' she wrote to Christopher on 16 September, 1977. 'Veronica rang me up on Tuesday asking if I could lunch with her on Thursday and meet her father ... I must confess to feeling nervous ("dentist feeling" – do you remember?). Well I hadn't been there more than five minutes when he and his second wife arrived. We embraced and he nearly cried – it was very touching. No look of Papa but a strong Bentinck appearance – a nose hooked and rather fleshy like Uncle Freddy's – lots of white hair which had been auburn. His wife had brought along photographs of him in his youth and there he did look like our Dad in his young clean-shaven days . . . I was sitting alone with him when he turned his head slightly away from me and there was a sudden flash of something from the past. I don't know what it was – but for a second or two he looked young – and then when he faced me again he was just a frail old man.'

Freya reassured her brother that the reason that his real family had not recognised his existence was that *they did not know about it*. Over the years, all documentary evidence relating to the story had presumably been systematically destroyed, and those who did know had kept their mouths firmly shut. In a matter of moments she put to rest the demons that had haunted George all his life as a result of his mistaken belief that his real family had rejected him.

'Of one thing,' Freya wrote to Christopher, 'Veronica and George are both convinced, that Mark never knew of the existence of a son and believe he was taken away from Beaumont and to France to separate him from Alice.' She told Christopher that she found George 'altogether delightful'. 'I stayed about a couple of hours,' she added, 'and Veronica drove me to the bus station. She was overwhelmed by the success of the meeting. George rang me up this morning to say how happy he was.'

Right up to his death in 1978, Papa steadfastly refused to believe that the story was true. On her last visit to Sledmere in his lifetime, Aunt Freya made one last courageous attempt to make a dent in his armour. If pecuniary gain was his motive, she asked, why had George waited to make this disclosure till he was over eighty years old? If his aim had been to prove a connection with a famous family, why had he chosen the relatively obscure Sykeses, virtually unknown outside Yorkshire, and not some more celebrated name such as the Grosvenors, the Cecils, the Russells or, closer to home, the Cavendish-Bentincks? And if the imposture had been plotted, why the choice of the name Carter for the mother, a name not remembered at Sledmere except by considerable family effort? And lastly and finally, why did the rest of George's family, his three sons and three daughters, want no part in this attempt to establish his origins, and why did he seek it, except as a matter of feeling, other than by the accident of his delirium? But Richard was unyielding. 'I still think the Mrs Roberts saga is nonsense,' he told Uncle Christopher.

Early in the year 2000, soon after this book had been commissioned, I went myself to meet my new cousin, Veronica Roberts, for the first time. Her husband Ben, a professor of Trade Union Studies, greeted my wife and I at the door of their house in Golders Green, and ushered us in. There standing in the hall was a woman who reminded me so strongly of my late and beloved Aunt Freya, that any doubts I might have harboured about the truth of the story were swept away in an instant. We instantly embraced and never drew breath for the rest of the evening. Amongst the things I remember her telling me was that the only relic of Mark that her father owned was an inkwell which he had given to Alice, and which was made from the foot of a pony he had owned as a child. Perhaps the most moving thing of all was that Alice had told George that she dreamed about Mark every night of her life. She never married because she never loved anyone again as she had loved him.

NOTES

The bulk of the Sykes papers are lodged in the Brynmor Jones Library, University of Hull – catalogue reference DDSY. The remaining papers are in the Library at Sledmere House and are referred to as SLP. Papers relating to Jessica Sykes and Christopher Sykes (Sykey) are lodged in the East Riding Archives, Beverley and are to be found amongst the Strickland-Constable papers. (S–CP)

CSLB: Christopher Sykes Letter Books, 1715–1790.
RSLB: Richard Sykes Letter Books, 1749–1761.
SFH: Sykes Family History, Mark Sykes, MSS.

PROLOGUE

1 *Yorkshire Post*, 24 May 1911.
2 *Mark Sykes*, Roger Adelson. 1975, p. 137.
3 *Yorkshire Post*, 24 May 1911.
4 MS account of her childhood by E.S. (Property of Mrs Tessa Scott).
5 *Yorkshire Post*, 24 May 1911.

CHAPTER I

1 *Descriptions of East Yorkshire: Leland to Defoe*, ed. D. Woodward, East Yorkshire Local History Society, 1985, p. 20.
2 DDSY/62/34.
3 *Some Particulars of the Life and Experience of Nicholas Manners Printed for the Author in 1785 in His Own Words.* York Minster Library.
4 DDSY/62/38.

5 SFH, p. 43.
6 *History of England*, T. B. M. Macaulay, 1849, Vol. 1, p. 341.
7 'A Man of Property'. Joan Kirby, *Northern History*, Vol. 37, December 2000, p. 73.
8 *Ralph Thoresby, the Topographer*, D. H. Atkinson, 1885, p. 246.
9 *A Tour Through the Whole Island of Great Britain*, Daniel Defoe, 1991, pp. 276, 277.
10 *High St Hull & Biographical Sketches*, John Symons, 1862, pp. 92, 93.
11 *Works*, Horace Walpole, 1798, Vol. 2, p. 536.
12 *The Economics of Elysium*, J. Popham, Vol. 2, p. 47. S.E.O.
13 RSLB, 1749–61, p. 1.
14 RSLB, 1749–61, p. 4.
15 SFH, p. 51.
16 RSLB, p. 5.

17 DDSY/101/47.

18 SFH, p. 51.

19 SLP, 1770–1782, p. 40.

20 RSLB, p. 17.

21 RSLB, p. 39.

22 SLP, 1770–1782, p. 40.

23 RS-JOTC, p. 7

24 RS-JOTC, p. 7.

25 RS-JOTC, p. 7.

26 *A Hundred British Spas*, Kathleen Denbigh, 1981, p. 139.

27 DDSY/101/47.

28 SFH, p. 52.

29 RSLB, p. 16.

30 SFH, p. 64.

31 RSLB, p. 187.

32 Copy to follow.

33 *The Alarming History of Medicine*, Richard Gordon, 1921, p. 100.

34 RSLB. p. 127.

35 RSLB, p. 42.

36 RSLB, p. 108.

37 RSLB, p. 231.

38 RSLB, p. 276.

39 RSLB, p. 283.

40 RSLB, p. 208.

41 RSLB, p. 107.

42 RSLB, p. 51.

43 DDSY/102/2.

44 SFH, p. 63.

45 SLP, 1604–1779, p. 85.

46 SLP, 1604–1779, p. 83.

47 SFH, p. 44.

48 SFH, p. 73.

49 SLP, 1641–1769, p. 118.

50 RSLB, p. 59.

51 DDSY/106/9.

52 RSLB, p. 77.

53 RSLB, p. 22.

54 RSLB, p. 287.

55 RSLB, p. 115.

56 SFH, p. 58.

57 RSLB, p. 263.

58 DDSY/102/2.

59 RSLB, p. 142.

60 RSLB, p. 165.

61 RSLB, p. 125.

62 RSLB, p. 176.

63 RSLB, p. 226.

64 SFH, p. 62.

65 SLP, 1604–1779, p. 88.

66 RSLB, p. 187.

67 RSLB, p. 213.

68 RSLB, p. 156. Usquebaugh = whisky.

69 RSLB, p. 34.

70 DDSY/101/47.

71 RSLB, p. 28.

72 RSLB, p. 26.

73 RSLB, p. 38.

74 SFH, p. 58.

75 SFH, p. 69.

76 SFH, p. 67.

77 RSLB, p. 97.

78 SFH, p. 70.

79 Ibid.

80 *Private Palaces*, Christopher Sykes, **0000**, p. 96.

81 SFH, p. 70.

82 RSLB, p. 112.

83 RSLB, p. 163.

84 RSLB, p. 166.

85 RSLB, p. 221.

86 RSLB, p. 222.

87 RSLB, p. 235.

88 RSLB, p. 246.

89 RSLB, p. 265.

90 SFH, p. 81.

91 RSLB, p. 302.
92 RSLB, p. 140.
93 RSLB, p. 141.
94 RSLB, p. 142.
95 RSLB, p. 178.
96 RSLB, p. 244.
97 RSLB, p. 335
98 RSLB, p. 339.
99 RSLB, p. 342.
100 SFH, p. 65.

CHAPTER II

1 SFH, p. 66.
2 SFH, p. 92.
3 SFH, p. 66.
4 SFH, p. 66.
5 RSLB, p. 44.
6 DDSY/101/48.
7 DDSY/101/50.
8 DDSY/101/50.
9 SFH, p. 83.
10 *The Diary of a Yorkshire Gentleman*, ed. David and Susan Neave, 2001, p. 23.
11 DDSY/101/50.
12 Christopher Sykes Diaries, entry 146, 25 May 1858.
13 SLP, 1770–1782, p. 1.
14 SFH, p. 99.
15 James Williamson, *The Elements of Euclid*, 1781.
16 SFH, p. 101.
17 SFH, p. 95.
18 SFH, p. 96.
19 SFH, p. 94.
20 SFH, pp. 102, 103.
21 Christopher Sykes Account Book (hereafter CSAB), cols. 2, 3.

22 CSAB, cols. 2, 3.
23 SLP, 1604–1779, p. 150.
24 SLP, 1604–1779, p. 153.
25 SLP, 1604–1779, p. 166.
26 SLP, 1604–1779, p. 172.
27 SLP, 1770–1782, p. 10.
28 'The Sledmere Scene', from an unpublished MS by Peter Atkinson, p. 2.
29 From *An Old Acct. of Ld. Bathurst Estate at Wetwang*. East Rising Record Office (hereafter ERRO), DDCV, parcel 110.
30 *A Tour Through England and Wales*, Daniel Defoe, Everyman Edition II, p. 235.
31 *Descriptions of East Yorkshire*, ed. Jan Crowther, East Yorkshire Historical Society, 1992, p. 28.
32 From *The Great Landowners of East Yorkshire 1530–1910*, Barbara English, 1990, p. 64.
33 RSLB, p. 286.
34 CSLB, 1775–1790, p. 4.
35 CSLB, 1775–1790, p. 5.
36 'Mr Perfects Design of the Plantations' (drawing in the Library at Sledmere).
37 DDSY/102/9.
38 *Works*, Horace Walpole, 1798, Vol. 2, p. 544.
39 *A General View of the Agriculture of the East Riding*, H. E. Strickland, 1812, p. 182.
40 DDSY/102/10.
41 DDSY/102/10.
42 SLP, 1770–1782, p. 32.
43 CS to W. E. Egerton of Tatton, Muniments, John Rylands

Library, University of Manchester, EGT/6/2/1.

44 DDSY/102/12.
45 DDSY/102/11.
46 CSLB, 1775–1790, p. 17.
47 *Trees and the English Landscape*, Paul Edwards, 1962, p. 15.
48 ERRO, DG/38/133.
49 SLP, 1780–1852, p. 18.
50 *The Beauties of England: Or Original Delineations – Topographical, Historical and Descriptive of Each County*, John Bigland, 1812, Vol. 16, p. 409.

CHAPTER III

1 SLP, 1783–1793, p. 1.
2 SLP, 1783–1793, p. 161.
3 SFH, p. 90.
4 SLP, 1780–1852, p. 78.
5 SFH, p. 86.
6 SLP, 1783–1793, p. 7.
7 DDSY/102/14.
8 CSLB, 1793–1793, p. 92.
9 SLP, 1780–1852, p. 99.
10 DDSY/106/15.
11 *Life in the English Country House*, Mark Girouard, 1978, p. 262.
12 *The Younger Pitt*, John Ehrman, 1969, p. 5.
13 *The Younger Pitt*. Ehrman, p. 5.
14 *Historical Memoirs*, Nathaniel Wraxall, 1884, Vol. 2, pp. 77, 78.
15 *Historical Memoirs*, Wraxall, p. 78.
16 *The Younger Pitt*, Ehrman, p. 102.
17 *Criticisms on the Rolliad*, Joseph Richardson, 1784.

18 *The Younger Pitt*, Ehrman, p. 217.
19 SLP, 1780–1852, p. 117.
20 DDSY/101/68.
21 SLP, 1780–1852, p. 122.
22 *England in the Age of Improvement*, Asa Briggs, 1999, p. 76.
23 DDSY/102/15.
24 DDSY/101/21.
25 DDSY/101/21.
26 *Diary and Letters of Madame D'Arblay*, 1893, p. 54.
27 SLP, 1783–1793, p. 1.
28 SLP, 1783–1793, p. 16.
29 SLP, 1783–1793, p. 29.
30 SLP, 1783–1793, p. 39.
31 SLP, 1783–1793, p. 128.
32 SLP, 1783–1793, p. 102.
33 CSLB, 1775–1790, p. 49.
34 CSLB, 1775–1790, p. 108.
35 CSLB, 1775–1790, p. 115.
36 CSLB, 1775–1790, p. 116.
37 CSLB, 1775–1790, p. 134.
38 DDSY/101/62.
39 CSLB, 1775–1790, p. 134.
40 CSLB, 1775–1790, p. 134.
41 Egerton Papers, J. Rylands Library, University of Manchester, 3/8/2/37.
42 DDSY/101/62.
43 DDSY/101/62.
44 *A Literary History of Wallpaper*, E. A. Entwisle, 1960, p. 13.
45 DDSY/101/62.
46 SLP, 1783–1793, p. 234.
47 SLP, 1783–1793, p. 243.
48 DDSY/101/68.
49 CSLB, 1790–1795, p. 84.
50 DDSY/102/14.

51 DDSY/101/68.

52 SLP, 1783–1793, p. 235.

53 DDSY/101/62.

54 DDSY/101/62.

55 CSLB, 1790–1795, p. 103.

56 *Country Life*, 14 October 1949, p. 1140.

57 DDSY/101/68.

58 DDSY/101/68.

59 DDSY/101/68.

60 SLP, 1780–1852, p. 220.

61 SLP, 1780–1852, p. 218.

62 DDSY/101/70.

63 DDSY/101/68.

64 DDSY/101/68.

65 From *The Bath* by Michèle and Robert Root-Bernstein, 1997.

66 DDSY/101/66.

67 DDSY/101/68.

68 DDSY/101/66.

69 *A Hundred British Spas*, Kathleen Denbigh, 1981, p. 49.

70 SLP, 1780–1852, p. 218.

71 SFH, p. 112.

CHAPTER IV

1 DDSY/106/15.

2 DDSY/102/13.

3 SLP, 1780–1852, p. 105.

4 *Random Records*, George Colman, 1830, Vol. 1, p. 67.

5 *The Life and Times of Frederick Reynolds*, 1826, Vol. 1, p. 58.

6 *The Life and Times of Frederick Reynolds*, p. 85.

7 *Westminster*, W. Teignmouth-Shore, 1910, p. 26.

8 *Great Public Schools*, 1893, p. 246.

9 Revd Simpson to Sir Christopher Sykes, 6 July, 1788, DDSY/101/68.

10 SLP, 1783–1793, pp. 86, 87.

11 SLP, 1783–1793, p. 143.

12 *Travels in England*, Carl Philipp Moritz, 1924, p. 20.

13 Matt Bramble to Dr Lewis, London, 20 May, in *The Expedition of Humphry Clinker*, Tobias Smollett, 1771.

14 Moritz, *Travels in England*, p. 21.

15 *Some Account of London*, T. Pennant, 3rd ed., 1793, p. 298.

16 *Works of Lord Byron*, ed. Thomas Moore, 1832, Vol. 2, p. 256.

17 *Boxing*, Viscount Knebworth, Vol. 11, held at the Lonsdale Library.

18 *Boxing*, Viscount Knebworth, p. 27.

19 *Yorkshire Reminiscences*, Revd M. Morris, 1922, p. 218.

20 *The Development of Transportation in Modern England*, W. T. Jackman, 1962, pp. 685, 696.

21 *A Journey Through England and Scotland to the Hebrides in 1784*, Faujas de Saint Fond, 1907, Vol. 1, pp. 124, 125.

22 *History of the British Turf*, J. C. Whyte, 1840, Vol. 1, p. 519.

23 SLP, 1783–1793, p. 178.

24 SFH.

25 DDSY/101/60.

26 DDSY/101/68.

27 DDSY/101/74.

28 CSAB, 1795.

29 DDSY/3/6/3.

30 *Light Come, Light Go*, Ralph Nevill, 1909, p. 108.
31 *Light Come, Light Go*, Nevill, p. 116.
32 *The Times*, 24 March 1812.
33 *Baily's Magazine*, February 1910, pp. 118–20.
34 *Scott and Sebright*, the Druid, 1912, p. 131.
35 LBCS, 1790–1795, p. 135.
36 *The Sporting Magazine*, 1807. 'Plumpers' were voters who guaranteed their vote to one candidate, although they had the right to vote for two or more.
37 *The History of Parliament: The House of Commons 1790–1820*, R. G. Thorne, Vol. 4, 1986, p. 568.
38 DDSY/101/74.
39 SFH, p. 112.
40 DDSY/101/68.
41 *The Bibliographical Decameron*, Revd T. F. Dibdin, 1817, pp. 58–60.
42 *The Bibliographical Decameron*, Dibdin, pp. 405, 406.
43 *The Bibliographical Decameron*, pp. 115–117.
44 *The Yorkshire Baronet*, H. M. Sykes, unpublished MS. SLP, p. 1.
45 'Came to bleed my chest.'
46 'Feel unwell all over.'
47 'I am not at all well.'
48 'A terrible headache.'
49 'Very unwell with nausea all day.'
50 'A superb day.'
51 'Head better. Outside a great deal. Return of Mark.'
52 DDSY/101/33.
53 DDSY/101/34.
54 *The York Chronicle*, 20 February 1823.

CHAPTER V

1 A ewe lamb, one year old.
2 *Saddle and Sirloin*, the Druid, 1912, p. 239.
3 *Kings of the Turf*, Thormanby, 1898, p. 168.
4 *Yorkshire Reminiscences*, Revd M. Morris, 1922, p. 217.
5 *Nimrod's Hunting Tours*, Nimrod, 1835, p. 365.
6 *Nimrod's Hunting Tours*, p. 365.
7 *The Sporting Magazine*, May 1808.
8 *Nimrod's Hunting Tours*, p. 365.
9 *Scott and Sebright*, the Druid, 1912, p. 13.
10 *Scott and Sebright*, the Druid, p. 327.
11 DDSY/101/72.
12 DDSY/101/72.
13 DDSY/101/72.
14 *Gentleman's Magazine*, November 1823, p. 451.
15 *Gentleman's Magazine*, November 1823, p. 451.
16 *Reminiscences of a Literary Life*, Revd Thomas Frognall Dibdin, 1836, p. 321.
17 *Saddle and Sirloin*, the Druid, p. 238.

18 *Kings of the Turf*, Thormanby, 1898, p. 167.

19 *Kings of the Turf*, Thormanby, 1898, p. 167.

20 *Sykes of Sledmere*, J. Fairfax Blakeborough, 1929, p. 78.

21 *Sykes of Sledmere*, Fairfax Blakeborough, p. 241.

22 *Nimrod's Hunting Tours*, p. 362.

23 *Saddle and Sirloin*, the Druid, p. 241.

24 *The Film of Memory*, Shane Leslie, 1938, p. 97.

25 *Sykes of Sledmere*, Fairfax Blakeborough, p. 153.

26 Emma Sykes to Christopher Sykes, 7 January 1854. S-CP ERA.

27 *Yorkshire Reminiscences*, Morris, p. 219.

28 *Victorian Wives*, Katherine Moore, 1974, p. 43.

29 E.S. to C.S., 29 September 1848, S-CP ERA.

30 E.S. to C.S., 1848, S-CP ERA.

31 E.S. to C.S., 1848, S-CP ERA.

32 E.S. to C.S., 1848, S-CP ERA.

33 *Yorkshire Reminiscences*, Morris, p. 220.

34 *Yorkshire Reminiscences*, Morris, p. 216.

35 *Kings of the Turf*, Thormanby, p. 167.

36 *Sykes of Sledmere*, Fairfax Blakeborough, p. 186.

37 *Sykes of Sledmere*, Fairfax Blakeborough, p. 123.

38 *Baily's Magazine*. January, 186X, p. 170.

39 *Sykes of Sledmere*, Fairfax Blakeborough, p. 218.

40 *Saddle and Sirloin*, the Druid, p. 226.

41 *Saddle and Sirloin*, the Druid, p. 233.

42 *Kings of the Turf*, Thormanby, p. 173.

43 *Saddle and Sirloin*, the Druid, p. 222.

44 Christopher Sykes Diaries, 13 February 1855, S-CP ERA.

45 Christopher Sykes Diaries, 1 April 1856.

46 *The Driffield Times*, 9 February 1861.

47 *The Driffield Times*, 9 February 1861.

48 *Saddle and Sirloin*, the Druid, p. 222.

49 *The Times*, 15 December 1863.

50 *The Illustrated London News*, 11 April 1863.

CHAPTER VI

1 *Sykes of Sledmere*, J. Fairfax Blakeborough, 1828, p. 127.

2 *Portrait of an Amateur*, Roger Adelson, 1975, p. 21.

3 *Yorkshire Reminiscences*, Revd M. Morris, 1922, p. 222.

4 *Travellers by Sea*, E. H. H. Archibald, 1962, p. 6.

5 *Travellers by Sea*, Archibald, p. 8.

6 *Travellers by Sea*, Archibald, p. 8.

7 *Travellers by Sea* Archibald, p. 9.

8 *Sykes of Sledmere*, Fairfax Blakeborough, p. 101.

9 *Yorkshire Reminiscences*, Morris, p. 229.

10 *Sykes of Sledmere*, Fairfax Blakeborough, p. 152.

11 *The Visitors' Book*, Christopher Simon Sykes, 1978, p. 32.

12 DDSY/104/168.

13 *Saddle and Sirloin*, the Druid, p. 246.

14 *Saddle and Sirloin*, the Druid, p. 246.

15 *Ashgill: The Life & Times of John Osborne*, J. B. Radcliffe, 1900, p. 40.

16 *Sykes of Sledmere*, Fairfax Blakeborough, p. 155.

17 This nickname was to distinguish him from his cousin Sir George Bentinck, known as 'Big Ben'.

18 *The Diaries of John Ruskin, 1843–1873*, 1958, p. 679.

19 *The Winnington Letters of John Ruskin*, 1969, p. 670.

20 T. G. Bowles to J.S., 13 March 1873. S-CP ERA.

21 Brown to J.S., 4 August 1874, Jessie Sykes Letters, S-CP ERA.

22 Mark Alston, *Christina. A. J. Sykes*, London, 1908.

23 C.S. to M.S., April 1856, S-CP ERA.

24 C.S. to M.S., May 1856.

25 The Marquis of Downshire to M.S., 5 November 1867, S-CP ERA.

26 T.S. to M.S., August 1867, S-CP ERA.

27 The Marquis of Downshire to M.S., 9 July 1868, S-CP ERA.

28 T.S. to C.S., October 1867, S-CP ERA.

29 Wrigglesworth to Mrs Baines, 8 October 1867, S-CP ERA.

30 Wrigglesworth to Mrs Baines, 11 October 1867, S-CP ERA.

31 C.S. to M.S., November 1867, S-CP ERA.

32 Letter to M.S., 9 February 1868, S-CP ERA.

CHAPTER VII

1 *Vanity Fair*, 4 August 1874.

2 *The Times*, 4 August 1874.

3 *The Times*, 4 August 1874.

4 *The Morning Post*, 4 August 1874.

5 C.S. to M.S., 4 August 1874, S-CP ERA.

6 *The Morning Post*, 4 August 1874.

7 DDSY/101/76.

8 'Britannia' to J.S.; August 1874, S-CP ERA.

9 Venetia to J.S., 30 August 1874, S-CP ERA.

10 DDSY/62/19.

11 DDSY/(5)/42/30.

12 Mrs Baines to M.S., November, 1874, S-CP ERA.

13 C.S. to M.S., 30 November 1874, S-CP ERA.

14 *Algernon Casterton*, Christina Anne Jessica Sykes, 1903.

15 'What a dream for a young woman.'

16 All the subsequent entries are from the Diary of Jessie Sykes, 1877–1878, S-CP ERA.

17 'I entreat you to believe that

you have left in me a friend on whom you can always count and for whom your memory will always remain a bright star.'

18 *The Astors*, Derek Wilson, 1993, p. 106.

19 *Complete Peerage*, V. Hardwicke, Vol. 4, p. 495, footnote (a).

20 *Memories of Fifty Years*, Lady St Helier, 1909, p. 269.

21 Lord Dufferin.

22 Lord Dufferin to J.S., 3 December 1877, S–CP ERA.

23 *The Astors*, Virginia Cowles, 1979, p. 96.

24 Later Duchess of Manchester.

25 Lord Dufferin to J.S., January 1878, S–CP ERA.

26 *Memories of Fifty Years*, Lady St Helier, p. 269.

27 Lord Dufferin to J.S., 6 March 1878, S–CP ERA.

28 *My Reminiscences*, Vol. 2, Lord Ronald Gower, 1883, p. 182.

29 Lord Dufferin to J.S., May 1878, S–CP ERA.

CHAPTER VIII

1 Diary of C.S., 4 June 1854. All subsequent diary entries are from Diaries of C.S. in S–CP ERA.

2 *Four Studies in Loyalty*, Christopher Sykes, 1946, p. 18.

3 *Letters of the Hon. Mrs Edward Twisleton*, 1928, pp. 10, 11.

4 Shabby.

5 *Four Studies in Loyalty*, C. Sykes, p. 21.

6 *Reminiscences*, Constance, Lady Battersea, 1923, p. 153.

7 *As We Were*, E. F. Benson, 1930, p. 297.

8 'Men of the Day'. *Vanity Fair*, November 1874.

9 *Lord Rosebery*, Marquess of Crewe, 1931, p. 120.

10 *The Candid Friend*, Herbert Vivian, 2 November 1901.

11 *Memoirs of Sixty Years*, Lord Warwick, 1917, p. 241

12 The visitors. Raby Castle to C.S., September 1867, S–CP ERA.

13 S–CP ERA.

14 *Lord Rosebery*, Marquess of Crewe, p. 120.

15 Lord Claud Hamilton to C.S., July 1867, S–CP ERA.

16 Sir Francis Knollys to C.S., 3 August 1870, S–CP ERA.

17 31 October, S–CP ERA.

18 3 August 1870, S–CP ERA.

19 3 August 1870, S–CP ERA.

20 Lord Claud Hamilton to C.S., 10 August 1870, S–CP ERA.

21 'Essence of Parliament', *Punch*, 1867.

22 *Things I Shouldn't Tell*, J. Field, 1924, p. 72.

23 S–CP ERA.

24 Ibid.

25 *Four Studies in Loyalty*, Sykes, p. 31.

26 Journal of Jessie Sykes, 5 November 1886, S–CP ERA.

CHAPTER IX

1 DDSY/4/6/70.

2 Lord Dufferin to J.S., 4 April 1879, S-CP ERA.

3 Sir George Wombwell to J.S., 9 April 1879, S-CP ERA.

4 Jessie's diary, August 1883, S-CP ERA.

5 Bay Middleton to J.S., 25 August 1881, S-CP ERA.

6 Scott to Neville, 17 Febrary 1881, Cardinal Newman's Library at Birmingham Oratory.

7 J.S. to Lady Herries, November 1882, SLP.

8 J.S. to Cardinal Manning, 20 November, 1882, SLP.

9 J.S. to C.M., 24 December 1882, SLP.

10 Scott to Neville, 17 February 1881, Cardinal Newman's Library at Birmingham University.

11 J.S. to Mr Creed, December 1882, S-CP ERA.

12 24 September 1882, SLP.

13 J.S. to C.M., 27 and 29 December 1882, SLP.

14 J.S. to C.M., 17 December 1882, SLP.

15 J.S. to C.M., 23 January 1883, SLP.

16 J.S. diary, 11 August 1883, S-CP ERA.

17 J.S. diary, December 1883, S-CP ERA.

18 *The Autobiography of Margot Asquith*, 1920, p. 96.

19 Lucien to J.S., 13 October 1884, S-CP ERA.

20 J.S. to Lucien, July 1885, S-CP ERA.

21 Lucien to J.S., 24 July 1885, S-CP ERA.

22 J.S. to Lucien, 4 October 1885, S-CP ERA.

23 J.S. to Lucien, 21 October 1885, S-CP ERA.

24 'I am deeply unhappy to leave my child, who is truly the only being in this world except you who I passionately wish to see again.'

25 J.S. to Lucien, 7 November, 1885, S-CP ERA.

26 J.S. to Lucien, 21 November 1885, S-CP ERA.

27 J.S. to Lucien, 15 December 1885. S-CP ERA.

28 J.S. to Lucien, 15 December 1885, S-CP ERA.

29 J.S. to Lucien, 20 December 1885, S-CP ERA.

30 J.S. to Lucien, 20 December 1885, S-CP ERA.

31 J.S. to Lucien, 20 February 1886, S-CP ERA.

32 J.S. to Lucien, 11 March 1886, S-CP ERA.

33 J.S. to Lucien, 14 April 1886, S-CP ERA.

34 J.S. to Lucien, 8 January 1887, S-CP ERA.

35 J.S. to Lucien, 8 January 1887, S-CP ERA.

36 J.S. to Lucien, 25 January 1887, S-CP ERA.

37 J.S. to Lucien, 5 Febrary 1887, S-CP ERA.

38 J.S. to Lucien, 24 Febrary 1887, S-CP ERA.

39 J.S. to Lucien, 5 March 1887, S-CP ERA.

40 J.S. to Lucien, 23 March 1887, S-CP ERA.

41 J.S. to Lucien, 28 March 1887, S-CP ERA.

42 J.S. to Lucien, 6 April 1887, S-CP ERA.

43 'Lucien gravely ill for eight days.'

44 J.S. to Lucien, 6 April 1887.

45 J.S. to Lucien, 6 April 1887, S-CP ERA. 'My sweetheart I embrace you a thousand times. I wish and pray with all my heart for your recovery . . . I feel that I could not live without you. I adore you.'

46 Paul Goldschmidt to J.S., 10 April 1887, S-CP ERA. 'I have received your dispatches. Poor Lucien died of pneumonia complicated by typhoid fever. The whole thing lasted no longer than fifteen days. He did not suffer. He spoke of you and asked me if you had sent a telegram. You are perhaps the only person who knows what a loss I have suffered and for my part I know how much he loved you and just what you have lost in him. Know without fear that your secret is in good hands . . .'

47 'How I Achieved Success', Mark Sykes, Ideas, 6 June 1914.

48 Lord Randolph Churchill, R. F. Foster, 1981, p. 371.

49 The Visitors' Book, C. S. Sykes, 1978, p. 57.

50 J.S. to Cardinal Manning, 24 December 1882, SLP.

51 J.S. to Lucien, 31 December 1886, S-CP ERA.

52 'The Slums of Victorian London', H. J. Dyos, Victorian Studies, Vol. 19, p. 19.

53 Sir Eldon Gorst, Peter Mellini, 1977, p. 24.

54 J.S. to Jack Gorst, 25 March 1892, S-CP ERA.

55 Jack Gorst to J.S., 26 October 1889, S-CP ERA.

56 Sir Eldon Gorst, Mellini, p. 26.

57 Jack Gorst to J.S., 15 April 1890, S-CP ERA.

58 Jack Gorst to J.S., 2 June 1890, S-CP ERA.

59 Sir Eldon Gorst, Mellini, p. 27.

60 Sir Eldon Gorst, Mellini, p. 27.

61 Jack Gorst to J.S., 16 October 1890, S-CP ERA.

62 Jack Gorst to J.S., 7 April 1891, S-CP ERA.

63 Jack Gorst to J.S., 3 July 1891, S-CP ERA.

64 Jack Gorst to J.S., 24 July 1891, S-CP ERA.

65 Jack Gorst to J.S., 15 August 1891, S-CP ERA.

66 Jack Gorst to J.S., 28 August 1891, S-CP ERA.

67 Jack Gorst to J.S., 19 March 1892, S-CP ERA.

68 Jack Gorst to J.S., March 1892, S–CP ERA.

CHAPTER X

1 'Britannia' to J.S., 14 December 1886, S–CP ERA.

2 J.S. to Lucien, 8 January 1887, S–CP ERA.

3 J.S. to Lucien, 22 January 1887, S–CP ERA.

4 J.S. to Lucien, 25 January 1887, S–CP ERA.

5 J.S. to Lucien, 24 Febrary 1887, S–CP ERA.

6 *Mark Sykes*, Shane Leslie, 1923, p. 30.

7 'How I Achieved Success', Mark Sykes, *Ideas*, 6 June 1914.

8 *Mark Sykes*, Leslie, p. 11.

9 *Mark Sykes*, Leslie, p. 10.

10 'How I Achieved Success', Sykes, p. 00.

11 *Mark Sykes*, Leslie, p. 9.

12 *Never Forget: A Biography of George F. S. Bowles*, Julia. M. Budworth, 2001.

13 'How I Achieved Success', Sykes, p. 00.

14 *Mark Sykes*, Leslie, p. 33.

15 *Mark Sykes*, Leslie, p. 32.

16 *Mark Sykes*, Leslie, p. 35.

17 *Mark Sykes*, Leslie, p. 35.

18 *Mark Sykes*, Leslie, p. 31.

19 *Mark Sykes*, Roger Adelson, 1975, p. 41.

20 *Mark Sykes*, Leslie, p. 37.

21 *Mark Sykes*, Leslie, p. 38.

22 *Mark Sykes*, Leslie, p. 33.

23 'How I Achieved Success', Sykes, p. 00.

24 *Diary of Sydney Bowles*, Chatsworth Papers, Chatsworth House.

25 DDSY/2/1/2a.

26 *Mark Sykes*, Roger Adelson, p. 52.

27 *Mark Sykes*, Leslie, p. 48.

28 *Mark Sykes*, Leslie, p. 52.

29 *Eton and Kings*, M. R. James, 1926, pp. 221–3; *Letters to a Friend*, ed. G. McBryde, 1956, p. 9.

30 M.S. to E.G., 25 July 1902, DDSY/2/1/2a.

31 DDSY/5/42/30.

32 DDSY/5/42/30.

33 SLP.

34 *The Morning Post*, 13 January 1898.

35 The massive private residence on Piccadilly of the Duke of Devonshire.

36 *The Morning Post*, 13 January 1898.

37 *The Morning Post*, 13 January 1898.

38 *The Morning Post*, 14 January 1898.

39 *The Times* and *The Morning Post*, both 14 January 1898.

40 *The Morning Post*, 14 January 1898.

41 *The Morning Post*, 15 January 1898.

42 *The Times*, 15 January 1898.

43 *The Times*, 18 January 1898.

44 *The Times*, 19 January 1898.

45 *The World*, 26 January 1898.
46 *The Times*, 19 January 1898.
47 *The Times*, 26 April 1898.

CHAPTER XI

1 *Diary of Sydney Bowles*, Chatsworth Papers, Chatsworth House.
2 M.S. to Henry Cholmondeley, late 1897, DDSY/2/1/1.
3 *Today*, Tel Aviv-Yafo.
4 M.S. to H.C., February 1898, DDSY/2/1/1.
5 *Through Five Turkish Provinces*, Mark Sykes, 1900, p. 2.
6 *Through Five Turkish Provinces*, Sykes, p. 3.
7 'Narrative of a Journey East of Jebel El-Druse', Mark Sykes. *Palestine Exploration Fund Quaterly Statement for 1899*, p. 47.
8 'Narrative of a Journey East of Jebel El-Druse', Sykes, p. 50.
9 'Narrative of a Journey East of Jebel El-Druse', Sykes, p. 51.
10 'Narrative of a Journey East of Jebel El-Druse', Sykes, p. 54.
11 'Narrative of a Journey East of Jebel El-Druse', Sykes, p. 55.
12 M.S. to E.G., 16 April 1900, DDSY/2/1/2a.
13 J.S. to the Prince of Wales, 1896, S-CP.
14 Albert Edward to T.S., 1 November 1898, SLP.
15 M.S. to H.C., 6 December 1898, DDSY/2/1/1.
16 M.S. to E.G., 20 October 1900, DDSY/2/1/2a.
17 *Through Five Turkish Provinces*, Sykes, p. 1.
18 *Through Five Turkish Provinces*, Sykes, p. 22.
19 *Through Five Turkish Provinces*, Sykes, p. 23.
20 *Through Five Turkish Provinces*, Sykes, p. 24.
21 *Through Five Turkish Provinces*, Sykes, p. 33.
22 *Through Five Turkish Provinces*, Sykes, p. 35.
23 *Through Five Turkish Provinces*, Sykes, p. 54.
24 *Through Five Turkish Provinces*, Sykes, p. 66.
25 *Through Five Turkish Provinces*, Sykes, p. 76.
26 *Through Five Turkish Provinces*, Sykes, p. 82.
27 *Through Five Turkish Provinces*, Sykes, p. 86.
28 *Through Five Turkish Provinces*, Sykes, p. 87.
29 *Through Five Turkish Provinces*, Sykes, p. 105.
30 M.S. to E.G., 20 October 1900, DDSY/2/1/2a.
31 *Sidelights on the War*, J. Sykes, 1900, p. 3.
32 M.S. to H.C., January 1900, DDSY/2/1/1.
33 M.S. to E.G., 26 February 1900, DDSY/2/1/2a.
34 M.S. to E.G., DDSY/2/1/2a.
35 M.S. to E.G., 2 April 1900, DDSY/2/1/2a.

36 M.S. to E.G., 4 April 1900,
   DDSY/2/1/2a.
37 M.S. to E.G., 11 April 1900,
   DDSY/2/1/2a.
38 M.S. to E.G., 17 April 1900,
   DDSY/2/1/2a.
39 M.S. to R.D., 24 June 1900,
   DDSY/2/1/3b.
40 M.S. to E.G., 4 September 1900,
   DDSY/2/1/2a.
41 M.S. to R.D., 8 August 1900,
   DDSY/2/1/3b.
42 M.S. to E.G., 20 August 1900,
   DDSY/2/1/2a.
43 M.S. to E.G., 1 September 1900,
   DDSY/2/1/2a.
44 M.S. to H.C., 30 December
   1900, DDSY/2/1/1.
45 'How I Achieved Success',
   Sykes, p. 00.
46 M.S. to R.D., January 1901,
   DDSY/2/1/3b.
47 M.S. to E.G., 13 December
   1901, DDSY/2/1/2b.
48 M.S. to E.G., 15 May 1902,
   DDSY/2/1/2c.
49 M.S. to E.G., 2 February 1902,
   DDSY/2/1/2c.
50 M.S. to E.G., May 1902,
   DDSY/2/1/2c.
51 M.S. to E.G., 22 May 1902,
   DDSY/2/1/2c.
52 M.S. to E.G., 19 June 1902,
   DDSY/2/1/2c.
53 M.S. to E.G., 20 September
   1901, DDSY/2/1/2b.
54 M.S. to R.D., January 1901,
   DDSY/2/1/3b.
55 *Tactics and Military Training*, G.

D'Ordel, ed. M. Sykes and E.
Sandars, 1902.
56 M.S. to E.G., summer 1902,
   DDSY/2/1/2c.
57 M.S. to E.G., 30 September
   1900, DDSY/2/1/2a.

CHAPTER XII

1 M.S. to E.G., 1 November
   1902, DDSY/2/1/2c.
2 M.S. to E.G., 13 November
   1902, DDSY/2/1/2c.
3 M.S. to E.G., 20 November
   1902, DDSY/2/1/2c.
4 M.S. to E.G. Browne,
   20 November 1902, DDSY/2/
   1/2c.
5 M.S. to E.G., 11 April 1903,
   DDSY/2/1/2d.
6 M.S. to E.G., 23 September
   1903, DDSY/2/1/2d.
7 *Mark Sykes*, Shane Leslie, 1923,
   p. 101.
8 *The Army and Navy Illustrated*,
   14 February 1903.
9 *The Spectator*, 21 February 1903.
10 M.S. to E.S., DDSY/2/1/2d.
11 M.S to E.S., December 1903,
   DDSY/2/1/2d.
12 *Dar-ul-Islam*, M. Sykes, 1904,
   p. 18.
13 *Dar-ul-Islam*, Sykes, p. 18n.
14 *Mark Sykes*, Leslie, p. 99.
15 *Mark Sykes*, Leslie, p. 161.
16 *Algernon Casterton*, C. A. J.
   Sykes, 1903.
17 H. B. Tree to J.S., 2 August
   1904, SP.

18 *The Macdonnells*, C. A. J. Sykes, 1905.

19 *Mark Alston*, C. A. J. Sykes, 1908.

20 J.S. to M.S., 24 April 1906, SP.

21 M.S. to E.S., 23 July 1904, DDSY/2/1/2e.

22 M.S. to E.S., DDSY/2/1/2e.

23 *Gertrude Bell*, E. Burgoyne, 1958, p. 197.

24 M.S. to E.S., 22 February 1905, DDSY/2/1/2.

25 M.S. to E.S., 6 April 1905, DDSY/2/1/2d.

26 M.S. to E.S., 15 April, 1905, DDSY/2/1/2d.

27 J.S. to M.S., 6 September 1905, SP.

28 DDSY/23/10.

29 M.S to H.C., 20 August 1905, DDSY/2/1/1.

30 J.S to M.S., 6 September 1905, SLP.

31 M.S. to H.C., 2 September 1905, DDSY/2/1/1.

32 M.S. to E.S., May 1906, DDSY/2/1/2d.

33 M.S. to E.S., 11 May 1906, DDSY/2/1/2d.

34 E.S. to M.S., 26 March 1906, SLP.

35 E.S. to M.S., 15 April 1906, SLP.

36 E.S. to M.S., 12 May 1906, SLP.

37 M.S. to H.C., 8 August 1905, DDSY/2/1/1.

38 M.S. to Edmund Sandars, 3 September 1907, DDSY/2/1/6.

39 DDSY/2/10/12.

40 N.H. to T.S., 1997, SP.

41 Interview with Christopher Sykes.

42 Interview with Christopher Sykes.

43 Interview with Freya Elwes.

44 *Much of Life is Laughter*, Harold E. Gorst, 1936, p. 270.

45 *Mark Sykes*, Leslie, p. 208.

46 *Mark Sykes*, Roger Adelson, 1975, p. 134.

47 *Mark Sykes*, Leslie, p. 213.

CHAPTER XIII

1 *The Malton Messenger*, 27 May 1911.

2 M.S. to W. H. Brierley, 30 January 1912, YAS MS 729.

3 M.S. to E.S., July 1911, DDSY/2/1/2e.

4 M.S. to E.S., 24 July 1911, DDSY/2/1.

5 M.S. to E.S., 9 August 1911, DDSY/2/1/2e.

6 M.S. to E.S., 3 September 1911, DDSY/2/1/2e.

7 M.S. to W.B., 18 October 1911, YAS MS 729.

8 M.S. to W.B., 23 October 1911, YAS MS 729.

9 *Much of Life is Laughter*, Harold E. Gorst, 1936, p. 213.

10 A MS account by a Mr Goulton. SP.

11 *Hansard*, 1911, Vol. 32, p. 106.

12 *Much of Life is Laughter*, Gorst, p. 214.

13 *Mark Sykes*, Shane Leslie, 1923, p. 218.

14 *Much of Life is Laughter*, Gorst, p. 271.

15 *Mark Sykes*, Leslie, p. 228.

16 M.S to E.S., July 1909, DDSY/ 2/1/2e.

17 Obituary 'The Late Lady Sykes', SLP.

18 *Daily Mail*, 4 June 1912.

19 *Mark Sykes*, Roger Adelson, 1975, p. 150.

20 *Mark Sykes*, Adelson, p. 150.

21 M.S. to E.S., March 1913, DDSY/2/1/2f.

22 Louise de Lichtervelde to W.B., 15 March 1912. BIHR AB 8/ 65/3.

23 M.S. to W.B., January 1912, YAS MS 729.

24 M.S. to W.B., 9 February 1912, YAS MS 729.

25 M.S. to W.B., 9 February 1912, YAS MS 729.

26 M.S. to W.B., 3 July 1914, YAS MS 729.

27 M.S. to W.B., 5 July 1914, YAS MS 729.

28 M.S. to W.B., 6 July 1914, YAS MS 729.

29 M.S. to W.B., 8 July 1914, YAS MS 729.

30 *Sunday Chronicle*, 20 April 1913.

31 *The Saturday Review*, 28 March 1914.

32 *Mark Sykes*, Leslie, p. 223.

33 *The Scarborough Post*, 19 August 1910.

34 M.S. to W.C., 24 August 1914,

Winston S. Churchill, Martin Gilbert, 1972, Vol. 3, Comp. Pt 1, p. 52.

35 M.S. to E.S., 5 November 1914, DDSY/2/1/2f.

36 *Winston S. Churchilll*, Gilbert, p. 582.

37 M.S. to E.S., February 1915, DDSY/2/1/2f.

38 M.S. to O. Fitzgerald, 4 March 1915, DDSY/2/1/3.

39 MS account of her childhood, by Petsy Scrope, in the possession of her daughter, Tessa Scott.

40 *Mark Sykes*, Leslie, p. 252.

41 *Letters from Tsar Nicholas to Tsarita Alexandra*, www.alexanderpalace.org/letters.

42 Quoted in *Mark Sykes*, Adelson, p. 225.

43 M.S. to W.B., September 1916, YAS MS 729.

44 From an unpublished MS by Angela Sykes in the possession of Hector MacDonnell.

45 Letter to the author, SP.

46 Interview with Freya Elwes.

47 M.S. to E.S., 23 April 1917, DDSY/2/1/2f.

48 M.S. to E.S., 30 April 1917, DDSY/2/1/2f.

49 M.S. to E.S., 17 November 1918, DDSY/2/1/2f.

50 David Lloyd George to E.S., 9 December 1918, SP.

51 *Mark Sykes*, Leslie, p. 279.

52 'You are my helpmeet and my liberator.'

53 *Mark Sykes*, Leslie, p. 301.

54 *Much of Life is Laughter*, Gorst, p. 282.

55 *Mark Sykes*, Leslie, p. 298.

56 *Mark Sykes*, Leslie, p. 299.

57 'You have been my helper and my liberator.'

58 *Eastern Morning News*, 26 February 1919.

CHAPTER XIV

1 Quoted in *The Visitors' Book*, C. S. Sykes, 1978, p. 208.

2 *Sykes of Sledmere*, J. Fairfax Blakeborough, 1929, p. 200.

3 Letter to the author from Nino Hunter.

4 Unpublished MS by Angela Sykes, in the possession of Hector MacDonnell.

5 Interview with Harman Grisewood.

6 R.S. to C.S., 25 August 1967, SP.

7 R.S. to C.S., 23 November 1972, SP.

8 Cecil Beaton Diaries, 1 November 1925 (the Literary Executors of Sir Cecil Beaton).

9 Cecil Beaton Diaries, 6 June 1925.

10 *Mercury Presides*, Daphne Fielding, 1954, p. 102.

11 *Cyril Connolly. Journal and Memoir*, ed. David Pryce Jones, 1983, p. 195.

12 C.C. to Noel Blakiston, Christmas. *A Romantic Friendship: The Letters of Cyril Connolly to Noel Blakiston*, 1975, p. 334.

13 *Cyril Connolly. Journal and Memoir*, Pryce Jones, p. 196.

14 *The Lands of Nonsuch*, unpublished MS in the collection of the University of Tulsa, Series II: Writings, 13.4.

15 E.S. to F.E., 27 February 1929, SP.

16 C.S. to R.S., November 1930 and February 1931, SLP.

17 Fielding, *Mercury Presides*, p. 160.

18 R.S. to C.S., 17 May 1975, SP.

19 Interview with Theresa 'Baby' Jungman.

20 *Cecil Beaton*, Hugo Vickers, 1985, p. 84.

21 Interview with Lady Dorothy Lygon.

22 Interview with Harman Grisewood.

23 Letter to the author from Nino Hunter.

24 Interview with Lady Sibell Rowley.

25 Interview with Lady Dorothy Lygon.

26 Cecil Beaton Diaries, 1 November 1925.

27 F.E. to A.S., 15 June 1931.

28 A.S. to F.E., 8 June 1931.

29 William Irons to Winifred Irons, 3 April 1932, SLP.

30 Interview with Harman Grisewood.

31 *Twenty-One Years*, R. S. Churchill, 1965, p. 96.

32 *Randolph*, Brian Roberts, 1984, p. 107.

33 *Sunday Dispatch*, 11 September, p. 2.

34 *Randolph*, Roberts, p. 108.

35 Interview with Lady Dorothy Lygon.

36 *Evelyn Waugh*, Selina Hastings, 1994, p. 266.

37 MS account of Richard's war by Col. Rupert Alec-Smith, SP.

38 R.S. to Archie Scott, November 1941, SP.

39 Adrian 'Bunty' Scrope to R.S., 24 September 1942, SP.

40 Adrian 'Bunty' Scrope to R.S., 24 September 1942, SP.

41 C.S. to R.S., 27 September 1942, SP.

42 C.S. to V.S., October 1942, SP.

43 Interview with Lady Morrison Bell.

44 Interview.

45 Interview with Lady Ebury.

CHAPTER XV

1 C.S. to V.S., '30th of some month or other', 1944, SLP.

2 C.S. to V.S., SLP.

3 Interview with Jack Clarke.

4 Obituary of Christopher Sykes by Harman Grisewood.

5 Obituary, *The Times*, December 1986.

6 Interview with Lady Sibell Rowley.

7 C.S. to R.S., 3 December 1941, SLP.

8 Interview with John Richardson.

9 Interview with the late Mrs Odile Hourani.

10 C.S. to R.S., 29 September 1942, SLP.

11 C.S. to R.S., 8 March 1943, SP.

12 Interview with the late Mrs Odile Hourani.

13 Angela Antrim to Freya Elwes, 5 August 1953, SP.

14 R.S. to C.S., 29 August 1965, SLP.

15 R.S. to C.S., 25 August 1967, SLP.

16 V.S. to R.S., December 1960, SPL.

17 R.S. to Rupert Alec-Smith, 26 June 1970, SLP.

18 R.S. to C.S., 14 January 1971, GUA.

19 R.S. to R.A.-S., 18 November 1970, GUA.

20 C.S. to R.S., 4 November 1976, GUA.

21 R.S. to C.S., 4 February 1975, GUA.

22 R.S. to C.S., 24 February 1977, GUA.

EPILOGUE

1 *Mark Sykes*, Roger Adelson, 1975.

2 C.S. to F.E., 6 June 1976, GUA.

3 Extract from *My Unexpected Brother*, unpublished MS by Christopher Sykes.

4 Extract from *My Unexpected Brother*, Sykes.

5 Interview with Veronica Roberts.

SELECT BIBLIOGRAPHY

Adelson, Roger, *Mark Sykes: Portrait of an Amateur*, 1975.

Allfrey, Anthony, *Edward VII and his Jewish Court*, 1991.

Archibald, E. H. H., *Travellers by Sea*, 1962.

Asquith, Margot, *The Autobiography of Margot Asquith*, 1920.

Atkinson, Peter, *The Sledmere Scene* (MS in possession of Sledmere Estate Office).

Baily's Magazine.

Benson, E. F., *As We Were*, 1930.

Bigland, John, *The Beauties Of England: Or Original Delineations – Topographical, Historical and Descriptive of Each County*, 1812.

Blakiston, Noel (ed.), *A Romantic Friendship: The Letters of Cyril Connolly to Noel Blakiston*, 1975.

Briggs, Asa, *England in the Age of Improvement*, 1999.

Budworth, Julia M., *Never Forget: A Biography of George F. S. Bowles*, 2001.

Burgoyne, E., *Gertrude Bell*, 1958.

Byron, Lord, *Works of Lord Byron*, ed. Thomas Moore, 1832.

Churchill, R. S., *Twenty-One Years*. 1965.

Clark, Norman, *All In The Game*. 1935.

Cokayne, Gec (ed.), *The Complete Peerage*, 1887–1898.

Cowles, Virginia, *The Astors*, 1979.

The Marquess of Crewe, *Lord Rosebery*, 1931.

Crowther, Jan (ed.), *Enclosure Commissioners and Surveyors of the East Riding*, East Yorkshire Local Historical Society, 1986.

—— *Descriptions of East Yorkshire*, East Yorkshire Local Historical Society, 1992.

D'Arblay, Mme, *Diary and Letters of Madame D'Arblay*, 1893.

Defoe, Daniel, *A Tour Through the Whole Island of Great Britain*, ed. P. N. Furbank and W. R. Owens.) 1991.

Denbigh, Kathleen, *A Hundred British Spas*, 1981.

de Saint Fond, Faujas, *A Journey through England and Scotland to the Hebrides in 1784*, 1907.

Dibdin, Revd T. F., *The Bibliographical Decameron*, 1817.

—— *Reminiscences of a Literary Life*, 1836.

The Dictionary of National Biography.

Dixon, Henry Hall, 'the Druid', *Saddle and Sirloin*, 1912.

—— *Scott and Sebright*, 1912.

Dowling, Vincent, *Fistiana*, 1841.

Ehrman, John, *The Younger Pitt*, 1969.

English, Barbara, *The Great Landowners of East Yorkshire*, 1990.

Entwisle, E. A., *A Literary History of Wallpaper*, 1960.

Fairfax Blakeborough, J., *Sykes of Sledmere*, 1929.

Field, J., *Things I Shouldn't Tell*, 1924.

Fielding, Daphne, *Mercury Presides*, 1954.

Foster, R. F., *Lord Randolph Churchill*, 1981.

Fromkin, David, *A Peace to End All Peace*, 1989.

Gentleman's Magazine, in the *Illustrated London News*, 18XX–19XX.

Gilbert, Martin, *Winston S. Churchill*, 1972.

Girouard, Mark, *Life in the English Country House*, 1978.

Gordon, Richard, *The Alarming History of Medicine*, 1921.

Gorst, Harold E., *Much of Life is Laughter*, 1936.

Gower, Lord Ronald, *My Reminiscences*, 1883.

Great Public Schools, 1893.

Hastings, Selina, *Evelyn Waugh*, 1994.

Hey, David, *Yorkshire from AD 1000*, 1986.

Hobson, J. S., *Sledmere And The Sykes Family: A Dissertation*, B.J.L. D88–1561.

Jackman, W. T., *The Development of Transportation in Modern England*, 1962.

James, M. R., *Eton and Kings*, 1926.

Knebworth, Viscount, *Boxing*, XXXX.

Leslie, Shane, *Mark Sykes*, London, 1923.

—— *The Film Of Memory*, 1938.

Mellini, Peter, *Sir Eldon Gorst: The Overshadowed Proconsul*, 1977.

Moore, Katherine, *Victorian Wives*, 1974.

Morris, Revd M. C. F., *Yorkshire Reminiscences*, 1922.

Neave, David and Susan Neave (eds.), *The Diary of a Yorkshire Gentleman*, 2001.

Nevill, Ralph, *Light Come, Light Go*, 1909.

Nimrod, *Nimrod's Hunting Tours*, 1835.

Pennant, T., *Some Account of London*, 3rd edition, 1793.

Popham, J., *The Economics of Elysium: A Landscape, Economic and Social History Principally Recording the Contribution of Sir Christopher Sykes 1770–1801* (MS in possession of Sledmere Estate Office).

Pryce Jones, David (ed.), *Cyril Connolly: Journal and Memoir*, 1983.

Radcliffe, J. B., *Ashgill: The Life & Times of John Osborne*, 1900.

Roberts, Brian, *Randolph*, 1984.

Root-Bernstein, Michèle and Robert Root-Bernstein, *The Bath*, 1997.

Ruskin, John, *The Diaries of John Ruskin, 1843–1873*, 1958.

—— *The Winnington Letters of John Ruskin*, 1969.

Sambrook, Pamela, *Country House Brewing in England: 1500–1900*, 1996.

Sheahan, J. J., *History of Kingston-upon-Hull*, 19XX.

St Helier, Lady, *Memories of Fifty Years*, 1909.

Strickland, H. E., *A General View of the Agriculture of the East Riding*, 1812.

Sykes, Christopher, *Four Studies in Loyalty*, 1946.

Sykes, Mark, *Though Five Turkish Provinces*, 1900.

—— *Dar-ul-Islam*, 1904.

Teignmouth-Shore, W., *Westminster*, 1910.

'Thormanby', *Kings of the Turf*, 1898.

—— *Kings of the Hunting Field*, 1899.

Thorne, R. G., *The History of Parliament: The House of Commons 1790–1820*, 1986.

Vaughan, E. T. (ed.), *Letters of the Hon. Mrs Edward Twisleton*, 1928.

Vickers, Hugo, *Cecil Beaton*, 1985.

Whyte, J. C., *History of the British Turf*, 1840.

Wilson, Derek, *The Astors*, 1993.

Wraxall, Nathaniel, *Historical Memoirs*, 1884.

INDEX

Addison, Joseph, 54
Adelson, Roger: *Mark Sykes*, 377–8
Agar, Harry, 312
Agnew, Joan, 146
Ailesbury, Maria, Marchioness of, 205
Aitken, Max, 338
Albert, Prince Consort: death, 178
Alec-Smith, Rupert, 334–7, 370
Alexandra, Princess of Wales (*later* Queen), 178, 181
Alice, Princess of Monaco, 221
Alliance Assurance Company, 233, 250, 253
Ampleforth College, 318
Anderson, Susanna, 22
Andrew, John, 70
Anglesey, Henry Cyril Paget, 5th Marquess of, 339
Annesley, William Richard, 4th Earl, 168, 170, 172–3
Annual Register, 88
Anthony, Father, 357
Antrim, Angela, Countess of (*née* Sykes; Mark/Edith's daughter): birth, 284; moves into Sledmere, 302; and father's visits to Sledmere on leave, 307, 309; upbringing, 314; sculpting, 317; social life at Sledmere, 321; appears in brother Richard's films, 322; in earthquake (1931), 329; and brother Daniel's opium addiction, 363; marriage, 363; and illegitimate half-brother, 379
Antrim, Randal McDonnell, 8th Earl of, 364
Apperley, Charles James ('Nimrod'), 116, 123
Arch, Arthur, 109
Arundell, Ivy, Lady, 336
Asquith, Herbert Henry, 280, 283, 287, 289
Astor, John Jacob III and Charlotte, 158–9, 164
Astor, Waldorf, 158

Baghdad Proclamation (March 1917), 305
Bagshawe, Edward, 312
Baines, Mary, 153–4
Bainton, Christopher, 77
Balfour, Arthur James, 284
Balkan crisis (1914), 197
Bankhead, Tallulah, 340
Banks, Mary, 22

Baring, Sir Evelyn (*later* 1st Earl of Cromer), 207–8
Barker, Walter, 312
Bath, 82–3
Bath, Thomas Henry Thynne, 5th Marquess of, 336
Bayley, John, 61
Beaton, Cecil, 319, 325–6, 328, 332, 354
Beatty, Admiral of the Fleet David, 1st Earl, 367
Beaumont College, Windsor, 217, 220
Beaumont, Richard, 56–7, 61, 65, 83
Beck, Egerton, 221, 224, 231, 278
Beckley, Ann, 153–4
Beit, Alfred, 332
Bell, Freddy, 164
Bell, Gertrude, 269–70
Bell, Lilah Morrison, 340
Bellingham (5th Bt's valet), 198–9
Belmont, August, 159
Belmont, Percy, 159
Bence-Jones, Dr, 134
Beresford, Lord Charles, 185
Beresford, Robert, 231
Bigland, John, 54
Bingham, Lady Lavinia, 173–4
Blakiston, Noel, 321
Boer War: Mark in, 249–56; Jessie writes on, 259
Bouillon, Franklin, 303
Bower, Robert, 177
Bowles, Dorothy (Thomas's daughter), 222
Bowles, George, 216, 249
Bowles, Sydney (Thomas's daughter), 222, 235
Bowles, Thomas Gibson, 146–7, 216, 222
Bowring, Wilfred, 217–18
boxing (prize-fighting), 92
Braithwaite, Richard, 207, 210, 292
Bramah, Joseph, 152
Brantingham Thorpe, Yorkshire, 181–2, 187, 327
Brasenose College, Oxford, 88, 97
Bridgeman, Diana, 327
Bridlington, 51
Brierley, W.H., 282, 285–6, 294, 296, 306, 373
Bristol, 83–4

Britton, George, 82–4
Brocklesby, Mary, 22
Broughton, Sir Thomas, 67
Brown, Lancelot ('Capability'), 48–9, 53–4, 86
Brown, Rawdon, 145
Browne, Edward Granville, 262
Brussels: Mark studies in, 221–2
Buckingham Gate, London, 288, 290
Bucknill (lawyer), 229–30
Burdett, Sir Francis, 88
Burdet(t), Sir Francis and Elizabeth, Lady, 18
Burke, Edmund, 60
Burney, Fanny (Mme d'Arblay), 63
Butler, Samuel: *The Way of All Flesh*, 124
Byron, George Gordon, 6th Baron, 91
Byron, Thomas, 95

Cadoual, Georges, 102
Callaghan, James, 373
Callwell, General Sir Charles Edward, 304
Cambridge: Mark (6th Bt) attends (Jesus College), 224–6, 249; Richard (7th Bt) attends (Trinity College), 319–20
Cambridge, George William Frederick Charles, Duke of, 179, 181
Campbell-Bannerman, Sir Henry, 279
Canada: Sir Tatton II and Jessie visit, 160, 165
Cardwell, Norman, 354, 356
Carlisle, Frederick Howard, 5th Earl of, 66, 75
Carlton House Terrace, London (No.13), 128
Carr, John, 53, 58, 66–7
Carter, Alice, 377–82, 385–6
Carter, Tom, 123, 379
Carter, Will, 379
Cassidy (butler), 315, 336, 346
Castle Cary, Somerset, 336
Castle Farm, Sledmere, 49, 53
Castle Howard, Yorkshire, 5, 24, 52, 66
Cavendish, Lord Charles, 319, 325–6
Cavendish-Bentinck, Frederick (Jessie Sykes's brother), 159–60, 165, 263
Cavendish-Bentinck, George (Jessie Sykes's brother), 156, 159
Cavendish-Bentinck, George (Jessie Sykes's father; 'Little Ben'), 144, 219, 283
Cavendish-Bentinck, Prudence Penelope (Jessie Sykes's mother; 'Britannia'), 145–7, 150–1, 211–14
Cavendish-Bentinck, Venetia *see* James, Venetia
Cazalet, Zara, 369
Cecil, Lord Hugh, 289
Chalmers, Sir George, 36
Chambers, Dr, 21, 35, 38
Channon, Sir Henry ('Chips'), 327, 331

Chaplin, Henry, 179, 339
Charles Edward Stewart, Prince ('the Young Pretender'), 14
Charlotte (Bessy's personal maid), 51
Chesterfield Street, London, 242, 258
Chetwynd, Lady Florence (*née* Paget), 339
Chetwynd, Sir George, 339
Chifney, Sam, 104
Chirnside (Australian horse-breeder), 139
Cholmondeley, Beatrice, 174–5
Cholmondeley, Henry: and 1911 fire, 1–2; as Sledmere land agent, 220, 223, 235; and Mark's travels in Middle East, 235, 238, 244; and Mark's mission to locate mother in Boer War, 250; and Mark's experiences in Boer War, 254; Mark dines with on return from South Africa, 257; as best man at Mark's wedding, 263; and birth of Mark's son Richard, 272; finds Eddlethorpe as home for Mark, 275; and Jessie's appearance at horse sale, 284; Mark loses patience with, 293; and rebuilding of Sledmere, 295; helps Edith manage estate after Mark's death, 313; Scrope succeeds as estate manager, 321
Cholmondeley, Hugh, 174–5
Cholmondeley, Katherine Lucy (*née* Sykes; 4th Bt's daughter): birth, 124; marriage and children, 125, 148, 174; and birth of 7th Bt Richard, 272
Churchill, Lord Randolph (Winston's father), 205
Churchill, Randolph (Winston's son), 331–3
Churchill, (Sir) Winston, 300–1
Clark, Jack, 349–53, 374
Clark, Lilian, 350, 353
Clarke, Sir Edward, 231–3
Clayburg, Jack, 365
Cleaver, Revd William, 52, 68
Clements (surgeon), 134
Cleveland, Catherine Lucy Wilhelmina, Duchess of, 151, 205
Cleveland, Henry George Powlett, 7th Duke of, 151
coaching: in 18th century, 93
Coates, Audrey, 237
Cochrane, Sir Thomas, 169
Cocks, Katherine, 173
Cocteau, Jean, 362
Coe, Bob, 324, 327, 332
Collett (architect), 275
Collings, Robert, 22
Colman, George, 87
Connolly, Cyril, 320–1, 327
Constable Burton, Yorkshire, 66
Constantinople: Mark Sykes in, 269, 272
Conyngham, Elizabeth, Marchioness (*née* Denison), 39

Cooper, Lady Diana, 331–3
Cooper, Duff, 331–2
Cooper, Mary Ashley, 328
Cooper, Richard (coachman), 51
Corrigan, Laura Mae, 331
Courtney, John, 38
Coward, Noel, 365
Cowlam Farm, near Sledmere, 46
Crewe, Robert Offley Ashburton Crewe-Milnes, Marquess of, 179, 181
Cunard, Maud Alice, Lady ('Emerald'), 331, 333
Curzon of Kedleston, George Nathaniel Curzon, Marquess, 268
Cutsem, Bernard van, 365

Dardanelles campaign (1915), 300
Darwin, Erasmus, 59
De Bunsen, Sir Maurice William, 302–3
Defoe, Daniel, 10–11, 13, 46
Denison, Joseph, 26–7, 33, 38–9, 44–5, 50, 95
Denison, Sarah (née Sykes; Joseph's first wife), 39, 44–5
Denison, William Joseph, 39
Derby, Edward John Stanley, 18th Earl and Dorothy, Countess of, 352–3, 370
Devonshire, Andrew Cavendish, 11th Duke of, 345, 346
Devonshire, William Spencer Cavendish, 6th Duke of, 109
Dibdin, Revd Thomas Frognall, 107–9, 121
Dickens, Cedric, 217
Dickens, Henry, 217, 220
Dillon, John (MP), 286–7
Dillon (Sir Tatton II's valet), 156, 160–1
Disraeli, Benjamin, 279
Dixon (nurseryman), 47
Dixon, Henry Hall ('the Druid'), 95, 104, 115, 117, 122–3, 127, 131–2, 134, 142
Dixon, Sophia, 114
Dixon, William Willmott ('Thormanby'), 115, 122–3, 129
Doddington Hall, Cheshire, 67
Donegall, Edward Chichester, 6th Marquess of, 332
D'Ordel, Major-General George (i.e. Mark Sykes and Edmund Sandars): Tactics and Military Training, 259–60, 264
D'Ordel, Prometheus (i.e. Mark Sykes and Edmund Sandars): D'Ordel's Pantechnicon, 266
Dorothy (housekeeper), 348–9
Dowbiggin (firm), 127
Dowling, Richard ('Doolis'), 214, 224, 253, 255, 259
Downside College, Somerset, 318

Doxford (Lord Derby's maid), 353
Doyle, Sir Arthur Conan, 266
Duff, Sir Michael, 324
Dufferin and Ava, Frederick Temple Hamilton-Temple, 1st Marquess of, 160–1, 164–6, 190, 207
Dufferin and Ava, Harriet, Marchioness of, 160–1
Duke, Doris, 330–3, 366
Duke, Sir James, 271
Dundas, Henry (later 1st Viscount Melville), 60, 78
Dunn, Jo, 325
Dunn, Robert, 47, 82
Dunning, John, 59
Duntz, Marie, 277
Dupplin, George, Viscount, 184

East Yorkshire Militia, 56
Eddlethorpe, Yorkshire, 123, 274–6, 278, 287, 302
Eden, Miss (governess), 128
Edge, Bella, 25, 33–4
Edge, Dicky, 25
Edge, Kitty, 25
Edge, Thomas, 25
Edward, Prince of Wales (later King Edward VII): on Sir Tatton II's dress, 142; avoids Sir Tatton II's wedding, 150; marriage, 178; social life, 178–9; relations with and treatment of Christopher ('Sykey'), 179, 181–7, 205; Jessie intervenes with to help Christopher, 242
Edwardes, James, 109
Egerton, Lady Charlotte, 169
Egerton, Mary Elizabeth see Sykes, Mary Elizabeth, Lady
Egerton, Sir Thomas, 30
Egerton, Mr & Mrs William, 50, 56, 61, 67
Egremont, John Wyndham, 1st Baron, 367–8
Egypt, 207–9, 215–16
Elizabeth the Queen Mother: stays at Sledmere, 347
Ellenborough, Edward Law, 1st Baron, 103
Ellis, Tom see Howard de Walden, 8th Baron
Ellis, William, 54
Elwes, Freya (née Sykes; Mark/Edith's daughter; 'Moot'): birth, 269; father takes to Constantinople as child, 270; childhood and upbringing, 273, 276, 307, 314; moves into Sledmere, 302; father sees on leave form Paris Peace Conference, 309; marriage, 321; and Richard's temper, 328; in earthquake (1931), 329; Christmas visits to Sledmere, 356–8; on Daniel Sykes, 360, 364; learns of and meets illegitimate half-brother, 378, 384–5

Elwes, Richard: marriage to Freya, 321; visits Sledmere, 356–7
Erskine, Mary, 324

Farmer, Captain, 334
Farmiloe family, 336
farming methods: in 18th century, 45–7
Ferrit, Parson, 19
Ferstel, Baron Heinrich, 193, 195
Feversham, Charles Duncombe, 3rd Earl of ('Sim'), 330
Fischbein, Bill, 362
Fitzgerald, Oswald, 301
Flames of Desire (film), 322
Flandin, Etienne, 303
Flat Top Farm, Hilderthorp, 51
Flatters (chauffeur), 316
Foulis, Decima Hester (*née* Sykes; Christopher/Elizabeth's daughter): birth, 50; upbringing, 88; and brother Mark's engagement and marriage to Henrietta, 98; marriage, 118
Foulis, John Robinson, 98, 118
Foulis, Mark, 118
Foulis, Sir William, 118, 148, 167
Fox, Charles James, 59, 61
Fox, Robert, 349
France: Britain at war with, 78, 102; and settlement of Ottoman Empire, 302–3, 307
Frankland, Sir Thomas, 70
Franklin, Benjamin, 59
Franz Ferdinand, Archduke of Austria, 300
Frijs, Magens, 156
From Toe Dancing to Tonsure (film), 322

Gainsborough, Thomas: *The Morning Walk*, 74
Gardiner, Thomas, 224, 227–8, 250
George III, King, 59, 80
George V, King, 300
Gibbs, John, 134
Gilbert, Revd James, 101–3, 129
Gilliat, John Francis Gray (Jack), 338, 340
Gilliat, John, Jr, 340–1
Gilliat, Lily (*formerly* Marchioness of Anglesey), 338–41
Gilliat, Simon, 340–1
Glanely, William James Tatem, 1st Baron, 314
Gold, Jack, 319, 326
Goldschmidt, Paul, 203–4
Goodall, Nellie ('Zellie'), 343
Gorst, Harold (Edith Sykes's brother), 278, 286, 288, 310
Gorst, John Eldon (Jack), 207–10, 240
Gorst, Sir John Eldon (Jack & Edith's father), 240, 263
Gorst, Mary, Lady (*née* Moore), 263, 277
Gotherd (Jessie Sykes's maid), 156, 161, 198–200, 213, 223

Gower, Lord Ronald, 166
Grant, Sir Francis, 129
Granta (magazine), 249
Grayson, Tom (groom), 129, 212–13, 215, 222, 267
Great Western (steamship), 136
Green Howards (regiment), 334–6
Gregory, William, 124
Grenfell, Field Marshal Francis Wallace, 1st Baron, 215
Grenville, Thomas, 106
Grimston, John, 66
Grimston, Thomas, 73, 75, 79
Grisewood, Harman, 318, 326, 330, 358–9
Grosvenor Street, London, 204, 223
Guest, Cynthia (*later* Talbot), 326
Guinness, Lady Evelyn, 340
Guinness, Tanis, 325, 327–8
Gutenberg Bible, 109–10, 121
Guthrie, Edward, 21

Haig, Field Marshal Douglas, 1st Earl, 319
Hall, Dr, 81
Hall, Sam (wine merchant), 43–4
Halme, George, 97
Hamid Bey, Sheikh, 239–40
Hamilton, Lord Claud, 182–4
Hamilton, William (artist), 306
Hardinge, Arthur (*later* Viscount), 173
Harewood House, near Leeds, 24, 66, 69
Harper, Revd George, 97
Hartington, Spencer Compton Cavendish, Marquess of (*later* 8th Duke of Devonshire), 179
Hastings, Henry Rawdon-Hastings, 4th Marquess of, 179
Hatry, Eric, 327
Haycock, Lieut., 334
Heathcote, Gilbert, 168, 175
Heathcote, Father William, 217, 220
Heberieh, 240–1
Hedonville, Count d', 130
Hejaz, 303
Herbert, Aubrey, 287
Herries, Angela, Lady, 191, 192
Herring, Thomas, Archbishop of York, 14
Heugelmüller, Baron, 190
Hewland, Arthur, 153
Hickey, William, 137
Hilderthorp, near Bridlington, 51–2
Hildyard, Robert, 119
Hill, Lady Alice, 147–9
Hill, Theopilus, 85, 106–7
Hirsch, Lucien de: love affair and correspondence with Jessie Sykes, 195–203, 213–14; illness and death, 203–4
Hirsch, Baron Maurice de, 195–6
Hirst, Sam, 21

Hirtzel, Sir Arthur, 309
Hobman, Hesketh, 15
Hobman, John, 16
Hobman, Randolph, 26, 28
Holland, Elizabeth, Lady, 106
Home Rule Bill (1914), 297
Hooton Hall, Cheshire, 67
Hope-Nicholson family, 361
Hopper, John, 56
Hornak, Marno, 361–3
Hornak, Odile see Hourani, Odile
Horner (electrician), 317
Hornsby, Thomas, 40
Hotham, Charles, 114
Houghton, John, 72
Hourani, Odile (formerly Hornak), 361–3
Howard, Brian, 327
Howard de Walden, Blanche, Lady (Tom's mother), 220
Howard de Walden, Thomas Evelyn Scott-Ellis, 8th Baron, 214–15, 219–20, 310
Hunter, Hylda (née Gorst), 314, 322
Hunter, Nino, 276, 306, 314–16, 318–19, 326
Huntly, Alexander Gordon, 7th Marquess of, 117
Hussein ibn Ali, Sherif and Emir of Mecca, 303–4
Hussey, Christopher, 77
Hussey, Mr & Mrs (York innkeepers), 130–1

Ireland: Mark Sykes serves in, 264; and Home Rule, 297
Irons, William, 329
Isa Kubrusli: accompanies Mark on Middle East travels, 238–40, 244, 247–8; death, 262

Jackson, Foakes, 225
Jackson, 'Gentleman' John (boxer), 92, 115
Jackson, John (jockey), 104
Jacksons of Hammersmith (contractors), 296
Jacob-el-Arab, 262
James, Arthur, 236
James, Montague Rhodes, 225, 239, 275
James, Venetia (née Cavendish-Bentinck), 152, 236–7
Jay, Daniel, 226, 228, 233
JC, Miss (visitor to 2nd Bt and Bessy), 61–2
Jeffreys, Thomas: Yorkshire Atlas, 45
Jesus College, Cambridge see Cambridge
Johnson, Samuel, 86
Johnson, Tom, 92
Jungman, Baby, 325, 327
Jungman, Zita, 325, 327

Kay, Sir John Lister, 94
Kedleston, Derbyshire, 68, 70

Kenneally, Michael, 347–8
Kennedy, Joseph, Jr, 338
Kent, William, 15, 49
Kernochan, Mr & Mrs (of Newport), 159
Kilnwick House, 66, 79
King, Sir Henry Seymour, 280
King, John, 107
Kipling, Rudyard, 266
Kirby Hall, Yorkshire, 67
Kirkby, Mark, 9, 11–12, 23, 36, 176
Kirkby, Richard, 17
Kitchener, Field Marshal Horatio Herbert, 1st Earl, 301–2
Kitteridge, Ben, 324
Knebworth, Edward Anthony James Lytton, Viscount, 92
Knollys, Francis, 1st Viscount, 182–3

Langley, W.H., 130
Lascelles, Edwin, 24, 49, 66
Lawrence, Sir Thomas, 100, 126
Lawson, Richard, 25, 27
Lazenby, Parson, 19
Leeds, 12–13
Leeds, Francis Osborne, 5th Duke of, 76, 78
Legard, Sir J., 75
Leibowitz, Annie, 373
Lennox Gardens, London, 265
Leslie, Sir Shane, 263
Levant Consular Service, 273
Leveson-Gower, Frederick, 173
Lewis, Sam, 223
Lichtervelde, Louise de ('Madame'), 271, 274, 278, 292–3
Life Hill, Sledmere (farm), 49, 53–4, 74–5
Lightoler, Thomas: The Gentleman and Farmers Architect, 54
Lillingstone, Luke, 47
Lindley, Alice, 328–9
Lloyd George, David, 279, 283–4, 308
Lockwood, Mark Henry, 114
Londonderry, Theresa Susey Helen, Marchioness of, 287
Lords, House of, 283–4
Lott, Frederick, 380–1
Lott, (Frederick) George (Sir Mark Sykes's illegitimate son), 379–86
Lott, Marjorie, 382
Lott, Mary (née Page), 380–1
Loudovici, Mademoiselle de ('Mouzelle'), 314, 327, 335, 344–5, 356, 365
Lovat, Siomon Fraser, 15th Baron ('Shimi'), 338, 365
Lowndes (machine designer), 80–1
Lucan, Anne, Countess of (née Brudenell), 169
Luck, Dorothy, 20
Lycett-Green, Candida, 372–3

Lygon, Lady Dorothy ('Coote'), 310, 325–8, 333
Lygon, Lady Sibell, 327, 360

McAlister, Ward, 158
MacEwan (servant), 224, 238, 240
McGregor-Petrie, Hamish, 372
Mainwaring, Emma, 114
Maister, Colonel Henry, 56, 58, 61, 86
Maister, Nathaniel, 73
Malcolm, Sir Ian, 289
Malton, Thomas, 76
Manchester, Louise, Duchess of (*later* Duchess of Devonshire), 179
Manners, Nicholas, 11
Manners, Lord Robert, 19, 25
Manning, Henry Edward, Cardinal Archbishop of Westminster, 191–4, 206
Maramatte, Sledmere (farm), 49, 53
Marlborough Club, 184
Marriott, Nancy, 61
Marshall, Marion, 346
Marshall, William, 46
Marson (quarry foreman), 68
Martin, Charles Bower, 114
Martyns of Cheltenham (plasterwork firm), 297
Masterman, Elizabeth, 99
Masterman, Henry, 98
Matasek, Eduard, 208
Maude, General Sir Stanley, 305
Maunsell, Captain, 248
Max-Muller, Wanda Maria, Lady, 236
Maxwell, General Sir John Grenfell, 301
Mellon, Paul, 365
Mendoza, Dan, 92
Menethorpe (farmhouse), 275
Messel, Oliver, 331–2
Middle East: Mark travels in, 235, 238–40, 244–8, 260, 261–2, 269–72, 273; Mark complains of westernisation, 265–6; Sykes-Picot Agreement and post-war settlement of, 303, 305
Middleton, Captain George ('Bay'), 190
Middleton, Henry Willoughby, 4th Baron, 105
Middleton, Michael Willoughby, 11th Baron, 325, 379
Mills, James, 227
Mitchell, Mary, 22
Monaco: Mark Sykes studies in, 221
Moncrieff, Sir David, 117
Montagu, Drogo, 325
Montagu, Lady Mary Wortley, 31
Montrose, Violet Hermione, Duchess of, 205
Moore, Nurse, 51
More O'Ferrall family, 365
Morice, Parson, 19
Moritz, Carl Philipp, 90

Morris, Revd Mr, 125–6, 129
Morris (tutor), 89
Mostell Priory, 16
Mulgrave, Henry Phipps, 3rd Baron (*later* 1st Earl), 79
Mussolini, Benito, 333
Myton Carr, Yorkshire (estate), 47

Napoleon I (Bonaparte), Emperor of the French, 78, 101–3
Nelson, Admiral Horatio, 1st Viscount, 80
Neville, Henry, 173
Newcastle, Thomas Pelham-Holles, 1st Duke of, 86
Newman, C.S., 152
Newman, John Henry, Cardinal, 191
Nicholas II, Tsar, 304
Nicholson, Lizzie, 277
Niven, David, 365
Norfolk, Henry Fitzalan-Howard, 15th Duke of, 192
Norreys, Montagu Arthur Bertie, Lord, 192
Norris, Robert, 19, 27, 34
North, Frederick, Lord, 58
Northcliffe, Alfred Harmsworth, Viscount, 292

O'Connor, Sir Nicholas, 273
Ohanessian, David, 296
Oliphant, Lancelot, 307
Orwell Park, near Ipswich, 151
Osbaldeston, George, 116
Osborne House, Isle of Wight, 127
Osborne, John (jockey/trainer), 142
Osterley Park, Middlesex, 151
Otley, Mark, 114
Ottley, William Young, 106
Ottoman Empire *see* Turkey

Pakenham, Sir William, 249, 377, 379, 381
Palestine Exploration Fund, 239
Palmer, Edward, 238
Pardoe, Richard & Son, 17
Paris Peace Conference (1919), 308
Parker, Sir Thomas, 19
Parma, Charles III Bourbon, Duke of, 172
Parrington, Jean, 328
Pattenhorne, Revd Mr, 192
Paul, Parson, 20, 26
Pearson (bank manager), 232
Pearson, John Loughborough, 143
Pelham, Henrietta, 114
Pelham, Henry, 18, 86
Pennant, Thomas, 91
Pennyman, Sir James, 60
Perfect, John, 15–17
Perfects (Pontefract nurserymen), 16
Perrins, Isaac, 92

Photo Richard (film company), 322
Pickering, Henry, 27
Picot, François Georges: draws up Agreement on Middle East with Mark Sykes, 303, 305
Pitt, William, the Younger, 59–61, 63–4, 78, 80
Ponthieu, John de, 29–32, 38
Ponthieu, Josias de, 29–30
Ponthieu, Maria de (née Sykes; Parson Sykes' daughter; 'Polly'), 28–33, 36–7
Porter, Thomas, 22
Powis, Violet, Countess of, 327
Pozzi, Father Dunstan, 314–15, 322–3, 345, 357
Price, Richard, 59
Priestley, Joseph, 59

rabbits: rearing and marketing, 46
Raby Castle, 180
Rambler, The (journal), 259
Ramsay, Robert, 137–8
Ramsden, Frederick, 173
Ramsden, Sir John, 168, 175
Rees, Mattie, 210
Reynal, Eugene, 324
Reynolds, Frederick, 87
Rhodes, John, 34–5
Richardson, John, 361–2
Richardson, Samuel: Clarissa, 10
Richmond-Brown, Charles, 334
Robbins, John, 126
Roberts, Ben, 386
Roberts, Veronica, 378–80, 382–6
Robertson, Dicky, 382
Rockingham, Charles Watson-Wentworth, 2nd Marquess of, 59, 66
Rolling Stones (pop group), 373
Romney, George: portrait of Christopher (2nd Bt) and wife, 7, 74–5, 126, 329
Rose, Joseph, 69–72, 75–6, 80, 306
Rosebery, Archibald Philip, 5th Earl of, 179–80, 187
Rosse, Michael, 6th Earl of, 325
Roxburghe, John Ker, 3rd Duke of, 107
Royal Naval and Military Tournament, 299–300
Royston, Charles, Viscount ('Champagne Charlie'), 179
Ruskin, John, 145, 268
Russell of Killowen, Charles, 1st Baron, 228, 230–2
Russia: Bolshevik revolution (1917), 304; and division of Turkish Empire, 304
Ryskamp, Charles, 110

Sagar (wallpaper-hanger), 73
St Albans, William Amelius Aubrey de Vere, 10th Duke of, 184

Saint Fond, Faujas, 93–4
St Helier, Susan Elizabeth Mary, Baroness, 165
St Mary's church, Sledmere, 192, 371
St Quintin, Sir William, 49
Salton, Walter, 156
Sanday (sheep breeder), 114
Sandars, Edmund, 249, 259, 266, 275, 300, 309
Sanguinetti (moneylender), 223, 250
Saunders, William, 73
Scarsdale, Nathaniel Curzon, 1st Baron, 68
Schreiber, Gaby, 362
Scott, Archibald, 337
Scott, Sir George Gilbert, 144
Scott, George Gilbert, Jr, 191–2
Scott, Mrs (cook), 345, 364
Scrope, Adrian ('Bunty'): marriage to Petsy, 321, 330; succeeds Henry Cholmondeley as estate manager, 321, 330; regulates 3rd Bt Richard's finances, 330, 333; enlists in Second World War, 334; resigns from Sledmere position, 337–8
Scrope, Everilda (née Sykes; Mark/Edith's daughter; 'Petsy'): birth, 275; moves into Sledmere, 302; and father's death, 309; marriage, 321, 330; takes over husband's management duties in Second World War, 334, 337
Sea Birds Preservation Act (1869), 178
Seamore Place, Mayfair, 181, 186–7
Searle, George, 104
Settrington, Yorkshire (estate), 98–100, 113
Shawe, William, 21
Shelburne, William Petty, 2nd Earl of (later 1st Marquess of Landsdowne), 59–60
Sidall, Thomas, 21
Simpson (6th Bt's valet), 232
Simpson, Dr, 112
Simpson, Revd John, 53, 69, 86, 89
Sirius (paddle-steamer), 136
Skeffington, William, 81–2
Slaney, Nannette Kenyon, 340
Sledmere House: burnt (1911), 1–3, 281–2; described, 5–8, 55, 62, 84–5, 107, 127–8; Richard Sykes builds, 9, 17–19, 22–4; landscaping, 15–16, 24–5, 48–9; inventory (1755), 22–4; Christopher (2nd Bt) improves estate, 45, 47–50, 53–5, 62, 64; enclosure and land value, 47, 49; The Avenue, 47–8; Christopher (2nd Bt) occupies, 57–8; ice-house, 58; Orangery, 64–5, 77, 85, 126, 140; Christopher (2nd Bt) re-designs and furnishes house, 65–73, 75, 85; wallpaper introduced, 72; hunting banned by Christopher, 74–5; Gallery, 75–6; Library and book collection, 75–6, 107–8, 154–5, 285, 296; Malton

Sledmere House – *cont.*
  watercolour of (1795), 76–7; debts, 100;
  Mark (3rd Bt) moves into, 100; horse-
  breeding stud, 104–5; art works, 106,
  342–3; art and books sold, 120; Sir Tatton
  I occupies, 120; home-brewed 'Old
  October' ale, 122, 130; redecorated under
  4th Bt, 128; servants, 128, 153, 212,
  344–52; stud sold by Sir Tatton II, 139;
  gardens destroyed by Sir Tatton II, 140; Sir
  Tatton II rebuilds stud, 142–3, 270–1, 313;
  water supply and sewerage inadequacy,
  152–3; Jessie reorganises and renovates,
  153–5, 219–20; income falls (1881–9), 194;
  new drainage system installed, 220;
  Christmases at, 222–3, 356–8, 371;
  rebuilding after fire, 282–3, 285, 294–6,
  305; Edith and children move into in First
  World War, 302; memorial brasses, 312;
  electric power-station, 316–17; Connolly
  visits and writes on, 321–2; inter-war social
  life, 321–5, 327; film-making at, 322;
  Richard (7th Bt) inherits and improves,
  323; financial crisis under Richard (7th Bt),
  329; rocked by earthquake (1931), 329;
  recovers solvency, 333; in Second World
  War, 335, 337; author's recollections of life
  at, 342–55; repaired after Second World
  War, 342; stud thrives, 342; nannies and
  governesses, 343; organ installed, 354–5;
  shooting- and house-parties, 364; Richard
  (7th Bt) devotes widowhood years to,
  371–2; opened to public, 373
Sledmere village: site, 11; *see also* St Mary's
  church
Smith, John Hugh ('Little John'), 261–2, 265,
  310
Smith, Mary, 189
Smith, Samuel (Westminster headmaster),
  87–8
Snarl, The (Cambridge journal), 249
Snarry, Jacob, 121–2, 136, 142
Snarry, James, 142
South Africa *see* Boer War
Southey, Robert, 90
Stafford, Joseph, 44
Stallard (Lord Derby's butler), 352
Stanley, Sir Thomas, 67
Stansfield, Major Guy, 337
Stavordale, Henry Fox-Strangways, Lord, 327
Sterne, Laurence, 18
Storrs, Sir Ronald, 310
Street, George Edmund, 144, 192, 372
Strickland, Freddy, 2
Stuart (Lord Derby's under-butler), 352
Styan (butler), 51
Sullivan (Lord Derby's valet), 353
Sunrise, The (Jessie's journal), 259

Swain, Revd E.G., 225
Swaine, Dr, 134
Sydenham, Dr Thomas, 20
Sygrove, Arthur, 141
Sykes Dyke, near Carlisle, 12
Sykes family: background, 12–13
Sykes, Anna Maria (*earlier* Edge; Richard II's
  second wife), 25
Sykes, Arabella (author's sister): birth, 346
Sykes, Christina Anne Jessica (Jessie), Lady
  (*née* Cavendish-Bentinck; 5th Bt's wife):
  portrait, 7; marriage, 144, 146–7, 150–1;
  character and interests, 145–6, 155;
  reorganises and renovates Sledmere, 153–5;
  writings, 154, 259, 266–7; charitable work,
  155, 206–7, 292; marriage relations, 155–6,
  163, 190, 195–7, 199–200, 213, 221, 223;
  friendship with Magens Frijs, 156; in North
  America with husband, 156–65; on
  Christopher (Sykey), 187; birth of child,
  189; affairs, 190–1; converts to Catholicism,
  191–2; attempts to persuade husband to
  build Westminster Cathedral, 192–5; love
  affair and correspondence with Lucien de
  Hirsch, 195–204, 213–14; travels with
  husband, 198–203, 207–8, 213; social life
  in London, 204–5; drinking, 206, 210, 219,
  223, 227, 285, 290; nickname ('Lady Satin
  Tights'), 206; attachment to Gorst, 207–10;
  and son Mark's upbringing and education,
  211, 216–18; debts and gambling, 219–21;
  223, 226, 228–30, 250, 253–4; relations
  with son Mark, 220, 226, 228, 235–6, 258,
  284; celebrates Christmas at Sledmere, 222;
  husband formally disclaims responsibility for
  debts, 224, 226; husband deserts, 226–7;
  husband makes settlement on, 226; attempts
  divorce proceedings, 227; and court case
  against husband, 228–30, 232–4, 235;
  accompanies Mark to Middle East, 235,
  238; helps brother-in-law Christopher,
  242–3; moves to Chesterfield Street, 242;
  and Mark's efforts to arrange settlement of
  debts, 244, 250–4; departs for Boer War,
  249–50; attends Mark's wedding, 263;
  dislikes Louise de Lichtervelde, 271–2; and
  birth of grandson Richard, 272; ill health,
  285; death and funeral, 290, 292; and
  Mark's illegitimate son, 377, 380–1;
  Algernon Casterton, 154, 267; *The
  Macdonnells,* 267; *Mark Alston,* 268; *The
  New Reign of Terror in France,* 267; *Side
  Lights on the War in South Africa,* 259
Sykes, Sir Christopher, 2nd Bt: raises
  regiment in Napoleonic Wars, 7, 77–80;
  Romney portrait, 7, 74–5, 126, 329; birth,
  37; studies, 39–40; courtship and marriage,
  40–2; accounts and domestic management,

42–4; children, 44–5, 50; improves
Sledmere estate, 45, 47–50, 53–5, 62, 64;
home and family life, 51–2; education of
children, 52–3, 86, 88, 97; architectural
designs, 53–4, 65–7; moves into Sledmere
House, 57–8; elected MP for Beverley,
60–1; entertaining, 61; buys London house,
62; parliamentary silence, 63–4; wealth, 64;
redesigns and furnishes house, 65–73, 75,
84–5; gives up politics, 69; field sports, 74;
absence from Sledmere, 79–84; takes waters
at spas, 82; health decline and death, 82–4,
100, 117

Sykes, Christopher (4th Bt's son; 'Sykey'):
birth, 124; at Cambridge, 127; on father's
failing health, 132; and brother Tatton,
144, 147, 148–9, 167; character and social
life, 167–73, 179; at Sledmere, 171, 173,
175; considers career, 171–2, 175–6;
attempts family history, 176; as Member of
Parliament, 177–8, 283; as object of
practical jokes, 179–86; relations with
Prince of Wales, 179, 181–7; bankruptcy
and ill health, 236, 242–3; friendship with
Jessie, 236, 242; Prince of Wales helps,
242–3; death, 243

Sykes, Christopher (Christopher/Elizabeth's
son): birth, 50; upbringing and education,
53, 86, 88; on mother's illness, 81

Sykes, Christopher (Mark/Edith's twin son):
birth, 275; upbringing, 277; in father's
military pageant, 300; moves into Sledmere,
302; schooling, 309, 318; at father's funeral,
311; on loss of father, 313; attends horse-
sales with mother, 314; friendship with
Connolly, 321; appears in Richard's film,
323; on Richard's Rolls-Royce, 323; unhurt
in private plane crash, 325; wartime
caricature, 334; congratulates Richard on
engagement, 338; revisits Sledmere, 342,
358; character and career, 358–9; on
brother Daniel, 360, 362–3; and Richard's
hostility to Labour, 373–4; receives letter
about unknown illegitimate half-brother,
377–9, 383–6; Four Studies in Loyalty, 359;
High Minded Murder, 359; Wassmuss, 359

Sykes, Christopher Simon (Richard/Virginia's
son): birth, 342; upbringing at Sledmere,
343–50, 365; behaviour and dress as
teenager, 369; and mother's death, 371;
loses automatic rights to visit home, 377;
meets illegitimate uncle, 386; The Visitor's
Book, 349

Sykes, Daniel (1632–97), 13

Sykes, Daniel (Mark/Edith's son): birth, 306;
father sees on leave from Peace
Conference, 309; education, 314; life-style,
320; and mother's death, 326, 360;

character and career, 360–4; homosexuality,
360–2; opium addiction, 362–4

Sykes, Decima Hester (Christopher/
Elizabeth's daughter) see Foulis, Decima
Hester

Sykes, Decima Twyford, Lady (née
Woodham; 1st Bt's wife): marriage, 36;
lives at Sledmere, 50; Tatton visits, 95;
death, 96

Sykes, Dorothy (née Twigge; Joseph's wife;
'Dolly'), 28

Sykes, Edith, Lady (née Gorst; 6th Bt Mark's
wife): Mark meets and corresponds with,
241–2, 244, 248–9, 252, 254–9, 261–3;
Mark proposes marriage to, 260; joins Mark
in Constantinople, 263; wedding, 263;
encourages Mark's political career, 264;
London home with Mark, 265;
accompanies Mark on Palestine holiday,
269; children, 269–70, 284; with Mark on
journey to Aleppo, 273–4; family life, 276;
and son's tantrum, 278; and Mark's
experiences in Commons, 283, 286, 288;
and Mark's activities in First World War,
300–1; invites family children to Sledmere,
306, 314; letters from Mark abroad in war,
307; manages Mark's election campaign
during wartime absence, 308; and Mark's
health decline and death, 308–9; contracts
Spanish flu in Paris, 309; interest in horse-
breeding, 313; widowhood, 313;
deteriorating relations with son Richard,
320, 324–6; death, 325–6; and son Mark's
illegitimate child by Alice Carter, 377

Sykes, Elizabeth (Christopher/Elizabeth's
daughter), 50, 88

Sykes, Elizabeth, Lady (née Tatton; 2nd Bt's
wife; Bessy): Romney portrait, 7, 74–5,
126, 329; marriage, 40–2; pregnancies and
children, 43–4, 50–1; miscarries, 51; moves
into Sledmere House, 57; improves house,
61; presented at Court, 62–3; and death of
favourite dog, 68; dislikes political life, 69;
weak health, 80–2; maiden name, 374

Sykes, Elizabeth Beatrice (4th Bt's daughter),
124–5, 127–8

Sykes, Emma Julia (4th Bt's daughter): birth
and upbringing, 124–5, 128; room
repapered, 128; marriage, 148

Sykes, Henrietta (author's sister): birth, 346;
and father's death, 377

Sykes, Henrietta (née Masterman; 3rd Bt's first
wife): marriage, 98–9; books and reading,
110; writings, 111; death and will, 112–13;
Lawrence portrait of, 126; The Yorkshire
Baronet, 110–11

Sykes, Jane (née Hobman; Richard's first
wife), 15–17

Sykes, Jeremy (author's brother), 343–4

Sykes, Jessie *see* Sykes, Christina Anne Jessica

Sykes, Joseph (1723–1805), 21, 24, 27–8, 32–3, 57

Sykes, Louisa Anne (4th Bt's daughter): birth and death, 124–5

Sykes, Lucy (3rd Bt's niece), 114

Sykes, Revd Sir Mark ('Parson'), 1st Bt: on brother Richard's fondness for port, 19; poem on building of Sledmere, 22; visits Richard, 26; and daughter Polly, 28, 32; and Richard's death, 35; character and appearance, 36; marriage and children, 36–7; inherits Sledmere, 37; financial speculations and interests, 38, 38–9; lives at Sledmere, 50, 56; Baronetcy, 56–7; decline and death, 56–7; and eulogy to wife, 96

Sykes, Sir Mark, 3rd Bt: birth, 44, 50; education, 86–9, 97; engagement and marriage to Henrietta, 98–9; adds Masterman to surname, 99; gambling and debts, 100–2; moves into Sledmere on death of father, 100; commands local regiment in Napoleonic wars, 102, 298; as MP for York, 103; wins case against Gilbert, 103; horse-breeding and racing, 104–5; hunting, 105; book and art collecting, 106–10, 120–1; death and will, 113–14; second marriage (to Mary Elizabeth Egerton), 113; Lawrence portrait of, 126

Sykes, Sir Mark, 6th Bt: and Turkish Room, 6; researches family history, 23; birth and christening (as Tatton Benvenuto Mark), 189; received into Catholic Church, 192, 211; upbringing, 211–15; early ill-health and travels abroad, 215–16, 218; schooling, 217–18; acting and story-telling, 218, 226; writings, 218, 261, 265–6, 268, 274; relations with mother, 220, 226, 228, 235–6, 258–9, 284; withdrawn from school, 220–1; studies in Monaco and Brussels, 221–2; appearance, 222; at Cambridge University (Jesus College), 224–6; testifies in parents' court case, 232–3; effect of parents' court case on, 235; exploration and travel in Middle East, 235, 238–40, 244–8, 260, 261–2, 269–73; meets and corresponds with Edith Gorst, 241–2, 244, 248–9, 252, 254–9, 261–2; efforts to arrange final settlement between parents, 244, 250–3; serves in Boer War, 249–57; returns to Sledmere from Boer War, 256–66; writes as 'D'Ordel' with Edmund Sandars, 259–60, 266; proposes marriage to Edith, 260; wedding, 263; as Private Secretary to George Wyndham in Ireland, 264–5; home and family life, 265, 276–8,

288; children, 269, 272, 284, 306; post in Constantinople, 269, 272; differences with Gertrude Bell, 270; moves to and improves Eddlethorpe, 274–5; as illustrator and caricaturist, 277, 285, 289–90, 306; stands and loses in 1910 parliamentary elections, 278–80; elected MP for Central Hull (1911), 280–1; busy schedules, 282, 288, 298; and rebuilding of Sledmere after 1911 fire, 282–3, 285, 294–6, 305; parliamentary and political activities, 283–9, 296–9; maiden speech on Middle East, 285–7; and father's illness and death, 292–4; and mother's death, 292; organises military pageants, 299–300; raises and funds 'Wagoner's Special Reserve', 299; seconded to War Office in Great War, 301; draws up Agreement on Turkish Empire ('Sykes-Picot Pact'), 303, 305; meets Tsar, 304; wartime visits to Sledmere, 305–6; attends Paris Peace Conference (1919), 308–9; health decline on return at war's end, 308–9; re-elected (1918), 308; death and funeral, 309–11; memorial brass in Sledmere church, 312; illegitimate son by Alice Carter, 377–81, 386; *The Caliphs' Last Heritage*, 274; *Dar-ul-Islam: A Record of a Journey through Ten of the Asiatic Provinces of Turkey*, 261, 265–6; *Through Five Turkish Provinces*, 249, 258

Sykes, Mark (1st Bt's son), 36

Sykes, Martha (*née* Donkin; Richard III's second wife), 27–8

Sykes, Mary (*née* Kirby; Richard III's wife), 13

Sykes, Mary Anne (*née* Foulis; 4th Bt Tatton's wife): courtship and marriage, 114, 118–20; married life, 121; birth of children, 124; and children's upbringing, 125, 136; welfare and charity work, 125–6; reorganises household, 128; death and funeral, 133

Sykes, Mary Elizabeth (4th Bt's daughter): birth, 124; father refuses permission to marry, 125; and father's failing health, 132; and brother Tatton's infatuation with Lady Alice Hill, 147–8; excluded from Sledmere, 152; and Jessie's running of Sledmere, 154; and brother Christopher, 177

Sykes, Mary Elizabeth (*née* Egerton; 3rd Bt's second wife), 112–13

Sykes, Nicholas (author's brother), 346

Sykes, Nicholas (Parson's nephew), 57

Sykes, Sir Richard, 7th Bt: birth, 272; childhood illness, 273; upbringing, 276, 314; father calms tantrum, 278; moves into Sledmere as child, 302; schooling, 309, 318–19; at father's funeral, 311; attends horse-sales with mother, 314; boyhood at

Sledmere, 315, 317; character and behaviour, 317–21, 326–8, 366–70, 372–3; at Cambridge, 319–20; piano- and organ-playing, 319, 327, 354–5, 369, 372; relations with mother, 320, 324–6; film-making, 322–3; extravagance and entertaining, 323–4, 327, 329; inherits and improves Sledmere, 323; financial crisis, 329–30; ditched by Doris Duke, 331; involved in brawl in Venice, 331–3; military service in Second World War, 334–7; invalided out of army, 337; courtship and marriage, 338–9; life at Sledmere, 350–1, 353–4, 356; motor cars, 350; and children's upbringing, 353; cosseted by Jack Clark, 353; friendship with brother Christopher, 359; anecdotes on past, 366–8; marriage relations, 370; and wife's death, 371; changes name to Tatton-Sykes, 373; death, 374; told of illegitimate half-brother, 384–6

Sykes, Richard (1570–1645), 12

Sykes, Richard (1678–1726): background and career, 9, 13, 176; portrait, 9; visits property, 9–12; second marriage and child, 27, 34; and niece Polly de Ponthieu's decline and death, 32–3

Sykes, Richard (1706–1761): moves to and develops Sledmere, 9, 13–19, 22–3, 67–8; first marriage (to Jane), 15–17; appointed High Sheriff, 18; gout and other ailments, 19–21, 35; servants, 21–2; second marriage (to Anna Maria), 25; hunting and entertaining, 26; portrait, 27; improves Sledmere land, 47, 64

Sykes, Sir Richard (unrelated), 373

Sykes, Sophia Frances (4th Bt's daughter): birth, 124; marriage, 125, 148; paintings, 126–7, 297

Sykes, Sir Tatton, 4th Bt: portraits, 7, 9, 126, 129; birth, 50; upbringing, 53; education, 86–9; in London to study law, 89–92, 94–5; learns to box, 92–4, 115; visits Sledmere from London, 93–4; horse-breeding and racing, 94–7, 104–5, 130–2; walking and physical toughness, 95, 114–16; works in Hull bank, 95; attachment to sister-in-law Henrietta, 99; moves to Westow, 104, 120; succeeds brother Mark and inherits estate, 113, 114; buys and breeds sheep, 114–15; courtship and marriage, 114, 118–20; horsemanship, 116–17, 123–4, 129; country pursuits and interests, 117–18, 122–3; occupies Sledmere, 120; daily routine and diet, 121–3; children, 124–5; social life and entertaining, 128–30; dress, 129, 132; health decline and death, 132–4;

reputation, 132, 135; funeral and memorial, 134–5

Sykes, Sir Tatton, 5th Bt: and house fire (1911), 1, 3–4, 282; birth and upbringing, 124; on father's bringing up children, 124–5; qualities and character, 136; travels, 136–9, 143, 198–203, 207–8, 213, 215–16, 218; sells Sledmere stud, 139; destroys gardens, 140; dress, 141–2; hypochondria, 141, 200; horse-breeding and racing, 142–3, 270–1; builds and restores churches, 143–4, 192, 222, 270; marriage, 144, 150; earlier infatuations, 147–9; mental decline, 148–9; in USA and Canada with Jessie, 148–9, 156–65; neglects water and sewerage facilities at Sledmere, 153; daily routine and habits, 155; marriage relations, 155–6, 163, 190, 195–7, 200, 213, 221, 223; birth of son, 189–90; considers building Westminster Roman Catholic Cathedral, 193–5; eating habits, 200; on son Mark's shape, 222; hangs Mark's dogs, 223, 378; formally disclaims responsibility for Jessie's debts, 224; deserts Jessie with unsettled debts, 226–7; sued in court for unpaid debts, 228–34, 235; fails to attend brother Christopher's funeral, 243; son Mark arranges settlement of mother's debts with, 244, 250–3; approves Mark's marriage to Edith, 263; depicted in Jessie's novel Mark Alston, 268; relations with Louise de Lichtervelde, 271; and birth of grandson Richard, 272; grandchildren visit, 277–8; plans rebuilding of Sledmere after fire, 282; and Jessie's death and funeral, 290, 292; final illness, death and funeral, 292–4; threatens to disinherit son Mark for affair with Alice Carter, 377, 380

Sykes, Sir Tatton, 8th Bt: apprehensions of lift, 6; schooling, 343; and mother's death, 371; inherits Sledmere, 377

Sykes, Virginia, Lady (née Gilliat; 7th Bt Richard's wife): courtship and marriage, 338–9, 341; social life and entertaining, 355–6, 364–5; on husband's sensitivity to past, 368; embraces fashions of youth, 369–70; illness and death, 370–1; marriage relations, 370

Sykes, William (1500–1577), 12

Sykes-Masterman, Sir Mark see Sykes, Sir Mark, 3rd Bt

Tait, Archibald Campbell, Archbishop of Canterbury, 150

Talbot, Lady Gertrude, 147

Talbot, Lady Gwendolyn, 192

Talbot (nanny), 343

Tattersall, Richard, 94, 132

Tatton, Frances, 114
Tatton, Thomas, 114
Tatton, William (2nd Bt Christopher's father-in-law), 40
Tatton, William (2nd Bt Christopher's nephew), 72
Tatton-Sykes, Sir Richard *see* Sykes, Sir Richard, 7th Bt
Telford, John and George (nurserymen), 47, 50
Temple Newsam, Yorkshire, 66
Tennant, Sir Charles, 196
Tennant, Margot (*later* Countess of Oxford and Asquith), 195–6
Territorial Army: Mark Sykes's campaign for recruitment, 298
Thelwell (schoolteacher), 214
Thesiger, Frederic Augustus (*later* 2nd Baron Chelmsford), 238
Thirkleby Park, near Thirsk, 70
Thompson, Mr Baron (judge), 103
Thompson, Stephen, 67
Thornton, Mary, 22
Tinniswood (crammer head), 318–19
Tinsley, Dr, 271
Todd, Revd H.J., 120
Tomline, George, 151
Toronto, 160–1
Tovell, James, 227
Townshend, Thomas, 57
Tracey, Mrs (housekeeper), 212
Tracy, George, 119
Tree, Herbert Beerbohm, 267
Truslove, John, 23
Tuesday Club (Conservative Party), 289
Turkey (Ottoman Empire): Mark's views on British alliance with, 272; in First World War, 300, 302–3; divided under post-war settlement, 303–5
Turley, Mrs (Lord Derby's housekeeper), 353
Turner, Louisa, 114
Twigge, Nicholas, 28
Twistleton, Ellen, 168

United States of America: Sir Tatton II and Jessie visit, 156–62

Vauban, Sébastien le Prestre de, 214
Venice: brawl in, 331–3
Victor, Ed, 349
Victoria, Queen: widowhood, 178
Vivian, Daphne (*later* Marchioness of Bath), 319, 324, 327–8; *Mercury Presides*, 323
Vivian, Herbert, 179

Wagoner's Special Reserve (military), 299
Walker, James, 177
Wallace, David, 207

Walmisley, Parson, 27
Walpole, Horace, 15; 'On Modern Gardening', 49
Walton, J. Lawson, 228, 230–2
Waterford, Blanche, Marchioness of, 190
Waterford, John Henry de la Poer, 5th Marquess of, 179
Watson, William, 312
Waugh, Evelyn, 331, 333; *Brideshead Revisited*, 320
Wellbank, James, 22
Wellington, Arthur Wellesley, 1st Duke of, 128
Wentworth Woodhouse, Yorkshire, 66, 366
Westminster: Roman Catholic Cathedral, 193–5
Westminster, Elizabeth Mary, Marchioness of, 168
Westminster, Hugh Lupus Grosvenor, 1st Duke of, 142–3, 197
Westminster, Richard Grosvenor, 2nd Marquess of, 168
Westminster School, 86–8
Westow, Yorkshire, 104, 120
Westwang, Yorkshire (estate), 47
Westwood, Regimental Sergeant-Major, 334
Wetmore, George Peabody, 157
Wetmore, William Shepherd, 157
Weymouth, Dorset, 82–3
Weymouth, Henry Thynne, Viscount, 327
Wheldrake Hall, near York, 42, 50–2
White, Sir Luke, 280
White, Thomas, 48, 50, 53–4
Whitley park, Yorkshire, 65
Wignall, Mrs (cook), 316–17, 336, 345
Wilberforce, William, 61
William (2nd Bt's valet), 51
Wilson, Sir Charles, 238
Wilson, Harold, 373
Wilson, Sergeant Robert, 79
Wilson, Walter, 289, 309
Wimborne, Alice, Viscountess, 326
Winstanley, Harold, 352–3
Wolds (Yorkshire): farming, 45–6
Wombwell, Sir George, 190
Worsley, William, 177
Wraxall, Nathaniel, 59
Wrigglesworth, Richard, 148–9, 153
Wyatt, Samuel, 67–8, 71, 77
Wyndham, George, 264–5
Wyndham, John *see* Egremont, 1st Baron
Wyvill, Sir Marmaduke, 66

Yatton, John, 34
Yorkshire Post: on 1911 fire, 4
Yorkshire Wolds Gentlemen and Yeomanry Cavalry, 79–80, 102
Young, Robert, 228
Yussuf Haddad, 262

P.S.

Ideas,
interviews
& features ...

About the author

2 A Slightly Rebellious Spirit:
Louise Tucker talks to
Christopher Simon Sykes

4 Life at a Glance

5 Top Ten Favourite Books

10 A Writing Life

12 A Photographer's Diary

Read on

16 If You Loved This, You Might Like ...

18 Find Out More

A Slightly Rebellious Spirit

Louise Tucker talks to Christopher Simon Sykes

The Big House details the lives of your ancestors minutely, but apart from your spell as a hippy and a mention of your photographic career there is little to tell us about you. Could you fill in the gaps?

I had a very conventional upper-class upbringing. A French governess taught me at home until I was eight, then I was sent away to prep school in Berkshire where my grandmother lived and we all, me and my brothers, went there, then I went to Eton. Until I was 18 I only ever went to Sledmere so it was a very sheltered childhood.

My great passion at Eton was art, painting and drawing to start with and then pottery. I used to spend all my life in the art schools mostly because all the interesting people, the cool guys, hung out there. I also got involved in cinema and wanted to be a film director – in those days there were no film schools but art colleges ran film courses – so I went to Ravensbourne College of Art. I never wanted to go to Cambridge or Oxford and, I realize now, if I had the choice again I still wouldn't go because I'd have ended up in some upper-class enclave at some Oxford college. But I didn't stay at Ravensbourne that long because the course wasn't terribly good. It was new and we used to spend an awful lot of time doing building work: they used the students as free labour for constructing their studio. Photography was part of the course and while I was there I got offered a job as an assistant photographer by somebody I met when I was up in London so I went to do that for a year. It was mostly pack-shots for advertising but I used to use the studio after hours and get my friends in and practise. So I started off doing portraits, children, weddings and that sort of thing. I got into interiors through a friend of mine, interior decorator David Mlinaric, who wanted to do a book. I said, 'Well, I've never done interior photography,' and he said, 'Well, I've never written a book, so we'll just sort of muddle along together.' He sent me to photograph a few of the places and that's how I taught myself to photograph interiors. Like all people when they start out I was scratching along doing this and that: I did a wedding that appeared in *Vogue* and through that I did odds and ends for their Living pages, then my big break came when I went on the Rolling Stones' tour in 1975 to take photos for a book.

Have you always lived in London?
Yes, since I started work I've always lived in London, but I keep a bolthole in Yorkshire. I rent a house on the estate, the castle farm. It's one of the houses built by my ancestor, Sir Christopher Sykes, so it's a little older than the big house. ▶

❛ I've always been interested in families, having endlessly been told stories about my ancestors and all the portraits. It's become a bit of a standing joke among my friends. ❜

LIFE
at a Glance

BORN

23 June 1948

EDUCATED

Eton and Ravensbourne
College of Art

CAREER

Photographer and
author specializing in
architectural and garden
photography and
architectural subjects
and social history

BOOKS

Include *Black Sheep,
Ancient English Houses,
The National Trust
Country House Album,
The Rolling Stones on Tour*
and *The Gardens of
Buckingham Palace*

FAMILY

Married with two
children. Lives with his
second wife, the stage
designer, Isabella Bywater,
and her daughter in North
London.

A Slightly Rebellious Spirit *(continued)*

◀ **The book creates an incredible sense of
connection and continuity. What is it like to
have such a strong sense of family and of
place?**
I suppose it's difficult to say because I was
brought up in a close-knit family and didn't
really know much else until I left home. I've
always been interested in families, though,
having endlessly been told stories about my
ancestors and all the portraits. It's become
a bit of a standing joke among my friends
and indeed my wife, 'Oh God, not the Sykes
family again!' We are still close-knit, close in
that we always get on when we see each other,
but we don't interfere in each other's lives.
I almost feel more comfortable with my
brothers and sisters than with anyone else
because I don't have to try very much.

**Many of your ancestors kept detailed
diaries as well as writing letters. The latter
are rare in an email-obsessed era, but do
you keep a diary?**
I keep a photographic diary. When I was at
art school I did a lot of black and white
photography and I used to have my own
darkroom. Then when I got married in 1982
and my children were born I started keeping
day-to-day photo diaries to record them
growing up. I have about ten years of them.
I still do it every day, except now it's digital.
I've never really kept a written diary except
when I went on tour with the Stones.

**Sledmere lends itself to constant
redecoration, refurbishment,
relandscaping, whether forced by fire or**

otherwise. Do you think this is particular to your family, or is it a very English obsession, home and garden being such priorities?

I think it's both English and generational. Generations like to leave their mark on the house. My brother, who's been living there since my father died in 1978, has done a lot of redecoration. My father would probably turn in his grave at some of the things he's done, but it's rather nice because he's added to it and some additions will stay there forever.

Each new generation seems to rid the house of something belonging to the last. For example, one Tatton gets rid of the books and the next gets rid of the horses. Is there anything that you would get rid of, either now or at any time in history, or is there something you wish that they had kept?

There's nothing I'd get rid of, but I think it's very sad that the books got sold. Unfortunately when hard times come, unless the person in charge is a fanatical lover of them, they'll be sold first. It's a pity because it would have been one of the greatest private libraries ever put together. My brother needed some money recently and he sold something from the library, a collection of prints that no one ever saw, and of course he'd rather sell that than a painting.

Which of your ancestors would you most like to meet? And least?

I'd love to have met my grandfather. It's very sad to me that I didn't know him because he died so young. He sounded absolutely ▶

TOP TEN FAVOURITE BOOKS

(In no particular order)

The Lion, the Witch and the Wardrobe
C.S. Lewis

Great Expectations
Charles Dickens

Cider With Rosie
Laurie Lee

Of Human Bondage
Somerset Maugham

The End of the Affair
Graham Greene

Brideshead Revisited
Evelyn Waugh

The Bonfire of the Vanities
Tom Wolfe

Wild Swans
Jung Chang

A Good Man in Africa
William Boyd

A Fine Balance
Rohinton Mistry

A Slightly Rebellious Spirit *(continued)*

◄ extraordinary. I'm sure he was exasperating and didn't suffer fools but he was also funny and clever, a real live wire, and he had enormous energy which I would have loved. He was 39 when he died in 1919 and I was born in 1948 so if he'd lived into his eighties I would have known him. I wouldn't have liked to meet his father, Sir Tatton – the nasty Sir Tatton, the slightly mad one – he sounded too difficult. The other one I would have liked to meet is Richard Sykes, the builder of the house, because he sounded so jolly and jovial, someone who really enjoyed his life.

> ⸜ This book was totally motivated by my fascination with my family. ⸝

Your dedicatee is your grandfather. Like you he was a writer and a traveller. Was he your inspiration?
In a funny way he was. He wanted to write a biography of Sledmere – he started a family history and he covered the eighteenth century – and I'm sure he would have finished it if he hadn't died. He also did something else which was incredibly useful: he had all the eighteenth-century letters transcribed by a typist in London so there are twenty volumes of letter books in the library at Sledmere and I didn't have to struggle with all that handwriting. Also, I began to feel it was my destiny to do this.

Your grandfather Mark and your grandmother Edith occupy much of the latter half of the book, yet there is no picture or photograph of them together or of him with his children. Why is that?
Ah, that was our mistake. There was a picture

of him with his family but it slipped through the net ... I've included one here to make up for that.

Why do you think that your grandfather, very much the happy family man, spent so much time away from home?
I think he was incredibly driven, one of those people who couldn't sit still, a real achiever. I'm sure he didn't have very happy memories of Sledmere, and I think that's a lot to do with his very unhappy childhood.

Why do you think Jessie, your great-grandmother, had only one child?
She did say that the marriage was only consummated because she managed to get Tatton drunk. I suspect there was very little sex and once he had an heir he wasn't going to bother. I think he was terrified of women and neurotic to the point of insanity. ▶

A Slightly Rebellious Spirit *(continued)*

◄ **What was the most surprising thing that you discovered?**
The most unexpected things were the love letters from Jessie which not only detailed her love affair with this young German but also told one details of her life with Tatton that nobody had possibly begun to hint at, extraordinary things like him pulling her hair and bullying her. That was quite shocking really. Reading those letters made me feel so sad for her, she pours her heart out in them, it was just tragic that she was pushed into this miserably unhappy marriage. The whole thing was ghastly: she was dead at 54, drank herself to death, and yet she must have been the most wonderful person, a very passionate and highly intelligent woman who in another life would probably have had a lovely time.

What did you learn about yourself while writing this? For example, were there any 'eureka' moments when you recognized yourself in your ancestors? Who do you think you take after, if anyone?
You certainly see family traits coming through. I remember when we were children that we were obsessed with rather macabre things, like ghost stories, and that runs in the family. When my grandfather went to Cambridge he was taught by M.R. James, the great ghost story writer, and they used to discuss ghosts. We're also not very conventional as a family, that seems to run right through, there's a slightly rebellious spirit.

> ❡ I decided the best way to start was to go up to Sledmere and stay in the house. So in February 2002 I spent six weeks there and went through all Richard Sykes's letter books. ❡

8

Does such a history allow you a different sense of self, in that you feel its weight and its responsibility as well as its security and comfort?

For my brother, or any person who is born the first son, it immediately excludes them from doing anything that they want to do, and it's not the sort of responsibility that I would want. I'm rather relieved that it hasn't fallen on my shoulders.

Where did you start your research, and how long did it take?

I decided the best way to start this book was to go up to Sledmere and stay in the house. So in February 2002 I spent six weeks there and went through all Richard Sykes's letter books, writing down all the bits that I thought would interest me. Then I wrote the first chapter and in a way once I'd done that one it freed me. The rest of the book was written in London in the London Library and I would alternate trips up to the house with writing. So I did some research, wrote a couple of chapters, did a bit more research then wrote another couple of chapters.

How long did it take?

A year's research and about a year's writing.

What did you enjoy most, the writing or the research, or were they inseparable?

Yes, I'd say they were inseparable and I loved both. With all research you get quite fed up with it at the time, but looking back it was a very happy period. I spent a lot of time in the Brynmor Jones library in Hull which is ▶

❛Don't try to be clever. That's the best piece of advice I've ever been given – writing is not some gift that is only given to special people which you can only do if you use clever words; just tell the story in as simple a way as possible. ❜

9

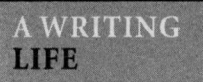
When do you write?
Best in the morning.

Where do you write?
The London Library.

Pen or computer?
Computer.

Silence or music?
Silence.

How do you start a book?
Just start. The great thing is to write something down, that's the best cure for writer's block.

And finish?
Consciously one thinks that the ending of a book is very important so I thought the way to end this was to have me leaving the house after my father died, but then I remembered this funny conversation I had with my brother and it's actually a very good way of ending it.

Do you have any writing rituals or superstitions?
No, absolutely not.

Which living writer do you most admire?
I have to say, having read *A Fine Balance* by Rohinton Mistry, I do think he is a most extraordinary writer.

A Slightly Rebellious Spirit *(continued)*

◄ one of the best archives in the country. I used to go there every day – work, have lunch at the local pub – I loved that. It certainly made me want to write more. I mean it's not the first book I've written, because I've written quite a few, but it's the first book I've done since I wrote *Black Sheep*, which came out in 1982, that was my own idea and all my own research.

What motivates you to write?
This book was totally motivated by my fascination with my family. In a funny way I would like to write a book about my childhood – I'd like to write something autobiographical. I might do it one day.

What are you writing next?
A film script based on the epilogue of *The Big House* for Robert Fox Limited, the production company.

Fiction, ever?
Well, the film script is partly fiction because I have to make up what people say. I've never tried it and I have a great admiration for people who write fiction.

Is there any book that you wish you had written?
That's a difficult question. My favourite book is *Great Expectations* and, God, I wish I'd written anything by Charles Dickens because there is a man who understands how to tell a sweeping story yet always with a message.

Why do you write?
Because I love writing. I never thought of

myself as a writer: in the 1970s I was inspired by seeing a book called *Album of a Century*, a wonderful book of Lartigue's photos of his own life put together by Richard Avedon, and I thought it would be fun to create the diary of a century using the photographs of one family. I found photos of the Sykes family going back to the 1850s and, working with a very good art director, we put together a dummy. I was then introduced to Ed Victor – this was a long time ago when he was just an agent working in some other agency – and he said, 'This is a great idea. Would you like me to try and get it published for you?' Of course we said yes, and he took us to meet George Weidenfeld. I had envisaged this book would be photographs with captions, but at the end of the meeting George said, 'Well, I think it's a brilliant idea and I'd like you to write 50,000 words to go with it.' I looked absolutely horrified and said, 'I can't do that. I can't write.' 'Don't be ridiculous,' replied George, 'anybody can write. Go and have a go at it and if it's no good I'll get someone here to do it. But I'll give you one piece of advice: don't try to be clever.' That's the best piece of advice I've ever been given – I realize he was saying to me that writing is not some gift that is only given to special people which you can only do if you use clever words; just tell the story in as simple a way as possible. Now people tell me that the way I write is very easy to read and I feel that I can say I'm a writer. ■

I've read few books that have been as striking as that. I'm astonished that it didn't win the Booker Prize.

What's your guilty reading pleasure or favourite trashy read?
I absolutely love detective stories and I would never call P.D. James a trashy read but I think *The Murder Room*, the last one I read, is absolutely gripping. I like a proper detective story.

A Photographer's Diary

By Christopher Simon Sykes

THROUGHOUT MY LIFE I have always kept some kind of photographic diary illustrating my day-to-day life.

I have a great series of snapshots from childhood. When I showed this one to my children, they cooed, 'Ooh, Dad, you were so sweet in those days!'

The photograph shows me and my sister, Arabella, standing with my father and his pack of lurchers, all of which lived in the house.

My big break as a photographer came in 1975 when I was hired by the Rolling Stones to take photographs for a tour diary.

Here I am backstage with Andy Warhol.

Many of the diaries chronicle the years in which my children, Lily and Joby, were growing up.

This is a shot of them today.

These days I also have another family, my second wife Isabella Bywater, a stage designer, and her daughter B. ▶

Here they are standing in front of one of my photographs from the Rolling Stones tour, which were exhibited at the Getty Images Gallery in the summer of 2003.

We also have a Jack Russell, Gussie, who rules our life.

She is not as cute as she seems and has a very sharp set of teeth. She lives with us in London and keeps the burglars away.

I see quite a lot of my five brothers and sisters. This is a favourite shot of me with my brothers and my son.

The Sykes boys ∎

If You Loved This,
You Might Like ...

Knole and the Sackvilles; Knole, Kent
Vita Sackville-West
Sackville-West's histories of the family home that she didn't inherit since she wasn't a first-born son.

Orlando
Virginia Woolf
Often reputed to be based on Sackville-West's own sense of loss at not being able to own and live in Knole, owing to her gender, Woolf's tale of a first-born son who becomes a daughter is a satirical take on generational history and primogeniture.

A Country House at Work: Three Centuries of Dunham Massey
Pamela Sambrook
The details of running a country house, in this case the home of the Earls of Stamford, told through the stories of all those connected to it.

The diaries of James Lees-Milne
Several volumes starting with *Ancestral Voices: Diaries 1942–43* and currently reaching 1998–2002 with *Ceaseless Turmoil*. Lees-Milne's diaries offer a remarkable window into over half a century of social history. See also www.jamesleesmilne.com/books.

Fathers and Sons: The Autobiography of a Family
Alexander Waugh
The story of four generations of the Waugh

family, told from the perspective of the relationship between fathers and sons.

Pride and Prejudice
Jane Austen
When Elizabeth Bennett refuses to marry for money, she throws not only her mother but Georgian values into turmoil. Young women in Jane Austen's day were expected to marry well, not for love, whereas men needed an heir for their property as much as a wife. Family battles over what is most important – romance, respectability or revenue – are at the centre of this witty classic.

Brideshead Revisited
Evelyn Waugh
A pre-First World War tale of the relationship between an aristocratic family, its magnificent house and their rapidly diminishing future. Charles Ryder meets Sebastian at Oxford and is fascinated by him, then by his family. Slowly, however, he recognizes that the distance between them cannot be broached.

The Remains of the Day
Kazuo Ishiguro
A loyal and long-serving butler of an English country house in the 1930s finds his values and fidelity tested by the arrival of a new housekeeper and the discovery that his master has links to the Nazis. ∎

Find Out More

Sledmere House
The house and gardens are open every year
from the end of April until mid-September.
Details of prices, opening hours and other
events can be found on the website, at
www.sledmerehouse.com.

WATCH

Gosford Park, *directed by Robert Altman*
The McCordle family invite their friends and
family for a weekend shooting party at their
country house. In the course of 48 hours the
rigid order of servants and aristocrats will
be overturned. Set in the 1930s, the film
depicts a world on the brink of extinction
as war approaches. Stars Maggie Smith,
Michael Gambon, Kristin Scott Thomas
and Charles Dance.

The Remains of the Day, *directed by
James Ivory*
The enduring appeal of the English country
house is given the Merchant–Ivory treatment
in this adaptation of Ishiguro's Booker-Prize-
winning novel. Anthony Hopkins stars as the
devoted butler whose life is turned upside
down by the arrival of love, in the form of
a new housekeeper (played by Emma
Thompson), and the corruption of war.

Brideshead Revisited
(TV series available on DVD)
Jeremy Irons and Anthony Andrews star as
Charles Ryder and Sebastian Flyte in this
much-acclaimed adaptation of Waugh's
novel. At the time of writing a film of the
book is due for release in late 2005. ∎